# IN THEORY

# RADICAL THINKERS

"A golden treasury of theory" Eric Banks, *Bookforum*

"Beautifully designed...a sophisticated blend of theory and thought" Ziauddin Sardar, *New Statesman*

## SET 1 ($12/£6/$14CAN)

**MINIMA MORALIA**
Reflections on a Damaged Life
THEODOR ADORNO
ISBN-13: 978 1 84467 051 2

**FOR MARX**
LOUIS ALTHUSSER
ISBN-13: 978 1 84467 052 9

**THE SYSTEM OF OBJECTS**
JEAN BAUDRILLARD
ISBN-13: 978 1 84467 053 6

**LIBERALISM AND DEMOCRACY**
NORBERTO BOBBIO
ISBN-13: 978 1 84467 062 8

**THE POLITICS OF FRIENDSHIP**
JACQUES DERRIDA
ISBN-13: 978 1 84467 054 3

**THE FUNCTION OF CRITICISM**
TERRY EAGLETON
ISBN-13: 978 1 84467 055 0

**SIGNS TAKEN FOR WONDERS**
On the Sociology of Literary Forms
FRANCO MORETTI
ISBN-13: 978 1 84467 056 7

**THE RETURN OF THE POLITICAL**
CHANTAL MOUFFE
ISBN-13: 978 1 84467 057 4

**SEXUALITY IN THE FIELD OF VISION**
JACQUELINE ROSE
ISBN-13: 978 1 84467 058 1

**THE INFORMATION BOMB**
PAUL VIRILIO
ISBN-13: 978 1 84467 059 8

**CULTURE AND MATERIALISM**
RAYMOND WILLIAMS
ISBN-13: 978 1 84467 060 4

**THE METASTASES OF ENJOYMENT**
On Women and Causality
SLAVOJ ŽIŽEK
ISBN-13: 978 1 84467 061 1

## SET 2 ($12.95/£6.99/$17CAN)

**AESTHETICS AND POLITICS**
THEODOR ADORNO, WALTER BENJAMIN, ERNST BLOCH, BERTOLT BRECHT, GEORG LUKÁCS
ISBN-13: 978 1 84467 570 8

**INFANCY AND HISTORY**
On the Destruction of Experience
GIORGIO AGAMBEN
ISBN-13: 978 1 84467 571 5

**POLITICS AND HISTORY**
Montesquieu, Rousseau, Marx
LOUIS ALTHUSSER
ISBN-13: 978 1 84467 572 2

**FRAGMENTS**
JEAN BAUDRILLARD
ISBN-13: 978 1 84467 573 9

**LOGICS OF DISINTEGRATION**
Poststructuralist Thought and the Claims of Critical Theory
PETER DEWS
ISBN-13: 978 1 84467 574 6

**LATE MARXISM**
Adorno, Or, The Persistence of the Dialectic
FREDRIC JAMESON
ISBN-13: 978 1 84467 575 3

**EMANCIPATION(S)**
ERNESTO LACLAU
ISBN-13: 978 1 84467 576 0

**THE POLITICAL DESCARTES**
Reason, Ideology and the Bourgeois Project
ANTONIO NEGRI
ISBN-13: 978 1 84467 582 1

**ON THE SHORES OF POLITICS**
JACQUES RANCIÈRE
ISBN-13: 978 1 84467 577 7

**STRATEGY OF DECEPTION**
PAUL VIRILIO
ISBN-13: 978 1 84467 578 4

**POLITICS OF MODERNISM**
Against the New Conformists
RAYMOND WILLIAMS
ISBN-13: 978 1 84467 580 7

**THE INDIVISIBLE REMAINDER**
On Schelling and Related Matters
SLAVOJ ŽIŽEK
ISBN-13: 978 1 84467 581 4

# IN THEORY

## NATIONS, CLASSES, LITERATURES

*Aijaz Ahmad*

VERSO

London • New York

First published by Verso 1992

This edition published by Verso 2008


1 3 5 7 9 10 8 6 4 2

**Verso**
UK: 6 Meard Street, London W1F 0EG
USA: 180 Varick Street, New York, NY 10014-4606
www.versobooks.com

Verso is the imprint of New Left Books

ISBN-13: 978-1-84467-213-4

**British Library Cataloguing in Publication Data**
A catalogue record for this book is available from the British Library

**Library of Congress Cataloging-in-Publication Data**
A catalog record for this book is available from the Library of Congress

Printed and bound by ScandBook AB, Sweden

# Contents

# Acknowledgements

'Jameson's Rhetoric of Otherness and the "National Allegory"', which appears as Chapter 3 of this book, was originally published in *Social Text* (no. 17, New York, Fall 1987) and is reprinted here with only minor corrections. Chapter 4, on Salman Rushdie's *Shame*, appeared under a different title as one of the Occasional Papers on History and Society (Second Series, Number XXXIV) issued by the Centre of Contemporary Studies, Nehru Memorial Museum and Library, Teen Murti House, New Delhi. It was then reprinted in *Economic and Political Weekly* (vol. XXVI, no. 24, Bombay, 15 June 1991). Chapter 5, on the work of Edward Said, was first presented in two sessions of the Fellows Seminar at the Centre of Contemporary Studies. Subsequent versions of it were then presented in two sessions of the Seminar on Methodology in the History Department of Delhi University, in a Seminar at the Centre of Historical Studies at Jawaharlal Nehru University, in the English Department at Yale and as a faculty lecture at Sarah Lawrence. It has subsequently been issued as an Occasional Paper by the Centre of Contemporary Studies. Material which appears here in Chapters 1, 2, 7 and 8 has its origins in Seminar presentations at the History Department of Delhi University and the English Department of Jawaharlal Nehru University in the summer of 1988. A summary of tentative formulations then appeared as '"Third World Literature" and the Nationalist Ideology' in *Journal of Arts and Ideas* (nos 17–18, New Delhi, June 1989). A much lengthier version was published subsequently under the title 'Disciplinary English: Third-Worldism and Literary Theory', both as an Occasional Paper by the Centre of Contemporary Studies and as a chapter in Svati Joshi, ed., *Re-thinking English: Culture, Literature, Pedagogy* (New Delhi: Trianka, 1991). In other words, all this material has been in gestation, for three years or so, even though the statement of my positions is more systematic and elaborate in the present book. I am grateful to journals and institutions which have been hospitable to those earlier versions of my writing, and to audiences who helped me think my thoughts more accurately. The list of individuals who helped me in that process is, alas, too long for me to acknowledge all my debts. I must perforce limit myself only to those who have been very much involved in the making of this book as it now stands, in ways that can be acknowledged in a tangible form.

Michael Sprinker read the entire manuscript with astute and affectionate attention to each detail, giving me the benefit of his close readings with unswerving generosity, some local disagreements notwithstanding. Kumkum Sangari also read the whole manuscript, much of it in several versions, and the book would not have been what it is without her criticism, advice and support. Sumit Sarkar and Tanika Sarkar read much of the manuscript and gave me invaluable advice on many points, as did Talal Asad and Harbans Mukhia who read the penultimate version of the chapter that has been for me the most difficult to write. Bruce Robbins thought that I had a book before I thought so myself; his enthusiastic involvement in the conception of the book and in the publication of what appears here as Chapter 3 should not be construed, though, as agreement with what follows in later chapters. Ibrahim Noor Shariff and John Loose took over a number of responsibilities, personal and intellectual, which I was unable to undertake myself. Among friends and scholars who helped me in numerous ways, I must mention my special debt to Ravinder Kumar, Director of the Centre and the Library where I have been a Fellow while most of this book was written. I have drawn on his magnificant knowledge of Indian history, his support as a senior colleague and his kindness as a personal friend more freely and variously than I can recount.

The immediate and personal conditions of one's production loom large in life but appear only in the margins of print. The generosity of my children, who chose to go on happily with their lives through my long absences, has been not only a cause of extraordinarily pleasurable wonder for me but also the largest single source of what sanity or confidence I possess. A circle of friends in Delhi, only a few of whose names appear in these acknowledgements, kept alive in me the belief that what I had to say made, on the whole, considerable sense. Such belief, in the resolve to say things which go against the contemporary current, does not come easy and certainly cannot come if one in any degree feels alone. The opportunity to speak from within a structure of solidarities, shared with children in some ways and with adults in some others, is always a rare privilege.

# INTRODUCTION

## Literature among the Signs of Our Time

The unity of this book is not of a chronological, disciplinary or even narrative kind, though it includes chronologies and narratives aplenty. This unity is rather, as I conceive of it, theoretical and thematic. The notable development in literary studies, as these have evolved in all the English-speaking countries over the past quarter-century or so, is the proliferation, from a great many critical positions, of what has come to be known simply as 'theory'. Gerald Graff has quite rightly pointed out that this explosion of 'theory' is an 'outcome of a climate of radical disagreement' regarding signifying cultural practices and modes of interpreting them, and that this 'dissentual culture' is as much a product of the new forms of knowledge which have arisen since World War II to destabilize the established ways of intellectual inquiry as it is a consequence of the politicizations which have occurred in the wake of postwar demographic shifts in the metropolitan universities and the students' movements of the 1960s.[1] That emphasis is worth retaining. It is also arguable, however, that dominant strands within this 'theory', as it has unfolded *after* the movements of the 1960s were essentially over, have been mobilized to domesticate, in institutional ways, the very forms of political dissent which those movements had sought to foreground, to displace an activist culture with a textual culture, to combat the more uncompromising critiques of existing cultures of the literary profession with a new mystique of leftish professionalism, and to reformulate in a postmodernist direction questions which had previously been associated with a broadly Marxist politics – whether communist, or social democratic, or inspired by some other strand in the labour movements around the globe. For the historic 'New Left' as it arose in Britain, the reference points had been Hungary and Suez, supplemented then by the crisis of labourism itself; in the United States, those sorts of energies had been associated first with Cuba and then with Vietnam, with the ambiguous liberalism of the Democratic Party itself becoming a very considerable issue. In France, terminologies were slightly different, but the wars in Indochina and Algeria had played the same constitutive role in the imaginations of the Left before the ascendancy of structuralism – in the perspective of High Gaullism, of course. Literary debates in these three cultures presumed those realities up to, and somewhat beyond, 1968. The notable achievement of 'the children of '68' is that they did not even intend to give rise to a political formation that might organize any fundamental solidarity with the two million workers who are currently unemployed in France. Debates about culture and literature on the Left no longer presume a labour movement as the ground on which they arise; 'theory' is now seen, by Graff among many others, as a 'conversation' among academic professionals.

This explosion of theory as conversation and reformulation has been, in one major aspect, a matter of catching up with many kinds of very diverse continental developments: Benjamin, the Frankfurt School, Lukács; linguistics, hermeneutics, phenomenology, structuralism, poststructuralism; the Voloshinov/Bakhtin circle; Gramsci; Freud, and the Lacanian Freud; and so on. More and more critics and theorists of literature on the Left have sought, then, to combine these diverse continental insertions with debates and preoccupations specific to the Anglo-American academy – for example, 'Commonwealth Literature', 'minority discourse', counter-canon, multiculturalism, the location of non-European immigrant intelligentsia in structures of metropolitan hegemony – to produce theoretical articulations quite novel in quality and kind. These theoretical and thematic combinatorics have had the effect not only of focusing attention on particular areas of concern but also, frequently, of reformulating much older and recalcitrant issues both of minorities within these societies and of imperialism and colonialism, as regards the archive of Western knowledges and the question of cultural domination exercised by countries of advanced capital over imperialized countries.

## I

I do not intend to offer yet another survey of a theoretical formation so diversely – and, often enough, eclectically – constituted, even though many of these framing references will be discussed at appropriate length. Central to the thematics of the present book is, rather, a particular political configuration of authors and positions which has surfaced in particular branches of literary theory, clustered around questions of empire, colony, nation, migrancy, post-coloniality, and so on, as these questions have been posed from the 1960s onwards – first under the insignia of certain varieties of Third-Worldist nationalism and then, more recently and in more obviously poststructuralist ways, *against* the categories of nation and nationalism. I do not offer here what one may call a 'survey of the field', as it were, even for this more defined and delimited area within contemporary literary theory. Instead of assembling the sort of eclectic catalogue of authors and titles that one routinely encounters in literary-critical essays these days, I have tried to concentrate on a very few positions which have been, I believe, seminal and defining.

The specifically Foucauldian ideas of 'archaeology' and 'discourse' would be such defining positions in the epistemological field, for example, as would be Said's notion of 'Orientalism' in the field of Colonial Discourse Analysis, owing not so much to theoretical rigour as to its emotive impact; the Saidian notion, of course, presumes the Foucauldian epistemological position. Once a powerful position of that kind has been put in place and recognized as defining, many other writers may come to inhabit the field marked by such a position, and what I have wanted to do is to interrogate not the variations of subsequent inhabitation but the modalities of primary definition – hence the emphasis not on cataloguing the numerous names and writings of those who have participated in these debates, but on narrowing the focus to those particular ideas which have generated so many others. This has been necessary also because as one examines the principal trajectories in these areas of literary study over the past two decades, one is impressed by how very much the increasing dominance of the poststructuralist position has had the effect, in the more recent years, of greatly extending the centrality of *reading* as the appropriate form of politics, and how theoretical moorings tend themselves to become more random, in this proliferation of readings, as much in their procedures of inter-textual cross-referentiality as in their conceptual constellations.

The issue of Marxism is surely not external to these theoretical developments, either in their generality or in the specific texts where issues of colony and empire are foregrounded. In the 1960s and early 1970s, before structuralism and poststructuralism rose to dominance in the Anglo-American academy, many literary critics who wrote about questions of colony and empire did so with some sympathy for the Marxist position even as a Third-Worldist kind of nationalism was often the main inspiration, and an Althusserian kind of Marxism was itself a key moment in the initial impact of structuralism, especially in Britain.[2] Some authors – notably Fredric Jameson, whose intervention I discuss in Chapter 3 – even write from explicit and avowed Marxist positions. Some other ways of dealing with Marxism are, however, more common. One is the outright dismissal of it, without any sustained engagement and with one or more quite familiar polemical designations: 'modes-of-production narrative', 'positivist', 'historicist', 'empiricist', even 'Orientalist' and 'oxymoronic', and many others. Equally common is the practice of treating Marxism as a method primarily of *reading*, an analytic of textual elucidation among other such analytics, so that discrete statements or concepts may be lifted out of the political praxis that is implicit in the theoretical unity of Marxism and combined, instead, with statements and concepts manifestly irreconcilable with any conceivable Marxist position.

There is, of course, a much older tradition – and a Marxist one at that – which has treated Marxism essentially as an epistemology and mainly in the twin realms of culture and aesthetics. Perry Anderson has quite rightly emphasized that a certain distancing from political economy in favour of philosophy, the habit of reading Marx in relation both to great philosophers of the past and to the main developments in the bourgeois academy, and a preoccupation with cultural superstructures in general and literary production in particular, were all hallmarks of most of the more influential theorists of what has come to be known, largely due to Anderson's own characterization, as 'Western Marxism'.[3] These prior shifts have doubtless left an imprint upon the work of those contemporary literary theorists of the Anglo-American academy who are at all open to that tradition, but some other features are more fundamental.

The lack of a sizeable and home-grown tradition of communist politics and Marxist cultural criticism has meant that the process of importation leaves much more room for eclectic borrowings and academic abstractions. The fact that radical literary theory of the kinds I discuss in this book has really come to the fore *after* the mass anti-imperialist movements of the 1960s were over – in the period of Reagan and Thatcher, really – has meant that there is, of course, no accountable relation with the non-academic political field in general but also, as I argue in Chapter 1, that Marxism itself is generally not a formative theoretical position in the first place, even in academic work; as a rule it is subordinated to a prior theoretical position, of a nationalist and/or poststructuralist kind. To the extent that American Marxism had itself produced major work in political economy in the quarter-century up to 1975 – as, for example, from the publishing house of *Monthly Review* – the striking feature of American literary theory of the last two decades is the paucity of influence from that tradition.[4] Finally, the eclectic invocation of particular Marxist propositions and of individual Marxists like Gramsci is a characteristic, in this recent phase, of radical literary theory *in general*, very much including those who are otherwise quite hostile to the specific underpinnings of Marxist theory and political practice; eclecticism of theoretical and political positions is the common ground on which radical literary theory is, on the whole, constructed. It is not uncommon, in fact, to come across texts of contemporary literary theory which routinely appropriate discrete Marxist positions and authorial names while explicitly debunking the theory and history of Marxism as such.

This reduction of Marxism to an element among other elements in the analytics of textual reading means – at the very least, and even where the hostility is less marked – that the problem of the determinate set of mediations which connect the cultural productions of a period with other kinds of productions and political processes, which is one of the central problems of Marxist cultural historiography, is rarely addressed with any degree of rigour in precisely those branches of literary theory where issues of colony and empire are most lengthily addressed.[5] Similarly, it would be hard to think of a Marxism which would not foreground, in any discussion of theory, the issue of the institutional sites from which that theory emanates; the actual class practices and concrete social locations, in systems of power and powerlessness, of the agents who produce it; the circuits through which it circulates and the class fractions who endow it with whatever power it gains; hence the objective determination of the theory itself by these material co-ordinates of its production, regardless of the individual agent's personal stance towards these locations and co-ordinates. To the extent that the determination of cultural production is even more complexly mediated than are other superstructures such as law or politics, and to the extent that literary and literary-critical production continues to have a far more individualized character than production in, say, public architecture or advertising, the relative autonomy of cultural production in general and of the literary field in particular is obvious enough – as is, concomitantly, the very considerable role of the individual theorist's agency. 'Determination' does not mean, in other words, the kind of entrapment of which structuralists and Foucauldians speak; it refers, rather, to the givenness of the circumstance within which individuals *make* their choices, their lives, their histories.

It would not be too difficult to demonstrate, in fact, that for ontology as much as politics, and on the individual level as much as on the collective, the role of human agency is much more circumscribed in all those modern epistemologies which are based upon the exorbitation of language than it is in the Marxist epistemology as such.[6] These realities of autonomy and agency do not, however, negate the durable realities of class belonging, institutional location and periodization of production in general. A difficult but also pressing question for theory, one would have thought, would consist of the proper specification of the dialectic between objective determination and individual agency in the theorist's own production. This would be an especially pressing issue – not so much in the form of censorship as of self-censorship and spontaneous refashioning – as the radical theorist takes up the role of a professional academic in the metropolitan university, with no accountable relation with classes and class-fractions outside the culture industry. The characteristic feature of contemporary literary radicalism is that it rarely addresses the question of its own determination by the conditions of its production and the class location of its agents. In the rare case where this issue of one's own location – hence of the social determination of one's own practice – is addressed at all, even fleetingly, the stance is characteristically that of a very poststructuralist kind of ironic self-referentiality and self-pleasuring.

This book is not offered as yet another contribution to literary theory as it is currently constituted, nor as an extension of the discussions of colony and empire as they are at present conducted within branches of this theory. The intention, rather, is to mark a break with the existing theoretical formation both methodologically and empirically, and to base alternative ways of periodization, for theoretical production as a whole and for individual authors, not on discrete developments within literary theory but at points of confluence between literary theory, other kinds of theories and the world whose knowledge these theories offer. This necessarily involves raising the suppressed questions of institutional site and individual location while negotiating the dialectic between the relatively autonomous status of literary theory as such, as a distinct form of cultural practice, and its determination, in a last instance which is not infinitely postponable, by the world of political and economic materialities which surrounds and saturates it. In the process, of course, one also examines the structured inscriptions of class and gender in the very linguistic and narrative constructions of some exemplary texts in the evolving counter-canons of the new metropolitan radicalisms. To the extent that I am concerned mainly with those branches of literary theory which raise the issues of colony and empire, and inevitably think themselves through categories of nation, nationalism and the Third World, the book offers some minimal expositions of these categories as well and attempts to locate them in those prior political histories which gave them their content before the categories became assimilated, mostly in very unsystematic ways, into literary theory as such.

This task of categorical specification is relatively easier in the case of the concept of a 'Third World' where the recapitulation of a certain history can easily clarify the many (and often contradictory) uses for which this concept has been variously deployed. The issue of nationalism is much more difficult to settle, because nationalism is no unitary thing, and so many different kinds of ideologies and political practices have invoked the nationalist claim that it is always very hard to think of nationalism at the level of theoretical abstraction alone, without weaving into this abstraction the experience of particular nationalisms and distinguishing between progressive and retrograde kinds of practices. Theoretical debates as well as global historical accounts are rendered all the more opaque when the category of 'nationalism' is yoked together with the category of 'culture' to produce the composite category of 'cultural nationalism'. Unlike the political category of the state, the regulatory and coercive category of law, institutional mechanisms such as political parties or class organizations like trade unions, 'culture' generally and the literary/aesthetic realm in particular are situated at great remove from the economy and are therefore, among all the superstructures, the most easily available for idealization and theoretical slippage. As these categories have been historically constituted, they have been endowed with an inherent tendency towards national and civilizational singularization. The ideology of cultural nationalism is based explicitly on this singularizing tendency and lends itself much too easily to parochialism, inverse racism and indigenist obscurantism, not to speak of the professional petty bourgeoisie's penchant for representing its own cultural practices and aspirations, virtually by embodying them as so many emblems of a unified national culture. Cultural domination is doubtless a major aspect of imperialist domination as such, and 'culture' is always, therefore, a major site for resistance, but cultural contradictions within the imperialized formations tend to be so very numerous – sometimes along class lines but also in cross-class configurations, as in the case of patriarchal cultural forms or the religious modes of social authorization – that the totality of indigenous culture can hardly be posited as a unified, transparent site of anti-imperialist resistance.

The difficulties of analytic procedure which arise from such complexities of the object of analysis itself are further compounded by the very modes of thought which are currently dominant in literary debates and which address questions of colony and empire from outside the familiar Marxist positions, often with great hostility towards and polemical caricature of those positions. First, the term 'culture' is often deployed as a very amorphous category – sometimes in the Arnoldian sense of 'high' culture; sometimes in the more contemporary and very different sense of 'popular' culture; in more recent inflations that latter term, taken over from Anglo-American sociologies of culture, has been greatly complicated by the equally amorphous category of 'Subaltern consciousness' which arose initially in a certain avant-gardist tendency in Indian historiography but then gained currency in metropolitan theorizations as well.[7] Meanwhile, the prior use of the term 'cultural nationalism', and of other cognate terms of this kind, in Black American literary ideologies since the mid 1960s – not to speak of the Negritude poets of Caribbean and African origins, the Celtic and nativist elements in Irish cultural nationalism, or the Harlem Renaissance in the United States – then endows the term, as it is used in American literary debates, with another very wide range of densities. Used in relation to the equally problematic category of 'Third World', 'cultural nationalism' resonates equally frequently with 'tradition', simply inverting the tradition/modernity binary of the modernization theorists in an indigenist direction, so that 'tradition' is said to be, for the 'Third World', always better than 'modernity', which then opens up a space for defence of the most obscurantist positions in the name of cultural nationalism.[8] There appears to be, at the very least, a widespread implication in the ideology of cultural nationalism, as it surfaces in literary theory, that each 'nation' of the 'Third World' has a 'culture' and a 'tradition', and that to speak from within that culture and that tradition is itself an act of anti-imperialist resistance. By contrast, the principal trajectories of Marxism as they have evolved in the imperialized formations have sought to struggle – with varying degrees of clarity or success, of course – against both the nation/culture equation, whereby all that is indigenous becomes homogenized into a singular cultural formation which is then presumed to be necessarily superior to the capitalist culture which is identified discretely with the 'West', and the tradition/modernity binary, whereby each can be constructed in a discrete space and one or the other is adopted or discarded.[9]

## II

Apart from thematic clarifications of a general nature, this Introduction offers, in its lengthiest section, a basic summation of the fundamental dialectic – between imperialism, decolonization, and the struggles for socialism – which in my view constitutes the contradictory unity of the world in our epoch. Some clarification of this issue, however generalized or abbreviated, appears to me to be the necessary backdrop against which issues of nation, nationalism, colony, empire, post-coloniality, and so on, need to be posed, in literary or any other theory. From this basic political clarification I return, then, in Chapter 1, to sketch broadly the conditions – both intellectual and political – under which literary theory has developed in the Anglo-American academy and which have shaped, decisively, the very terms in which those key issues have been posed. My interest here is mainly in the postwar period and especially in developments since the 1960s, even though I begin with some earlier background. The structure of the argument is very much determined, though, by the fact that this material was presented initially as Seminar lectures in the Indian academic situation, which has left its imprint on the structure of citations and the very thrust of the polemic. That discussion of the genesis of Anglo-American literary radicalism is then extended into Chapter 2, where I offer a critique of recent counter-canonical trends in the literary academy, both in terms of (a) the conditions of literary production which initially gave rise to a Third-Worldist outlook and (b) those sociological moorings of the relevant sections of literary intelligentsia which predispose them towards those particular kinds of counter-canonicity.

An essay which I published some years ago, on Jameson's conception of the 'national allegory' as the determinate form of cultural production in the 'Third World', appears here as Chapter 3 and offers a detailed engagement with what I take to be both a representative and also theoretically the most sophisticated statement of a position that arises – naturally as it were – from those larger grids of literary radicalism which I examine more generally in the first two chapters. Since that text is now part of a well-known exchange, I have reproduced it here with only some minor factual corrections but without any major revisions. Nevertheless, I should now like to offer two clarifications. It has been a matter of considerable personal irritation for me that my essay appeared at a time when Jameson was very much under attack precisely for being an unrepentant Marxist. There remain at least some circles where almost anything that was so fundamentally critical of him was welcome, so that my article has been pressed into that sort of service, even though my own disagreement had been registered on the opposite grounds – namely, that I had found that particular essay of his not rigorous enough in its Marxism. Meanwhile, my disagreement with Jameson on Third-Worldist nationalism has also been assimilated far too often into the sort of thing which we hear nowadays from the fashionable poststructuralists in their unbridled diatribes against nationalism as such. My disagreements had been far more specific. I refuse to accept that nationalism is the determinate, dialectical opposite of imperialism; that dialectical status accrues only to socialism. By the same token, however, it is only from the prior and explicit socialist location that I select particular nationalist positions for criticism, even at times very harsh denunciation; a critique of nationalism without that explicit location in the determinate socialist project has never made any sense for me, either politically or theoretically. Nor do I accept that nationalism is some unitary thing, always progressive or always retrograde. What role any given nationalism would play always depends on the configuration of the class forces and sociopolitical practices which organize the power bloc within which any particular set of nationalist initiatives become historically effective. That position cuts against both Third-Worldist nationalism and poststructuralist rhetorical inflations, and implies at least two things. It recognizes the actuality, even the necessity, of progressive and revolutionary kinds of nationalism, and it does not characterize nations and states as coercive entities *as such*.

Very affluent people may come to believe that they have broken free of imperialism through acts of reading, writing, lecturing, and so forth. For human collectivities in the backward zones of capital, however, all relationships with imperialism pass through their own nation-states, and there is simply no way of breaking out of that imperial dominance without struggling for different kinds of national projects and for a revolutionary restructuring of one's own nation-state. So one struggles not against nations and states as such but for different articulations of class, nation and state. And one interrogates minority nationalisms, religious and linguistic and regional nationalisms, transnational nationalisms (for example Arab nationalism) neither by privileging some transhistorical right to statehood based upon linguistic difference or territorial identity, nor by denying, in the poststructuralist manner, the historical reality of the sedimentations which do in fact give particular collectivities of people real civilizational identities. Rather, one strives for a rationally argued understanding of social content and historic project for each particular nationalism. Some nationalist practices are progressive; others are not.

Chapter 4, on the representation of women and the issue of postmodern, upper-class migrancy in Salman Rushdie's novel *Shame*, serves, in the thematic organization of the book, as something of a bridge between several quite distinct issues which I address in different ways throughout. There is, first, the privileging of certain kinds of texts and certain forms of interrogation and reading – mainly the issues of nation, state, post-coloniality, the Third World – in the recent counter-canonical trends in the Anglo-American academy. What kind of reading obtains, I am curious to know, if one were fundamentally to change the questions, raising the issue of 'nation' and 'post-coloniality' only in a subordinate register and foregrounding, instead, the issue of gender, class, the late-capitalist moment of Rushdie's preoccupations with migrancy, and his ideological convergence with the available metropolitan grids of modernism and postmodernism? How oppositional would these kinds of texts, so celebrated in the counter-canonical trends of the academy, then turn out to be? I have also argued, in several places in this book, that the development of those counter-canonical trends has undergone two distinct phases – the first dominated by certain varieties of Third-Worldist nationalism; the latter, more recent, marked much more decisively by a poststructuralist debunking of all nations and nationalisms as mere myths of origin and as essentialist, coercive totalizations. If Jameson's text – which I examine in Chapter 3 – was a late and authoritative statement of that earlier position, Rushdie's novelistic enterprise greatly facilitates the consolidation of the latter tendency. The enterprise itself was so widely admired, in turn, partly because of this particular convergence between the novelist and his avant-garde critics.

Finally, my treatment of the issue of migrancy in the rhetoric of Rushdie's fiction is connected both with Chapter 2, where I examine the literary tropes in ideologies of immigration in more general terms, and with the latter section of Chapter 5 where I examine Edward Said's way of privileging the migrant intellectual – the 'figure of exile', as he calls it – in his specification of the typology of 'colonial' and 'post-colonial' intellectuals. Needless to add, the ideological ambiguity in these rhetorics of migrancy resides in the key fact that the migrant in question comes from a *nation* which is subordinated in the imperialist system of intra-state relationships but, simultaneously, from the *class*, more often than not, which is the dominant class within that nation – this, in turn, makes it possible for that migrant to arrive in the metropolitan country to join not the working classes but the professional middle strata, hence to forge a kind of rhetoric which submerges the class question and speaks of migrancy as an ontological condition, more or less. What concerns me eventually is not this or that novel or theoretical articulation but the relation between the internal structure of such rhetorical forms and the historical co-ordinates within which they arise. Rushdie's book in this chapter, like Jameson's essay in the earlier one, comes up for discussion mainly for illustrative purposes in a much wider argument.

Chapter 5, on the work of Edward Said, is the lengthiest in the book, for obvious reasons. This is not the place to indicate the complexity of the thematics of that chapter, but it is worth emphasizing that within the trends I examine in this book, Said's *œuvre* is by far the most magisterial, the most influential but also possibly the most ridden with ambivalence and inner contradiction – in particular texts, between one text and another, and between the earlier and later phases of his work. So his work exemplifies, very starkly, virtually all the main moments in the evolution of literary theory which I trace in the book as a whole. *Orientalism* is, undoubtedly in the entire career of literary theory, the grandest of all narratives of the connection between Western knowledge and Western power (in terms of the civilizational and even ontological continuities which Said purports to find in Western 'Orientalism' as a whole, from Athenian drama up to the present moment, the book actually offers us a narrative far more 'grand' than anything Marxism could muster for a mode of production), and in its underpinnings and in both explicit and implicit ways it is a very uncompromising document of Third-Worldist cultural nationalism. Yet the main methodological innovation of the book was to articulate these familiar themes in stridently Foucauldian terms, thus effecting an early bridge between that kind of nationalism and a particular variant of poststructuralism. Over a period of time, and especially after the sentencing of Rushdie, Said himself has taken to debunking states and nations as coercive mechanisms *tout court*.[10] The evidence of his latest essays puts him much more squarely within the poststructuralist milieu. There are, of course, other kinds of poststructuralisms – derivations of Derrida and Lacan, for example – which have also intervened with great force in redefining the questions of colony and empire in literary theory. It remains the case, however, that Said is undoubtedly the central figure and that he has at least influenced, if not always directly defined, virtually all the main positions which have had the greatest influence in determining the approaches to questions of colony, empire, nation and post-coloniality as these questions have surfaced in literary theory since the publication of *Orientalism* in 1978.

The brief discussion of 'Marx on India' in Chapter 6, the shortest in the book, is occasioned here formally by Said's attack on Marx in *Orientalism* precisely on the issue of India,[11] but I also had some other aspects in mind. Polemical dismissals of Marxism, without any detailed engagement with Marx's thought, are now a fairly common feature of French poststructuralism and of the straightforwardly right-wing ideas which have arisen in its wake.[12] There has been, since *The Order of Things*, a pose of weariness and wry contempt.[13] This is duplicated, then, in the whole range of Anglo-American literary poststructuralisms – and not only literary, nor only poststructuralisms – where one routinely encounters a dense system of mutual citations and invocations of Foucault and/or Said which portrays Marx as an Orientalistic enthusiast of colonialism, based almost always on that same passage which Said quotes.[14] A striking feature of this portrayal of Marx as an Orientalist, based as it is on some journalistic observations about India, is that it never even refers to how those same observations may have been seen by India's own anti-imperialist historians. My short chapter here is designed not to examine the question of 'Marx on India' in any exhaustive manner but to offer some comments in relation to these particular phenomena and to insist on a kind of detailed engagement which that polemical stance seeks always to pre-empt. What is at issue here, even more than in the previous chapters, is not any particular text of literary theory but the kind of 'common sense' which so much of contemporary theory has gathered to itself.

I have tried to indicate in the very title of Chapter 7, on the conceptual category of 'Indian Literature', the merely exploratory and provisional status of the material presented therein. I offer this material in print with much trepidation, considering that there are many in India far more competent than I who can and do write on these matters. Apart from indicating, in a speculative sort of way, some directions that some of my own future work might take, there are at least two other circumstances which have occasioned these remarks. There was the more limited but at one point more immediate question as to what teachers of *English* might do in India – a question not of my choosing but simply there in the situation in which these thoughts were initially formulated. Addressing some of the issues I raise in this chapter appeared to me to be far more worthwhile, for a teacher of English in India in search of a research agenda, than the not-so-pressing matter of writing yet another article – or book – on Bacon, or Dickens, or whatever. But there was also another question which arose from within the literary side, as it were, of the present book itself. Having argued that 'Third World Literature' is, despite its polemical charge, an impossible category both politically and epistemologically, I did not wish to be understood as saying that the only alternative was 'national' literature, yet I did – and *do* – want to say that the most pressing research agendas for literary critics and theorists can arise only out of the situations which they in fact live. Metropolitan countries accumulate cultural artefacts from the whole world; something called 'world literature' may arise out of these processes of accumulation, and the category may even have relevance in a context where these countries also import, in the same sweep, proletarian as well as professional strata from all parts of the globe, who in turn press the metropolitan university to expand its curricula. No such accumulation obtains in the imperialized formations such as India, and 'world literature' in that situation exists only as an abstraction or, at best, a universalist aspiration.

One inevitably returns, then, to 'Indian Literature'. What one wishes to avoid in this situation is the possibility – in fact, the pressure – of replicating the procedures through which the European bourgeoisies formulated the premisses and contours of their 'national' literatures in the period of their class hegemony and colonial expansion. What one finds in India is an unfinished bourgeois project: certain notions of canonicity in tandem with the bourgeois, upper-caste dominance of the nation-state; a notion of classicism part Brahminical, part borrowed from Europe; the ongoing subsumption of literary utterances and cultures by print capitalism; accommodation with 'regional' languages but preoccupation with constructing a supralinguistic 'Indian Literature' based on an idealized Indian self defined largely in terms of what Romila Thapar has eloquently called 'syndicated Hinduism'; textual attitudes towards lived histories; notions of literary history so conventional as to be not even properly bourgeois; and so on. The issues I raise in that chapter are addressed to the problem of obstructing and displacing that project, in the literary domain. The imagined readership for it are those who share the same concerns but who are also, I am sure, far more competent. Within the structure of the present book, though, the chapter stands as something of a counterpoint against my earlier criticism of 'Third World Literature' as both a political and an epistemological category.

Chapter 8, on Three Worlds Theory, concludes, then, a particular debate – not on the repercussions of this theory for literary study, but on the history and political status of the Theory itself. The implications for literary theory are spread over all the earlier chapters, and this summation of a history is designed to provide the basic frame to fit all the secondary pieces. In a detailed recapitulation of the context in which the Bandung Conference took place, I summarize the overall political situation in Asia and Africa within which the term 'Third World' first arose, to connote a meaning very different from the one it subsequently acquired. Then I clarify three quite different elaborations of the meanings of this term – the Nehruvian, the Soviet and the Chinese, schematically speaking – which have given it both its emotive power and its high degree of imprecision, since a user of it could then aspire to carry all three meanings without being responsible for any one of them, replicating and even greatly extending its ambiguity in subsequent usages. The key fact about the post-colonial history of this so-called Third World is that each nation-state came under the dominance of a distinct national bourgeoisie (existing or emergent) as it emerged from the colonial crucible and was then assigned a specific location in the international division of labour as it is organized by imperialism, so that the period has come to be characterized not by greater unity but by increasing differentiation and even competitiveness among these states. The consequences of this structural lack of any sort of unified project, and the primacy instead of mutual competitiveness, are there to be witnessed in a wide range of developments throughout this period.

Thus it is not for nothing that a great many of the wars fought during this period, including the highly destructive and virtually insane Iran–Iraq War (quite comparable, in its inhumanity and scale of devastation, to the

American invasion of Iraq) have been between countries of the so-called 'Third World'. Similarly, the unbearable pressure of the stupendous rise in petroleum prices, perfected in the engineering of the Arab–Israeli War of 1973 and much admired in Third-Worldist circles at the time, actually benefited the imperialist economies and wrecked that majority of the imperialized ones which did not themselves produce oil. The structural link between the oil-producing countries of the Gulf and the petrodollar economy of imperialism is therefore a vivid illustration of the fact that speaking of a unified 'Third World' – in a global context in which producers of industrially strategic raw materials seek a *world price* without a massive compensatory mechanism for those countries in the backward zones which rely on them – is at least, to put it very, very mildly, an extremely misguided notion. It is in this double motion – the differential assimilation of each of the national-bourgeois states into the structure of imperialist capital, the mutual competitions and even warfare among the Asian and African states – that the so-called Third World has kept on collapsing into its constituent units, starting certainly with the Sino-Indian War of 1962, if not earlier, and decisively since petrodollars became a linchpin of the imperialist economy and a force of destruction in the non-oil-producing countries in the imperialized world.

It is useful, I think, to raise issues of theoretical accuracy and political responsibility with regard to a cultural theory which either constructs a counter-canonicity based upon the cultural productions of these dependent, mutually competing national bourgeoisies and homogenizes it into a 'Third World Literature', or simply throws up its hands and retreats into its poststructuralist ideological location and metropolitan privilege. But then, the very fortunes of these national bourgeoisies, not to speak of their cultural productions, have been determined, on the whole, by that fundamental dialectic of our times which has mediated – to devastating effect – the relationship between imperialism, decolonization and socialism. It is to this generality, therefore, that we now turn.

## III

As the movements of the mid sixties got going, the essential global reality was composed of a triangular contradiction that had been developing for some twenty years and came to be condensed in the Indochina War. For those two decades immediately after World War II had witnessed three process of immense magnitude.

First, there was the unstoppable dynamic of decolonizations throughout Asia and Africa; dissolution of the British Indian Empire in 1947 was doubtless a key moment, but the process reached particular intensity in Africa a decade later, starting with the independence of Ghana in 1957 and the decolonization of Algeria in 1962. Even where this dynamic was to be contained and reversed, as in Palestine, it was the intensification of this particular colonial reality, combined with the forces released by the Algerian War, which gave Arab nationalism its essential energy, for two decades or more. If the war of 1948 had been the immediate proximate cause for the (Nasserite) Free Officers to start plotting their coup in Egypt, the Arab defeat in 1967 led directly to the uprising in Aden which led to the first – albeit short-lived – socialist republic in the Arab world. And it is the eventual acceptance of the colonial aspect of the Israeli reality which has demonstrated, in more recent years, the full exhaustion of the nationalism of the Arab national bourgeoisie.

Decolonization, however, was no uniform matter. All classes and all political ideologies, from landowners of various sorts to fully fledged national bourgeoisies, and from the most obscurantist to the most revolutionary, had contended for leadership over the anti-colonial movements, with diverse consequences in different parts of the world. Anti-colonial struggle was itself, in other words, a riven terrain. If in most places decolonization came under the leadership of the national bourgeoisie (considerably well developed in India, petty and mercantile in Kenya, with many variants in between), all the socialist revolutions that occurred in Asia and Africa between 1949 and 1978 were those where the national bourgeoisie had been sidelined and socialist hegemony established in the course of the anti-colonial struggle. Even in China, where there had been a much older issue of semi-colonialism in the form of territorial concessions, a comprador bourgeoisie (in the exact sense) and the Kuomintang's complete reliance on foreigners, it was in the course of the anti-Japanese struggle that the People's Army had managed to break out of its liberated zones and lead a national revolution. This dynamic of an anti-colonial struggle being transformed into a socialist struggle was, of course, much clearer in the countries of Indochina and Southern Africa, which then won their wars of liberation much later, in the mid 1970s.

In *some* countries, in other words, decolonization tended to converge with what was clearly the second important aspect of the global contradiction as it emerged in the aftermath of the Second World War – namely, the *actuality* of the struggle for socialism. For while the victory of the Chinese Revolution in 1949 – even more than the Red Army's advances into the backward zones of East-Central Europe in the course of World War II – promised the emergence of a bloc of socialist countries, the French defeat in Indochina in 1954, the intensification of the Cuban Revolution from 1959 onwards, the immense expansion of the Communist Party in Indonesia under Sukarno, the persistence of the Communist movement in the Philippines even after the defeat of the so-called Huk Rebellion, the electoral victory of the Communist Party of India in Kerala in 1957 and the consequent emergence of the world's first elected Communist government there, the substantial presence of Communist Parties in Southern Europe in both the electoral and the outlawed zones of politics, and numerous such developments (in Iraq and Sudan, in Southern Africa, in Latin America) seemed to promise that the socialist dynamic was itself on the ascendant, certainly in the poorer zones of the globe but also on the margins of Western Europe itself, in many forms.

I shall return to some of these elements in a moment, but it is as well to remember that the question of communism in the southern margins of Western Europe was not entirely settled until after the defeat of the Portuguese Revolution and the decline of the PCI after the 1976 elections in Italy. We might also recall that the US-sponsored bloodbath into which the *Unidad Popular* government had been dissolved in Chile, the one country where revolutionary socialism had taken legislative power through electoral means, was a key element underlying Enrico Berlinguer's slogan 'Simple majority is not enough' and in the subsequent emergence of the more bizarre forms of the doctrine of 'historic compromise'. The *fear* that Italian communism might have to face the fate of Chile was palpable, before other kinds of disorientation set in. Within Hispanic America, the Chilean slaughter also brought to a virtual close the revolutionary dynamic that had been unleashed by the Cuban Revolution and had passed through a number of guerrilla movements, notably in Colombia, Peru, Bolivia, Venezuela; in the succeeding years, only the Sandinistas were provisionally to succeed and then to be decisively disorganized by a combination of domestic economic collapse, regional isolation and imperialism's global triumph. The Portuguese Revolution at the southwestern tip of Europe, meanwhile, was part of that larger dynamic which had brought the revolutionary Left to power in Portugal's African colonies, with the help of Soviet arms. These overlapping histories which connect Chile with Italy, Nicaragua with Gorbachev's global perestroika, Angola with Portuguese communism and Soviet weaponry, and even the defeat of the Portuguese Revolution with subsequent sequestration and defeat of the revolutions in the former Portuguese colonies, should lay to rest any idea that the world is really divisible into the discrete singularities of First, Second and Third.

What these two dynamics – of decolonization, and of very considerable expansion of socialist bases in many of the poorer countries – tended to conceal for many years, however, was the sheer power – eventually to prove decisive – of the third element which constituted the global contradiction of the postwar years and came to determine even the relation between decolonization and socialist revolution, while greatly exacerbating the internal crises of communist states and movements. For this same period witnessed the historically unprecedented growth, unification and technological power of capitalism itself, with fully globalized circuits of production and circulation, without colonial divisions and with increasing modernization of travel, transport and communication technologies, with far-reaching consequences for the international division of labour, not to speak of the technologies and effectiveness of subsequent imperialist wars – of destruction, and of prolonged encirclement – against the emerging socialist states and movements in the backward zones. If the Second World War had resolved the problem of disarticulation between productive capacity and market demand which had been the central element in the Depression of the 1930s, and if the war itself had made viable the production of new kinds of technologies (for example computers, nuclear energy), postwar expansion introduced the characteristically American form of the Fordist regimes of industrial accumulation – first into Western Europe and Japan, eventually into some regions of Latin America and Asia as well.[15]

Not only did the the United States emerge as the hegemonic capitalist power, but by the end of World War II its levels of accumulation were already far greater than Britain or France had ever enjoyed even at the height of the colonial period; in 1945, it alone accounted for roughly half the world's output. One of the many contradictory consequences of decolonization within a largely capitalist framework was that it brought all zones of capital into a single, integrated market, entirely dominated by this supreme imperialist power. It was in the context of this historically unprecedented opportunity that the United States was then to launch itself on a period of enormous uninterrupted growth which lasted into the late 1960s, even the early 1970s; to lead Western Europe and Japan into full postwar recovery and a boom which is not yet quite over, despite the recessionary pressures of the past decade; and to emerge as the dominant power globally, including the zones which old colonialisms had vacated, with the power to assimilate into its own hegemony the newly independent national-bourgeois states and first to isolate, then decisively to disorganize, those poorer countries which had opted out of the system of the national-bourgeois states in favour of a non-capitalist form of development.[16]

The more recent *global* triumph of imperialism has come after so much else – principally, the disorientations of what might have become a bloc of socialist countries; the enormous expansion and then the containment, finally the defeat, of the socialist offensives in the underdeveloped zones – that we now forget how this imperialist triumph actually *began* in the immediate postwar years – not in the backward but in the advanced and intermediate zones, expanding then, over the next forty years or so, from there to the rest of the world.[17] Within the United States immediately after the war, the unprecedented capitalist growth was combined with – was, in fact, the very basis for – equally unprecedented levels of anti-communist mobilizations, putting in place the McCarthyist terror in society at large, the Eisenhower–Dulles combination in charge of the state, a 'military-industrial complex' (Eisenhower's own phrase) in charge of corporate capital, and the merged AFL–CIO to marginalize the radical segment of the working-class movement and to incorporate the unions into that imperialist consensus which was buttressed materially by new and spectacular levels of consumption.

The capitalist zones of Europe were then made safe through containment of existing socialisms (unbearable military and economic pressure on the Soviet Union which played an incalculable role in strengthening the Stalinist reaction there and throughout Eastern Europe), combined with warfare (Greece, with eighty thousand dead), fascism (Spain, Portugal), division and occupation (Germany), threat of war and actual military might (the Truman Doctrine; NATO; the deployment of nuclear weapons; a quarter of a million 'Allied' – mainly American – troops stationed permanently in West Germany; huge military-industrial complexes in Britain and France), as well as enormous investment and spectacular growth (the Marshall Plan; the Eurodollar economy; generalized Fordism) which laid the foundations for the welfare state and the conservative kind of social democratic compact for European labour – not to speak of the beefing-up of the old West European colonial armies in those zones where colonialism was being challenged under the leadership not of the national bourgeoisie but of the Marxist Left (the British in Malaya; the French in Indochina; the Portuguese in Southern Africa during the 1960s and 1970s). The formative years of this overwhelming structure provided the immediate backdrop against which Togliatti was to announce, in effect, in the one industrial country where the Communist Party had emerged from the war as the main national force, that socialist revolution was simply not on the cards in Western Europe. Whether Togliatti was being plainly realistic or packaging a Stalinist sell-out in democratic phrases, subsequent historians have not been able quite to determine.

This consolidation and postwar expansion in all the homelands of advanced capital, reflected as much in the imperialist military machine as in the globalized corporate economy, meant that throughout this period capital was to command enormous power to condemn every country which even attempted to introduce socialism to a perpetual war economy under conditions of acute scarcity and low levels of social development, with no prior experience of even a bourgeois democracy, let alone a socialist one. Every one of these states became, in the very moment of inception and for many years thereafter, a national-security state – always with a high degree of regimentation, frequently sequestered and pauperized as well.[18] This meant, in turn, that the worst potentialities of Stalinist bureaucratism, which not only stifled dissent in the name of national security but created vast distortions in the economy, with eventual degeneration into sheer corruption and nepotism, had the maximum chance of realization. There simply was no line that could be clearly drawn between what was a consequence of unbearable external pressure and what was simply inherent in the very mode of the command economy which the Stalin regime first introduced into the Soviet Union after the dissolution of the New Economic Policy ('primitive socialist accumulation' it was once called in a peculiar twist of terminologies) and which was then extended into the East-Central European countries of what became Comecon, becoming thereafter the model for 'socialist construction' as such. Nor could one quite tell how much that external pressure had actually reinforced the internal distortion.[19]

In foregrounding the scope and constancy of the imperialist pressure, in other words, I do not at all wish to minimize the significance of factors which were rooted primarily in the histories of the communist movements themselves and only secondarily shaped by external pressure. For example, it is eminently arguable that international socialism's inability to rectify the two great splits which occurred in its history – between communism and social democracy in the course of the Bolshevik revolution and then the Sino–Soviet split in the early 1960s, which had the net effect of determining social democracy's rightward drift as well as the hardening first of the Bolshevik and subsequently of the Maoist positions – had as much to do with the fragmentation and eventual liquidation of the communist regimes as with the imperialist pressure itself. It is equally arguable that the full imperialist triumphs of 1989 were dialectically correlated with the Hungary of 1956, the Czechoslovakia of 1968, and the lapsing of the Khrushchev reforms within the Soviet Union; all available evidence seems to suggest that it was not in the age of Stalin himself but after the suppression of the reform movements that increasingly larger sections of the Soviet and East European populations and intelligentsias actually gave up on regimes of 'existing socialism' – and that *despite* the very considerable improvement in the economic conditions of their lives. What I wish to emphasize in foregrounding the imperialist dimension is the sheer intractability of the extremely unfavourable material conditions under which socialism's battles had to be fought, both internally and externally. The inherited anachronisms of those backward societies were bad enough, and the Marxist tradition of documenting what went wrong in the history of 'existing socialisms' is too voluminous for even preliminary citation, but the upshot, in any case, of this additional combination (Stalinist distortion, and distortions as a consequence of scarcity, pressure and duress) was that the kind of societies which actually emerged in the Soviet Union and East-Central Europe simply had no reasonable chance to inspire West European or American working classes towards socialism, while the closure of those societies, resulting from that same combination, meant also that there was no free space within them where socialism had even a chance to fight for reasserting itself. Even E.P. Thompson, the legendary anti-Stalinist of British socialism, has had to concede that

> war (1917–1921 and 1941–45 and the expectation of invasion in the 1930s) and cold war thereafter were necessary conditions for the historic formation of Stalinism and of its Brezhnevite aftermath: in the exaltation of military priorities, the imposition of command economies and suppression of consumer demand, the enhancement of ideological paranoia, the strengthening of internal security forces, the 'two camps' diplomacies, the outlawing of dissent, and all the rest.[20]

*On its own terms*, the economic performance of most of these countries was actually not bad. The Soviet Union did double its living standards in the quarter-century after the war and made further gains in the next decade, up to 1980; the number of people with more than a secondary education rose from twelve million in 1960 to over forty million by 1985, and the number of trained scientists exceeded those in Western Europe and Japan together.[21] People in several of the Comecon countries lived even better than those in the Soviet Union. China started with a far more backward industrial base and infrastructural development than India, but its subsequent performance has been incomparably superior both in terms of aggregate accumulation and in the material security of the vast majority of its people. Cuban performance has likewise been better than that of comparable countries in the Caribbean and Central America – all this with no imperialist loot, no Marshall Plans, and under conditions of extreme duress. But none of these countries is ever judged on its economic performance in relation to its own past, its inherited environment, its regional location: China is not compared with India, Cuba with Haiti, Bulgaria (once a periphery of the Ottoman Empire) with Turkey (the central formation of that empire). What matters is that Vietnam has failed utterly to become a Singapore, China simply is not Japan or California, Cuba is not Miami. In other words, it is the superior power of the material productions of advanced capitalism which sets the terms of comparison, in war and in peace. The countries which have experimented with non-capitalist paths have thus had to struggle not only with the inherited anachronisms of their own past, not only with the imperialist denial to them of a secure existence, not only with the structural distortions of their own command economies and centralizations of political and administrative power, but also with a comparison with the consumption patterns of the imperialist countries and the hegemonic assertions of their cultural products and aspirations – a comparison which has been made all the more palpable with each phase in the development and globalization of the electronics media and the (dis)information technologies.

The enormous revolutionary upheavals in Cuba, Indochina and Southern Africa, not to speak of vibrant communist movements in a dozen other countries, served to conceal the fact that it was precisely in the 1960s that the 'existing socialisms' of the Comecon countries entered their double-edged crisis, in both the political and economic domains. This crisis was brought about by the failures of the reform movements on the one hand and, on the other, by the onset of a secular decline in the overall *rates* of growth and their eventual inability to make a transition from extensive industrialization, which had marked the years immediately following the war, to an intensive technological revolution in the means of production, of the kind advanced capitalism was already embarked upon. This failure was as much a consequence of the costs of military confrontation which imperialism was able to impose, leading to acute scarcity of resources and sectoral imbalances, as it was owed to bungled allocation of priorities favouring the bureaucracy, both at the micro-level of managerial decision-making and at the macro-level of central planning. It was the economic side of the crisis – the failure to make a transition from extensive to intensive industrialization, inevitably leading to rising social and ecological costs of whatever further industrialization did take place – which eventually proved decisive. But the failure of the system to correct itself politically, to construct an egalitarian social space where problems could be openly faced and alternative ways of building socialism could be found, meant also that the further gains in living standards which continued through the 1970s (albeit at a slower pace) accomplished nothing by way of restoring the lost political hegemony, since there was now no collective consent to bear comparative scarcities, nor to accept the coercive ways in which the entirely salutary project of building secular, multi-ethnic, multinational societies was being implemented. The paradox, of course, is that once those regimes of 'existing socialism' had decisively and violently disjoined the socialist project from issues of a superior morality and a fuller democracy, 'socialism' became a mere authoritarian developmentalism, promising not much more than economic security and rising living standards, so that the regimes which had so distorted the project were then judged not only from the standpoints of morality and democracy (glasnost, the scandals of bureaucratic privilege) but also from the standards of commodity fetishism set in the advanced capitalist countries, projected as the very essence of universal well-being and increasingly internalized by populations – especially the intelligentsias – in the Comecon countries.

As Blake once put it: 'Unacted desire breeds pestilence'. Regimes which had so severely circumscribed the possibilities of acting on socialism's emancipatory desires were then faced with – were at length overthrown by – the 'pestilence' of commodity fetishism, as it enveloped the disgruntled populations to such a degree that they succumbed to the most extreme ideas of the American and West European Right. So it is that the movements that came to power in 1989 and constitute the majority inside Russia as well – aided, surely, by imperialism, but with the momentum of mass mobilizations – have turned out to be not only reactive but reactionary, in the strict sense.[22] On some key issues – distribution of wealth, public responsibility for basic human needs, collective ownership of the major means of production, struggle against imperialism, struggle against religious forms of alienation, the desirability of multi-ethnic and multinational polities, solidarity with non-European countries – these are regimes of distinctly Right reaction. In most sections of the Left in Britain and North America – with a few worthy exceptions, of course – this entire upheaval has been greeted as the collapse of an evil empire, the outbreak of the spirit of liberty, and the salutary reassertion of social movements based on identity: national, religious, ethnic, linguistic, local, individual, and so on.[23]

All that has come later. The ambiguity of the period covered in this book – the persistence, up to the 1970s, of the socialist offensive in many of the directly imperialized formations; the receding of revolutionary horizons in Western Europe; the many distortions of the Comecon countries; the sheer power and productivity of advanced capital; but also the highly visible brutality of imperialist war – was that the radicalism which arose in the United States in 1968 or thereabouts did not, except in some small pockets, believe in the desirability of socialism in its own country or in any realistic possibility of a revolutionary movement in the West, while its counterparts among the Parisian intelligentsia seemed to believe more in Surrealism than in socialism and quickly settled into poststructuralisms and New Philosophies which were directly hostile to Marxism and to the idea of any historical role for the working class. The overwhelming majority of the Left in the metropolitan countries actually believed – whether it said so in so many words or not – that the combination of the Fordist regimes of accumulation and the welfarist compact for industrial labour, which had underwritten the anti-communist consensus in the advanced capitalist countries, was the best possible choice for their own countries, and what they now needed to do was to refine the democratic premisses of liberal-capitalist regimes on their own terms.[24]

Starting with the Algerian and Cuban revolutions, and greatly expanding under the influence of the Indochinese and Southern African revolutions as well as the guerrilla movements in half a dozen Latin American countries, anti-war movements grew to massive proportions in all the advanced capitalist countries, but virulent anti-communism was so rampant – especially in the United States, the country which counted the most – that these movements could be organized only in opposition to strictly military intervention. The issue of an active solidarity with the *socialist* projects in Cuba or Indochina was posed only by the groupings which were immediately branded as ultra-Left, while the anti-war movement as a whole was arrested at the pedagogical level of simply affirming the rights of small nations to determine their sovereign future. Any militant mass struggle for socialism became, in these formulations, more or less synonymous with the anti-colonial nationalism of the underdeveloped; socialism, in other words, was poor man's capitalism. The fact that the socialist revolutionary dynamic was much stronger in East Asia and Southern Africa than in zones of advanced capitalism, and the further fact that it was in the course of the anti-colonial struggles that the socialist movements of Asia and Africa had in the main grown, seemed to obscure, in the meantime, the much larger fact that decolonization had given power in most (and in the most populous, the largest, the relatively more developed) countries not to revolutionary vanguards but to the national bourgeoisie poised for reintegration into subordinate positions within the imperialist structure. Instead, the lone fact of decolonization itself came to be seen, for the so-called Third World, as the kernel of the revolutionary process, while the class projects of the post-colonial regimes seemed to matter less and less. The next logical step, then, was to declare nationalism itself as the determinate answer to colonialism and imperialism.

The whole of this contradiction – revolutionary anti-colonialism; the most advanced socialist political practice in the most backward peasant economy; the direct, historic, prolonged combat between socialism and imperialism; the utterly unequal balance of forces – was condensed in the Vietnam War. We need not go over the aspects that are well enough known: the construction of socialist hegemony in the course of the anti-colonial struggle against the French; the seamless transfer of capitalist interest in Indochina from French colonialism to American imperialism; the nuanced handling by the Vietnamese of the historic Sino-Soviet split; the combined and uneven development of the revolution in the three Indochinese countries; the carpet bombings, the devastation, but also the eventual defeat of the most advanced imperialist war machine by an ill-equipped army of peasants. The memory of that revolutionary heroism shall remain. What eventually proved decisive, however, was what came after the revolutionary victory: the impossibility of building anything resembling socialism in a land so utterly devastated in all its human and natural resources. Vietnam was simply left with little more than hunger and horror to redistribute, and with no power, not even remotely, to seek as much as an iota of reparations. It is a measure of how much the American Left has needed to suppress the memory of Vietnam in the process of normalizing itself into a professionally responsible stratum that it organized no movement of any proportions either to demand from its state that it undertake reparations or to mobilize resources from the citizenry to help rebuild what their rulers and armies had destroyed so utterly.

Within Vietnam, the strictest forms of control were required for sheer survival, but controls of that order leave little room for socialist democracy, plenty of room for bureaucratic degeneration; internationally, continued and vicious American policies of sequestering the Vietnamese Revolution meant an inordinate reliance upon the Soviet state, with all the predictable consequences. The extreme kinds of scarcity and destitution which had required the most far-reaching domestic controls gave rise, inevitably, to further stagnation, even to some degree of nepotism, graft, the black market, mutual competition for the smallest quantity of goods, ethnic animosities over resources and markets. Literal devastation of the land meant that agricultural production was barely enough to feed the surviving population, but lack of development resources for a country reduced to rubble meant also that no dramatic improvement in production was possible. American imperialism had made sure that the material dimensions of the Vietnamese Revolution would collapse utterly, with not even scraps to retrieve.

When this material devastation brought in its train the inevitable disorientations in the social and political domains, those who believe in the moral grandeur of revolutions but not in the brute reality of the material conditions in which people actually build their lives and their revolutions were thoroughly disillusioned. The predominantly (and after the mid 1970s, increasingly) anti-communist Left of the metropolitan variety, having already dismissed the discussion of material realities as 'vulgar Marxism' and 'economic determinism', held the Vietnamese themselves responsible for those failures, then consigned them to the remotest margins of its own memory. Thus it was that Vietnam, the great victor of anti-imperialist war, became the showcase not of socialism but of the impossibility of building socialism. This sense of failure was to be repeated, then, in the rest of Indochina, in Southern Africa, in Nicaragua, and (so far to a lesser extent, but already visibly) in Cuba. None of the small places where great revolutions had occurred had the space, the time, the material resources, the assistance, the conditions of peace to make possible the correction of the distortions which inevitably arise in the course of collective human projects of such magnitude, undertaken in conditions so very punishing.

## IV

A rough periodization is also possible. A very large number of sovereign states emerged in Asia and Africa during the first twenty years after the Second World War, mainly under the hegemony of the respective national bourgeoisies and subordinated to regimes of advanced capital. The next decade, 1965–75, was dominated by the wars of national liberation which had a distinctly socialistic trajectory, even though the level of prior economic development and the scale of imperialist devastations preempted the possibility that socialist construction would have a reasonable chance. These two phases of the anti-colonial movements were over by the mid 1970s, and the revolutions which broke out in the next few years occurred mainly in countries which had *not* been directly colonized – Iran, Ethiopia, Afghanistan – and regardless of their respective rhetorics – either of Islam or of communism – the essential historic function of these revolutions was to dismantle the structures of the antecedent monarchical regimes and replace them with regimes of the modern, professional salariat and those sectors of the merchants' capital which had previously been repressed by the monarcho-bourgeoisie. The beginning of the 1980s, then, marked a new phase in which the regimes of the national bourgeoisie had already been assimilated into the imperialist structures, and any revolutionary potential had been successfully denied to states which arose out of the wars of national liberation, so that the full imperialist hegemony was established in Asia and Africa precisely (and paradoxically) in the very phase in which the advanced capitalist societies are experiencing the long wave of a recessionary cycle.

On the whole, decolonization came more quickly and more smoothly where the national bourgeoisie was firmly in the saddle, and the process was sometimes speeded up where there was even the prospect of further radicalization.[25] The actual processes of decolonization were, of course, diverse. In Kenya, for example, where the formation of an indigenous bourgeoisie had been obstructed by the growth of modern farming owned directly by the British and of a trading class composed mainly of foreign (notably Indian) strata, guerrilla warfare was organized through an alliance of the educated middle class and the subordinated farming communities, in which the issue of race provided the main ideological cement. In other places, notably Malaya, the country was decolonized *after* the defeat of the revolutionary forces had been secured. The fact remains, however, that this process of the transfer of governmental power from the colonial to the post-colonial state of the (existing or emergent) national bourgeoisie, otherwise known as decolonization, had been largely completed by the mid 1960s, regardless of the different paths whereby each nation-state gained its sovereignty. The next decade then witnessed the most intense and prolonged revolutionary wars in those zones of traditional colonialism – notably in Indochina and Southern Africa – where the nascent bourgeoisie, such as it was, had been sidelined by the socialist Left and the colonial question therefore converged with socialist revolution. The overwhelming fact of the Chinese Revolution, seizing state power in 1949 and remaining a key defining polarity until after the end of the Cultural Revolution, exercised enormous influence on anti-colonial struggles throughout this period, from the end of the Second World War up to the mid 1970s. The equally decisive reality of the revolutionary wars in Indochina which raged during these years – first against the French, then against the Americans – again reveals the fact that the issue of socialism was the one with which both imperialism and the movements of bourgeois nationalism had to contend, as a great many nation-states of Asia and Africa emerged from the colonial crucible.[26] As a historical abstraction, however, and essentially for analytic purposes, we may say that while the first two decades of this period gave rise to a very large number of sovereign regimes of the national bourgeoisie (the fact that such a regime arose in India was, after all, as decisive as the fact that it did not in China), the next decade, 1965–75, was a phase predominantly of the revolutionary wars of national liberation.[27]

Those wars were mainly over by the mid 1970s, and the two great colonial questions which remained unresolved, in Israel and South Africa, were questions of very recalcitrant kinds of *settler* colonialism. What proved decisive in South Africa, of course, was the fact that the majority of the indigenous population had not been evicted, that there was a consolidated class of the African proletariat, that the alliance between the African National Congress (ANC) and the Communist Party survived and the ANC was able to defend and expand its political hegemony among the majority of the population, that revolutions in the Portuguese colonies created a favourable environment for struggles in Namibia and South

Africa, and that these factors combined to precipitate a crisis both of economy and of authority for the apartheid regime. In Palestine, by contrast, the only analogue for that situation is the political hegemony of the PLO among the Palestinians; none of the other key elements of the South African situation obtains. In addition, imperialist stakes are far higher in Israel than they ever were in South Africa. Zionism has succeeded in becoming one of the most powerful ideologies of the advanced capitalist countries, and the Zionist state has been the main beneficiary of the global sympathies generated by the Nazi concentration camps.

It is owing to the *totality* of these contrasting realities that the formations of the metropolitan Left, as much as the states of advanced capitalism, have displayed remarkably contrasting attitudes towards these surviving colonialisms. While the apartheid regime came increasingly under attack in the very countries to which it looked for sustenance, support for the Zionist regime has also kept growing throughout the imperialist state system, including the Arab state system; it is indicative that the Warsaw Pact countries remained the main international supporters of the PLO throughout the Brezhnevite 'period of stagnation', and that far-reaching accommodation with Israel is a notable feature of the ongoing global perestroika. Such discrepancies contributed to the relative success of the ANC, on the one hand, and on the other to Israel's increasing power to dictate its terms as it moved from the appropriation of the West Bank, Gaza and the Golan Heights to the invasion of Lebanon and, more recently, the most brutal suppression of the Palestinian *intifada*, in the classic colonial fashion. The metropolitan Left paid its homage to these contrasting situations by mobilizing support for the ANC but accepting the Zionist credentials to the extent that the settler–colonial origins of the Zionist state, and the numerous distortions of the Israeli polity which are owed directly to those origins, are now not even a part of the discourse of that Left.

The main point for the discussion at hand is that anti-colonial nationalism – both in the form of the nationalist ideologies and post-colonial states of the national bourgeoisie, and in the form of the revolutionary wars and post-revolutionary states of the socialist Left – was a key constitutive element of the global configuration until the late 1970s. Because the last decade of even that period was dominated by revolutionary movements which had combined their anti-colonialism with programmes of fundamental transformation for their own polities, it was mistakenly assumed by the metropolitan Left which came of age during the 1960s that progressive social change at home was intrinsic to anti-colonial nationalism as such. It was against this background that the specifically Chinese version of the Three Worlds Theory gained its widest global currency, and nationalism – and, for cultural theorists, the ideology of cultural nationalism – was designated as the determinate answer to imperialist (postmodernist?) culture. In those Asian countries where Maoism gave rise to substantial communist movements, there was at least an emphasis on the culture of the peasantry against that of the dominant classes; in the metropolitan versions, the whole of the 'Third World', with all its classes singularized into an oppositionality, was idealized as the site, simultaneously, of alterity and authenticity.

By the 1980s, this global configuration was undergoing a historic sea-change. The post-revolutionary states which grew out of the socialist currents of anti-colonial nationalism had been contained and consigned to the worst kind of ossification of the productive forces. Anti-communist ideologies which had permeated most of the new radicalisms were now mobilized to *prove* that socialism does not work. In the process, there was a certain shift in the attitude towards the Soviet Union itself. While the revolutionary wars were going on, it had been difficult for the more truthful even within the anti-communist Left to ignore entirely the contradiction that an internally bureaucratized society was in every single case the main supplier of the material and diplomatic support which made those wars possible; it was, after all, in the so-called 'period of stagnation' (the Brezhnev years) that so many of the revolutions had in fact taken place, with direct Soviet assistance, and it is at least arguable that the crisis of the apartheid regime was intensified somewhat later owing to the demise of the racist regimes in the surrounding countries and to the tenacity of the ANC itself, all facilitated by Soviet arms. As the metropolitan Left came to shelve its identifications with post-revolutionary societies of Indochina and Southern Africa, that memory, and what it had meant for the oppressed peoples of Asia and Africa, was simply suppressed; the subsequent Gorbachev years were to help that willed amnesia greatly. What remained was the memory only of the failures, the distortions, the bureaucratization; that there had also been other kinds of solidarities no longer mattered.

In the post-colonial states where the nationalism of the national bourgeoisie had been expected to work all kinds of wonders, one witnessed, on the one hand, enormous consolidation of the national bourgeoisie itself, with its ability to take hold of the Non-Aligned Movement and the North–South dialogue over terms of trade; and, on the other, the stagnation, increasing dependence, dictatorial brutality, religious millenarianism, and general fracturings of polity and society – despite, and frequently because of, imperialist aid, investment and patronage. The anti-colonial content had been realized already; what remained of this nationalism seemed either to evaporate or to cause havoc. The Iranian Revolution was perhaps the last great event to offer any considerable lease on life for a full flowering of cultural nationalism in the journals of the metropolitan Left, so that literary theory itself felt compelled to defend Islam against its misrepresentations in the American media even as Khomeini consigned the Iranian Left to the dungeons.[28] It took a principally *literary* event – the macabre sentencing of Salman Rushdie for selling certain novelizations of Islam to British and American corporate publishing – for protest campaigns against Khomeini to envelop that very literary intelligentsia which had never bothered when that same clerical state had not only sentenced but tortured and actually killed countless communists and other patriots. When the degeneration of the Iranian state into clerical fascism became unmistakable, the last remaining illusion of Third-Worldist cultural nationalism finally had to be abandoned. What, then, to replace it with? Socialism had already been renounced as the determinate name of imperialism's negation. Nationalism – the whole of it – also now went. This is the redoubled vacuum which, in the radicalized versions of metropolitan literary theory, poststructuralism is now to fill.

## V

Facts require explanations, and all explanations, even bad ones, presume a configuration of concepts, which we provisionally call 'theory'. In other words, theory is not simply a desirable but a *necessary* relation between facts and their explanations. That anti-colonial nationalism was a tremendous historical force until about the mid 1970s is a fact. That this force declined sharply in the succeeding years is also a fact. So is the defeat of the revolutionary movements which sought to replace colonial societies with socialist societies, and so is the assimilation of the nationalism of the national bourgeoisie into the globally overarching imperialist structure. It is also a fact that a very unequal kind of war between imperialism and socialism has raged in a great many places around the globe throughout most of this century, and that this war has now been won by imperialism, for the remainder of this century at least. It is not possible to pose questions about colony and empire, and about their representations in cultural products, without possessing a theory of such facts.

Marxism provides a particular constellation of concepts to account for facts of this order. Within this conceptual apparatus, there is plenty of room for internal development and debate – which accounts for the most intense kinds of disagreements among Marxists themselves, as can be seen in a small way in the severity of my criticisms of Fredric Jameson in Chapter 3. The preceding two sections of this chapter offer an outline of my own understanding of recent history in accordance with the way I understand those concepts, and this brief (non-literary) detour has been necessary because the way we pose questions of colony and empire, in literary or any other theory, depends very much on how we understand the history of materialities within which these questions obtain their objects and densities. The objective, in other words, is to make explicit the premisses from which I offer my own readings of literary theory, as well as to prepare the theoretical ground from which it is then possible to argue that both Third-Worldist cultural nationalism and the more recently fashionable postmodernisms offer false knowledges of real facts.

Other Marxists may well disagree with at least part of my account, and shared understanding may well be the richer for such disagreements. But a theoretical position that dismisses the history of materialities as a 'progressivist modes-of-production narrative', historical agency itself as a 'myth of origins', nations and states (all nations and all states) as irretrievably coercive, classes as simply discursive constructs, and political parties themselves as fundamentally contaminated with collectivist illusions of a stable subject position – a theoretical position of that kind, from which no poststructuralism worth the name can escape, is, in the most accurate sense of these words, *repressive* and *bourgeois*.[29] It suppresses the very conditions of intelligibility within which the fundamental facts of our time can be theorized; and in privileging the figure of the reader, the critic, the theorist, as the guardian of the texts of this world, where everything becomes a text, it recoups the main cultural tropes of bourgeois humanism – especially in its Romantic variants, since the dismissal of class and nation as so many 'essentialisms' logically leads towards an ethic of non-attachment as the necessary condition of true understanding, and because breaking away from collective socialities of that kind inevitably leaves only the 'individual'– in the most abstract sense epistemologically, but in the shape of the critic/theorist concretely – as the locus of experience and meaning, while the well-known poststructuralist scepticism about the possibility of rational knowledge impels that same 'individual' to maintain only an ironic relation with the world and its intelligibility.[30] I might add that this issue of irony and non-attachment as regards literary poststructuralism of the kind under discussion here surfaces in a variety of ways: in the actual practice of the individual critics, in the ideological positions they advocate, and in the heavily charged ways in which conditions of postmodern 'migrancy' and the image of the theorist as 'traveler' are foregrounded.[31]

As one now examines that branch of literary theory which poses those questions, one is struck by the fact that while the privileging of cultural nationalism as the determinate political energy of our time takes place under one or another variant of the Three Worlds Theory, the subsequent move *against* nationalism – all of it – is made under a completely different theoretical signature, that of poststructuralism. The two moments – politically, for and against nationalism; theoretically, Third-Worldism and poststructuralism – remain discrete and epiphenomenal, even though the more outlandish of the poststructuralists have tried to combine them. What this branch of literary theory has lacked is a larger configuration of concepts that may produce a systematic periodization of its own practices and of that world to which it constantly refers, so that it may overcome the discreteness of *moments* and their second-order explanations.[32] That is, I suppose, another way of saying that in renouncing Marxism and in developing a shrill rhetoric against historicism – not just the positivist and geneticist current in it, but historicism as such – avant-gardist literary theory has turned its back on modes of thought that might help it to grasp at least its own history.

My starting point in the present book, briefly put, is that the sizeable changes we have witnessed in the situation(s) of literary theory over the past quarter-century have occurred within the context of monumental and extremely rapid shifts in the economic and political orderings of the world, and that the surrender, in rapid succession, first to a Third-Worldist kind of nationalism and then to deconstruction – to poststructuralism generally, in fact – on the part of that branch of literary theory which is most engaged with questions of colony and empire conceals, instead of explaining, the relationships between literature, literary theory and that world of which these purport to be the literature and the theory. By the same token, then, the vicissitudes and even re-enactments of those more global realities in the shifting frames of literary theory become intelligible only if we connect the theory with the determinate and shaping forces of our time, not *through* poststructuralism but by examining, as a considerable issue in itself, the historical co-ordinates of the rise and fall of cultural nationalism as the master-code of this theory in its earlier phase, and then the turn away from activist kinds of politics – even nationalist politics – as this theory fully develops its poststructuralist complicities. I can illustrate this point with reference to a phenomenon that will be summarized here in very general outline but will receive considerable elaboration in the main body of this book.

We know that this branch of literary theory privileged cultural nationalism as the determinate ideological form of resistance against the dominant imperialist culture throughout the 1970s; but then, increasingly in the 1980s, nationalism itself, in all its forms, came to be discarded as an oppressive, coercive mechanism. I write at considerable length in Chapters 1 and 2 about factors which contributed to the predominance of cultural nationalism for a time, and the sea-change in the fortunes of nationalist ideology within literary theory in the later years – as we go, for instance, from *Orientalism* to the later work of Said himself, or from Fredric Jameson to a whole host of lesser and later critics like Homi Bhabha – needs, of course, to be traced in relation to developments internal to literary theory itself. But the precise terms in which this shift away from cultural nationalism has taken place would be unintelligible without taking into account the ascendancy of poststructuralism, with its debunking of all myths of origin, totalizing narratives, determinate and collective historical agents – even the state and political economy as key sites for historical narrativization.

The newly dominant position of poststructuralist ideology is the fundamental enabling condition for a literary theory which debunks nationalism not on the familiar Marxist ground that nationalism in the present century has frequently suppressed questions of gender and class and has itself been frequently complicit with all kinds of obscurantisms and revanchist positions, but in the patently postmodernist way of debunking *all* efforts to speak of origins, collectivities, determinate historical projects. The upshot, of course, is that critics working within the poststructuralist problematic no longer distinguish, in any foregrounded way, between the progressive and retrograde forms of nationalism with reference to particular histories, nor do they examine the even more vexed question of how progressive and retrograde elements may be (and often are) combined within particular nationalist trajectories; what gets debunked, rather, is nationalism *as such*, in more or less the same apocalyptic manner in which cultural nationalism was, only a few years earlier, declared the determinate answer to imperialism.

Needless to add, a number of tendencies within 'Western Marxism', especially as they developed in the 1960s, contributed considerably to the latter ascendancy of poststructuralism. If Marcuse finally came to abandon the category of class and to locate the revolutionary dynamic in the realms of the erotic and the aesthetic, Adorno's extreme pessimism in *Minima Moralia* found its analogue in Sartre's proposition, in *Critique of Dialectical Reason*, that the category of 'scarcity' makes it virtually inevitable that any 'fused group' which comes to power will undergo bureaucratic degeneration. The central case, so far as literary theory is concerned, was of course that of Althusser, who has exercised very considerable influence on 'theory' on both sides of the Atlantic and whose affinities with structuralism are well enough known.[33] It is also significant that Althusser's conception of ideology simultaneously as an 'unconscious', as 'a system (with its own logic and rigour) of representations', as 'the "lived" relation between men and the world',[34] and as something which saturates virtually all conceivable 'apparatuses' in political society (the state),[35] makes it remarkably homologous with the concept of 'discourse' as it was to be developed in poststructuralist thought – chiefly by his renegade pupil Michel Foucault, with whom he shared a deep antipathy towards humanism, even though the two clashed on the status of Marxism, the historic role of the working class and, above all, the issue of practical involvement in communist politics.[36] And there is, of course, the accidental matter of temporal adjacency; even though the historical moment of 'Western Marxism' in its continental unfolding was largely different, its moment of arrival in the Anglo-American academy in fact coincided with the arrival of poststructuralism itself, in the mid to late 1970s. Philosophical affinity of discrete elements facilitated, then, the acceptance of great many poststructuralist positions among literary theorists who came to it through the Althusserian route.

That poststructuralism, arising initially in fields as diverse as anthropology and philosophy, has given literary theory its present terms of thought, is obvious enough. But these changing fortunes of the nationalist ideology in the trajectories of literary theory are determined also – more decisively though less self-consciously on part of the theorists themselves – by the actual fortunes of the national-bourgeois state in the decolonized countries. The years between 1945 and 1975 may be roughly designated the high period of decolonization. The first half of this thirty-year period witnessed the Chinese Revolution, the Korean War and the decolonization of great many countries, including India, under the leadership of the national bourgeoisie, both medium and petty. The significant fact about this earlier phase is that neither the Chinese Revolution nor the Independence of India made much impact upon the literary intelligentsia – either in Britain as it recovered from the ravages of World War II, or in the United States as it descended into the most rabid kind of postwar reaction. Rather, it was in France that the successive shocks of the colonial wars in Indochina and North Africa, coming hot on the heels of the Nazi Occupation of France itself, tended to polarize the intelligentsia; the well-known confrontation between Sartre and Camus was the specific expression of a much broader polarization.

In the Anglo-American academy, the radicalizing impact came in the second phase of decolonization – ushered in, schematically speaking, by the Cuban Revolution (1958–9), Algerian independence (1962) and the onset of the Third Indochina War with the introduction of American troops during the Kennedy Administration. The Vietnam War was, of course, the central fact of the whole of this second phase, but the phase had two distinct and principal aspects: revolutionary wars of national liberation, mainly in countries of Indochina and Southern Africa, on the one hand; and, on the other, the consolidation of the national-bourgeois state in the majority of the Asian and African states that had been newly constituted as sovereign nations, where the expanding dynamic of global capitalism was bringing unprecedented growth and wealth to the newly dominant classes. This fundamental distinction between the revolutionary project in the countries under siege and of national-bourgeois consolidation in the rest was often erased from the dissenting ideologies that arose in the Anglo-American academy – except, of course, in those relatively small groups that had Marxist leanings or communist affiliation. In the anti-war movements of this period, the predominant sentiment was that of anti-colonialism, and the bulk of the mobilization, including the main organizers (the role of the Church and pacifist groups is usually understated in accounts from the Left), represented the political traditions essentially of decent liberalism thrown into agony by the scale of savagery and the number of American deaths. What this anti-war sentiment affirmed was the right of national self-determination, and it was in this period of the ascendancy of the national-bourgeois state that cultural nationalism – that is, the characteristic form of the nationalism of the national bourgeoisie – was declared to be the determinate ideological form for progressive cultural production.

This tendency was greatly augmented by the radical sectors of the Afro-American intelligentsia which identified deeply with the emergent groups in newly independent African countries, and by the students from Asia, Africa and the Caribbean who faced various kinds of racism in the Anglo-American academy and resisted that pressure by positing against it the literary documents and cultural practices of the social configurations that were dominant in their own societies but commanded no status in the Western canonical formations. This was a defensive ideology of parochial pride necessitated by the superior power of the metropolitan – predominantly white – academy, with the student coming to represent, in his own eyes as much as in his hosts', the culture of his nation and his newly independent state.[37] Meanwhile, the national-bourgeois state partly basked in the reflected glory of the wars of national liberation, hence in the general valorization of nationalism as such; in part, it was seen as the very expression of the aura of particular leaders – Nasser, Nehru, Nkrumah, Sukarno, Nyerere, Kenyatta, and others – who had led the movements of anti-colonial consolidation. Now, as the stagnation of that type of post-colonial state has become more obvious in more recent years, and as the perception of that stagnation coincided chronologically with the ascendancy of poststructuralism in literary theory, cultural nationalism itself is currently in the process of being discarded as illusion, myth, totalizing narrative.

These monolithic attitudes towards the issue of nationalism–shifting rapidly from unconditional celebration to contemptuous dismissal – are also a *necessary* outcome of a radical theory that is none the less pitched self-consciously against the well-known Marxist premisses and therefore comes to rely, consecutively and at times simultaneously, on the nationalistic versions of the Three Worlds Theory and deconstructionist kinds of poststructuralism. An obvious consequence of repudiating Marxism was that one now sought to make sense of the world of colonies and empires much less in terms of classes, much more in terms of nations and countries and races, and thought of imperialism itself not as a hierarchically structured system of global capitalism but as a *relation*, of governance and occupation, between richer and poorer countries, West and non-West. And whether one said so or not, one inevitably believed that ideas – 'culture' was the collective term in most mystifications, or 'discourse', but it mainly meant books and films – and not the material conditions of life which include the instance of culture itself, determine the fate of peoples and nations. All kinds of visionary hopes were provisionally attached to the ideologies of decolonization. With the colonial relationship broken, the newly independent states were expected to combat imperialism with their nationalist *ideologies*, regardless of what classes were now in power and irrespective of the utter inadequacy of the nationalist ideology as such, even at its best, to protect a backward capitalist country against the countless pressures of advanced capitalism, so long as the confrontation takes place within an imperialist structure – which is to say, on capitalist terms. When the limits of the nationalism of the national bourgeoisie became altogether evident, the hostility towards rigorous kinds of Marxism that had been assimilated from the postmodern avant-garde made it impossible for this literary theory to produce a rationally historicized autocritique of its own prior enthusiasms for that kind of homogenized nationalism. Instead, poststructuralism itself was offered as the determinate answer to nationalism, while – in at least some versions – some discrete elements of Marxism (not to speak of feminism) were reworked into the subordinate clauses of poststructuralism. We thus have a specific conjunction of elements: a radical literary theory in the moment of repudiating the Marxist component of its own past; the rise and fall of the national-bourgeois state in the 'Third World' as the object of this radicalism's passion; capitalism's global offensive and, by the late 1980s, its global triumph; the ascendancy, in the theoretical realm, of poststructuralism. The rise and fall of nationalist ideology in the recent history of this literary theory is thus conjoined with other theoretical developments as well as with more directly political developments in the world.

1

# Literary Theory and 'Third World Literature': Some Contexts

The issue of assembling and professionalizing a new area of literature, namely 'Third World Literature', has arisen primarily in the metropolitan university, in England and North America for the most part, which is responding to quite specific kinds of pressures by appropriating particular kinds of texts, and by devising a new set of categories within the larger conceptual category of Literature as such. We may begin, then, by summarizing some of the pressures – literary, cultural, political pressures – as well as the general ideological conjuncture which impels them – and, through them, *us* – first to speak of a unitary category of Third World Literature and then to reproduce that very ideology, on an extended scale, in all we think and say about that category.[1] The directly political contexts which gave rise to the Three Worlds Theory in the first place, before it became a literary-critical matter, will be addressed in Chapter 8, towards the end of the book. The pressures and paradoxes I examine in this chapter, and also in the next, take institutional and pedagogical forms. Through these forms, I trace lineages of particular intelligentsias and then connect the practices of these intelligentsias with their largely unrecognized global determinations in order, precisely, to prepare a theoretical ground for examining the fairly widespread proposition that nationalism of one kind or another is the determinate ideological imperative in the cultural productions of the 'Third World' in the era of colonialism and imperialism. That proposition will be examined directly in Chapter 3.

I might add that I had initially felt reluctant to speak of these matters in the context of Indian debates because this matter of 'Third World

Literature' is connected, really, with the context of the metropolitan university and the teaching of Literature in *that* situation, but it has been necessary to engage with these questions here for obvious reasons. So fundamental and even genetic is the Indian university's relation with – indeed, dependence upon – its British and American counterparts that knowledges produced there become immediately effective here, in a relation of imperial dominance, shaping even the way we think of ourselves. So, in examining the pressures which impel the metropolitan university to devise new categories for conceptualizing cultural productions in our part of the world, I am speaking also of pressures which are exerted *by* the metropolitan university upon the already-subordinated Indian university. Nowhere is this parasitic intellectual dependence of the Indian university upon its metropolitan counterparts so obvious as in the teaching of English. And, typically, this dependence tends to be greater at the higher, more elite levels of English teaching in India: the more privileged universities, the handful of the elite colleges, those among the university faculties who are the most lavishly armed with degrees, foreign experience, lists of publications, academic ambitions. It is with disorientations of elite scholarship in our institutions that I am here implicitly most concerned.

In declaring nationalism to be the main political imperative of our era, the theoretical positions of 'Third World Literature' and 'Colonial Discourse Analysis' would tend to subvert, with overt intent or not, the rich history of our oppositional and radical cultural productions, which have more often than not come out of communist political practice and, more broadly, from inside a political culture deeply marked by Marxism. What we need to do is to build vastly better knowledges on the basis of that heritage; to revert, instead, from the Marxist critique of class, colony and empire to the emptiness of a Third-Worldist nationalism is politically and theoretically a regression. Inclusion of some writers from the 'Third World' in our existing curricula would surely be a gain, but a relatively less significant one, especially if it is done in an eclectic sort of way and without negotiating the consequences of the fact that 'literature' from other zones of the 'Third World'– African, say, or Arab or Caribbean – comes to us not directly or autonomously but through grids of accumulation, interpretation and relocation which are governed from the metropolitan countries.

By the time a Latin American novel arrives in Delhi, it has been selected, translated, published, reviewed, explicated and allotted a place in the burgeoning archive of 'Third World Literature' through a complex set of metropolitan mediations. That is to say, it arrives here with those processes of circulation and classification already inscribed in its very texture. About this contradictory role of imperialism which simultaneously unifies the world, in the form of global channels of circulation, and distributes it into structures of global coercion and domination, I shall say a great deal throughout this book. Suffice it to say here that even as we open ourselves up to the widest possible range of global cultural productions, it is best to keep in view the coercive power of the very channels through which we have access to those productions. Internationalism, in other words, has been one of the constitutive traditions of the Left, but in this age of late capitalism it is best to recognize that certain kinds of internationalism also arise more or less spontaneously out of the circuits of imperialist capital itself, and the lines between the internationalism of the Left and the globalism of capitalist circuits must always be demarcated as rigorously as possible.

It is in the metropolitan country, in any case, that a literary text is first designated a Third World text, levelled into an archive of other such texts, and then globally redistributed with that aura attached to it. It is useful, therefore, to demystify the category of 'Third World Literature' which is emerging in the metropolitan university now as something of a counter-canon and which – like any canon, dominant or emergent – does not really exist before its fabrication. What, we may ask, are the conditions within which this new subdiscipline of Literature, namely 'Third World Literature', has been assembled? My summary treatment of these conditions will emphasize a specific grid of four mutually reinforcing elements: (a) the general backgrounds and the contemporary situation of literary theory itself; (b) the new availability and increasing influence in the metropolitan countries of a large number of literary texts composed by non-Western writers; (c) the increasing numbers and therefore far greater social assertion there of immigrant professional strata from non-Western countries; and (d) the arrival, during that same period, of a new political theory – namely, the Three Worlds Theory – which eventually had the widest possible circulation in many variants, including, especially, the one popularized by certain sections of the Parisian avant-garde which saw in it – at a certain stage of its evolution, before settling down into straightforward right-wing positions – a convenient alternative to classical Marxism – convenient, I might add, because one could thus retain, and even enhance, one's radical credentials. Only the first of these elements – the backgrounds and contexts of contemporary literary theory itself – will be addressed in this chapter; Chapter 2 will take up the rest. This somewhat schematic commentary on the contexts of metropolitan literary Third-Worldism will then make possible fuller discussions of the authors and texts which constitute this ideological tendency, the Three Worlds Theory as such, the constitutive role of nationalism in that theory, and some alternative starting points.

## I

As regards the contemporary situation of literary theory, it is as well to recall that even the more advanced sectors of English Studies during the period between the two World Wars were dominated by four main – and in some significant respects overlapping – tendencies: the practical criticism of I.A. Richards;[2] the conservative, monarchist, quasi-Catholic criticism of T.S. Eliot; some elements of avant-gardist modernism which nevertheless remained much less theorized in the English-speaking countries than in continental Europe; and the then newly emergent 'New Criticism' of Ransom, Tate and others in the United States.[3]

The impulse to resist these exclusivist – and, in many areas, technicist – emphases was stronger in England, where there had been a much older tradition of socially conscious literary study. The *Scrutiny* group, led by F.R. Leavis, assimilated the pedagogical value of practical criticism, making its salutary move to define objective criteria for literary analysis to displace the aristocratic notions of literary 'taste', while also insisting on locating the texts of English literature in the larger narrative of English social life. More recent critiques of the Leavisite tendency have documented this group's own deep complicity in the ideologies of the Tory middle class; Leavis's own almost messianic vision of English Studies as the determinate mode of cultural salvation for England has been documented often enough.[4] There was also, however, a populist kind of radicalism in their positions.[5] That populist edge was what Raymond Williams picked up, and then combined with his own Welsh working-class background, as well as with the kind of radicalism that had once brought him into the Communist Party, even as he returned from the war and started working on his magisterial survey in *Culture and Society*. Over the next twenty years or so, he produced a large number of studies – including *The Country and the City*, possibly the most moving book of literary criticism ever written in the English language – which went over the same territory that had been marked earlier by Leavis, remapping it in highly original, radical and persuasive ways. By the time Williams died, in 1988, he had revamped the very terms in which English Studies had conceived of the relation between literature, culture, society and history. I do not mean that Williams ever came to command the kind of power that, let us say, Eliot had once commanded – and continues to command in some circles, especially in *our* university departments and among the genteel literati. One could safely say, however, that between Leavis's Tory populism and Williams's increasingly Marxist perspectives – and the kinds of thinking these two represented, the influences they exercised – the more advanced sectors of the academic literary intelligentsia in British universities continued to grapple relatively more steadily with the social matrix of literary production, even at the height of the Cold War.

In some ways, this British development was in sharp contrast with the American, which will be discussed below, and this too can be briefly clarified if we take a slightly more extended look at Williams's career. He had started exercising his broad influence in Britain with the publication of *Culture and Society* (1958), at about the same time as Northrop Frye published his *magnum opus*, *Anatomy of Criticism* (1957), when the careers of the likes of Paul de Man and Harold Bloom also got going. In other words, while the reaction against 'New Criticism' in the United States moved increasingly into the questions of genre, conservatively defined, or towards deconstruction and associated positions, the critique of I.A. Richards and Leavis in England moved leftward. Nor was it a solitary endeavour, even though Williams's later ruminations about how alone he felt at the time deserve our respect.[6] For it was precisely at the time when the intellectual climate in the United States had solidified into the worst kind of Cold War anti-communism that the Communist Party Historians' Group was assembled as a collective enterprise and began changing the British intellectual landscape.[7] Two members, Maurice Dobb and Christopher Hill, had published substantial work before,[8] but their assertion as a group, as well as the best work of each of them, came after the war – the period being inaugurated, so to speak, with the publication of Dobb's *Studies in the Development of Capitalism* in 1946. That kind of research, of course, provided a sustaining climate for work like Williams's, so far as strictly literary and cultural studies were concerned, but it is worth remarking that much more than simple sustenance from a cognate academic discipline is involved here. There were, of course, personal associations which, judging from available evidence, seem not to have broken down entirely, even though Williams dissociated himself from the party after returning from the war, but then there is also the fact that several of these historians made immeasurable contributions to cultural studies directly. Victor Kiernan is a substantial critic of literature in his own right, and Hill himself is one of the most authoritative scholars of Milton and of seventeenth-century 'culture' generally[9] – not to speak of E.P. Thompson, whose first major work was a study of William Morris[10] and whose *The Making of the English Working Class* (1963) should be one of the fundamental texts for any Cultural Studies Programme, anywhere in the world. That ensemble of intellectual productions was one part – and surely a shaping part – of the milieu in which Williams's own intellectual formation took place, even though he kept his distance from Marxism at that time. But there were other things as well, such as the adult education work in which Williams found partnerships with intellectuals like Hoggart,[11] and direct political activism in such organizations as the Campaign for Nuclear Disarmament (CND), which proved equally sustaining and, for Williams himself, a bridge both towards the 'New Left', when that emerged as a distinct tendency in the 1960s, and into the lived pressure of collective engagements which helped him define for himself, over the years, a much finer Marxism than anything he had known in his youth.

Williams's was a peculiar odyssey, quite the reverse of what happens so very often when the commitments and passions of youth give way to professional incorporation and increasing embourgeoisement. Williams's intellect, always cautious and always reluctant to press too far beyond thresholds of existing convictions, kept moving leftward. What he had gained in the writing of the earlier books he never lost, but the culture of his ideas in, say, *Problems of Materialism and Culture* (1980) is doubtless much wider, more to the Left, more theoretically grounded. But then, as one reads the two posthumous collections of his essays, *The Politics of Modernism* and *Resources of Hope* (1989), one is struck by the fact that in those closing years of his life his mind had become, if anything, more passionate. *Culture and Society* had doubtless had enormous impact in Britain, though much less in the United States. Even so, right up to and after the publication of *The Country and the City* (1973), Williams was seen only as a very distinctive kind of literary/cultural critic, and his continuing activist affiliation with the Left throughout that period – preserved now in such documents as *Mayday Manifesto* (1968) – was seen as not central to his critical enterprise, partly because of the ambiguous relationship Williams himself had maintained with theoretical Marxism.

The real turn came, in fact, in the mid 1970s and after. In part, of course, Williams's turn towards theoretical Marxism at this juncture was connected with the introduction, mainly via *New Left Review*, of many texts of continental Marxism (Gramsci to Colletti, Althusser to Goldmann) into the British Isles. But, characteristically, it took the form of rethinking the existing categories of his own thought. His recovery and reconsideration of the categorical apparatus that had been in the background of *Culture and Society*, which he now published in *Keywords* (1976; enlarged, revised edition 1984), precisely at the time when he was working on his *Marxism and Literature* (1977), has the status, I think, of a symptomatic caesura, connecting his earlier work with the later but also beginning to form a line of clear demarcation. This task of reconsideration then took the shape of what is to my mind a very moving book in its own right, *Politics and Letters* (1979), in which Williams submitted himself to sustained questioning, at once courteous and firm, by Marxist scholars of a younger generation, responding with reflections on his own work with astonishing – and, in the fullest sense of the word, *enabling* – veracity. The work of his last decade went from strength to strength thereafter, though the breadth of its engagements was hardly to be contained in a given book. In the process, Williams helped to sustain a level of critical discourse not easily dislodged by the kind of new fashions and new orthodoxies that came to dominate literary studies – in sections of the British Left itself but, even more, in the United States.

For the American intellectual formation had been different in significant ways. There was no working-class culture of the kind England had had since at least the Chartists. The chief characteristics of the bourgeois revolution in the United States had been that (a) it was carried out by a section of the settler population against the colonial regime which had constituted that population in the first place; and (b) bourgeois hegemony was established before the full consolidation of the classes of industrial capitalism, and under a leadership ideologically as advanced as in revolutionary France but drawn, in its class composition, substantially from the plantation economy of slaveowners, with the predominantly commercial and petty capitals of New England occupying a subordinate position. The contradictory consequence was that the American Revolution was, simultaneously, in some fundamental ways even more advanced than the French, while it retained some aspects so retrograde that its full elaboration spanned virtually a whole century and was completed only in 1864 with the destruction of the plantation economy and the assimilation of the slave population first into sharecropping and then increasingly into wage-labour circuits.

The origins of English Romanticism are inseparable from the anti-capitalist passions of Blake, and it had the Cromwellian radicalism of Milton in its past; even Wordsworth and Coleridge had been, before their respective Tory conversions, radical supporters of the Jacobin content in the French Revolution. The main currents of American Romanticism were, by contrast, oracular and transcendentalist, optimistic and confident; this one can see readily if one were to pause and think what 'transcendence' might have meant to, say, Blake and Emerson respectively. In the nineteenth-century American pantheon it is only in people like Frederick Douglass – in the songs and narratives of the slaves; in Sojourner Truth, in John Brown, in radical Abolitionism – that one sees the Cromwellian element, but the racism of the American literary Establishment has been such that even the inclusion of Douglass in this pantheon has been only a recent and is still a very sectoral matter; all the rest is consigned to the obscurity of 'minority literature'. Among the great American poets of that time, Whitman is of course the most 'Jacobin', but it is symptomatic of this oracular tendency in American Romanticism that whenever Whitman errs, he errs into sugariness and mist. The experience which had produced this Romanticism – especially in the dominant, Emersonian current – was not the experience of industrial capitalism, as in England, but that of a society of independent petty commodity producers, which was the predominant mode of existence for the middling classes of the Eastern seaboard until the mid nineteenth century.

The case of Emily Dickinson, the most moving nineteenth-century American poet and one of the most thoroughly nuanced literary intelligences ever to be born in the United States, is indicative in this regard. She wrote some of her greatest poems in the years of the American Civil War, and the pain of them is quite as excruciating as in Blake; yet, except for a handful of oblique references and metaphors, that decisive experience of her generation is entirely absent from her work. Lacking other sorts of traditions and communities, she seems to have been driven to experience her deepest pains in a privacy that had been radically separated, in order to be understood, from the public and the political. I do not mean that either Emerson or Dickinson was even remotely conservative by persuasion, in the way that British Tories always are; nor do I mean that other currents were not there, even within the dominant tradition. There is the overwhelming presence of Mark Twain, for example, in the latter part of the nineteenth century. And if one steps out of the dominant tradition, there is of course a large body of writings by women who tell us a great deal about the stresses of embourgeoisement in a gendered society, not to speak of Black literature, which documents in very straightforward ways much of the pain and cruelty upon which the splendour of America has been built.

What I do mean, however, is that the tradition of letters American modernism inherited from its own elite past had rarely been informed by energies of the working class; was dominated largely by the boundless and somewhat philistine optimism of New England's petty commodity producers; and had made a truce, by and large, with the racism and mercantilism of its own society. Even as this mercantilism and petty commodity production in New England, as well as the slave society of the South, gave way, in the latter half of the nineteenth century, to the social predominance of large-scale industrial capital, the critical issue for masters of American fiction, such as Henry James, was whether the ruling class of this new industrial society would learn the leisured manners of European aristocracy, or descend into the purest forms of commodity fetishism. A particular tension in James's work, of course, is that he is more or less equally attracted and repelled by both the aristocratic arrogances of the European cultural elite and by the forms of self-aggrandizing bourgeois individualisms that were taking shape in the USA more firmly and visibly than in Europe. What the cost of this unprecedented American growth was – for the immigrant, the Black, the poor farmer of the Midwest – James did not, at any rate, care about much.

It is hardly surprising, in this context, that American modernism turned out to be deeply conservative and elitist, often with racist overtones. Of the four poets – Pound, Eliot, Stevens and Williams – who are commonly considered the masters of American modernism, only Williams had even a populist strand.[12] Admittedly, the 1930s also experienced a sudden wave of literary and cultural radicalism, but the two remarkable things about that radicalism are (a) the fact that it left behind no body of radical critical thought, even on the order of, let us say, Christopher Cauldwell in England; and (b) the quickness with which it disappeared as a *literary* phenomenon, leaving little trace upon the subsequent postwar literary culture even though it left behind many undercurrents in the larger society which then fed, more or less silently, into the rise of the New Left during the 1960s. After World War II, as the USA consolidated its position as the leading capitalist power in the world, so immense was the right-wing national consensus, so pathological the anti-communist phobia, that those lonely figures, such as Kenneth Burke, who continued to do serious radical work in literary and cultural theory were thoroughly marginalized.

The cumulative weight of this cultural configuration has been such that when 'New Criticism' appeared on the horizon – with its fetishistic notions of the utter autonomy of each single literary work, and its post-Romantic idea of 'Literature' as a special kind of *language* which yields a special kind of knowledge – its practice of reified reading proved altogether hegemonic in American literary studies for a quarter-century or more, and it proved extremely useful as a pedagogical tool in the American classroom precisely because it required of the student little knowledge of anything not strictly 'literary' – no history which was not predominantly literary history, no science of the social, no philosophy – except the procedures and precepts of literary formalism, which, too, it could not entirely accept in full objectivist rigour thanks to its prior commitment to squeezing a particular ideological meaning out of each literary text. The favourite New Critical text was the short lyric, precisely because the lyric could be detached with comparatively greater ease from the larger body of texts, and indeed from the world itself, to become the ground for analysis of compositional minutiae; the pedagogical advantage was, of course, that such analyses of short lyrics could fit rather neatly into one hour in the undergraduate classroom. This pedagogical advantage, and the attendant detachment of 'Literature' from the crises and combats of real life, served also to conceal the ideology of some of the leading lights of 'New Criticism' who were quaintly called 'Agrarian Populist' but were really bourgeois gentlemen of the New South, the cultural heirs of the old slaveowning class. What is even more significant, however, is that 'New Criticism' reached its greatest power in the late 1940s, as the USA launched the Cold War and entered the period of McCarthyism, and that its definitive decline from hegemony began in the late 1950s as McCarthyism, in the strict sense, also receded and the Eisenhower doctrine began to give way to those more contradictory trends which eventually flowered during the Kennedy era – those golden years of US liberalism which gave us the Vietnam War. The peculiar blend of formalist detachment and deliberate distancing from forms of the prose narrative, with their inescapable locations in social life, into reified readings of short lyrics was, so to speak, the objective correlative of other kinds of distancing and reifications required by the larger culture.

The first dissent against New Criticism came at this transitional time – from critics like Northrop Frye, who retained the conception of Literature as a special language yielding a special kind of knowledge, but insisted also that individual literary texts simply could not be discussed outside some larger narrative. What Frye wanted, of course, was that any given poem or novel should be placed within a wider, formalist narrative of all-encompassing genres and literary modes. His preferred text was not so much the short lyric as the longer narrative poem, preferably in the genre of romance or comedy, which are as a rule much less tainted by the stresses of lived socialities. Literature's true residence was still, in any case, in the metaphysical, preferably religious, Sublime: the poem, we were told, writes itself through the poet, and the closed, self-reproducing history of genres is the true history of civilization's deep structures in which the individual poet performs only a communicative and incidental function, as the site of more or less linguistic elaboration. This kind of literary-critical training was later to prove helpful in paving the way for structuralism, as well as what came to be known as Discourse Theory: language doing the speaking through human beings, human agency constituted by discourse itself, with each genre now seen either as a distinct discourse or, alternatively, as a specific form in Literature's discursive regularities. The job of the critic came to reside, therefore, in the power of these regularities to generate enunciations, more or less infinitely. The training also facilitated various kinds of Romantic, anti-humanist irrationalisms, through its emphasis both on extra-rational inspiration, thus reiterating the Romantic trope of poet as prophet and oracle, and on writing emanating neither from the pressures of history and society nor from the writer's own choice, but from literature's power to write itself through the medium of the writer. The crucial period of Frye's intellectual formation, from *Fearful Symmetry* (1947) to *Anatomy of Criticism* (1957), encompassed the heyday of McCarthyism, and it was after the appearance of the latter work that his influence became, for a time, decisive.

The figures who came to dominate the US literary scene from the 1960s onwards – figures like Paul de Man and Harold Bloom – had emerged towards the end of this transition from Dulles-style, pathological anti-communism to the Kennedy-style, hard-edged 'liberal' imperialism – the transition, one might say, from Korea to Vietnam. The political origins of de Man's ideas are, of course, far more complex and disagreeable, given his own Nazi associations, to which he never confessed or faced up publicly during his lifetime, but certain broad emphases may also be identified. Bloom's early work had the effect, first, of privileging the Romantic Movement as *the* modern movement, thus extending the tendencies which were already there in Frye and Cleanth Brooks but taking them further in Nietzschean directions; and, second, of locating the difference of later texts in the anxieties produced by earlier ones, so that the field of textual production becomes contentious and conflictual, while the history of such productions and contentions itself remains strictly textual. Even though Bloom was later to be greatly disturbed by the ascendancy of deconstruction, he was entirely incapable of mounting a *theoretical* counter-offensive because of his essentially untheoretical, literary-critical bent and his prior complicity in the Romantic, the religious, the prophetic and the oracular –

Emersonian in one breath, Nietzschean in another, biblical in yet another. That same privileging of Romanticism is there in de Man's early work, even though it was mediated even then by his own preference for reading the Romantics themselves through Heidegger. It is at least arguable that his later slide into Derridean positions was facilitated by the specifically Heideggerian forms of anti-rationalism. The overall thrust of American deconstruction was in any case highly technicist, shorn of whatever political radicalism there might have been in the original French formation; the net effect was to make the text entirely hermetic. If the New Critics had privileged the isolated text in order to contemplate its beauty and principle of coherence, deconstruction isolated it for identifying the principle of dissolution inherent in its very textuality; but the closure of the text, its hermetic distancing, was in either case the precondition for its reading. That Frye, Bloom and de Man were all attracted, in their respective ways, by versions of the irrational, the religious and the Romantic contributed to a structure of feeling in American literary criticism which was implicitly already hostile to rationalism and therefore particularly receptive to sloganeering against the Enlightenment, and so on, when the fashion arrived from Paris.

If New Critical close reading had had the effect of offering a method which took the literary text out of the chitchat of leisured gentlemen, a method that could be taught to undergraduates in repeated fifty-minute doses, deconstructionist close reading became a fully fledged technology requiring specialist training that would span both the undergraduate and the graduate classrooms for about ten years. It was in the moment of the emergence of this full-scale technology – launched, paradoxically enough, in contemptuous dismissal of rationalism for its claims to scientificity – that literary criticism in the English-speaking countries gave way to what came to be known as literary theory. The general political climate which attended its birth and the technological hermeticism of textuality which is deconstruction's main concern have left their mark on the very structure of US literary theory, with the result that the younger critics who came to constitute the left wing of the US literary Establishment in the Carter and Reagan years were themselves hung, excruciatingly, between de Man and lessons of the Vietnam War. The mystique of Left professionalism, which grew alongside literary theory, was a precise expression of this self-division. If the lessons of the Vietnam War took one into politics, the technologism of theory took one deeper and deeper into mastery of the professional field, and radical literary theory, like any professional field, also developed a language and a way of referencing other signposts within it, which were inaccessible to those located outside its boundaries.[13]

## II

It was in the 1960s, in any case, that contentions were really sharpened, in the form of a three-way split. The great majority of teachers and critics have continued to function, in both Britain and North America, as if nothing much has changed since T.S. Eliot and the 'New Criticism'. An entirely new kind of literary avant-garde has also arisen, however, on both sides of the Atlantic, which functions now – alongside and in conflict with the conservative majority – under the insignia not of criticism but of theory. This shift in the governing insignia indicates, for the bulk of this avant-garde, both a continuity of perspective and a sea-change in method: the idea of the *specialness* of literature (special language, special kind of knowledge, answerable only to its own past practices and rules of composition – now invoked as forms of discourse – and not to the world outside the text) is retained and vastly complicated, but the analytic method refers now not to the enclosed world of 'literary criticism' but to a whole host of 'extra-literary' theoretical positions, from psychoanalysis to phenomenology, linguistics to philosophy. (Psychology, of course, was there even as early as Richards, but the resurfacing of Freud, via Lacan, in the new literary theory was of an entirely different kind.) In an accompanying move, 'Literature' undergoes both a deflation and an aggrandizement: it becomes, in one sort of reading, just *one* discourse among other discourses, with its *specialness* residing simply in the *difference* of its language; but in a much more radical and now quite pervasive displacement – which asserts that there is really nothing outside language, outside textuality, outside representation – *everything* becomes, in a sense, 'Literature'.

The *bulk* of this avant-garde is essentially technicist, much more so than poor old 'New Criticism' ever dreamed of being, but alongside this bulk there is also a minoritarian current within the avant-garde. Sometimes overlapping with that dominant current and sometimes resisting some of its technicist stridencies, but almost always – and increasingly so in the 1980s – needing to respond to that dominance in its own terms, this minoritarian current attempts to fashion, with lesser or greater success, politically informed readings. But the question of what constitutes political reading is itself greatly complicated for this radical current because of the character of its own intellectual formation as it went through graduate schools, solidified its theoretical bearings and affiliations, and began joining the profession during precisely the period about which Lentricchia has written with such elegance. He has described the shaping influences for this period (1957–77):

> Northrop Frye, Wallace Stevens, Frank Kermode, Jean-Paul Sartre, Georges Poulet, Martin Heidegger, Ferdinand de Saussure, Claude Lévi-Strauss, Roland Barthes, Jacques Derrida, and Michel Foucault have largely set the terms and themes of recent critical controversies in the country. Theodor Adorno, Walter Benjamin, Georg Lukács, Antonio Gramsci, Louis Althusser, Lucien Goldmann, and others in their tradition have a great deal to say to American critics, but in the period I have chosen to study they have not been shaping influences.[14]

Two clarifications about the inclusion of Sartre in the first list must be made. For if he was one of those who 'set the terms' for American criticism during that period, it was *not* through his growing concern with political engagement or his later turn towards Marxism but through his 'existentialism' and, specifically, his very early work, *The Psychology of Imagination*. Furthermore, the younger critics who came of age at this time read the later Sartre, if at all, not directly but through the disparaging critiques of Lévi-Strauss, Derrida, and others. More generally, Lentricchia's two contrasting lists – of those who 'set the terms', and of the absences – makes it quite clear that what came to be known later as 'Western Marxism'[15] was not a part of the intellectual formation of that generation of American critics, and by the time the more radical among them began to read these other kinds of theorists, their basic critical positions had been formed quite solidly by deconstruction, etc. When any sustained reading began of Gramsci, whose name was to be much abused in later theorizations, his work was as a rule read into a theoretical position already framed by Derrida and Paul de Man, Foucault and Lyotard; the question was how to assimilate Gramsci *into* this pre-existing structure. This, then, determined the nature of the 'political' readings which followed.

Politically more engaged in its earlier projects, increasingly more professionalized and confined to the academy since the recooling of America began in the latter 1970s, this minoritarian current of radicals in contemporary literary theory has its origins in those new groupings among students and teachers of the 1960s which had at that time begun to interrogate the very 'literariness' of the literary text, so as to locate it not in the history of genres and styles but in the larger history of the world itself. When Marxism had proposed such a worldly approach to literature, a confident American literary Establishment had dismissed it out of hand, as mere 'sociology'. Now, under mounting pressures, a whole range of people – only a few of them Marxist in any fashion or degree – have had to open up this buried continent of Literature to the scrutinizing gaze of history and politics. How this has come about is a complex tale, and this is not the occasion to tell it, but it is worth emphasizing that the emergence of this current – complex as it was, fragmented as it remained, and regardless of all its later detours and largely successful incorporation into poststructuralism – was connected, in its origins, with the crisis provoked in the Western academy first by the Algerian Revolution and then by the Vietnam War. It was in the crucible of those wars that at least some of the intellectuals of the contemporary West learned to question their own place in the world, and hence also to question the hegemonic closure of the texts upon which their epistemologies were based. One of the side-effects of that overall crisis was that Literature was pressed to disclose the strategic complicities whereby it had traditionally represented races – and genders – and empires.

The first breaks came, predictably, in France. For one thing, the 'Jacobin' element was much older, more deeply rooted, in the French universities, where even the most revered institutions had long been dominated not by an aristocracy, as in England, but by the petty bourgeoisie, thanks to the legacy of the Revolution itself. Then, in sharp contrast to the American variant of modernism, Paris, one of the main sites for the emergence of that modernism (Berlin and Vienna were, arguably, the other two), had become, by the early decades of this century, the home of the more radical, anti-bourgeois positions within modernism, such as the Cubist Movement or the more politically motivated strands in Dada and Surrealism. The inter-war years also witnessed the emergence of the first sizeable Marxist philosophical tradition in France (much later than in Germany or Russia or even Italy, but earlier and more articulated than in the predominantly Anglo-Saxon countries); the emergence also of mass labour and communist movements; the first Popular Front government; and the widely felt radicalizing influence of the Spanish Civil War. On the heels of all that came the Nazi Occupation, which gave numerous French intellectuals, especially those who actually fought in the underground Resistance, some imaginative understanding of the meaning of colonial subjection and the legitimacy of combat for liberation. Finally, it was in the *French* colonies, Indochina and Algeria, that the two great wars of anti-colonial national liberation broke out. For a whole generation of French writers, from Merleau-Ponty to André Malraux, support for the anti-colonial struggles was the natural extension of the anti-fascist struggles at home and the earlier movement of solidarity with the Republic in Spain; for others, the issues of colony and empire served to open up a whole range of other buried areas as well, from ontology to gendering. Thus, for example, Sartre's philosophical and literary radicalism from the late 1940s onwards, as well as Simone de Beauvoir's emergence in the 1950s as the seminal figure in modern feminism, are inseparable from the reshaping of their lives and ideas due to their involvement in the French anti-war movement during the Algerian Revolution; and it is symptomatic of the whole drift of modern French thought that the decisive attack on Sartre, mounted by Claude Lévi-Strauss – and mounted, precisely, in the name of the anthropological pre-modern – came towards the very end of the Algerian War.[16]

The two decades of the greatest radicalism in French thought – roughly from 1945 to 1965 – were also the decades in which the colonial question became the principal point of contention within French society, just as the rise and fall of American radicalism in the subsequent decade, from about 1965 to 1975, was also a direct consequence of the Vietnam War. Inside France, however, the years of the Indochinese and Algerian wars had coincided with the installation of a new-style, Fordist regime of capital accumulation, thanks largely to French acceptance of the Marshall Plan.

While the labour movement itself had gradually been tamed through the 1950s, facilitated further by the French Communist Party's convergence with its own bourgeoisie on the colonial question, the defeat in Indochina and the bloody combat in *colon*-dominated Algeria served to move large sections of the French population, including substantial sections of the intelligentsia, into the Right's embrace. The settlement of the Algerian War then paved the way for full-scale consolidation of High Gaullism. It was at this point that the ascendancy of structuralism and then of semiotics began – first in fairly radical variants, in keeping with the temper of the times, and then in increasingly formalist, domesticated directions. Both Lévi-Strauss and Roland Barthes, for example, had initially indicated affinities with Marxism, claiming for linguistics, in earlier phases of their respective careers, not so much an *ontological* primacy as, basically, a *methodological* efficacy. The real trends remained so unclear for so many years that the Events of 1968, when they burst upon the French scene, were widely viewed as the inaugural gesture of a new generation of radical, even revolutionary, intellectuals and militants, and *neither* as the process that propelled the worst kind of anti-communism to an hegemonic position among the Parisian avant-garde *nor* as the last rites for an antiquated form of capitalism which was soon to be replaced by a more efficient, more consumptionist form.[17] In the course of the decade following 1968, Paris was at length normalized. Many of the more strident members of the generation of '68, from Kristeva to Glucksmann, then passed into the ultra-Right of the 'New Philosophers', and the voices that came to dominate French intellectual life – Derrida and Foucault, Lyotard and Baudrillard, Deleuze and Guattari – quite comfortably announced 'the death of the subject', 'the end of the social', and so on.[18]

Developments in the USA were somewhat different. *There* 1968 was not a year of defeat or disorganization for the Left – such as it was. Rather, 1968, from the American point of view, was the year of the spectacular victories of the Vietnamese Tet offensive, the high point of the Black rebellion inside the country, the abdication of Lyndon Johnson, the hot summer of the anti-war movement. The historical underpinnings of the American anti-war movement were no doubt contradictory and ambiguous. On the one hand, the political underdevelopment of the United States was such that the anti-war movement could not even become a properly anti-imperialist movement, let alone a revolutionary one; for most of its participants, it was simply a movement against the direct involvement of the US armed forces in Vietnam, and it fizzled out as soon as Nixon started bringing back the troops. On the other hand, so massive was the mobilization of millions of people – men and women, Black and white – that they were able, over a decade or more, to put on the social agenda questions that had been suppressed for far too long.

There were four consequences for the teaching of literature; these can be listed here separately for the sake of clarity, though in actual fact there was considerable overlap among the forces and human agencies which produced them. First, the anti-war radicalism was combined with the preceding and in some ways overlapping Black Civil Rights Movement and what came to be known as Black Cultural Nationalism; colleges and universities were opened up for Black students and faculty as never before; and Black literature, which had never been taught in the US academy with any degree of coherence, now became a serious, albeit still very marginalized, discipline. Second, this confluence (or at least simultaneity) of the predominantly white anti-war movement and the many strands of Black oppositional politics opened up a much wider political space in which a whole range of other social agents, by no means *constituted* by those movements, nevertheless began to articulate their own agendas in new and much larger ways than previously; the movements of Hispanic-Americans and of Mexican agricultural labour within the USA are cases in point. It is significant that some of the more influential figures in that first wave of the contemporary Women's Movement in the USA which began to gather force in the late 1960s – figures as different as Shulamith Firestone and Adrienne Rich, Robin Morgan and Angela Davis – had been radicalized first within those other movements; it was only somewhat later that they began to think consistently of their own positions as women, of the larger history of those positions, and of the many modes of women's resistance, past and present. As a fully fledged women's movement gathered momentum – not centralized but dispersed at many sites, originating as much in a common history as in diverse local pressures – the impact began to be felt within the academy as well, and Women's Studies programmes were organized throughout the United States as never before; many would argue that it is precisely in the academy that the Women's Movement has made its largest gains. Third, and as a result of an equally diverse 'New Left' which was nevertheless based largely on campuses, Marxism itself made its first serious appearance as a theoretical position within the US academy.[19] The short-lived communist growth of the 1930s had doubtless given rise to many writers, intellectuals and teachers who were on the Left, either sympathetic towards communism or communists themselves. But they had been activists rather than theorists – indeed, many of them had thought of theoretical work and political practice as radical opposites – and as they began to be purged from the universities during the McCarthy era, they left behind a relatively meagre theoretical legacy, beyond the Leftist version of the well-known Reflection Theory of Realism, as regards presuppositions which governed the teaching of literature. What happened *now* was that as the student generation of the 1960s started teaching in the university during the 1970s, at least a few of them became serious Marxist intellectuals, dispersed as they were in several disciplines, including Literature. Given the absence of any real socialist movement outside the university, this was usually a very academic kind of Marxism; and, given the absence of a preceding Marxist cultural tradition, this new Marxism was frequently and fashionably combined with all sorts of other things, in all kinds of eclectic and even esoteric ways. The fact remains, however, that even these inroads were more than the US academy had ever known – unlike the European academy, where Marxism had had a much older presence. Fourth, and finally, there was the issue of colonialism and imperialism, which was addressed now, in any sort of systematic fashion, for the first time in the history of US literary criticism.

This last issue – that of colony and empire, and its relationship with Marxist cultural theory – is obviously central to my argument, but I need to make one further observation about this background before coming to the issue at hand – namely, that this issue of the literary representation of colony and empire in Euro-American literary discourses was posed in the US academy, from the beginning, not from Marxist positions but in response to nationalist pressures, so that the subsequent theorizing of the subject, even when undertaken by Marxists, proceeded from the already-existing nationalist premisses and predispositions. This becomes quite clear as soon as one looks at the actual pressures which opened up the question in the first place.

It is symptomatic, for example, that this issue was first posed in the colleges and universities of the USA *not* in relation to the uses of literature in the building and representing of empires in Asia and Africa, but in relation to the *Black* experience *within* the United States. In so far as African-American intellectuals have no historical or cultural basis for thinking of Greece and Rome, the Cathedrals of St Peter and St Paul, Dante and Shakespeare, as *their* cultural past – at least, not in an exclusive way – significant segments among them, starting most markedly with Martin Delaney and DuBois, have often looked to Africa for their cultural origins. African literature now made its appearance in the American literary syllabi under increased Black nationalist pressure, not so much as an object of critical inquiry as evidence of achievement; the right to teach Senghor and Diop, Soyinka or Ngugi, was won against such odds and so very provisionally that one could not possibly interrogate this emergent counter-canon as one was only too glad to interrogate the existing canonicities.[20] Second, opposition to the Vietnam War brought up, strictly within the field of literary studies, the question of how colony and empire had been represented in Western literatures. There has since been a considerable rereading of at least parts of the established canon. Gradually, it has dawned upon some that no reading of English and French literatures was possible without taking into account the constitutive presence of the colonial experience in these literatures: Shakespeare and Jane Austen, Samuel Johnson and George Eliot, Shelley and Tennyson, André Gide and St John Perse were all implicated in it, and the vocabulary of colonial racism was there even in texts that were ostensibly not about colonialism at all – *Wuthering Heights*, for example. As African literature was inserted into the American syllabi under Black nationalist pressure, anti-colonial nationalism was the theoretical insignia for rereading the dominant cultural texts of the colonizing West. By the time the theoretical category of 'Colonial Discourse Analysis' arose, however, this perfectly necessary rereading of the Western archive was extended to produce the more or less dubious claim that the whole of it was an archive of bad faith and 'Orientalist' deformation. Third – and more important from the theoretical point of view – was the issue of the exclusive emphasis, in the Western academy, on the experience of Europe and North America – corners of the globe which are relatively small if you look at the whole world. This is the point where the issue of cultural production in the larger, non-Western part of the world – in Asia, Africa, Latin America – came to be posed. In the fullness of time, the literary documents of this other kind of cultural production would be called 'Third World Literature', within a discourse that would speak of a fundamental, generic difference between West and non-West, redefined now as a binary opposition between First and Third Worlds – and an opposition, moreover, which was said to be partly an effect of colonialism but partly a matter also of civilizational, primordial Difference. If the whole history of Western textualities, from Homer to Olivia Manning, was a history of Orientalist ontology, Third World Literature was *prima facie* the site of liberationist practice. The two theoretical categories, 'Colonial Discourse' (or 'Orientalism', in the Saidian sense) and 'Third World Literature', were thus conjoined, even if the actual practitioners of the one or the other were differentially located in the division of academic labours. Inevitably, then, cultural nationalism of one kind or another continues to be the constitutive ideology of the theoretical positions from which these issues are raised.

## III

I have presented a very complex history in such telegraphic terms with three purposes in mind. First, I want to emphasize the sheer weight of reactionary positions in the Anglo-American literary formations. Second, I do want to stress the gains which have been made there since the 1960s, despite the havoc caused recently by the more mindless kinds of poststructuralism; for the first time in its history the metropolitan university is being forced, in some of its nooks and niches, to face issues of race and gender and empire in a way it has never done before. One simply has to compare the nature and breadth of today's debates on these issues with the absence of such debates in the 1950s, and even the 1930s, to grasp the degree of change. But, third, I also want to stress that the political vagrancy of much of the radical literary intelligentsia in the USA is such that it has been difficult – so far impossible, in fact – to constitute a properly Marxist political or literary culture, on any appreciable scale. The fundamental and constant danger faced by each radicalism – whether

Black, or feminist, or Third-Worldist – is the danger of embourgeoisement. And the triple signs under which radical movements of this kind are at length assimilated into the main currents of bourgeois culture itself are the signs, these days, of Third-Worldist nationalism, essentialism, and the currently fashionable theories of the fragmentation and/or death of the Subject: the politics of discrete exclusivities and localisms on the one hand, or, on the other – as some of the poststructuralisms would have it – the very *end* of the social, the *impossibility* of stable subject positions, hence the *death* of politics as such. In more recent years, of course, we have also witnessed many attempts to reconcile Third-Worldist nationalism with poststructuralism itself.

These possibilities of internal erosion, which exist within the body of the radical discourse as it were, are then greatly augmented, from the outside, by the enormous pressures of the lingering Thatcherite–Reaganite consensus in the metropolitan culture at large. This consensus, especially aggressive now in the moment of imperialism's greatest triumph in its history, is unwilling to grant any considerable space to fundamental dissent of *any* kind, so that demands even for simple decency – that non-Western texts be integrated into the basic syllabi, that women have the right to abortion or equal pay or the writing of their own history, that normative pressures concede ground to individual sexual choice – are construed as mad attacks on Western civilization and 'family values', and as outright degenerations against which 'the American mind', as Alan Bloom tendentiously calls it, needs to defend itself. I cannot analyse the structure of that pressure here, but a particular consequence is that the individual practitioner of academic radicalism comes to occupy so beleaguered a space that any critical engagement with the limitations of one's own intellectual and political formation becomes difficult. The Right's attack tends, rather, to confirm the sense of one's own achievement. This power of the Right more or less to dictate the terms of engagement, not only in the academy but (even more so) in the culture at large, is surely not a *creation* of the university-based Left – it is, rather, evidence of the Right's power, and sets the objective limits for the Left itself. This pressure on the public space available for dialogues and projects of the Left also has the potential, however, of disorientating further theoretical development inside the restricted space that still does exist.

Those younger literary theorists in Britain and North America who had come out of the student movements of the late 1960s and early 1970s, and started their academic careers more or less after the cooling of America began with Nixon's second Presidential term and as Britain started skidding from the Wilsonian variants of Labourism to outright Thatcherite reaction, found their radicalism caught in a series of contradictions. The *international situation* which had framed much of their radicalism had been intensely revolutionary: the Vietnam War, the Chinese Cultural Revolution, the wars of liberation in the Portuguese colonies, the immensely powerful figures of Fidel and Che Guevara, the victory of *Unidad Popular* in Chile, the student uprisings from Mexico City to Paris to Lahore. Their *academic* training, meanwhile, had been an affair mainly of choosing between 'New Criticism' on the one hand, Frye and Bloom and Paul de Man on the other. Few enough had negotiated, by then, their way through Lukács; Gramsci was then almost entirely unknown in the English-speaking world, and much of the best of Raymond Williams was yet to come. The gap between what moved them politically and what they were doing academically was large enough, but then there was the 'movement' of which they had been, unevenly, a part. Those who were politically the most involved rarely found a coherent organizing centre for their activity once the intensity of the mobilization had peaked; those who found such a centre, for good or ill, disappeared into the anonymity of direct political work; few enough finished their PhDs, and those who did rarely gained the academic sophistication to become theorists. Those who became theorists had been, as a rule, only marginally involved in the *political* movement. Most of them had known the 'movement' mostly in its other kinds of social emphases: certainly the music, the alternative readings of Laing and Marcuse, surely the occasional demonstration – but there had been, through it all, the pressure to write brilliant term papers and equally brilliant dissertations. It was, in other words, mostly the *survivors* of the 'movement' who later became so successful in the profession. Radicalism had been, for most of them, a state of mind, brought about by an intellectual identification with the revolutionary wave that had gripped so much of the world when they were truly young; of the day-to-day drudgeries of, say, a political party or a trade union they had been (and were to remain) largely innocent.

By the time they had secured their teaching positions, the international situation itself had changed. In the metropolises, the Civil Rights Movement had been contained through patronage for segments of the Black petty bourgeoisie, the political content of the anti-war movement frittered away after the retreat of US troops from Vietnam, and Paris itself was normalized soon after the uprising. The cycles of economic recession and stagnation which set in during the early 1970s had the effect, furthermore, of putting the movements for social justice on the defensive. In the imperialized world, meanwhile, Chile was decisively beaten, Cuba contained, China largely incorporated, and the wave of anti-capitalist revolutions was mainly over by the mid 1970s. The revolutionary states which arose at that time were encircled economically and derailed by invasions and insurgencies that were engineered through surrogates; none of them, from Angola to Vietnam, was allowed to become a model of development for post-colonial societies. The revolutionary upheavals which occurred thereafter – in Ethiopia or Afghanistan, for example – had problematic beginnings at best, originating in the radical sectors of the military. Their subsequent development was no better than that of other regimes based on the 'progressive' *coups d'état* elsewhere in Asia and Africa. In other words, for the revolutionary movements and states of the post-colonial world, this was a period of retreat and even outright disorientation.

In a parallel movement, moreover, this was also a period of increasing consolidation of the bourgeois nation-state in much of the rest of the post-colonial world. The international focus shifted accordingly, from revolutionary war ('Two, Three, Many . . . Vietnams') to such strategies for favourable terms of incorporation within the capitalist world as the Non-Aligned Movement, the North–South Dialogue, UNCTAD, the New Economic Order, the Group 77 at the United Nations, or commodity cartels such as OPEC. If in 1968 the epoch had seemed to belong to the revolutionary vanguard, it seemed to belong now, as the 1980s dawned, to the national bourgeoisie. Radical thought in the universities paid its homage to this new consolidation of the post-colonial national bourgeoisies by shifting its focus, decisively, from socialist revolution to Third-Worldist nationalism – first in political theory, then in its literary reflections.

It was in this moment of retreat for socialism, and resurgence of the nationalism of the national bourgeoisie, that the *theoretical* category of 'Third World Literature' arose, as did the new emphasis on analyses of the 'Colonial Discourse', pushing the focus of thought not into the future but into the past. Since nationalism had been designated during this phase as the determinate source of ideological energy in the Third World by those same critics who had themselves been influenced mainly by poststructuralism, the disillusionment with the (national-bourgeois) state of the said Third World which began to set in towards the later 1980s then led those avant-garde theorists to declare that poststructuralism and deconstruction were the determinate theoretical positions for the critique of nationalism itself. Edward Said is thus quite astute in describing Ranajit Guha, and by extension the Subalternist project as a whole, as 'poststructuralist'.[21] This same tendency can be witnessed in a great many of the more recent literary theorists themselves, as exemplified by Homi K. Bhabha among others. The positioning of poststructuralism as the alternative to nationalism is thus quite evident in his own definition of the project as he has assembled it in *Nation and Narration*:

> My intention was that we should develop, in a nice collaborative tension, a range of readings that engaged the insights of poststructuralist theories of narrative knowledge. . . . The marginal or 'minority' is not the space of a celebratory, or utopian, self-marginalization. It is a much more substantial intervention into those justifications of modernity – progress, homogeneity, cultural organicism, the deep nation, the long past – that rationalize the authoritarian, 'normalizing' tendencies within cultures in the name of national interest . . . (p. 4)

Bhabha, of course, lives in those material conditions of *post*modernity which presume the benefits of modernity as the very ground from which judgements on that past of this *post-* may be delivered. In other words, it takes a very modern, very affluent, very uprooted kind of intellectual to debunk both the idea of 'progress' and the sense of a 'long past', not to speak of 'modernity' itself, as mere 'rationalizations' of 'authoritarian tendencies within cultures' – in a theoretical *mélange* which randomly invokes Lévi-Strauss in one phrase, Foucault in another, Lacan in yet another. Those who live within the consequences of that 'long past', good and bad, and in places where a majority of the population has been denied access to such benefits of 'modernity' as hospitals or better health insurance or even basic literacy; can hardly afford the terms of such thought. The affinities of class and location then lead Bhabha, logically, to an exorbitant celebration of Salman Rushdie which culminates in pronouncements like the following, itself assembled in the manner of a postmodern pastiche:

> America leads to Africa; the nations of Europe and Asia meet in Australia; the margins of the nation displace the centre; the peoples of the periphery return to write the history and fiction of the metropolis. The island story is told from the eye of the aeroplane which becomes that 'ornament that holds the public and the private in suspense'. The bastion of Englishness crumbles at the sight of immigrants and factory workers. The great Whitmanesque sensorium of America is exchanged for a Warhol blowup, a Kruger installation, or Mapplethorpe's naked bodies. 'Magical Realism', after the Latin American boom, becomes the literary language of the emergent post-colonial world. (p. 6)

It is doubtful, of course, that 'magical realism' has become 'the literary language of the emergent post-colonial world', any more than the 'national allegory' is the unitary generic form for all Third World narrativities, as Jameson would contend. Such pronouncements are now routine features of the metropolitan theory's inflationary rhetoric. Not all his collaborators write in accordance with his prescription, but Bhabha's own essay at the end of the volume makes a very considerable effort, albeit in very arcane ways, to pre-empt other kinds of critiques of nationalism by offering such familiar plays on 'poststructuralist theories'.

For these more recent developments in 'theory', especially for those sections of literary theory which surely set the terms for dealing with issues of empire, colony and nation, this general situation had peculiarly disorientating effects. In one kind of pressure, politics as such has undergone remarkable degrees of diminution. Any attempt to *know* the world as a whole, or to hold that it is open to rational comprehension, let alone the desire to change it, was to be dismissed as a contemptible attempt to construct 'grand narratives' and 'totalizing (totalitarian?) knowledges'. The theorist spoke often enough of imperialism and nationalism, sometimes as dialectical opposites but increasingly as twin faces of the same falsity, but the main business of radicalism came to reside in the rejection of rationalism itself (the Enlightenment project, as it came to be called).[22] Only

Power was universal and immutable; resistance could only be local; knowledge, even of Power, always partial. Affiliations could only be shifting and multiple; to speak of a stable subject position was to chase the chimera of the 'myth of origins'. In some American dilutions of this theory of the dispersal and fracturing of historical subjects, the idea of 'inquiry', which presumes the possibility of finding some believable truth, was to be replaced with the idea of 'conversation' which is by its nature inconclusive. This idea of theory as 'conversation', may at times pass itself off as Bakhtinian dialogism, but in reality it moves inevitably in one of two possible directions.

The more common one is doubtless that of a peculiarly American kind of pluralism, with no small hint of politeness, accommodation and clubby gentlemanliness, albeit expressed in avant-gardist critical circles in the Barthesian language of 'pleasure of the text', 'free play of the Signifier', etc. The alternative direction, on the other hand, is a more sombre one, for if we accept the more extreme versions of the Foucauldian propositions (a) that whatever claims to be a *fact* is none other than a truth-*effect* produced by the ruse of discourse, and (b) that whatever claims to resist Power is already constituted as Power, then there really is nothing for Theory to *do* except to wander aimlessly through the effects – counting them, consuming them, producing them – and in the process submitting to the interminable whisperings of Discourse, both as Origin and as Fate. This theory-as-conversation also has a remarkably strong levelling effect. One is now free to cite Marxists and anti-Marxists, feminists and anti-feminists, deconstructionists, phenomenologists, or whatever other theorist comes to mind, to validate successive positions within an argument, so long as one has a long list of citations, bibliographies, etc., in the well-behaved academic manner. Theory itself becomes a marketplace of ideas, with massive supplies of theory as usable commodity, guaranteeing consumers' free choice and a rapid rate of obsolescence. If one were to refuse this model of the late-capitalist market economy, and dared instead to *conclude* a conversation or to advocate strict partisanship in the politics of theory, one would then be guilty of rationalism, empiricism, historicism, and all sorts of other ills – the idea of historical agents and/or knowing subjects, for example – perpetrated by the Enlightenment. One major aspect of this particular drift in the theory of the grand masters was summed up succinctly by Lyotard, no small master himself: the age of Marxism is over, 'the age of the enjoyment of goods and services' is here! The world was, in other words, bourgeois.

Much of the avant-garde literary theory of today comes out of such moorings, intellectual and political, with a distinctly consumptionist slant. Quite apart from the remarkable claim that politics resides mainly in radicalizing the practice of one's own academic profession, there has grown, because of equal allegiance to irreconcilable pressures, that same kind of eclecticism among the politically engaged theorists as among the more technicist, conservative ones; it is not uncommon to find, say, Gramsci and Matthew Arnold being cited in favour of the same theoretical position, as if the vastly different political allegiances of these two figures were quite immaterial for the main business of literary criticism. In some of these radicalized versions too, thus, that same market-economy model of theory obtains.

# 2

# Languages of Class, Ideologies of Immigration

Alongside the shifts in the fortunes of literary theory that were summarized in the previous chapter, the post-colonial era has also witnessed some fundamental shifts in the structure of literary production itself – especially in English and French, but also in other European languages – as regards that body of work from which the counter-canon of Third World Literature is typically assembled.

One of the peculiarities of this era is that with general expansion of schooling and the modern professions in many of the decolonized countries, there has come about not a decline but a great proliferation of literary texts composed and published in those countries but in languages that had been initially imported from Europe, ranging from English to Portuguese. India is now one of the world's largest markets for the production and dissemination of English-language books, and boasts of several very famous novelists in the language. Heinemann, the English publishing company, has a fat list of authors and books from Africa and the Caribbean; one, Wole Soyinka, who writes exclusively in English, has been canonized with the Nobel Prize. It is fair to say, I think, that these writers born in other global spaces – Rushdie and Ghosh, Armah and Achebe, Lamming and Harris, not to speak of dozens of others, especially from South Africa – have altered the traditional map of English fiction beyond recognition. One cannot say the same about poetry, nor perhaps about the similarly decisive alteration of Paris to the same degree by writers of the Francophone countries – not since the heyday of 'Negritude' – though there is a major, and increasing, African presence in French film and fiction as well, and North African interventions in French fiction are currently very much on the increase. This vastly increased production of literary texts in the metropolitan languages by writers of the ex-colonial countries obviously has to do with a great many things, in highly differentiated national situations across continents. I shall take up the contexts of English in the composition of literary studies in India in a subsequent chapter. Some general observations, however, must be made at the outset.

## I

In so far as the metropolitan language – English in the case of India – was the chief cultural and communicational instrument for the centralization of the bourgeois state in the colonial period, the continued use of this instrument in the dominant systems of administration, education and communication is, among other things, an index of the profound – almost genetic – cultural link between the colonial and post-colonial phases of the bourgeois state. The fact that English has proliferated, instead of declining, in this later phase indicates the greater elaboration and deeper penetration of the state into all aspects of civil society, through administration, profession, commerce, schooling, mediology; the state is the chief employer, the principal educator, the largest property-owner, the governor of electronics media. The literary pre-eminence of English is a reflection of this larger, overlapping grid. The main *cultural* claim of English during the colonial period was also a non-literary one. The claim, rather, was that India was internally so fragmented, so heterogeneous, such a mosaic of languages and ethnicities, that it needed a centralizing language to sustain its national unity – the 'nation' in this conception was coterminous with exigencies of administration and, indeed, with the state itself. Now, after decolonization, our inability to acknowledge that the civilizational complexity of India simply cannot be lived or thought through in terms of the centralizing imperatives of the nation-state we have inherited from the European bourgeoisie; our inability fundamentally to reorganize the relations between centre and region, or to invent more heterogeneous forms of unity that might be commensurate with the complexity of our society – all this has meant that those earlier semiotics of administration and profession, with English at their epicentre, have merely reproduced themselves on an extended scale. The claim of English to be a unifying force in India has been not diminished but enlarged. These enlarged uses of English in India, and of the metropolitan languages in virtually all the ex-colonial countries of Asia and Africa, are connected, furthermore. with the consolidation, expansion, increased self-confidence, increased leisure, increased sophistication of the bourgeois classes in these countries, including its middle strata, especially the modern petty bourgeoisie located in the professions and in the state apparatuses. Among all the countries of Asia and Africa which gained their independence after World War II, India has numerically by far the largest professional petty bourgeoisie, fully consolidated as a distinct social entity and sophisticated enough in its claim to English culture for it to aspire to have its own writers, publishing houses, and a fully fledged home market for English books.

This is not the place to review the complexities of this situation, but there has clearly developed, in all the cosmopolitan cities of the country, an English-based intelligentsia for whom only the literary document produced in English is a *national* document; all else is regional, hence minor and forgettable, so that English emerges in this imagination not as *one* of the Indian languages, which it undoubtedly is, but as *the* language of national integration and bourgeois civility. One of the consequences of a large home market is that many of the more prominent Indian writers of English – in sharp contrast to the Caribbean ones, for example – choose to live inside India, which undoubtedly helps to consolidate their claim to represent – indeed to *embody* – the Indian national experience, for their readerships here as well as abroad, while the shared medium of English serves to strengthen that tie, and the metropolitan perceptions of that tie, between the writers based inside India and those who have migrated to the metropolitan countries. Anita Desai and Bharati Mukherjee thus become two faces of the same currency, so to speak, in the global category of Third World Literature. The fact that India offers far greater democratic freedom than virtually any other ex-colonial country means, of course, that a wide range of dissents can be expressed inside the country, largely eliminating the circumstances which have often forced writers from many other countries into political exile.

These post-colonial consolidations and expansions have not occurred in some vacuum, ahistorically. During the colonial period itself, the 'national' intelligentsia which operated on the all-India scale, and which very much included some of the fractions of the national*ist* intelligentsia, had arisen predominantly from the upper and middle castes and from inside the pursuits and professions that were closest to the institutions of the (colonial) state: administration, law, commerce, English-language journalism, teaching staffs of colleges and universities. There was already, during the colonial period, a distinct hierarchical divide between the 'national' functions of the intelligentsia, which were carried out in English, and the regional functions, which were carried out in the indigenous languages – sometimes by the same people, but at distinct sites. This was as true of the Indian National Congress as of the Muslim League or the Communist Party; as much of journalism or social science as of the colonial administration and the financial, industrial or commercial transactions of the private sector. This basic divide was lived in individual lives through all kinds of variations, even among the famous leaders. From Rammohun to Gandhi, and from Rajgopal Acharya to Maulana Muhammad Ali, there had been a great tradition of bilinguality and polyglot ease in communication. Nehru could speak Urdu and Hindi well but wrote only in English; Jinnah could not function much beyond English; Azad was an erudite scholar of Arabic and Persian, read English haltingly but was one of the great masters of Urdu in this century. Some of these patterns have survived, but with variations that are pertinent for our present argument. The 'national' intelligentsia is now rooted much more decisively in English than in any of the indigenous languages.[1] Hindi now commands far greater space in the electronic media and popular culture (clearly in the North but, through cinema and television, in the South as well). Really productive kinds of bilinguality are probably on the decline, and English is now in the process of emerging as a major language for fiction-writing by the greatly talented. These shifts in the post-colonial period have further augmented the tendency – among the metropolitan intellectuals especially, but also in large sectors of the bourgeois intelligentsia inside India – to view the products of the English-writing intelligentsia of the cosmopolitan cities as the central documents of India's *national* literature. This transcontinental partnership in perception, in essence a class alliance, is by now quite firmly established.

One can hardly attempt here to recapitulate the extensive and complex debates that have taken place, and must repeatedly take take place, about the role of English in India, nor can one easily summarize what tentative thoughts one may have on this issue. The intent, in any case, is not to debunk the role of English in India in any ahistorical fashion, or to force the argument in some indigenist direction. One cannot reject English now, on the basis of its initially colonial insertion, any more than one can boycott the railways for that same reason. There is reason to believe, in fact, that even the linguistic formation which was eventually shaped into Sanskrit came, in its own time, from elsewhere, as did, wave after wave, the ancestors of the vast majority of the people who now inhabit at least the Gangetic plains. History is not really open to correction through a return passage to an imaginary point centuries ago, before the colonial deformation set in, or before the insertion of Islam before that, or, earlier still, before the invasion of what are generally called the 'Aryan' tribes. Indian civilizational ethos, if there is one, is in any case deeply marked by the processes of Indianization of idioms and instruments – even peoples, who were initially strangers, sometimes predators, in this land. English is simply one of India's own languages now, and what is at issue at present is not the possibility of its ejection but the mode of its assimilation into our social fabric, and the manner in which this language, like any other substantial structure of linguistic difference, is used in the processes of class formation and social privilege, here and now.

In social processes at large, this privileging of a particular language is indicated by its uses in state administration, in those more powerful sections of the media which are considered 'national', in higher institutions of education and research, in its differential availability to the propertied and the working classes respectively, in the greater access it provides to the job market and hence the great prestige that attaches to the person who commands it with fluency, and so on. Once these processes are fully in place, with the bourgeoisie and the professional segments of the petty bourgeoisie fully incorporated in them, two things about 'literature', at the very least, become self-evident for all those who are thus incorporated. First, it seems inevitable that if an archive of a 'national' literature is to be assembled, it can be done only in *this* language. Second, as regards individual texts, only those that become available in *this* language can be said to have a *representative* character, so far as the 'national' literature is concerned; all else is 'regional', and a 'regional' novel, let us say, can become part of the 'national' archive only in so far as it is represented, either in full translation or through some extended summary and/or commentary, in the language designated already, through official proclamation or not, as the one appropriate for the construction of the 'national' archive.

We might add that if the inevitability of such processes has become self-evident to those who participate in the reproduction of this structure, that is not so simply because the structure serves their interests and opens up a privileged field for them. Those interests are surely there, but the materiality of this self-evidence originates not in the literary field but in those much larger processes, largely political and non-literary, which constitute this field in the first place; the dominant language of society, like the dominant ideology itself, is always the language of its ruling class. Nor can this privileging of the English literary text in the 'national' media and archive – not to speak of the metropolitan university and the literary Establishment – be altered in any significant degree unless much else changes in areas far beyond literary studies *per se*.

## II

Literature produced in the ex-colonial countries but produced directly in languages which had been imported initially from Europe provides one kind of archive for the metropolitan university to construe the textual formation of 'Third World Literature'; but this is not the only archive available, for the period after decolonization has also witnessed great expansion and consolidation of literary traditions in a number of indigenous languages as well. There are, of course, great regional variations even of this phenomenon, but as a generalization one might say that in most regions of the subcontinent, the writers of the indigenous languages have historically come from slightly lower rungs of the professional petty bourgeoisie and/or the more traditional sectors of petty property. This too is changing now, though, since systems of state patronage are creating interests in the indigenous languages at fairly high levels of affluence as well. One has only to think of the expansion of Hindi literature – and of the language itself, through the electronic media and whatnot – since Independence, to understand what I mean. Not much of this kind of literature is directly available to the metropolitan literary theorists because, erudite as they usually are in metropolitan languages, hardly any of them has ever bothered with an Asian or African language. But parts and shades of these literatures also become available in the West, essentially in the following three ways.

By far the greater part of the archive through which knowledge about the so-called Third World is generated in the metropolises has traditionally been, and continues to be, assembled within the metropolitan institutions of research and explication, which are characteristically administered and occupied by overwhelmingly Western personnel. Non-Western individuals have also been employed in these same institutions – more and more so during the more recent, post-colonial period, although still almost always in subordinate positions. The archive itself is dispersed through myriad academic disciplines and genres of writing – from philological reconstruction of the classics to lowbrow reports by missionaries and administrators; from Area Study Programmes and even the central fields of the Humanities to translation projects sponsored by Foundations and private publishing houses alike – generating all kinds of classificatory practices. A particularly large mechanism in the assembly of this archive has been the institutionalized symbiosis between the Western scholar and the local informant, which is frequently re-enacted now – no doubt in far more subtle ways – between the contemporary literary theorist of the West, who typically does not know a non-Western language, and the indigenous translator or essayist, who typically knows one or two.

This older, multidisciplinary and somewhat chaotic archive is greatly expanded in our own time, especially in the area of literary studies, by a developing machinery of *specifically* literary translations – a machinery not nearly as highly developed as the one that exists for the circulation of texts among the metropolitan countries themselves, but not inconsiderable on its own terms. Apart from the private publishing houses and the university presses which may publish such translations of their own volition or under sponsorship programmes, there are state institutions such as the Sahitya Akademi in India, as well as international agencies such as UNESCO, not to speak of the American 'philanthropic' foundations such as the Rockefeller-funded Asia Society, which have extensive programmes for such publications. Supplementing these translations are the critical essay and its associated genres, usually produced by an indigenous intellectual who reads the indigenous language but writes in one of the metropolitan ones. Some of this kind of writing becomes available in the metropolises, creating versions and shadows of texts produced in other spaces of the globe, but texts which frequently come with the authority of the indigenous informant. And, of course, literatures of South America and parts of the Caribbean are directly available to the metropolitan critic through Spanish, Portuguese, French and English, which are, after all, European languages. Entire vocabularies, styles, linguistic sensibilities exist now in English, French, Italian, for translations of so-called Third-World texts from Spanish and Portuguese. North American and European theorists can either read those literary documents directly, or – in case they are not entirely proficient in Spanish or Portuguese – can nevertheless speak of those literatures with easy familiarity thanks to the translatability of the originals. It is usually on the model of the Latin American text, in fact, that texts from Asia and Africa are customarily read, in order to obtain a homogeneous 'Third World Literature'.

In other words, over the past three decades or so a vast archive of texts has accumulated, which is available to the metropolitan university to examine, explicate, categorize, classify, and judge as to its worthiness for inclusion within its curriculum and canon. At the level of this greatly expanded archive of books produced in the ex-colonial countries but written in or translated into Western languages, a direct dialogue between, let us say, a Haitian and an Indian novelist could really take place, and something called 'Third World Literature', with its own generic classifications and categorizations, could ensue from that archival nearness; the irony of that operation would undoubtedly be that a Third World Literature would arise on the basis of Western *languages*, while Third-Worldist ideology is manifestly opposed to the cultural dominance of Western *countries*.

I referred above to an equally great – or perhaps greater – expansion in the number of literary utterances, printed or not, in the indigenous languages which are *not* translated into the metropolitan ones. These do not belong to any unified archive; many, in fact, have no archival existence at all. It is difficult to see how these other kinds of cultural productivities – not archival but local and tentative, generated not by colonialism *per se* or by the East/West binary oppositions but by histories at once older, more local, more persistent, more variegated and prolix, more complexly and viscerally felt – are to be accommodated within a unitary archive of a 'Third World Literature', with its own system of genres and categories. I have in mind here genres which are essentially oral and performative, sites of production located at great remove from the great cities, entire linguistic complexes as yet unassimilated into grids of print and translation. It is not clear to me what status these other kinds of productivities have with regard to the techno-managerial expertise that goes into the categorical construction, generic specification, dissemination, warehousing, and safeguarding of the inventories of 'Third World Literature'.

## III

No archive, however vast, gathers new significance and force by itself. After all, the machinery of accumulation, translation and gloss for texts from Asia and Africa has been cranked up in the metropolitan countries for two hundred years or so; it did give rise to what Edward Said calls 'Orientalism', but not to the category of 'Third World Literature', which is brand new and indicates a sea-change in the social situation now prevailing in those same countries. For this is the first time large ethnic communities from various ex-colonial countries have gathered in the metropolises in such a way that considerable segments are making historically new kinds of demand for inclusion in the salaried, professional middle class and its patterns of education, employment, consumption, social valuation and career advancement.

This is in some fundamental ways a reversal of the historic role of non-European minorities, especially in the United States, where the African-American minority has, of course, had a much older presence – since the earliest days of the slave trade and the colonization of the Americas. Even that largest and oldest of the ethnic minorities has been so constitutively handicapped by the racial structure that arose on the prior edifice of slavery, however, that as late as the inter-war years it had given rise to at most a very rudimentary and impoverished middle class;[2] both the achievements and the limitations of the Harlem Renaissance in the 1920s had been premissed on this obstructed development and delayed consolidation of the Black professional strata. But then – and even if we discount the few remnants of the indigenous population which had been exterminated in the process of that genocidal colonization – some other ethnic minorities had also been assembled over a century or more. Since the annexation from Mexico of what is now the US Southwest, the country has also been acquiring an increasingly larger number of working people of Hispanic origin, greatly augmented by the colonization of Puerto Rico and the current status of virtually the whole of Central America, including much of Mexico itself, as a fluctuating labour pool for the United States. After the Frontier in California had been reached and exceeded – right into the Philippines, for example, and with footholds all across the Pacific – new waves of immigrants came from East Asia as well: to build the great bridges, the underground tunnels, the railways; sometimes to work the mines; sometimes even to pick the fruit, the vegetables, the garbage. The structure of exploitation into which this colonial immigration is then slotted is the dark underbelly of the myth of America as the land of freedom and opportunity. In other words, the demographic evolution of the United States had followed a distinct pattern since the beginnings of slavery, and until after the Second World War the non-white population had remained mainly in the working class and in the army of the unemployed.

This social demography began experiencing some notable shifts by the time the postwar boom was fully in place and the Kennedy Administration took over, promising a 'New Frontier' for America. In a development of far-reaching consequence, the African-American commercial and professional strata expanded considerably. By then, there had already been a fully fledged critical discourse of a distinctive 'Black Literature' as an identifiable, self-conscious cultural category for over half a century, and the 'New Black Renaissance' of the 1960s – in part a repudiation of the very processes of embourgeoisement which Alaine Locke, in his famous essay 'The New Negro', had set up as the desired goal of the Harlem Renaissance of the 1920s[3] – therefore set the pattern for the subsequent assertions in other 'minority literatures', especially for the Puerto Rican groupings on the Eastern seaboard, the Chicanos mainly in the Southwest, Asian-Americans mainly in the Chinatowns of San Francisco and New York – for it was also during this same period that children of Hispanic and East Asian labouring classes entered American colleges in appreciable numbers. One may even suggest that it was initially on the pattern of 'Black Literature', as a distinct counter-canon with its own generic difference, that the later category of 'Third World Literature' had been in some respects modelled. If the latter was given a transnational character, that too was because no other ethnic minority in the United States, except the African-Americans and to a much lesser extent the Chicanos, is large enough to seek modification of the university and the associated canon exclusively in its own name.

The paradox about Britain, meanwhile, is that its non-European population remained relatively small throughout the colonial period, but then Black immigration – from Africa, the Caribbean, and principally from the Asian subcontinent – picked up appreciably after decolonization, so that only since the late 1960s has Britain, also, seen the coming-of-age of expanding new strata of Black British who have demanded, on the basis of schooling and professional competence, new kinds of middle-class representation premissed as much on non-racist assimilation into employment and property structures as on recognition of cultural difference. The normalizing category of 'Commonwealth Literature' addressed these pressures in the initial phase, and challenges to this British Council construct have gathered momentum more recently. The decisive fact, in any case, is that this same period has also witnessed – both in Britain and in the United States – vast new immigration from Asia which has supplemented, but also greatly transformed, the pre-existing Asian communities. This was a historically new kind of immigration. In Britain the working-class component remained very strong, but large segments of the professional strata and even of fully capitalist classes also came as immigrants and settlers. In the United States the shift was even more dramatic. The historic pattern of primarily European immigration was matched and then superseded by immigration from the empire: Arabs, Hispanics, but most of all Asians – and it is as well to remember that this was the first time, from the later 1960s on, that immigration from India became numerically significant and proportionately much larger than ever before.

That these were non-white Asians rather than the familiar white Europeans is significant enough, but equally crucial was the class shift. A majority of these Asians came not to do manual labour and join the working class, but to set up commercial enterprises or to join the professional petty bourgeoisie. Indian immigration into the United States was overwhelmingly petty-bourgeois and techno-managerial, while members of the Indian working classes went to sell their labour-power mostly in the Gulf region, secondarily in England. There is, of course, a working-class segment as well, and many among the petty bourgeois occupy only the lowest rung; the cultural schism between this poorer side of the immigration and the university-based intelligentsia tends, however, to be as large in immigration as it was in the home country. Supplementing the relative ease and security which personal incomes guaranteed for the more affluent, there was also the new technology of easily available air travel, telecommunications, audio and video cassettes, much quicker postal deliveries, and so on, which made it much easier than ever before in history to retain links with the home country.

Interwoven into these patterns of immigration is the ambiguous status of the incoming graduate student who comes from elsewhere, who studies under the full weight of the existing canonicity, who rebels against it, who counterposes other kinds of texts against the so-called canonical text, especially if any are available from his or her own part of the world. These other kinds of texts become, then, the ground, the document, even the counter-canon of her or his national self-assertion. This choice corresponds to the ambiguities of an existential kind, precipitated by the contradictions of the metropolitan, liberal, predominantly white university. It is by nature a site of privilege, and the student comes with the ambition of sharing this privilege. The liberal, pluralistic self-image of the university can always be pressed to make room for diversity, multiculturalism, non-Europe; careers can arise out of such renegotiations of the cultural compact. But this same liberal university is usually, for the non-white student, a place of desolation, even panic; exclusions are sometimes blatant, more often only polite and silent, and the documents of one's culture become little sickles to clear one's way through spirals of refined prejudice. Most such students never quite manage to break through these ambiguities of enticement and blockage; some return, but many get lost in the funhouse of disagreeable habitations and impossible returns. Out of these miseries arises a small academic elite which knows it will not return, joins the faculty of this or that metropolitan university, frequents the circuits of conferences and the university presses, and develops, often with the greatest degree of personal innocence and missionary zeal, quite considerable stakes in overvalorizing what has already been designated as 'Third World Literature' – and, when fashions change, reconciles this category even with poststructuralism. This, too, is by now a fairly familiar pattern.

But there is another kind of individual as well, and here I broach a factor which is very hard for me to discuss against the backdrop of India – I mean the factor of exile! And I do not mean people who live in the metropolitan countries for professional reasons but use words like 'exile' or 'diaspora' – words which have centuries of pain and dispossession inscribed in them – to designate what is, after all, only personal convenience. I mean, rather, people who are prevented, against their own commitment and desire, from living in the country of their birth by the authority of state – *any* state – or by fear of personal annihilation. In other words, I mean not privilege but impossibility, not profession but pain. Naked state terror in India has been directed so rarely at the *dominant* sectors of the literary intelligentsia that it may be difficult for those who have never lived in other zones of underdeveloped capitalism even to imagine the depth, the scope, the persistence of this kind of terror in large parts of the globe. This terror is not directed merely at the communist Left, for the communist Left in most countries of Asia and Africa is very small. Nor is it always rationally calibrated against the actual threat faced by the terrorizing regime; nor is the intensity equal in all parts of the globe where terror is practised. But it is worth remembering that there are entire national configurations, such as the Palestinian, whose intellectuals cannot speak – often cannot even be – inside what are their ancestral boundaries; that there have been whole decades when a Filipino, an Ethiopian, a Kenyan dissident had to choose between death, prison or exile; those who could manage to leave departed under duress. This again is a subject of such vast proportions that I cannot even begin to speak of it with any degree of coherence, but I do want to point out the irony that numerous intellectuals born in the outposts of empire cannot speak – frequently cannot even live – in their own countries, but have arrived, alive and speaking, in what Che Guevara once called 'the belly of the beast'– that is to say, the metropolitan city. Once in the metropolitan city, many have ended up in the metropolitan university, which tends to be more liberal than the kind of regime metropolitan capital prefers in Asia and Africa.

Immigration, in other words, has had its own contradictions: many have been propelled by need, others motivated by ambition, yet others driven away by persecution; for some there really is no longer a home to return to; in many cases need and ambition have become ambiguously and inextricably linked. No firm generalization can be offered for so large and complex a phenomenon, involving so many individual biographies. Nor is a uniform political choice necessarily immanent in the act of immigration as such. What we have witnessed, however, is that the combination of class origin, professional ambition and lack of a prior political grounding in a stable socialist praxis predisposes a great many of the radicalized immigrants located in the metropolitan university towards both an opportunistic kind of Third-Worldism as the appropriate form of oppositional politics and a kind of self-censoring, which in turn impels them towards greater incorporation in modes of politics and discourse already authorized by the prevailing fashion in that university.

Out of these reorganizations of capital, communications and personnel has come the image of 'theorist' as 'traveller', and of literary production itself as a ruse of immigration, of travelling *lightly*. Salman Rushdie's *Shame*, which I examine in Chapter 4, is only one of the scores of fictions of this period in which a fundamental connection between immigration and the literary imagination is sought or asserted. The fact that some of these intellectuals actually were political exiles has been taken advantage of, in an incredibly inflationary rhetoric, to deploy the word 'exile', first as a metaphor and then as a fully appropriated descriptive label for the existential condition of the immigrant as such; the upper-class Indian who *chooses* to live in the metropolitan country is then called 'the diasporic Indian', and 'exile' itself becomes a condition of the soul, unrelated to facts of material life. Exile, immigration and professional preference become synonymous and, indeed, mutually indistinguishable.

## IV

It is significant that although the category of 'Third World Literature' posited itself in terms of West and non-West, white and non-white, its reception among the African-American literary intelligentsia, among whom those terms have the most profound resonance, was at best contradictory. Many used it as a *descriptive* category, to signify a coalition of non-white minorities; 'Third World Women', for example, meant non-white women who needed to articulate a feminism different in some key respects from the high-bourgeois feminism of many white professionals, with oppressions of race and class layered together with the issue of gender. In another kind of emphasis, Black Third-Worldism was designed to broaden the perspective beyond the issue of African *origin*, to include more modern dimensions of the experience which was, in turn, shared with other coloured inhabitants of the inner cities, the ghettos, the *barrios*. 'Third World Literature', however, attracted few Black intellectuals. It was among teachers of Black Literature that the perception was immediate, even though it remained largely untheorized, that this category referred to literatures of the *other* minorities, the ones who were constituted not by slavery but by immigration. The commanding representatives of the African-American humanist tradition in this century – DuBois, Paul Robeson, Richard Wright, among them – had all been deeply moved by the revolutionary and anti-colonial currents on a global scale (virtually the last writing of DuBois had been a stirring homage to the Chinese Revolution; Wright was ecstatic about Bandung and the Non-Aligned Movement); but they had also known the specificity of African-American enslavement and its unique consequences, hence of the unique tie between this contemporary predicament and its African origin. This dual emphasis on the historical specificity of the African-American experience, on the one hand, and a guarded co-operation with advocates of Third World Literature, on the other, remained in place.

The Black academic intelligentsia was therefore open to establishing Third World Studies as a separate and adjacent field, but one that was not to encroach upon the distinct identity of Black Studies. This involved no small degree of wariness, partly because it is one of the distinguishing characteristics of the Asian immigrant's middle-class aspiration that even as he/she speaks constantly of non-Western origin, he/she wishes to join, within the United States, not the racially oppressed African-American community, but the privileged white middle class. It is also symptomatic that virtually all the theorizations of Third World Literature in the United States have come either from the immigrant or from that section of the elite white intelligentsia which normally pays scant attention to African-American literature and culture. There are, of course, *some* Black critics who participate in the production of this theory, and there are perhaps even some white critics who come to it from a prior interest in Black Literatures; but they – if and where they exist – are exceptions. In any case, it is in relation to the dominant, canonical tradition that 'Third World Literature' conceptually constitutes itself, even where it inadvertently appropriates the models and aspirations previously specific to the African-American.

That perfectly astute insistence on the specificity of Black experience in America, and on the historic roots of Black America's self-consciousness not in the generality of a 'Third World' but in the particularity of Africa, was, unfortunately, only part of the story. For apart from the almost spontaneously oppositionist positions which *any* Black intellectual, even of the most right-wing persuasion, feels compelled to adopt because of the racist juggernaut in which the whole of the African-American minority is held, this segment of the American intelligentsia has gone through those same processes of initially great radicalization in the 1960s, followed by increasing professionalization and embourgeoisement from the mid 1970s onwards, which has been characteristic of the United States as a whole. The process has been, if anything, more dramatic among the Black intelligentsia, and the irony is worth examining, however briefly.

The most radical phase of the Civil Rights Movement and the Black Nationalist Movements in the 1960s had coincided, paradoxically enough, with the phase of the most dynamic growth and expansion of American capital, thanks to the long wave of the postwar boom, the expansion of the military-industrial complex because of the Vietnam War, high rates of employment and spending, the still-existing US hegemony over its own capitalist partners as well as the world market generally. As a result, the system had at that particular juncture, before the crises came in the 1970s, a historically unprecedented capacity to absorb domestic challenges by incorporating into the margins of its own institutions the more professionally inclined elements of the radical intelligentsia, while the isolation through selective terror of the less compromising individuals and segments was facilitated by their relative isolation caused precisely by the increasing incorporation of the rest. The state-sponsored assassinations of Fred Hampton in his home and of George Jackson in prison, the decimation of the Black Panther Party in Chicago, Oakland, and other major centres, and the methodical disorganization of Black auto workers in Detroit, are all cases in point. It was in the process of this unfolding dynamic of insurrection and containment that the United States witnessed, from the mid 1960s on, a great expansion of educational and professional opportunity for the Black minority – vastly inadequate in terms of what it should have been, but *vast* in comparison with any earlier phase – under pressure of the Black insurrection but made economically feasible by the strength of US capital. By the time capitalist expansion slid into stagnation in the early 1970s, with the effects being felt in educational institutions in subsequent years, the benefits of that first decade had already engendered considerable embourgeoisement among Black campus communities. Retrenchment led, then, not to further radicalization but to a defensive relocation within the existing structures, supervised by faculties which were *socially* predominantly on the Right even though on the question of racial oppression they took, within parameters defined by the institutions, oppositional positions.[4] In outlook and aspiration, Black student bodies had been normalized even before the advent of Reaganism, becoming in their politics, except on the question of race, indistinguishable from the rest.

The twin emphases on professional aspiration and racial oppression produced considerable energy for identitarian politics and for defence of educational facilities, job protection, and so on. But, by the same token, little political energy was left for issues not related to professional advancement and racial identity. These social reorganizations of the Black academic intelligentsia led to a remarkable devolution in its own history. It was common among the Black intellectuals who came of age in the inter-war years to have some sort of sympathetic awareness of the Communist Party, while many, of course, started their careers in its publications. By contrast, the Black intelligentsia that came to prominence from the 1960s onwards was marked by its general lack of intellectual moorings in any kind of Marxism or in a politics marked by the communist movement. Figures like Angela Davis stand out in this regard precisely because they are the exceptions in a milieu where Black radicalism, as a distinct social category within American radicalism at large, is even farther removed from Marxism than are several quite distinct groupings in its white component. Feminism was the only progressive ideology which made any substantial new inroads into the Black academic community during this latter phase, as was true in the case of white intellectuals and students as well. The upshot was that with the exception of a very few, Black writers remained curiously disengaged from these larger debates about the contentions between imperialism and the imperialized formations on the global scale, and the consequences of these contentions for culture and literature as such, except from a strictly nationalist standpoint.

Meanwhile, there has been a very considerable shift in the composition of the archive which is to represent the Third World in the metropolitan university, creating new kinds of possibilities for certain kinds of Black critics. In the late 1960s and early 1970s, when the category of Third World Literature first emerged, it was to apply, more or less strictly, to texts that were actually produced *in* the non-Western countries, and it included texts produced in all epochs, including most prominently those from the pre-colonial epochs. The main idea at that time was to construct a counter-canon produced, constitutively, outside Europe and North America; one that displayed some civilizational differences (the word 'difference' was at that time written with a lower-case 'd', as something local and empirically verifiable, not to denote any epistemological category or perennial ontological condition). Documents of the African past were to be the testimonies of African-American heritage in the old continent, as Homer or Shakespeare were the documents of Western civilization; the same applied to Latin American, Caribbean, and Asian literary documents as well. This counter-canon was to be composed, in other words, of documents which referred to that which had been left behind, which had been there before the journey, and which was now to be recouped – by the descendant of the slave, the immigrant, the incoming student – as a resource of both memory and hope. This sense was to survive in very few theorists, and it survived notably in Jameson's treatment of the matter (discussed in Chapter 3), which simply would have no theoretical basis if the 'national allegory' were not to come from within the nation which the allegory was to narrate. As the elite immigrant intelligentsia located more or less permanently in the metropolitan countries began appropriating this counter-canonical category as their special preserve and archive, the emphasis kept shifting, from the epochal to the modern, erasing in the process the difference between documents produced within the non-Western countries and those others which were produced by the immigrant at metropolitan locations. With the passage of time, the writings of immigrants were to become greatly privileged and were declared, in some extreme but also very influential formulations, to be the only *authentic* documents of resistance in our time.[5] It was at this point that the singular ascendancy of Salman Rushdie began, and it is notable that apart from Edward Said himself, the critics who have played the key role in redefining literary Third-Worldism in relation mainly to the immigrant, and have also cemented the relationship between this immigrant phenomenon and postmodern ways of reading that archive, have usually been of Asian origin. Once this relationship between the immigrant intellectual, literary Third-Worldism, avant-garde literary theory in general and deconstructionist poststructuralism in particular had been cemented, a different kind of Black critic could then enter this scene of 'Race', Writing and Difference.[6]

## V

In short, there has been a very considerable aggregation of texts and individuals, but mere aggregation of texts and individuals does not give rise to the construction of a counter-canon. For the latter to arise, there has to be the cement of a powerful ideology, however incoherent and loosely defined. This cement eventually came to metropolitan literary theory in the shape of the Three Worlds Theory – especially after the later 1960s, in the global aftermath of the Chinese Cultural Revolution, and more so after the adoption of a certain brand of Maoism by some influential sections of the Parisian avant-garde, from Julia Kristeva to Jean-Luc Godard. Once these pressures of politics, texts, individuals, and certain kinds of radicalisms had opened up this still-expanding field of Third World Literature, it was only natural that a goodly number of other people – European and

American, white and non-white – would also start exploring it, from a whole range of diverse political positions, and that some would even want to invest their careers in it. The social collapse of the Comecon countries has, of course, complicated this matter of the 'Three Worlds Theory' a great deal, and it is likely that the category itself may now be abandoned altogether, more out of confusion than anything else, to be replaced simply with eclectic play, thus refurbishing the already hegemonic academic philosophies of 'Difference'.

We shall return to the political origins of the Three Worlds Theory, as well as some alternative ways of theorizing the global structure of imperialism in its current phase, in the concluding chapter of this book. Even in cultural theory as it has developed in the metropolitan countries, an exclusive emphasis on the nation, and on nationalism as the necessary ideology emanating from the national situation, has been a *logical* feature of Third-Worldist perspectives. For once the world is divided into three large unities, each fundamentally coherent and fundamentally external to one another, it is extremely difficult to speak of any fundamental differences within particular national structures – differences, let us say, of class or of gender formation. One is then forced, by the terms of one's own discourse, to minimize those kinds of differences, and to absolutize, on the other hand, the difference between, say, the First and the Third Worlds. The preferred technique among cultural theorists, then, is to look at 'Third World' literary texts in terms always of their determination by the colonial encounter, but rarely in terms of their determination by class and gender formations, or from the standpoint of what the needs of a socialist cultural production, quite beyond the issue of colonial determination, might be. We learn much, in other words, about Lamming and Achebe, Garciá Márquez and Rushdie, as their work negotiates a terrain marked by colonialism, but those same works are never examined from the perspective of socialism as the emancipatory desire of our epoch. The very terms of this discourse repress such alternative starting points, and those terms sit comfortably with the institutions – the university, the literary conference, the professional journal – which are in the business of authorizing such discourses. One would have thought that in any conflict between advanced capitalism and backward capitalism, the latter is bound to lose; socialism, therefore, has to be the third term of the dialectic, without which the antagonism of the other two terms simply cannot be resolved. If, however, socialist political and cultural practices are simply externalized *out* of our struggles, and if those practices are located only in some ideal place designated as the Second World, then a narrow nationalism can be the only insignia under which cultural production within the Third World can take place or be conceptualized.

The cognate subdisciplines of 'Third World Literature' and 'Colonial Discourse Analysis' emerged at a time when radical theory was in the process of distancing itself from the kind of activist culture that had started developing throughout Western Europe and North America during the period of the great anti-imperialist struggles in Indochina and Southern Africa. This distancing on the part of contemporary metropolitan radicalism from its own immediate past has led to other kinds of distancing as well. In terms of historical periodization, there appears to be in both these subdisciplines far greater interest in the colonialism of the past than in the imperialism of the present. In terms of social processes, interest has shifted from the 'facts' of imperialist wars and political economies of exploitation to 'fictions' of representation and cultural artefact. In terms of global spaces, one is hearing, as these subdisciplines now function in the United States, a lot less about the United States itself and a lot more about Britain and France. In terms of academic disciplines, much more prestige attaches now to Literature, Philosophy and radical Anthropology than to Political Economy. In terms of theoretical positions, Marxism is often dismissed as a 'modes-of-production narrative', a 'totalizing system', and so on, while engagements shift more towards Narratology, Discourse Analysis, Deconstruction, or New History of a Foucauldian kind.

To the extent that both 'Third World Literature' and 'Colonial Discourse Analysis' privilege coloniality as the framing term of epochal experience, national identity is logically privileged as the main locus of meaning, analysis and (self-)representation, which is, in turn, particularly attractive to the growing number of 'Third World intellectuals' who are based in the metropolitan university. They can now materially represent the undifferentiated colonized Other – more recently and more fashionably, the *post-colonial* Other – without much examining of their own presence in that institution, except perhaps in the characteristically postmodernist mode of ironic pleasure in observing the duplicities and multiplicities of one's own persona. The East, reborn and greatly expanded now as a 'Third World', seems to have become, yet again, a *career* – even for the 'Oriental' this time, and within the 'Occident' too.

3

# Jameson's Rhetoric of Otherness and the 'National Allegory'

In assembling the following notes on Fredric Jameson's 'Third World Literature in the Era of Multinational Capital'[1] I find myself in an awkward position. If I were to name the *one* literary critic/theorist writing in the USA today whose work I generally hold in the highest regard, it would surely be Jameson. The plea that generates most of the passion in his text – that the teaching of literature in the US academy be informed by a sense not only of 'Western' literature but of 'world literature'; that the so-called literary canon be based not upon the exclusionary pleasures of dominant taste but upon an inclusive and opulent sense of heterogeneity – is, of course, entirely salutary. And I wholly admire both the knowledge and the range of sympathies he brings to the reading of texts produced in distant lands.

But this plea for syllabus reform – even his marvellously erudite reading of Lu Xun and Ousmane – is conflated with – indeed, superseded by – a much more ambitious undertaking which pervades the entire text but is explicitly announced only in the last sentence of the last footnote: the construction of 'a theory of the cognitive aesthetics of third-world literature'. This 'cognitive aesthetics' rests, in turn, upon a suppression of the multiplicity of significant difference among and within both the advanced capitalist countries on the one hand and the imperialized formations on the other. We have, instead, a binary opposition of what Jameson calls the 'First' and the 'Third' worlds. It is in this passage from a plea for syllabus reform to the enunciation of a 'cognitive aesthetics' that most of the text's troubles lie. These troubles are, I might add, quite numerous.

There is doubtless a personal, somewhat existential side to my encounter with this text, which is best clarified at the outset. I have been reading Jameson's work now for roughly fifteen years, and at least some of what I know about the literatures and cultures of Western Europe and the USA comes from him; and because I am a Marxist, I had always thought of us, Jameson and myself, as birds of the same feather, even though we never quite flocked together. But then, when I was on the fifth page of this text (specifically, on the sentence starting with 'All third-world texts are necessarily . . . ' etc.), I realized that what was being theorized was, among many other things, myself. Now, I was born in India and I write poetry in Urdu, a language not commonly understood among US intellectuals. So I said to myself: '*All*? . . . *necessarily*?' It felt odd. Matters became much more curious, however. For the further I read, the more I realized, with no little chagrin, that the man whom I had for so long, so affectionately, albeit from a physical distance, taken as a comrade was, in his own opinion, my civilizational Other. It was not a good feeling.

## I

I too think that there *are* plenty of very good books written by African, Asian and Latin American writers which are available in English and which must be taught as an antidote to the general ethnocentricity and cultural myopia of the Humanities as they are presently constituted in these United States. If some label is needed for this activity, one may call it 'Third World Literature'. Conversely, however, I also hold that this term, 'the Third World', is, even in its most telling deployments, a polemical one, with no theoretical status whatsoever. Polemic surely has a prominent place in all human discourses, especially in the discourse of politics, so the use of this term in loose, polemical contexts is altogether valid. But to lift it from the register of polemics and claim it as a basis for producing theoretical knowledge, which presumes a certain rigour in constructing the objects of one's knowledge, is to misconstrue not only the term itself but even the world to which it refers. I shall argue in context, then, that there is no such thing as a 'Third World Literature' which can be constructed as an internally coherent object of theoretical knowledge. There are fundamental issues – of periodization, social and linguistic formations, political and ideological struggles within the field of literary production, and so on – which simply cannot be resolved at this level of generality without an altogether positivist reductionism.

The mere fact, for example, that languages of the metropolitan countries have not been adopted by the vast majority of the producers of literature in Asia and Africa means that the vast majority of literary texts from those continents are unavailable in the metropolises, so that a literary theorist who sets out to formulate 'a theory of the cognitive aesthetics of third-world literature' will be constructing ideal-types, in the Weberian manner, duplicating all the basic procedures which Orientalist scholars have historically deployed in presenting their own readings of a certain tradition of 'high' textuality as *the* knowledge of a supposedly unitary object which they call 'the Islamic civilization'. I might add that literary relations between the metropolitan countries and the imperialized formations are constructed very differently from such relations among the metropolitan countries themselves. Rare would be a literary theorist in Europe or the USA who does not command a couple of European languages besides his or her own; and the frequency of translation, back and forth, among European languages creates very fulsome channels for the circulation of texts, so that even a US scholar who does not command much beyond English can be quite well grounded in the various metropolitan traditions. Linguistic and literary relations between the metropolitan countries and the countries of Asia and Africa, on the other hand, offer three sharp contrasts to this system of textual exchanges among the metropolitan countries. Rare would be a modern intellectual in Asia or Africa who does not know at least one European language; equally rare would be, on the other side, a major literary theorist in Europe or the United States who has ever bothered with an Asian or African language; and the enormous industry of translation which circulates texts among the advanced capitalist countries grinds erratically and slowly when it comes to translation from Asian or African languages. The upshot is that major literary traditions – such as those of Bengali, Hindi, Tamil, Telegu and half a dozen others from India alone – remain, beyond a few texts here and there, virtually unknown to the American literary theorist.

One consequence, then, is that the few writers who happen to write in English are valorized beyond measure. Witness, for example, the characterization of Salman Rushdie's *Midnight's Children* in the *New York Times* as 'a Continent finding its voice' – as if one has no voice if one does not speak in English. Or Richard Poirier's praise for Edward Said in *Raritan* which now adorns the back cover of a recent book of Said's: 'It is Said's great accomplishment that thanks to his book, Palestinians will never be lost to history.'[2] This is the upside-down world of the *camera obscura*: not that Said's vision is itself framed by the Palestinian experience, but that Palestine would have no place in history without Said's book! The retribution visited upon the head of an Asian, an African, an Arab intellectual who is of any consequence and writes in English is that he or she is immediately elevated to the lonely splendour of a representative – of a race, a continent, a civilization, even the 'Third World'. It is in this general context that a 'cognitive theory of third-world literature' based upon what is currently available in languages of the metropolitan countries becomes, to my mind, an alarming undertaking.

I shall return to some of these points presently, especially to the point about the epistemological impossibility of a 'third-world literature'. Since, however, Jameson's own text is so centrally grounded in a binary opposition between a First and a Third World, it is impossible to proceed with an examination of his particular propositions regarding the respective literary traditions without first asking whether or not this characterization of the world is itself theoretically tenable, and whether, therefore, an accurate conception of *literature* can be mapped out on the basis of this binary opposition. I shall argue later that since Jameson defines the so-called Third World in terms of its 'experience of colonialism and imperialism', the political category that necessarily follows from this exclusive emphasis is that of 'the nation', with nationalism as the peculiarly valorized ideology; and, because of this privileging of the nationalist ideology, it is then theoretically posited that 'all third-world texts are necessarily . . . to be read as . . . national allegories'. The theory of the 'national allegory' as the metatext is thus inseparable from the larger Three Worlds Theory which permeates the whole of Jameson's own text. We too have to begin, then, with some comments on 'the Third World' as a theoretical category and on 'nationalism' as the necessary, exclusively desirable ideology.

## II

Jameson seems to be aware of the difficulties in conceptualizing the global dispersion of powers and populations in terms of his particular variant of the Three Worlds Theory ('I take the point of criticism', he says). And after reiterating the basic premiss of that theory ('the capitalist first world'; 'the socialist bloc of the second world'; and 'countries that have suffered colonialism and imperialism'), he does clarify that he does not uphold the specifically Maoist theory of 'convergence' between the United States and the Soviet Union. The rest of the difficulty in holding this view of the world is elided, however, with three assertions: that he cannot find a 'comparable expression'; that he is deploying these terms in 'an essentially descriptive way'; and that the criticisms are at any rate not 'relevant'. The problem of 'comparable expression' is a minor matter, which we shall ignore; 'relevance, on the other hand, is the central issue, and I shall return to it presently. First, however, I want to comment briefly on the matter of 'description'.

More than most critics writing in the USA today, Jameson should know that when it comes to a knowledge of the world, there is no such thing as a category of the 'essentially descriptive'; that 'description' is never ideologically or cognitively neutral; that to 'describe' is to specify a locus of meaning, to construct an object of knowledge, and to produce a knowledge that will be bound by that act of descriptive construction. 'Description' has been central, for example, in the colonizing discourses. It was by assembling a monstrous machinery of descriptions – of our bodies, our speech acts, our habitats, our conflicts and desires, our politics, our socialities and sexualities, in fields as various as ethnology, fiction, photography, linguistics, political science – that those discourses were able to classify and ideologically master colonial subjects, enabling the transformation of descriptively verifiable multiplicity and difference into the ideologically felt hierarchy of value. To say, in short, that what one is presenting is 'essentially descriptive' is to assert a level of facticity which conceals its own ideology, and to prepare a ground from which judgements of classification, generalization and value can be made.

As we come to the substance of what Jameson 'describes', I find it significant that First and Second Worlds are defined in terms of their production systems (capitalism and socialism, respectively), whereas the third category – the Third World – is defined purely in terms of an 'experience' of externally inserted phenomena. That which is constitutive of human history itself is present in the first two cases, absent in the third case. Ideologically, this classification divides the world between those who make history and those who are mere objects of it; elsewhere in the text, Jameson would significantly reinvoke Hegel's famous description of the master–slave relation to encapsulate the First–Third World opposition. But analytically, this classification leaves the so-called Third World in limbo; if only the First World is capitalist and the Second World socialist, how does one understand the Third World? Is it pre-capitalist? Transitional? Transitional between what and what? But then there is also the issue of the location of particular countries within the various 'worlds'.

Take, for example, India. Its colonial past is nostalgically rehashed on US television screens in copious series every few months, but the India of today has all the characteristics of a capitalist country: generalized commodity production, vigorous and escalating exchanges not only between agriculture and industry but also between Departments I and II of industry itself, and technical personnel more numerous than those of France and Germany combined. It is a very miserable kind of capitalism, and the conditions of life for over half the Indian population – roughly four hundred million people – are considerably worse than what Engels described in *The Condition of the Working Class in England*. But India's steel industry did celebrate its hundredth anniversary a few years ago, and the top eight of her multinational corporations are among the fastest-growing in the world, active as they are in numerous countries, from Vietnam to Nigeria. This economic base is combined, then, with unbroken parliamentary rule of the bourgeoisie since Independence in 1947, a record quite comparable to the length of Italy's modern record of unbroken bourgeois-democratic governance, and superior to the fate of bourgeois democracy in Spain and Portugal, two of the oldest colonizing countries. This parliamentary republic of the bourgeoisie in India has not been without its own lawlessnesses and violences, of a kind and degree now not normal in Japan or Western Europe, but a bourgeois political subjectivity *has* been created for the populace at large. The corollary on the Left is that the two communist parties (CPI and CPI–M) have longer and more extensive experience of regional government, within the republic of the bourgeoisie, than all the Eurocommunist parties combined, and the electorate that votes ritually for these two parties is probably larger than the communist electorates in all the rest of the capitalist world.

So – does India belong in the First World or the Third? Brazil, Argentina, Mexico, South Africa? And . . . ? But we *know* that countries of the Pacific rim, from South Korea to Singapore, constitute the fastest-growing region within global capitalism. The list could be much longer, but the point is that the binary opposition which Jameson constructs between a capitalist First World and a presumably pre- or non-capitalist Third World is empirically ungrounded in any facts.

## III

I have said already that if one believes in the Three Worlds Theory – hence in a 'Third World' defined exclusively in terms of 'the experience of colonialism and imperialism' – then the primary ideological formation available to a left-wing intellectual will be that of nationalism; it will then be possible to assert – surely with very considerable exaggeration, but possible to assert none the less – that 'all third-world texts are necessarily . . . *national allegories*' (original emphasis). This exclusive emphasis on the nationalist ideology is there even in the opening paragraph of Jameson's text, where the only choice for the 'Third World' is said to be between its 'nationalisms' and a 'global American postmodernist culture'. Is there no other choice? Could not one join the 'Second World', for example? There used to be, in Marxist discourse, a thing called 'socialist and/or communist culture' which was neither nationalist nor postmodernist. Has that vanished from our discourse altogether, even as the name of a desire?

Jameson's haste in totalizing historical phenomena in terms of binary oppositions (nationalism/postmodernism, in this case) leaves little room for the fact, for instance, that the only nationalisms in the so-called Third World which have been able to resist US cultural pressure and have actually produced any alternatives are those which are already articulated to and assimilated within the much larger field of socialist political practice. Virtually all the others have had no difficulty in reconciling themselves with what Jameson calls 'global American postmodernist culture'; in the singular and sizeable case of Iran (which Jameson forbids us to mention on the grounds that it is 'predictable' that we shall do so), the anti-communism of the Islamic nationalists has produced not social regeneration but clerical fascism. Nor does the absolutism of that opposition (postmodernism/nationalism) permit any space for the simple idea that nationalism itself is not some unitary thing with some predetermined essence and value. There are hundreds of nationalisms in Asia and Africa today; some are progressive, others are not. Whether or not a nationalism will produce a progressive cultural practice depends, to put it in Gramscian terms, upon the political character of the power bloc which takes hold of it and utilizes it, as a material force, in the process of constituting its own hegemony. There is neither theoretical ground nor empirical evidence to support the notion that bourgeois nationalisms of the so-called Third World will have any difficulty with postmodernism; they *want* it.

Yet there *is* a very tight fit between the Three Worlds Theory, the overvalorization of the nationalist ideology, and the assertion that 'national allegory' is the primary, even exclusive, form of narrativity in the so-called Third World. If this 'Third World' is *constituted* by the singular 'experience of colonialism and imperialism', and if the only possible response is a nationalist one, then what else is there that is more urgent to narrate than this 'experience'? In fact, there is *nothing else* to narrate. For if societies here are defined not by relations of production but by relations of intra-national domination; if they are forever suspended outside the sphere of conflict between capitalism (First World) and socialism (Second World); if the motivating force for history here is neither class formation and class struggle nor the multiplicities of intersecting conflicts based upon class, gender, nation, race, region, and so on, but the unitary 'experience' of national oppression (if one is merely the *object* of history, the Hegelian slave), then what else *can* one narrate but that national oppression? Politically, we are Calibans all. Formally, we are fated to be in the poststructuralist world of Repetition with Difference; the same allegory, the nationalist one, rewritten, over and over again, until the end of time: 'all third-world texts are necessarily . . . '

## IV

But one could start with a radically different premiss: namely, the proposition that we live not in three worlds but in one; that this world includes the experience of colonialism and imperialism on both sides of Jameson's global divide (the 'experience' of imperialism is a central fact of all aspects of life inside the USA, from ideological formation to the utilization of the social surplus in military-industrial complexes); that societies in formations of backward capitalism are as much constituted by the division of classes as are societies in the advanced capitalist countries; that socialism is not restricted to something called 'the Second World' but is simply the name of a resistance that saturates the globe today, as capitalism itself does; that the different parts of the capitalist system are to be known not in terms of a binary opposition but as a contradictory unity – with differences, yes, but also with profound overlaps. One immediate consequence for literary theory would be that the unitary search for 'a theory of cognitive aesthetics for third-world literature' would be rendered impossible, and one would have to forgo the idea of a metanarrative that encompasses all the fecundity of real narratives in the so-called Third World. Conversely, many of the questions that one would ask about, let us say, Urdu or Bengali traditions of literature may turn out to be rather similar to the questions one has asked previously about English/American literatures. By the same token, a *real* knowledge of those other traditions may force the US literary theorists to ask questions about their own tradition which they have not asked heretofore.

Jameson claims that one cannot proceed from the premiss of a real unity of the world 'without falling back into some general liberal and humanistic universalism'. That is a curious idea, coming from a Marxist. One would have thought that the world was united not by liberalist ideology – that the world was not at all constituted in the realm of an Idea, be it Hegelian or humanist – but by the global operation of a single mode of production, namely the capitalist one, and the global resistance to this mode, a resistance which is itself unevenly developed in different parts of the globe. Socialism, one would have thought, was not by any means limited to the so-called Second World (the socialist countries) but is a global phenomenon, reaching into the farthest rural communities in Asia, Africa and Latin

America, not to speak of individuals and groups within the United States. What gives the world its unity, then, is not a humanist ideology but the ferocious struggle between capital and labour which is now strictly and fundamentally global in character. The prospect of a socialist revolution has receded so much from the practical horizon for so much of the metropolitan Left that the temptation for the US Left intelligentsia is to forget the ferocity of that basic struggle which in our time transcends all others. The advantage of coming from Pakistan, in my own case, is that the country is saturated with capitalist commodities, bristles with US weaponry, borders on China, the Soviet Union and Afghanistan, suffers from a proliferation of competing nationalisms, and is currently witnessing the first stage in the consolidation of the communist movement. It is difficult, coming from there, to forget that primary motion of history which gives our globe its contradictory unity. None of this has anything to do with liberal humanism.

As for the specificity of cultural difference, Jameson's theoretical conception tends, I believe, in the opposite direction – namely, that of homogenization. Difference between the First World and the Third is absolutized as an Otherness, but the enormous cultural heterogeneity of social formations within the so-called Third World is submerged within a singular identity of 'experience'. Now, countries of Western Europe and North America have been deeply tied together over roughly the last two hundred years; capitalism itself is so much older in these countries; the cultural logic of late capitalism is so strongly operative in these metropolitan formations; the circulation of cultural products among them is so immediate, so extensive, so brisk, that one could sensibly speak of a certain cultural homogeneity among them. But Asia, Africa and Latin America? Historically, these countries were never so closely tied together; Peru and India simply do not have a common history of the sort that Germany and France, or Britain and the United States, have; not even the singular 'experience of colonialism and imperialism' has been in specific ways the same or similar in, say, India and Namibia. These various countries, from the three continents, have been assimilated into the global structure of capitalism not as a single cultural ensemble but highly differentially, each establishing its own circuits of (unequal) exchange with the metropolis, each acquiring its own very distinct class formations. Circuits of exchange among them are rudimentary at best; an average Nigerian who is literate about his own country would know infinitely more about England and the United States than about any country of Asia or Latin America or, indeed, about most countries of Africa. The kind of circuits that bind the cultural complexes of the advanced capitalist countries simply do not exist among countries of backward capitalism, and capitalism itself, which is dominant but not altogether universalized, does not yet have the same power of homogenization in its cultural logic in most of these countries, except among the urban bourgeoisie.

Of course, great cultural similarities also exist among countries that occupy analogous positions in the global capitalist system, and there are similarities in many cases that have been bequeathed by the similarities of socioeconomic structures in the pre-capitalist past. The point is not to construct a typology that is simply the obverse of Jameson's, but rather to define the material basis for a fair degree of cultural homogenization among the advanced capitalist countries and the lack of that kind of homogenization in the rest of the capitalist world. In context, therefore, one is doubly surprised at Jameson's absolute insistence upon Difference and the relation of Otherness between the First World and the Third, and his equally insistent idea that the 'experience' of the 'Third World' could be contained and communicated within a single narrative form. By locating capitalism in the First World and socialism in the Second, Jameson's theory freezes and dehistoricizes the global space within which struggles between these great motivating forces actually take place. And by assimilating the enormous heterogeneities and productivities of our life into a single Hegelian metaphor of the master–slave relation, this theory reduces us to an ideal-type and demands from us that we narrate ourselves through a form commensurate with that ideal-type. To say that all Third World texts are necessarily this or that is to say, in effect, that any text originating within that social space which is *not* this or that is not a 'true' narrative. It is in this sense above all that the category of 'Third World Literature' which is the site of this operation, with the 'national allegory' as its metatext as well as the mark of its constitution and difference, is, to my mind, epistemologically an impossible category.

## V

Part of the difficulty in engaging with Jameson's text is that there is a constant slippage, a recurrent inflation, in the way he handles his analytic categories. The specificity of the First World, for example, seems at times to be predicated upon the postmodernist moment, which is doubtless of recent origin; but at other times it appears to be a matter of the capitalist mode of production, which is a much larger, much older thing; and, in yet another range of formulations, this First World is said to be coterminous with 'Western civilization' itself, obviously a rather primordial way of being, dating back to Antiquity ('Graeco-Judaic', in Jameson's phrase) and anterior to any structuration of productions and classes as we know them today. *When* did this First World become First: in the pre-Christian centuries, or after World War II?

And at what point in history does a text produced in countries with 'experience of colonialism and imperialism' become a *Third World text*? In one kind of reading, only texts produced *after* the advent of colonialism could be so designated, since it is colonialism/imperialism which constitutes the Third World as such. But in speaking constantly of 'the West's Other'; in referring to the tribal/tributary and Asiatic modes as the theoretical basis for his selection of Lu Xun (Asian) and Sembene (African) respectively; in characterizing Freud's theory as a 'Western or First World reading' as contrasted with ten centuries of specifically Chinese distributions of the libidinal energy which are said to frame Lu Xun's texts – in deploying these broad epochal and civilizational categories, Jameson also suggests that the difference between the First World and the Third is itself primordial, rooted in things far older than capitalism as such. So, if the First World is the same as 'the West' and the 'Graeco-Judaic', one has, on the other hand, an alarming feeling that the *Bhagavad-Gita*, the edicts of Manu, and the Qur'an itself are perhaps Third World texts (though the Judaic elements of the Qur'an are quite beyond doubt, and much of the ancient art in what is today Pakistan is itself Graeco-Indic).

But there is also the question of *space*. Do all texts produced in countries with 'experience of colonialism and imperialism' become, by virtue of geographical origin, 'third-world texts'? Jameson speaks so often of '*all* third-world texts', insists so much on a singular form of narrativity for

Third World Literature, that not to take him literally is to violate the very terms of his discourse. Yet one knows of so many texts from one's own part of the world which do not fit the description of 'national allegory' that one wonders why Jameson insists so much on the category, '*all*'. Without this category, of course, he cannot produce *a* theory of Third World Literature. But is it also the case that he means the opposite of what he actually says: not that '*all* third-world texts are to be read . . . as national allegories' but that *only* those texts which give us national allegories can be admitted as authentic texts of Third World Literature, while the rest are by definition excluded? So one is not quite sure whether one is dealing with a fallacy ('all third-world texts are' this or that) or with the Law of the Father (you must write *this* if you are to be admitted into my theory).

These shifts and hesitations in defining the objects of one's knowledge are based, I believe, on several confusions, one of which I shall specify here. For if one argues that the Third World is constituted by the 'experience of colonialism and imperialism', one must also recognize the two-pronged action of the colonial/imperialist dynamic: the forced transfers of value *from* the colonialized/imperialized formations, and the intensification of capitalist relations *within* those formations. And if capitalism is not merely an externality but also a shaping force within those formations, then one must conclude also that the separation between the public and the private, so characteristic of capitalism, has occurred there as well, at least in some degree and especially among the urban intelligentsia which produces most of the written texts and is itself caught in the world of capitalist commodities. With this bifurcation must have come, at least for some producers of texts, the individuation and personalization of libidinal energies, the loss of access to 'concrete' experience, and the consequent experience of the self as an isolated, alienated entity incapable of real, organic connection with any collectivity. There must be texts, perhaps numerous texts, that are grounded in this desolation, bereft of any capacity for the kind of allegorization and organicity that Jameson demands of them. The logic of Jameson's own argument – that the Third World is constituted by the 'experience of colonialism and imperialism' – leads necessarily to the conclusion that at least some of the writers of the Third World itself must be producing texts characteristic not of the so-called tribal and Asiatic modes but of the capitalist era as such, much in the manner of the so-called First World. But Jameson does not draw that conclusion.

And he does not draw that conclusion at least partially because this so-called Third World is to him suspended outside the modern systems of production (capitalism and socialism). He does not quite say that the Third World is pre- or non-capitalist, but that is clearly the implication of the contrast he establishes – as, for example, in the following formulation:

> . . . one of the determinants of capitalist culture, that is, the culture of the western realist and modernist novel, is a radical split between the private and the public, between the poetic and the political, between what we have come to think of as the domain of sexuality and the unconscious and that of the public world of classes, of the economic, and of secular political power: in other words, Freud versus Marx . . .
>
> I will argue that, although we may retain for convenience and for analysis such categories as the subjective and the public or political, the relations between them are wholly different in third-world culture. (p. 69)

It is noteworthy that 'the radical split between the private and the public' is distinctly located in the capitalist mode here, but the *absence* of this split in so-called Third World culture is not located in any mode of production – in keeping with Jameson's very definition of the Three Worlds. But Jameson knows what he is talking about, and his statements have been less ambiguous in the past. Thus we find the following in his relatively early essay on Lukács in *Marxism and Form*:

> In the art works of a preindustrialized, agricultural or tribal society, the artist's raw material is on a human scale, it has an immediate meaning. . . . The story needs no background in time because the culture knows no history; each generation repeats the same experiences, reinvents the same basic human situations as though for the first time . . . . The works of art characteristic of such societies may be called concrete in that their elements are all meaningful from the outset . . . in the language of Hegel, this raw material needs no *mediation*.
>
> When we turn from such a work to the literature of the industrial era, everything changes . . . a kind of dissolution of the human sets in. . . . For the unquestioned ritualistic time of village life no longer exists; there is henceforth a separation between public and private . . . (pp. 165-7).

Clearly, then, what was once theorized as a difference between the pre-industrial and the industrialized societies (the unity of the public and the private in one, the separation of the two in the other) is now transposed as a difference between the First and Third Worlds. The idea of the 'concrete' is now rendered in only slightly different vocabulary: 'third-world culture . . . must be situational and materialist despite itself'. And it is perhaps that other idea – namely that 'preindustrialized . . . culture knows no history; each generation repeats the same experience' – which is at the root of now suspending the so-called Third World outside the modern modes of production (capitalism and socialism), encapsulating the experience of this Third World in the Hegelian metaphor of the master–slave relation, and postulating a unitary form of narrativity (the national allegory) in which the 'experience' of this Third World is to be told. In both texts, the theoretical authority that is invoked is, predictably, that of Hegel.

Likewise, Jameson insists over and over again that the *national* experience is central to the cognitive formation of the Third World intellectual, and that the narrativity of that experience takes the form exclusively of a 'national allegory'. But this emphatic insistence on the category 'nation' itself keeps slipping into a much wider, far less demarcated vocabulary of 'culture', 'society', 'collectivity', and so on. Are 'nation' and 'collectivity' the same thing? Take, for example, the two statements which seem to enclose the elaboration of the theory itself. In the beginning, on page 69, we are told:

> All third-world texts are necessarily, I want to argue, allegorical, and in a very specific way: they are to be read as what I will call *national allegories*, even when, or perhaps I should say, particularly when their forms develop out of predominantly western machineries of representation, such as the novel.

But at the end, on pages 85–6, we find the following: ' . . . the telling of the individual story and the individual experience cannot but ultimately involve the whole laborious telling of the experience of the collectivity itself.'

Are these two statements saying the same thing? The difficulty of this shift in vocabulary is that one may indeed connect one's personal experience to a 'collectivity' – in terms of class, gender, caste, religious community, trade union, political party, village, prison – combining the private and the public, and in some sense 'allegorizing' the individual experience, without involving the category of 'the nation' or necessarily referring back to the 'experience of colonialism and imperialism'. The latter statement would then seem to apply to a much larger body of texts, with far greater accuracy. By the same token, however, this wider application of 'collectivity' establishes much less radical difference between the so-called First and Third Worlds, since the whole history of realism in the European novel, in its many variants, has been associated with ideas of 'typicality' and 'the social', while the majority of the written narratives produced in the First World even today locate the individual story in a fundamental relation to some larger experience.

If we replace the idea of the 'nation' with that larger, less restrictive idea of 'collectivity', and if we start thinking of the process of allegorization not in nationalistic terms but simply as a relation between private and public, personal and communal, then it also becomes possible to see that allegorization is by no means specific to the so-called Third World. While Jameson overstates the presence of 'us', the 'national allegory', in the narratives of the Third World, he also, in the same sweep, understates the presence of analogous impulses in the US cultural ensembles. For what else are, let us say, Pynchon's *Gravity's Rainbow* or Ellison's *The Invisible Man* but allegorizations of individual – and not so individual – experience? What else could Richard Wright and Adrienne Rich and Richard Howard mean when they give their books titles like *Native Son* or *Your Native Land, Your Life* or *Alone With America*? It is not only the Asian or the African but also the American writer whose private imaginations must *necessarily* connect with experiences of the collectivity. One has only to look at Black and feminist writing to find countless allegories even within these postmodernist United States.

## VI

I also have some difficulty with Jameson's description of 'third-world literature' as 'non-canonical', for I am not quite sure what that *means*. Since the vast majority of literary texts produced in Asia, Africa and Latin America are simply not available in English, their exclusion from the US/ British 'canon' is self-evident. If, however, one considers the kind of texts Jameson seems to have in mind, one begins to wonder just what mechanisms of canonization there *are* from which this body of work is so entirely excluded.

Neruda, Vallejo, Octavio Paz, Borges, Fuentes, Garciá Márquez *et al.* – that is to say, quite a few writers of Latin American origin – *are* considered by the American academy to be major figures in modern literature. They, and even their translators, have received the most prestigious awards (the Nobel for Garciá Márquez, for instance, or the National Book Award for Eshleman's translation of Vallejo) and they are *taught* quite as routinely in Literature courses as their German or Italian contemporaries might be – perhaps more regularly, in fact. Soyinka was recently canonized through the Nobel Prize, and Achebe's novels are consistently more easily available in the US book market than are, for example, Richard Wright's. Edward Said, a man of Palestinian origin, has received virtually every honour the US academy has to offer, with distinct constituencies of his own; *Orientalism*, at least, is taught very widely, across several disciplines – more widely, it seems, than any other left-wing literary/cultural work in this country. V.S. Naipaul is now fully established as a major English novelist, and he does come from the Caribbean; he *is*, like Borges, a 'third-world writer'. Salman Rushdie's *Midnight's Children* was awarded the most prestigious literary award in England, and *Shame* was immediately reviewed as a major novel, almost always favourably, in virtually all the major newspapers and literary journals in Britain and the USA. Rushdie is a major presence on the British cultural scene and a prized visitor to conferences and graduate departments on both sides of the Atlantic. The blurbs on the Vintage paperback edition of *Shame*, based partly on a quotation from the *New York Times*, compare him with Swift, Voltaire, Sterne, Kafka, Grass, Kundera and Márquez. I am told that a doctoral dissertation has already been written about him at Columbia.[3] What else *is* canonization, when it comes to modern, contemporary, and in some cases (Rushdie, for example) relatively young writers?

My argument is not that these reputations are not well deserved (Naipaul, of course, is a different matter), nor that there should not be *more* such canonizations. But the representation of this body of work in Jameson's discourse as simply 'non-canonical' – that is, as something that has been altogether excluded from the contemporary practices of high textuality in the US academy – does appear to overstate the case considerably.

Jameson speaks of 'non-canonical forms of literature such as that of the third world', compares this singularized *form* to 'another non-canonical form' in which Dashiell Hammett is placed, and goes on to say:

> Nothing is to be gained by passing over in silence the radical difference of non-canonical texts. The third-world novel will not offer the satisfactions of Proust or Joyce; what is more damaging than that, perhaps, is its tendency to remind us of outmoded stages of our own first-world cultural development and to cause us to conclude that 'they are still writing novels like Dreiser and Sherwood Anderson'.

Now, I am not sure that realism, which appears to be at the heart of Jameson's characterization of 'Third World Literature' in this passage, is quite as universal in *that* literature or quite as definitively superseded in what Jameson calls 'first-world cultural development'. Some of the most highly regarded US fictionists of the present cultural moment, from Bellow and Malamud to Grace Paley and Robert Stone, seem to write not quite 'like Dreiser and Sherwood Anderson' but surely within the realist mode. On the other hand, Césaire became so popular among the French Surrealists because the terms of his discourse were contemporaneous with their own, and Neruda has been translated by some of the leading US poets because he is even formally not 'outmoded'. Novelists like García Márquez or Rushdie have been so well received in US/British literary circles precisely because they do not write like Dreiser or Sherwood Anderson; the satisfactions of their outrageous texts are not those of Proust or Joyce but are surely of an analogous kind, delightful to readers brought up on modernism and postmodernism. Césaire's *Return to the Native Land* is what it is because it combines what Jameson calls a 'national allegory' with the formal methods of the Parisian avant-garde of his student days. Borges, of course, is no longer seen in the USA in terms of his Latin American origin; he now belongs to the august company of the significant moderns, much like Kafka.

To say that the canon simply does not admit any Third World writers is to misrepresent the way bourgeois culture works – through selective admission and selective canonization. Just as modernism has now been fully canonized in the museum and the university, and as certain kinds of Marxism have been incorporated and given respectability within the academy, certain writers from the 'Third World' are also now part and parcel of literary discourse in the USA. Instead of claiming straightforward exclusion, it is perhaps more useful to inquire how the principle of selective incorporation works in relation to texts produced outside the metropolitan countries.

## VII

I want to offer some comments on the history of Urdu literature – not in the form of a cogent narrative, less still to formulate a short course in that history, but simply to illustrate the kind of impoverishment that is involved in the a priori declaration that 'All third-world texts are necessarily . . . to be read as national allegories'.

It is, for example, a matter of some considerable curiosity to me that the Urdu language, although one of the youngest linguistic formations in India, had nevertheless produced its first great poet, Khusrow (1253–1325), in the thirteenth century, so that a great tradition of poetry got going; but then it waited for roughly six centuries before beginning to assemble the first sizeable body of prose narratives. Not that prose itself had not been there; the earliest prose texts in Urdu date back to the fifteenth century, but those were written for religious purposes and were often mere translations from Arabic or Farsi. Non-seminarian and non-theological narratives – those that had to do with the pleasures of reading and the etiquettes of civility began appearing much, much later, in the last decade of the eighteenth century. Then, over two dozen were published during the next ten years. What inhibited that development for so long, and why did it happen precisely at that time? Much of that has to do with complex social developments that had gradually led to the displacement of

Farsi by Urdu, as the language of educated, urban speech and of prose writing in certain regions and groupings of Northern India.

That history we shall ignore, but a certain material condition of that production can be specified: many – though by no means all – of those prose narratives of the opening decades of the nineteenth century were written and published for the simple reason that a certain Scotsman, John Gilchrist, had argued within his own circles that employees of the East India Company could not hope to administer their Indian possessions on the basis of Farsi alone, and certainly not English, so that Fort William College was established in 1800 for the education of the British in Indian languages. For some time Farsi remained the most popular of all the languages taught at the College, but Gilchrist fancied himself as a scholar and exponent of the indigenous vernaculars, Urdu among them. He hired some of the most erudite men of his time and got them to write whatever they wanted, so long as they wrote in accessible prose. It was a stroke of luck even more than genius, for what came out of that enterprise was the mobilization of the whole range of speech patterns and oral vocabularies existing at that time (the *range* of vocabularies was in keeping with the pedagogical purpose) and the construction of narratives which either transcribed the great classics of oral literature or condensed the fictions that already existed in Arabic or Farsi and were therefore part of the cultural life of the North Indian upper classes. Thus the most famous of these narratives, Meer Amman's *Bagh-o-Bahaar*, was a condensation, in superbly colloquial Urdu, of the monumental *Qissa-e-Chahaar-Dervish*, which Faizi, the great scholar, had composed some centuries earlier in Farsi for the amusement of Akbar, the Mughal king who was almost an exact contemporary of the British Queen Elizabeth I.

But that was not the only impulse, and the publishing house of the Fort William College was in any case closed soon thereafter. A similar development was occurring in Lucknow, outside the British domains, at exactly the same time; some of the Fort William writers had themselves come from Lucknow, looking for alternative employment. Rajab Ali Beg Saroor's *Fasaana-e-Aja'ib* is the great classic of this other tradition of Urdu narrativity (these were actually not two different traditions but parts of the same, some of which were formed in the British domains, some not). In 1848, eight years before it fell to British guns, the city of Lucknow had twelve printing presses, and the consolidation of the narrative tradition in Urdu is inseparable from the history of those presses. The remarkable thing about all the major Urdu prose narratives which were written during the half-century in which the British completed their conquest of India is that there is nothing in their contents, in their way of seeing the world, which can reasonably be connected with the colonial onslaught or with any sense of resistance to it; by contrast, there is a large body of *letters* as well as poetry which documents that colossal carnage. It is as if the establishment of printing presses and the growth of a reading public for prose narratives gave rise to a kind of writing whose only task was to preserve in books at least some of that Persianized culture and those traditions of orality which were fast disappearing. It is only in this negative sense that one could, by stretching the terms a great deal, declare this to be a literature of the 'national allegory'.

The man who gave the language its first great publishing house, Munshi Naval Kishore, came somewhat later, however. His grandfather had been employed, like many upper-caste Hindus of the time, in the Mughal Ministry of Finance; his own father was a businessman, genteel and affluent but not rich. Naval Kishore himself had a passion for the written word; but like his father and grandfather, he also understood money. He started his career as a journalist, then went on to purchasing old handwritten manuscripts and publishing them for wider circulation. Over time he expanded into all sorts of fields, all connected with publishing, and gave Urdu its first great modern archive of published books. Urdu, in turn, showered him with money; at the time of his death in 1895, his fortune was estimated at one crore rupees (roughly half a million British pounds). He *had* to publish, I might add, more than national allegories, more than what came out of the experience of colonialism and imperialism, to make that kind of money.

But let me return to the issue of narration. For it is also a matter of some interest to me that the emergence of what one could plausibly call a novel came more than half a century *after* the appearance of those early registrations of the classics of the oral tradition and the rewriting of Arabic and Farsi stories. Sarshar's *Fasaana-e-Azaad*, the most opulent of those early novels, was serialized during the 1870s in something else that had begun in the 1830s: regular Urdu newspapers for the emergent middle classes.

Between the traditional tale and the modern novel, then, there were other things, such as newspapers and sizeable reading publics, much in the same way as one encounters them in a whole range of books on English literary history, from Ian Watt's *The Rise of the Novel* to Lennard J. Davis's more recent *Factual Fictions*. And I have often wondered, as others have sometimes wondered about Dickens, if the structure of Sarshar's novel might not have been very different had it been written not for serialization but for direct publication as a book.

Those other books, independent of newspapers, came too. One very prolific writer, whose name as it appears on the covers of his books is itself a curiosity, was Shams-ul-Ulema Deputy Nazir Ahmed (1831–1912). The name was actually Nazir Ahmed. 'Shams-ul-Ulema' literally means 'a Sun among the scholars of Islam', and indicates his distinguished scholarship in that area; 'Deputy' simply refers to the fact that he had no independent income and had joined the colonial Revenue Service. His training in Arabic was rigorous and immaculate; his knowledge of English was patchy, since he had had no formal training in it. He was a prolific translator of everything: the Indian Penal Code, the Indian Law of Evidence, the Qur'an, books of astronomy. He is known above all as a novelist, however, and he had one overwhelming anxiety: that girls should get a modern education (in this he represented the emergent urban bourgeoisie) but that they should nevertheless remain good, traditional housewives (a sentiment that was quite widespread, across all social boundaries). It was this anxiety that governed most of his fiction.

It is possible to argue, I think, that the formative phase of the Urdu novel and the narrativities that arose alongside that novel, in the latter part of the nineteenth century and the first decades of the twentieth, had to do much less with the experience of colonialism and imperialism as such and much more with two other kinds of pressures and themes: the emergence of a new kind of petty bourgeois who was violating all established social norms for his own pecuniary ends (Nazir Ahmed's own *Ibn-ul-Vaqt* – 'Time-Server', in rough English approximation – is a classic of that genre); and the status of women. Nazir Ahmed, of course, took conservative positions on both these themes, and was prolific on the latter, but there were others as well. Rashid-ul-Khairi, for example, established a very successful publishing house, the Asmat Book Depot, which published hundreds of books for women and children, as well as four of the five journals that came into my family over two generations: *Asmat*, *Khatoon-e-Mashriq*, *Jauhar-e-Nisvan*, *Banaat*, and *Nau-Nehaal*. English approximations for the last four titles are easy to provide: 'Woman of the East', 'Essence of Womanhood', 'Girls' (or 'Daughters'), and 'Children'. But the first title, *Asmat*, is harder to render in English, for the Urdu usage of this word has many connotations, from 'Virginity' to 'Honour', to 'Propriety', in a verbal condensation which expresses interrelated preoccupations. That these journals came regularly into my family for roughly forty years is itself significant, for mine was not, in metropolitan terms, an educated family; we lived in a small village, far from the big urban centres, and I was the first member of this family to finish high school or drive a car. The fact that two generations of women and children in such a family would be part of the regular readership of such journals shows the social reach of this kind of publishing. Much literature, in short, revolved around the issues of femininity and propriety, in a very conservative sort of way.

But then there were other writers, such as Meer Hadi Hassan Rusva, who challenged the dominant discourse and wrote his famous *Umrao Jan Ada* about those women for whom Urdu has many words, the most colourful of which can be rendered as 'women of the upper chamber': women to whom men of property in certain social milieux used to go for instruction in erotic play, genteel manners, literary taste, and knowledge of music. The scandal of Rusva's early-twentieth-century text is its proposition that since such a woman depends upon no one man, and because many men depend on her, she is the only relatively free woman in our society. He obviously did not like Nazir Ahmed's work, but I must also emphasize that the ironic and incipient 'feminism' of this text is not a reflection of any Westernization. Rusva was a very traditional man, and he was simply tired of certain kinds of moral posturing. Meanwhile, the idea that familial repressions in our traditional society were so great that the only women who had any sort of freedom to make fundamental choices for themselves were those who had no 'proper' place in that society – this subversive idea was to reappear in all kinds of ways when the next major break came in the forms of Urdu narrativity, in the 1930s, under the banner not of nationalism but of the Progressive Writers' Association, which was a cultural front for the Communist Party of India and had come into being directly as a result of the United Front Policy of the Comintern after 1935.

Critical Realism became the fundamental form of narrativity thereafter, for roughly two decades. 'Nation' was certainly a category used in this narrative, especially in non-fiction, and there was an explicit sense of sociality and collectivity, but the categories one deployed for that sense of collectivity were complex and several, for what Critical Realism demanded was that a critique of others (anti-colonialism) be conducted in the perspective of an even more comprehensive, multifaceted critique of ourselves: our class structures, our familial ideologies, our management of bodies and sexualities, our idealisms, our silences. I cannot think of a single novel in Urdu between 1935 and 1947, the crucial year leading up to decolonization, which is in any direct or exclusive way about 'the experience of colonialism and imperialism'. All the novels I know from that period are predominantly about other things: the barbarity of feudal landowners, the rapes and murders in the houses of religious 'mystics', the stranglehold of moneylenders upon the lives of peasants and the lower petty bourgeoisie, the social and sexual frustrations of schoolgirls, and so on. The theme of anti-colonialism is woven into many of those novels, but never in an exclusive or even a dominant emphasis. In fact, I do not know of *any* fictional narrative in Urdu, in roughly the last two hundred years, which is of any significance and any length (I am making an exception for a few short stories here) in which the issue of colonialism or the difficulty of a civilizational encounter between the English and the Indian has the same primacy as, for example, in Forster's *A Passage to India* or Paul Scott's *The Raj Quartet*. The typical Urdu writer has had a peculiar vision, in which he or she has never been able to construct fixed boundaries between the criminalities of the colonialist and the brutalities of all those indigenous people who have had power in our own society. We have had our own hysterias here and there – far too many, in fact – but there has never been a sustained, powerful myth of a primal innocence, when it comes to the colonial encounter.

The 'nation' indeed became the primary ideological problematic in Urdu literature only at the moment of Independence, for our Independence too was peculiar: it came together with the Partition of our country, the biggest and possibly the most miserable migration in human history, the worst bloodbath in the memory of the subcontinent: the gigantic fratricide conducted by Hindu, Muslim and Sikh communalists. Our 'nationalism' at this juncture was a nationalism of mourning, a form of valediction, for what we witnessed was not just the British policy of divide and rule, which surely was there, but our own willingness to break up our civilizational unity, to kill our neighbours, to forgo that civic ethos, that moral bond with each other, without which human community is impossible. A critique of others (anti-colonial nationalism) receded even further into the background, entirely overtaken now by an even harsher critique of ourselves. The major fictions of the 1950s and 1960s— the shorter fictions of Manto, Bedi, Intezar Hussein; the novels of Qurrat ul Ain, Khadija Mastoor, Abdullah Hussein – came out of that refusal to forgive what we ourselves had done and were still doing, in one way or another, to our own polity. No quarter was given to the colonialist; but there was none for ourselves either. One *could* speak, in a general sort of way, of 'the nation' in this context, but not of 'nationalism'. In Pakistan, of course, there was another, overriding doubt: were we a nation at all? Most of the left wing, I am sure, said 'No'.

## VIII

Finally, I also have some difficulty with the way Jameson seems to understand the epistemological status of the Dialectic. For what seems to lie at the heart of all the analytic procedures in his text is a search for – the notion that there *is* – a unitary determination which can be identified, in its splendid isolation, as the source of all narrativity: the proposition that the 'Third World' is a *singular* formation, possessing its own unique, unitary force of determination in the sphere of ideology (nationalism) and cultural production (the national allegory).

Within a postmodernist intellectual milieu where texts are to be read as the utterly free, altogether hedonistic plays of the Signifier, I can well empathize with a theoretical operation that seeks to locate the production of texts within a determinate, knowable field of power and signification, but the idea of a *unitary* determination is in its *origins* a pre-Marxist idea. I hasten to add that this idea is surely present in a number of Marx's own formulations as well as in a number of very honourable, highly productive theoretical formations that have followed, in one way or another, in Marx's footsteps. It is to be seen in action, for example, even in so recent a debate as the one that followed the famous Dobb–Sweezy exchange and came to be focused on the search for a 'prime mover' (the issue of a unitary determination in the rise of the capitalist mode of production in Western Europe). So when Jameson implicitly invokes this particular understanding of the Dialectic, he is in distinguished company indeed.

But there is, I believe, a considerable space where one could take one's stand between (a) the postmodernist cult of utter non-determinacy and (b) the idea of a unitary determination which has lasted from Hegel up to some of the most modern of the Marxist debates. For the main thrust of the Marxist Dialectic, as I understand it, comprises a *tension*, a mutually transformative relation, between the problematic of a final determination (of the ideational content by the life-process of material labour, for example) and the utter historicity of multiple, interpenetrating determinations, so that – in Engels's words – the 'outcome' of any particular history hardly ever corresponds to the 'will' of *any* of those historical agents who struggle over that outcome. Thus, for example, I have said that what constitutes the unity of the world is the global operation of the capitalist mode of production and the resistance to that mode which is ultimately socialist in character. But this constitutive fact does not operate in the same way in all the countries of Asia and Africa. In Namibia, the imposition of the capitalist mode takes a directly colonial form, whereas the central fact in India is the existence of stable and widespread classes of capitalist society within a post-colonial bourgeois polity; in Vietnam, which has already entered a post-capitalist phase – albeit in a context of extreme devastation of the productive forces – the character of this constitutive dialectic is again entirely different. So while the problematic of a 'final determination' is surely active in each case, it is constituted differently in different cases, and in each case literary production will, in principle, be differently constituted.

What further complicates this dialectic of the social and the literary is that most literary productions, whether of the 'First World' or the 'Third', are not always available for that kind of direct and unitary determination by any one factor, no matter how central that factor is in constituting the social formation as a whole. Literary texts are produced in highly differentiated, usually overdetermined contexts of competing ideological and cultural clusters, so that any particular text of any complexity will always have to be placed within the cluster that gives it its energy and form, before it is totalized into a universal category. This fact of overdetermination does not mean that individual texts merely float in the air, or that 'Totality' as such is an impossible cognitive category. But in any comprehension of Totality, one would always have to specify and historicize the determinations which constitute any given field; with sufficient knowledge of the field, it *is* normally possible to specify the principal ideological formations and narrative forms. What is not possible is to operate with the few texts that become available in the metropolitan languages and then to posit a complete singularization and transparency in the process of determinacy, so that all ideological complexity is reduced to a single ideological formation and all narrativities are read as local expressions of a metatext. If one does that, one produces not the knowledge of a Totality, which I too take to be a fundamental cognitive category, but an idealization, either of the Hegelian or the positivist kind.

What I mean by multiple determinations at work in any text of considerable complexity can be specified, I believe, by looking briefly at the problem of the cultural location of Jameson's own text. This is, ostensibly, a First World text; Jameson is a US intellectual and identifies himself as such. But he is a US intellectual of a certain kind: not everyone is able to juxtapose Ousmane and Deleuze so comfortably, so well; and he debunks the 'global American culture of postmodernism' which, he says, is *the* culture of his country. His theoretical framework, moreover, is Marxist, his political identification is socialist – which would seem to place this text in the Second World. But the particular energy of his text – its thematics, its relation with those other texts which give it its meaning, the very narrative upon which his 'theory of cognitive aesthetics' rests – takes him deep into the Third World, valorizing it, asserting it, filiating himself with it, as against the politically dominant and determinant of his own country. Where (in what *world*?) should *I*, who do not believe in the Three Worlds Theory, place his text: in the First World of his origin, the Second World of his ideology and politics, or the Third World of his filiation and sympathy? And, if 'all third-world texts are necessarily' this or that, how is it that his own text escapes an exclusive location in the First World? I – being who I am – shall place it *primarily* in the global culture of socialism – Jameson's Second World, my name for a global resistance – and I shall do so not by suppressing the rest (his US origins, his Third World sympathies) but by identifying that which has been central to all his theoretical undertakings for many years.

These are obviously not the only determinations at work in Jameson's text. I shall mention only two others, both of which are indicated by his silences. His is, among other things, a *gendered* text. It is inconceivable to me that *this* text could have been written by a US *woman* without some considerable statement, probably a full-length discussion, of the fact that the bifurcation of the public and the private, and the necessity to reconstitute that relation where it has been broken – which is so central to Jameson's discussion of the opposition between First World and Third World cultural practices – is indeed a major preoccupation of First World women writers today, on both sides of the Atlantic. And Jameson's text is also determined by a certain *racial* milieu. For it is equally inconceivable to me that *this* text could have been written by a *Black* writer in the USA who would not also insist that Black Literature of this country possesses the unique Third World characteristic that it is replete with national allegories (more replete, I personally believe, than is Urdu literature).

I point out these obvious determinations of Jameson's text for three reasons. One is to strengthen my proposition that the ideological conditions of a text's production are never singular but always several. Second, even if I were to accept Jameson's division of the globe into three worlds, I would still have to insist, as my references not only to feminism and Black Literature but to Jameson's own location would indicate, that there is right here, within the belly of the First World's global postmodernism, a veritable Third World, perhaps two or three of them. Third, I want to insist that within the unity that has been bestowed upon our globe by the irreconcilable struggle between capital and labour, there are more and more texts which cannot easily be placed within this or that world. Jameson's is not a First World text; mine is not a Third World text. We are not each other's civilizational Others.

4

# Salman Rushdie's *Shame*: Postmodern Migrancy and the Representation of Women

The axiomatic fact about *any* canon formation, even when it initially takes shape as a counter-canon, is that when a period is defined and homogenized, or the desired literary typology is constructed, the canonizing agency selects certain kinds of authors, texts, styles, and criteria of classification and judgement, privileging them over others which may also belong in the same period, arising out of the same space of production, but which manifestly fall outside the principles of inclusion enunciated by that selfsame agency; in other words, a certain kind of dominance is asserted and fought for, and is in turn defined as the essential and the dominant. The history of modernism is significant in this regard. It was the modernist avant-garde itself which first posited modernism as a comprehensive negation, both formal and philosophical, of the canonical realism of nineteenth-century Europe, and claimed, moreover, that realism itself had been definitively broken, superseded and buried in the period of High Modernism – the quarter-century before 1940, let us say. In turn, the *triumph* of modernism is indicated today precisely in the fact that realist texts produced during that same period and in the same Euro-American spaces now find no significant place in the literary curricula and critical discourses pertaining to that period and place, regardless of the number, the worth or the social influence of such texts in their own time. And it is the hegemonic self-representation of modernism as an utter negation of realism which makes it virtually impossible now to see how many kinds of modernist narrativity – Kafka's, for example – have been *facilitated* by the machineries of representation developed in nineteenth-century Europe.

This canonical status of modernism seems to be at work even in relation to what has now come to be known as postmodernism. All sorts of distinct movements – Imagism, Surrealism, Dadaism, Cubism, and so on – during the period later came to be canonized under the unified rubric of modernism. Once that category had been set in motion as *the* art of the twentieth century, however, what came after it could only be seen in relation to it (that is, it could only be a *post*- of modernism itself). The hegemonic manoeuvre was evident, further, in the fact that any text which aspired to be included in the category of 'what came after' had (a) to have enough modernism within it and (b) also to diverge sufficiently in a new avant-gardist way. In either case, processes of canon formation meant also that certain kinds of questions could not now be asked. One could not read a modernist or postmodernist narrative from the standpoint of realism, for example, without being guilty of Derrida's famous 'metaphysic of presence'. The subordinating or even foreclosing of certain kinds of questions, the foregrounding of others, is the essential canonizing gesture.

Analogous procedures of privileging certain kinds of authors, texts, genres and questions seem to be under way now with regard to 'Third World Literature'. The essential task of a 'Third World' novel, it is said, is to give appropriate *form* (preferably allegory, but epic also, or fairy tale, or whatever) to the *national* experience. The range of questions that may be asked of the texts which are currently in the process of being canonized within this categorical counter-canon must predominantly refer, then, in one way or another, to representations of colonialism, nationhood, post-coloniality, the typology of rulers, their powers, corruptions, and so forth. There is no gainsaying the fact that these *are* among the great questions of the age. What is disconcerting, nevertheless, is that a whole range of texts which do not ask those particular questions in any foregrounded manner would then have to be excluded from or pushed to the margins of this emerging counter-canon. Worse still, a whole range of other kinds of questionings – pertaining to other sorts of literary influences and experiential locations, the political affiliations of the author, representations of classes and genders within the text, and myriad such issues – would then have to be subordinated to the primacy of the authorized questions: about 'nation', and so on. It is with these *other* questions that this chapter will be, in the main, occupied.[1]

## I

I have referred elsewhere to the great prolixity and heterogeneity of cultural productions in our spaces, both of archival and non-archivable kinds, which simply exceed the theoretical terms of 'Third World Literature'. Here, I want to look briefly at only one author – Salman Rushdie – who occupies a distinguished place at the very apex of 'Third World Literature', and at only one of his books – *Shame* – which has already become something of a classic of this counter-canon. What happens to one's own reading, I would be curious to know, if one changes, in any appreciable degree, the questions? Apart from changing the questions somewhat, my main interest in undertaking this exercise is not to attempt a *sufficient* reading of either the author or the book, in some radicalized version of New Critical etiquettes, but, rather, to offer a *symptomatic* reading of an ideological location which makes it possible for Rushdie to partake, equally, of the postmodernist moment and the counter-canon of 'Third World Literature'. For there now appears to be, in the work of the metropolitan critical avant-garde, an increasing tie between postmodernism and Third-Worldist canonizations. Thus, for example, whether we look at the literary critics who have done the most productive and influential work on this idea of a generic difference between the West and the 'Third World', or at the actual authors who are accorded central importance in this evolving counter-canon – García Márquez, Fuentes, Rushdie, among others – we find, first, that these critical positions are framed by the cultural dominance of postmodernism itself; and, second, that there is enough in the authors upon whom critical attention is so trained which is appropriable for those sorts of readings, usually with the text's own abundant complicity.

The same predominance of postmodernist etiquettes of reading is palpably present in other cognate subdisciplines that are evolving alongside 'Third World Literature', as the roster of those who undertake 'Colonial Discourse Analysis' would amply show. Nor is this subjection of the so-called 'Third World' text to postmodernist scrutiny something reserved for the best known; it now appears to be a fairly general tendency. Fredric Jameson occupies a different and distinctive position in all this because of (a) his arduous attempts to combine poststructuralism with Marxism; (b) his identification of 'Third World Literature' with 'naive' realism and, farther back, specifically with allegory; and (c) his upholding of 'Third World Literature' as a global Other of postmodernism itself, under the insignia of 'nationalism'. What is remarkable even in his readings, different and superior as they are, is that he too is preoccupied, when one looks at the totality of his 'mapping', with defining a *relation* between 'Third World Literature' and 'the global American culture of postmodernism'. For most other critics, even the *problem* of this relation hardly exists. What we find instead, in most cases, is that postmodernism, in one variant or another, has been imbibed already as the self-evident politics and procedure, and what remains to be done is the selection, appropriation and interpretation of the texts that are to be included in – or excluded from – the emerging counter-canon of 'Third World Literature'. It is in this space of overlap that Salman Rushdie makes, most forcefully, his mark.

That the author himself wants his three major novels thus far (*Grimus* is minor and, in some fundamental ways, both obscure and different) to be read as 'Third World' texts is made obvious enough in the main lines of thematics and plotting, and in the emphases that Rushdie has underscored whenever he has spoken in his own voice, whether within the novels or in the interviews and conference papers which have inevitably followed: the colonial determination of our modernity, the conditions and corruptions of post-coloniality, the depiction of the Zia and Bhutto periods in Pakistan as emblematic of Third World *caudillos* and dictators in general, myths of nationhood and independence, the myths and gods of India, Third World migrants in metropolitan cities, the world of Islam, and so on. The forms of narrativization, meanwhile, are diverse enough for critics to conjecture that they belong, in essence, to a generally non-Western, specifically Indian form of non-mimetic narration, derived, finally, from the *Ramayana* and the *Mahabharata* and exemplifying, in the words of Raja Rao, the characteristically Indian penchant for obsessive digressions and the telling of an interminable tale. This, of course, is Rushdie's own stance in *Midnight's Children*. It has not been possible, though, to sustain this idea of quintessential Indianness in the *form* of Rushdie's narrative techniques; the lines of descent from European modernism and postmodernism are too numerous. The necessary, though often unintended, consequence of these approaches – the preoccupation with Rushdie's portrayal of 'the Nation' and 'the Third World' on the one hand; with the digressive self-reflexivity ('Indianness'?) of his narrative technique on the other – has been the obscuring of his ideological moorings in the High Culture of the modern metropolitan bourgeoisie as well as the suppression of a whole range of questions which have little to do with either 'the Nation' or 'the Third World', but which I take to be quite central to the basic import of his narratives.

The more fundamental questions will become clearer as we come to the reading of the novel, but two features of the ideological subtext itself may be mentioned here in passing, so as to illustrate the general ambience of the work. Thus, Rushdie's idea of 'migrancy', for example, which is quite central to his self-representation both in fiction and in life, has come to us in two versions. In the first version, fully present in *Shame* and in the writings that came at more or less the same time, 'migrancy' is given to us as an ontological condition of all human beings, while the 'migrant' is said to have 'floated upwards from history'. In the second version, articulated more fully in the more recent writings, this myth of ontological unbelonging is replaced by another, larger myth of *excess* of belongings: not that he belongs nowhere, but that he belongs to *too many* places. This is one kind of thrust in Rushdie's work, which appears to refer to the *social condition* of the 'Third World' migrant but is replete also with echoes from both the *literary tradition* of High Modernism and the poststructuralist *philosophical positions*. But then, alongside this issue of 'migrancy', we also find in *Shame* an actual portrayal of Pakistan – and, in Rushdie's own words, 'more than Pakistan' – as a space occupied so entirely by Power that there is no space left for either resistance or its representation; whoever claims to resist is already enmeshed in relations of Power and in the logic of all-embracing violences. This one can see in numerous minor episodes of the novel, such as the breezy caricature of the 1970s armed movement in Baluchistan in its earlier portions, as much as in the fabrication of the central character, Sufiya Zinobia, as we shall seek to demonstrate below.

Between these two poles of ideological construction – the individual's freedom, absolute and mythic, that is derived from the fact that he belongs nowhere because he belongs everywhere; and an image of the public sphere of politics so replete with violence and corruption that any representation of resistance becomes impossible – Rushdie encompasses, in fact, a whole range of nuances that clearly do not constitute a philosophical unity but are the very nodal points through which the contemporary (post)modernist literary imagination passes as it negotiates its way out of Pound and Eliot, into the world of Derrida and Foucault. How very enchanting, I have often thought, Rushdie's kind of imagination must be for that whole range of readers who have been brought up on the peculiar 'universalism' of *The Waste Land* (the 'Hindu' tradition appropriated by an Anglo-American consciousness on its way to Anglican conversion, through the agency of Orientalist scholarship) and the 'world culture' of Pound's *Cantos* (the sages of Ancient China jostling with the princely notables of Renaissance Italy, with Homer and Cavalcanti in between, all in the service of a political vision framed by Mussolini's fascism). One did not have to belong, one could simply float, effortlessly, through a supermarket of packaged and commodified cultures, ready to be consumed.

This idea of the availability of *all* cultures of the world for consumption by an individual consciousness was, of course, a much older European idea, growing in tandem with the history of colonialism as such, but the perfection and extended use of it in the very fabrication of modernism (not just Pound and Eliot, but a whole range of modernists, from Herman Hesse to St John Perse) signalled a real shift, from the age of old colonialism *per se* to the age of modern imperialism proper, which was reflected also in the daily lives of the metropolitan consumers in a new kind of shopping: the supermarket. In the literary imagination of High Modernism this idea of cultural excess served, however, as a counterpoint against the far less sanguine notion that the fragmented self was the only truly modern self. Ideas of excess and disruption, unity and fragmentation, were held in this imagination in a tense balance. The chief characteristic of the metropolitan supermarket was that entirely diverse products (utensils, fabrics, jewellery, refrigerators, beds) could now be purchased under one roof, while also drawing upon the resources of different countries (Indian textiles alongside Manchester woollens; Persian carpets alongside French hosiery), making available a wide range of personal consumptions in a wholly impersonal setting. (The New Critical idea that each literary text constituted a self-enclosed and sufficient unit for analysis rehearsed, in a peculiarly displaced way, this ideological assertion of the supermarket that each commodity carried its own text within itself, with no reference to the origins which in fact saturate it or to the other commodity-texts which surround it.) The felt experience of the elite artist, in this same phase of modern capital, was that he too could now draw upon a whole range of cultural artefacts from around the globe (Indian philosophy, African masks, Cambodian sculpture).

This sense of cultural excess, however, was only part of the story. For that same artist was also subjected to those same processes of capitalist alienation which were inscribed now not only in the processes of production, to be suffered by the working class alone, but also in the very structure of social space as it was reconstituted in the modern city. The collage and the Cubist recompositions of perspective were the characteristic responses in the visual arts, and Eliot's *œuvre* came to occupy so central a position in the literary imagination of the Anglo-Saxon elite – and, in an act of characteristic subordination, in the imagination of the Anglophone colonial elite as well – because he combined this sense of cultural excess with equally strong invocations of 'Hollow Men' and 'Unreal City'. *The Waste Land*, with its fragmented surface, its polyglot ascription, its multicultural list of literary resource and ideological possibility, its malevolence towards working women and the sexuality of popular classes, its aristocratic affiliation, its dazzling technical resolution for the sense of unbelonging and inner ennui, is of course the central document of Anglo-Saxon modernism; *Ulysses* would be in most respects comparable, but most of its productive aspects come from the fact that it is *not* Anglo-Saxon. In none of the major modernists, however, was the idea of the fragmented self, or the accompanying sense of unbelonging, ever a source of great comfort; it came, usually, with a sense of recoiling, even some terror.

What is new in the contemporary metropolitan philosophies and the literary ideologies which have arisen since the 1960s, in tandem with vastly novel restructurings of global capitalist investments, communication systems and information networks – not to speak of actual travelling facilities – is that the idea of belonging is itself being abandoned as antiquated false consciousness. The terrors of High Modernism at the prospect of inner fragmentation and social disconnection have now been stripped, in Derridean strands of postmodernism, of their tragic edge, pushing that experience of loss, instead, in a celebratory direction; the idea of belonging is itself seen now as bad faith, a mere '*myth* of origins', a truth-effect produced by the Enlightenment's 'metaphysic of presence'. The truth of being, to the extent that truth is at all possible, resides now in occupying a multiplicity of subject positions and an *excess of belonging*; not only does the writer have all cultures available to him or her as resource, for consumption, but he or she actually belongs in all of them, by virtue of belonging properly in none. Rushdie puts it quite succinctly: 'the ability to see at once from inside and out is a great thing, a piece of good fortune which the indigenous writer cannot enjoy.'[2] As formulations of this kind become the manifest common sense of the metropolitan intelligentsia, dutifully reproduced in the literary productions and pronouncements of 'Third World intellectuals' located within that milieu, one wonders what these cultural positions – the idea of *origin* being a mere 'myth'; the doubleness of arriving at an *excess* of belonging by *not* belonging; the project of mining the resource and raw material of 'Third World Literature' for archival accumulation and generic classification in the *metropolitan* university – might have to do with this age of late capitalism in which the most powerful capitalist firms, originating in particular imperialist countries but commanding global investments and networks of transport and communication, proclaim themselves nevertheless to be *multi*nationals and *trans*nationals – as if their *origins* in the United States or the Federal German Republic were a mere myth, as if their ability to accumulate surplus-value from a dozen countries or more were none other than an *excess* of belonging.

If Derridean kinds of pressures move postmodernism in the direction of a self-reflexive celebration (one is free to choose any and all subject positions – beyond all structure and all system, in Edward Said's formulation – because history has no subjects or collective projects in any case), the political implications of Foucault's philosophical position and narrative structure tend not only to reinforce the impossibility of stable belonging and subject position but also to bestow upon the world a profound cage-like quality, with a bleak sense of human entrapment in Discourses of Power which are at once discrete and overlapping, many of which appear to be located in the archaeological layerings of the countless passages from the *ancien régime* to modernity, while others (the Discourse of Sexuality, for example) are perhaps located in Roman Antiquity. But there appears to be none that can be traced to an origin or a purpose or an interest. This history without systemic origins, human subjects or collective sites is nevertheless a history of all-encompassing Power, which is wielded by none and *cannot* be resisted because there is nothing outside the fabrications of Power – perhaps *ought not* to be resisted, because it is not only repressive but also profoundly productive. History, in other words, is not open to change, only to narrativization. Resistance can only be provisional, personal, local, micro, and pessimistic in advance. The enormous archival depth of Foucault's researches and the sumptuousness of his prose, we might add, stand in a peculiar relation to this definition of human possibility, as if the recovery and redefinition of the archive were, in the old humanist sense of the intellectual's vocation, a fundamentally redemptive act, and as if Foucault too believed – along with Whitehead, for example – that style was the essential morality of a writer's mind.

I do not mean to suggest that *Shame* is somehow a fictional fabrication derived from these sets of ideas which the author then applies to the social reality that engages his attention. Nor is it of any importance whether Rushdie has even read any or all of these other authors (though some phrases in *Shame* are doubtless modelled on phrases from *The Waste Land*). What I wish to specify, rather, is the context of the book's composition as well as its reception: the *kind* of author Rushdie is, the whole grid of predispositions which have gone into the making of such an imagination, the kinds of pleasures his book supplies to what was conceived of as its initial readership, which was primarily British, secondarily among the immigrant intelligentsia. In some basic ways, one is speaking not so much of Rushdie's intentions as of the conditions of his production – the very saturation of his thought, as it were, by the discursive conditions enveloping the site of his production.

It is important to recall here that Rushdie was not, until his recent and macabre sentencing by the Ayatollah Khomeini, an exile but a *self*-exile. Writers-in-exile often write primarily for readerships which are materially absent from the immediate conditions of their production, present only in the country from which the writer has been forcibly exiled, hence all the more vividly and excruciatingly present in the writer's imagination because their actuality is deeply intertwined with the existential suffering of exile and with the act of writing as such. The self-exile has no such irrevocable bond; he is free to choose the degree of elasticity of that bonding, and the material consequences of his migrancy necessarily bring him into a much more accountable relation with the readership which is materially present within the milieu of his productive work. This one recognizes not as a weakness or a strength of Rushdie's work but simply as one of its framing realities. Such a shared ambience between the writer and his primary readership may then be reinforced, or not, by ties, or lack of them, that are normally produced by one's own culture, one's own class and the range of choices which are then available and which one exercises, for better or worse, in the process of living and writing.

I shall return briefly to these particular moorings and the broader implications of Rushdie's work in the concluding section of this chapter. Before going on any further with such generalization, however, I want to look more closely at some aspects of *Shame* in order to clarify how these larger issues are embedded in the text of the novel itself. In the process, I shall offer some remarks on Rushdie's self-representation within the book, some more extended remarks on his representation of women in it, and on the implications of these, and of both his migrancy and his postmodernist allegiances, for his politics. The intention is not to offer a more adequate or even an alternative reading of either *Shame* or the rest of his growing corpus, less still to deny that the condition of post-coloniality may itself be *one* of the co-ordinates for reading such books, but simply to illustrate the sorts of questions and connections that become marginalized in the pursuit of a generic category of 'Third World Literature'.[3]

## II

We might as well begin with the author inside the book. Apart from the numerous things Rushdie has said in the course of his many interviews about his intentions in *Shame*, the narrative within the book itself is controlled transparently by repeated, direct, personal interventions on the part of the narrator – who is, for the purposes of our interpretation here, mainly Rushdie himself.[4] The first such intervention comes early, as soon as the author is through with his first chapter. After a significant description of his theme – Shame, and what causes it – he comes to himself, his book, his country:

> I tell myself this will be a novel of leavetaking, my last words on the East from which, many years ago, I began to come loose. I do not always believe myself when I say this. It is a part of the world to which, whether I like it or not, I am still joined, if only by elastic bonds. (p. 23)[5]

And:

> The country in this story is not Pakistan, or not quite. There are two countries, real and fictional, occupying the same space, or almost the same space. My story, my fictional country exists, like myself, at a slight angle to reality. I have found this off-centering to be necessary. . . . I am not writing only about Pakistan. (p. 24)

Then, after a short passage on the Farsi poet Khayyam, we are told: 'I, too, am a translated man. I have been *borne across*.' (pp. 23–4; original emphasis). Later in the novel, in the course of a poignant passage about his younger sister, Rushdie would also say, unmistakably about himself:

> Although I have known Pakistan for a long time, I have never lived there for longer than six months at a stretch . . . I have learned Pakistan by slices . . . however I choose to write about over-there, I am forced to reflect that in fragments of broken mirrors . . . I must reconcile myself to the inevitability of the missing bits. (pp. 70–71)

And finally:

> What is the best thing about migrant peoples and seceded nations? I think it is their hopefulness. . . . And what is the worst thing? It is the emptiness of one's luggage. . . . We have floated upwards from history, from memory, from Time.

As we begin to negotiate this imaginative territory marked by 'Pakistan', 'the East', 'seceded nation', etc., we should recall what Rushdie himself tells us in a different passage: that he had actually gone back to live in Pakistan but had left not because of political difficulty or economic pressure but because he had found the country 'suffocating' and 'claustrophobic'.[6] With that personal decision to leave one does not quarrel, because that kind of decision always *is* personal, but his 'leavetaking' is so very central to his public self-representation as well as to the structure of his fictions that one wants to locate at least the *literary* consequences – and precedents – of it somewhat accurately. With regard to his fictions and his general political stance, I think, this personal detail is to be seen not so much in relation to coloniality and its aftermath, nor with reference to the issue of dictatorship *per se*, but in the highly pressurizing perspective of modernism itself, which has been framed so very largely by self-exiles and émigrés – James and Conrad, Pound and Eliot, Picasso and Dalí, Joyce, Gertrude Stein, and so on – who had experienced the same kind of 'suffocation' in their own spaces of this globe, and were subsequently to leave behind immense resources of genre and vocabulary for delineating that predominant image of the modern artist who lives as a *literal* stranger in a foreign and impersonal city and who, on the one hand, uses the condition of exile as the basic metaphor for modernity and even for the human condition itself, while, on the other, writing obsessively, copiously, of that very land which had been declared 'suffocating'.

Nor was 'the East', and the itch to say some 'last words' about it, ever far from the imaginative topography of modernism. Rushdie seems to have taken as much from the many styles and ideologies in which 'the East' had been represented within the larger compass of the modernist moment (the debts of *Midnight's Children* to *Kim*, for example, are substantial; Kipling, one might recall, actually belongs within this moment, as does Orwell; and Conrad, coming in the middle, is of course one of the masters of it) as he has taken, on other scores, from García Márquez. Even the increasing insistence on self-exile as a positively enabling experience for writers is by no means new; what *is* new, and decidedly postmodernist, is the emphasis we find in *Shame* on the productivity, rather than the pain, of dislocating oneself from one's original community, as well as the idea, made much sharper in Rushdie's more recent writings, of multiple belongings. But this too fits, because the current metropolitan milieu, with its debunking of any 'myths of origin' and 'metaphysics of presence', does not really authorize any sustained acknowledgement of such pains.

The remarkable thing about the passages I have quoted above is, in any case, the handling of ambivalences and conditionalities. The irony of 'I tell myself', which is so clearly intended to suggest that what follows is mere self-persuasion, not the truth but a hallucination of truth, is poised so sharply against the power of that phrase, 'a novel of leavetaking' – and poised all the more sharply because *Midnight's Children* and *Shame* actually *are* novels of leavetaking: not from 'the East', surely but, more particularly, first from the country of his birth (India) and then from that second country (Pakistan) where he tried, half-heartedly, to settle down and couldn't – that the initial tone of self-mockery dissolves quickly into a characteristically modernist use of a particular brand of irony which comes into modernism from its antecedents in Romanticism and serves to destabilize not only the object of irony but also its author, who succumbs to what Franco Moretti has quite properly called a 'spell of indecision'.[7]

There is a quality of linguistic quicksand in all such passages, as if the truth of each utterance were conditioned by the existence of its opposite, and Rushdie seems forever to be taking back with one hand what he has given with the other: the will to take leave is poised against the impossibility of leavetaking; he has been coming loose but is still 'joined'; he is still joined but only by 'elastic' bonds, and he is not sure that he likes the fact of continued joining (joined, 'whether I like it or not'); he makes statements, but he does not believe in them; the fictive and the real coexist but do not correspond; not only his text but he, himself, exists 'at a slight angle to reality'; not his text but *he* is 'translated', 'borne across'; the translation occurs not on the semantic but on the existential level. These ambivalences propel him, then, to write a 'novel of leavetaking', about a country which is 'not quite Pakistan' and 'not only Pakistan' but *is*, in the most obvious ways, Pakistan. And the novel is something else as well: 'my last words on the East'! An audacious undertaking indeed, wider in some senses than Joyce's in *A Portrait of the Artist as a Young Man*, the book which I think Rushdie quite intentionally invokes, where Stephen, the alter ego of that Irish, colonized author, had also set out for self-exile so that, as he puts it in the concluding passages of that other book of leavetaking, 'I may learn in my own life and away from home and friends what the heart is and what it feels' and 'to forge in the smithy of my soul the uncreated conscience of my race'.

There is poignancy here, surely, but Rushdie's formulations are troubling on at least two counts. One is that it is always impossible, even in a work much larger than *Shame*, to say one's 'last words' about anything as amorphous as 'the East'; this idea – that there is some unitary thing called 'the East' about which some 'last words' can be said – is a figment of the colonial imagination, and Rushdie is simply overstating at least his capacities, if not also his intentions. That he begins the passage with a suggestion of self-mockery does not really retrieve the banal character of the assertion, since the book is replete with all sorts of banal statements about 'the East', including the assertion that the English word 'Shame' falls far short of the Urdu word '*Sharam*' because the latter is, as sentiment and notion and normative conduct, characteristically Eastern, hence exceeding the Western capacities of cognition and linguistic formulation; 'they' live after the death of tragedy, we are told, while 'we' presumably live in the grip of it. Second, there are remarkable contrasts between Rushdie's declarations and the phrases I have used from Joyce's little work of early modernism. There is still, in the young Joyce, a sense of 'home and friends', and even an accompanying sense of desolation in having to choose self-exile; there is also an intentionality, a choice, however tragic, as well as a full-blooded irony about one's own undertaking and about the kind of rhetoric which frequently accompanies such undertakings; remarkable in all this is the pun on the word 'forge'; nor is there any sense that the writer has 'floated upwards from history, from memory, from Time'.

Rushdie's stance is different. Pakistan – or India, for that matter – is precisely *not* home; neither the joining nor the coming loose has by now, with *Midnight's Children* behind him, the immediacy of a willed and necessary self-wounding that may require the language of iron and smithy; what we have, instead, is an image of tenuous and possibly flaccid rubber, 'elasticity'; and what impresses one about 'I, too, am a translated man. I have been *borne across*,' is that someone or something else, perhaps History itself, appears to be doing the translating, the bearing across. It is perhaps the lightness of being that comes from having 'floated upwards from history, from memory, from Time' which makes it possible for the author to mock himself into wanting to say his 'last words on the East', in a parody of the flip confidence that one would encounter later in Naipaul's *Among the Believers*. (*The Satanic Verses* can perhaps be read more appropriately as Rushdie's version of the world Naipaul describes there; Rushdie creates the greater knowing effect, but with a very uncanny overlap of stances.) As one returns from that phrase, 'last words on the East', to Stephen's 'in the smithy of my soul the uncreated conscience of my race', one senses the impossibility of that 'floating upwards' for anyone, migrant or not, who might have thought of 'migrancy' as personal need, because of the 'suffocation', but might yet be unwilling to make a fetish of his own unbelonging.

Parenthetically, I may emphasize that I do not wish to construe this juxtaposition of two texts – or rather, the two sets of brief quotations – as some kind of fixed difference between modernism and postmodernism. If Rushdie is a postmodernist at all, he is so precisely in the sense that his intellectual and artistic formation is essentially modernist, but there are distinct articulations and emphases in which he clearly exceeds that basic formation. I am reminded here of those passages in Lyotard where he argues that postmodernism is a set of tendencies within Late Modernism itself, which distinguishes itself primarily by *celebrating* human inability to experience reality as a totality, over and beyond its fragments. The attitude towards (self-)exile would be another such shift – but a shift connected with historically distinct moments within the continuum of the metropolises' High Culture in the century of modern imperialism.

'The East' would, of course, continue to haunt Rushdie for many years after the writing of *Shame*, right up to the present and most probably into the indefinite future. For one thing, self-exile rarely becomes a full naturalization even when class and culture can be fully shared, as even Henry James was to find out. British racism forecloses the option for people of colour in any case, even for a man of Naipaul's longings and identifications, let alone for Rushdie, with his monumental ambivalences about the culture of his origins as well as his activist and oppositional relationship with the culture of official Britain. The writing of *The Satanic Verses* on the one hand, and the fundamentalist fury that was unleashed against him thereafter, has made the non-elasticity of those bonds vivid in a particularly macabre way, which Rushdie himself nevertheless could not have foreseen when he wrote *Shame*. As regards the reading of that earlier novel in its own setting, however, what is even more significant than the attitude towards (self-)exile in these passages is the *connection* in Rushdie's utterances between (a) the project of saying some 'last words on the East'; (b) the ambition to write at one and the same time about Pakistan and also *more* than Pakistan ('the East' on the one hand, the typology of dictatorships on the other, as well as post-coloniality in general); (c) the sketchiness of the actual knowledge of Pakistan; and (d) the device of 'off-centering'. His declaration, furthermore, that he has 'learned Pakistan by slices' and must therefore reconcile himself 'to the inevitability of the missing bits', and to reflecting both the known and the not-known 'in fragments of broken mirrors', is at once a defence, very early in the book, before the reader has engaged with the greater part of the narrative, against the anticipated criticism that there is much missing from this judgement of the 'last words', as well as a positioning of the author which has both a formal and a political import. The confessed fragmentariness of the experience precludes, for example, the realist option, because what realism presumes, at the very least, is an integral experience which includes more than mere 'slices'. The narrativization of 'slices', in the form of 'fragments of broken mirrors' (the echo from *The Waste Land* here is, I think, intentional), only refurbishes the author's prior disposition towards modernism and postmodernism – that is to say, views of the world which would serve to validate further the ontological primacy of the fragment.

But the matter of the 'missing bits' is not so easily settled, purely as a problem begging for a formal resolution. It is at least arguable that no one ever knows their country whole, regardless of how much of their life is or is not actually lived within its borders; that the imaginative apprehension of totality is always constructed on the basis of those bits and slices of concrete experience which constitute any individual's life, migrant or not; that what eventually matters about any experience, felt or narrated, is not its partiality, because direct experience is always partial, but the quality of the particular 'bits' which constitute it and those others which remain outside the felt experience and therefore outside one's imaginative capacity as well. If one has 'known Pakistan for a long time' and yet, because of circumstance, 'learned' it only 'by slices', the question naturally arises: *which* 'slices' has one chosen to 'learn'? For, if we do not *choose* our own 'bits' of reality, those 'bits' will then be chosen for us by our class origin, our jobs, the circuits of our friendships and desires, our ways of spending our leisure time, our literary predilections, our political affiliations – or lack of them. There are no neutral 'bits', not even of not-knowing.

What Rushdie seems to know – from the inside, because of his own class origin – is the history of the corruptions and criminalities of Pakistani rulers; about these he says remarkably trenchant things, and his desire to disjoin himself from that history is both productive and, for the reader, very moving. The structure of this limited knowledge, circumscribed as it is within the experience of a decadent class to which he is joined by origin but from which he himself feels wholly alienated, only confirms, however, the world-view implied in his already-existing affiliations with modernism and postmodernism. Neither the class from which the Pakistani segment of his experience is derived, nor the ideological ensemble within which he has located his own affiliations, admits, in any fundamental degree, the possibility of heroic action; between the structure of felt experience and the politico-literary affiliation, therefore, the circle is closed. What this excludes – 'the missing bits' to which he must 'reconcile' himself – is the dailiness of lives lived under oppression, and the human bonding – of resistance, of decency, of innumerable heroisms of both ordinary and extraordinary kinds – which makes it possible for large numbers of people to look each other in the eye, without guilt, with affection and solidarity and humour, and makes life, even under oppression, endurable and frequently joyous. Of that other kind of life his fictions, right up to *The Satanic Verses*, seem to be largely ignorant; what his imagination makes of the subsequent experiences we shall find out only from later work. The infinite bleakness of *Shame*, its cage-like quality, is rooted, in other words, in what it excludes as much as what it actually comprises.

## III

Virtually everyone has noted, as Rushdie himself has, that *Shame* – which is almost exclusively about Pakistan, although a couple of episodes do take place in India – is a much more severe and despairing book, more bleak and claustrophobic, than *Midnight's Children*. The sense that Pakistan is a cage is already there, in the opening episodes, where the Shakil sisters – the three mothers of the 'peripheral hero', Omar Khayyam – are cloistered twice over: first by their father, the patriarch of the macabre mansion, with whose death the book begins, and then by themselves, after their one hedonistic night in which their son is conceived. And this sense of being trapped permeates the whole book, right up to the final dénouement where we find that even dictators cannot cross the 'frontier' and escape their cage.

In between, Bilquis is trapped in her 'elite actressy manner', her sentimentality, her 'horror of movement', her desire for sons and yet her lack of sons, as well as the crassness of her husband's ambitions, pieties and cruelties; Rani is trapped, likewise, in her own husband's infidelities and the rise and fall of his political career; Sufiya Zinobia – the heroine of the book, 'Shame' embodied – is trapped in her brain fever, her humiliation, and her volcanic urge to violence; her younger sister, Good News Hyder, is a much less substantial being, but she too is trapped, first in her superficiality and then, despite the marriage of her choice, in the constant demand on her fertility. The younger sister kills herself, the older kills her tormentors, but the cage never quite becomes anything other than itself.

We shall return to some of these characters presently, but first we should note the contrast with *Midnight's Children*, which had been about India, the country of Rushdie's own cherished childhood. What had given that earlier novel its narrative amplitude was the connection with autobiography – the baggage of memories that even a migrant – particularly a migrant – must carry. Pakistan, by contrast, is a society Rushdie never knew in those golden years before the uprooting. It is not 'teeming' (Rushdie's word for India, borrowed, significantly, from Kipling) for him with stories, and with the plenitude of life, because, as he himself puts it, he has learned it only in little slices, and because his own life's connection with that land – 'the new, moth-nibbled land of God', as he calls it – is so very tenuous. It is a country which he knows, beyond very personal affections, only as a polity, and primarily in the grotesqueries of its ruling class. Within the limits of that knowledge, the rage the book conveys is entirely well founded. The problem is that the experience of a certain class – rather, a ruling elite – is presented, in the rhetorical stance of the book, as the experience of a 'country'. Far from being about 'the East' or even about 'Pakistan', the book is actually about a rather narrow social stratum – so narrow, in fact, that Rushdie himself is able to portray all the major characters as belonging to a single *family*. This plot device of turning all the antagonists into relatives is a wonderful technical resolution for reflecting the monopolistic structure of dictatorial power and the very narrow social spectrum within which this power in Pakistan circulates. It also helps him to bypass the easy liberal dichotomy between military villains and civilian innocents; they are all of the same stripe. The main difficulty does not arise in his portrayal of this structure of power and cruelty at the apex; this he accomplishes, on the whole, superbly. The difficulty arises when this ferocious fable of the state is elided, again and again, in his own recurrent rhetoric throughout the book, with a society which is declared to be coterminous with this state structure, equally deformed and irretrievably marked by its purported civilization (Islam) and its genetic origin (the Partition), more catastrophically wounded even than Naipaul makes out India to be in *A Wounded Civilization*. The rulers and the ruled seem to be joined together, each mirroring the other, in a Satanic compact.

Thus the bulk of the narrative is focused on the careers, corruptions, ribaldries and rivalries of the two main protagonists in the political arena: Raza Hyder, an army officer whose origins and early career are quite different from Zia's but who comes increasingly to resemble him, and Iskander ('Isky') Harappa, who is modelled on the personality of Bhutto, the former Prime Minister. The problem, even here, is that those parts of the book which attempt to create fictional equivalents of the literal facts of recent Pakistani history tend too much towards parody, while many of the other parts tend too much towards burlesque. Both the parody and the burlesque are at times delicious, inventive, hilarious, but in re-creating the major strands of contemporary history in the form of a spoof, and then mixing up this spoof with all kinds of spooky anecdotes whose symbolic value is sometimes unclear and often excessive, Rushdie has given us a Laughter which laughs, unfortunately, much too often. The fictional equivalents of Bhutto and Zia are such perfect, buffoon-like caricatures, and the many narrative lines of the political parable are woven so much around their ineptitude, their vacuity, their personal insecurities and one-upmanships, their sexual obsessions, the absurdities of their ambitions and their ends, that one is in danger of forgetting that Bhutto and Zia were in reality no buffoons, but highly capable and calculating men whose cruelties were entirely methodical. It is this tendency either to individualize completely the moral failures of a ruling class (Bhutto, or Zia, or whoever, is a bad character) or to spread them far too widely through society at large (the country was *made* wrong; what else do you expect?) which gives to Rushdie's Laughter, so salutary in some respects, the ambience, finally, of the modern cartoon.

It is on this narrative line, and on the thematics gathered around it, that most readings of *Shame* have concentrated – and with reason. If the book is to be located in the counter-canon of 'Third World Literature', if it is to be read essentially as a document of post-coloniality, a myth of the 'Nation', a critique of dictatorship, a fictionalized biography of the Pakistani state, a dissent from the politics of Partition and of Islamicism, then surely *that* narrative, and all other narrative lines converging on that main one, should rightly be the point of focus. Who on the Left – and not only on the Left – could dissent from the abuse heaped on the likes of Zia, etc.? We can take infinite pleasure in the inventiveness and eloquence of the denunciations which are, because of their justness, our own; because we are already preoccupied with the twin problematics of the 'Third World' and the 'Nation', far too many of us are willing to set aside all sorts of things that the book says about women, minorities, servants, and others who are not of the ruling class. It is this very pleasure of those wide-ranging denunciations which makes it possible for the *New York Times*, let us say, to lift the book out of its immediate location and compare Rushdie's achievement in *Shame* – in one breath, as it were – with Sterne, Swift, Kafka, García Márquez, Günter Grass. What this particular angle on the book – the primary emphasis on the representation of the 'Third World' and the condition of post-coloniality on the one hand; the tradition of the Grotesque on the other – does, however, is to read the book back from the author's own declarations and foregroundings, according to etiquettes stipulated by critics and theorists of 'Third World Literature'. Thus there is, a certain complicity of a shared starting point between the author and his critics, generated largely by the very conditions in which the idea of a 'Third World Literature' has arisen, which I have tried to specify elsewhere in this book. This complicity inhibits, then, other possible starting points for our readings: the issue, in the midst of all the political claims that go back and forth between authors and critics, of Rushdie's own politics and affiliations, for example; or his representation of women and the related issue of a possible misogyny; or the aesthetic of despair that issues both from his overvalorization of unbelonging ('floating upwards') and his own location within the modernist trajectories, both early and late, which are more than merely formal.

These other issues are the ones I want, briefly, to address, but I am concerned here mainly with Rushdie's representation of women, for four reasons: women occupy so large a portion of all the narratives in the book; Rushdie himself has drawn attention to this fact directly, through the narrator, within the book and then in numerous interviews, congratulating himself for these representations; the issue of misogyny is a central issue in any sort of oppositional politics; and the absence of any substantial male figures from among the oppressed and oppositional strata in this book – the absence, for example, of the male sections of workers and peasants, political militants, the patriotic intelligentsia – is so complete that it is only by analysing the author's representation of women that we can obtain any clue as to what his imaginative relation with *all* such strata might in fact be. In other words, Rushdie has so often declared himself a socialist of sorts that it is both legitimate and necessary to see what this book might look like if we were to read it from the standpoint of – no, not socialism, simply some determinate energies of an emancipatory project: not only in its representation of rulers, but also in its representations of the oppressed.[8]

This is by no means an uncomplicated undertaking, for Rushdie is not, in the way Orwell always was, a misogynist plain and simple. Living in the contemporary milieu of the British Left, he has not remained untouched by certain kinds of feminism; and he is clearly aware, and quite capable of effective narrativization, of many kinds of women's oppression in our societies. The complication is of a different order, and politically far more devastating than mere lack of sympathy. It is only after taking into account that structure of sympathy and the kind of politics in which it is embedded that one can proceed to examine the more central issues in his representation of women, and then to relate those issues back to the generality of his political positions.

Thus, alongside the stories of Isky and Raza, which together constitute the main narrative frame, are the tribulations of their wives, Bilquis and Rani. These portraits are drawn far more sympathetically than the portraits of their husbands, and some of the most moving episodes in the book are associated with these women: the episode, for example, of the fire at the time of Partition which burns away 'the brocades of continuity and the eyebrows of belonging' from Bilquis's vulnerable female body, while she is left with nothing save the 'dopatta of honor' in which she wraps herself as an only refuge; and the other episode, towards the end, when Rani, sequestered once more on her rural estate, takes stock of her life and embroiders eighteen shawls on which she traces, in intricate representational design, the debaucheries and cruelties of her husband's full career. Equally powerful are those last images of Bilquis, whose adult life started with forced, fire-propelled nakedness, shrouding herself at the end, an aged woman with defeated dreams, in black veils, so as to make permanent the distance between herself and the male-dominated world in which she has been caged all her life. Similarly, the episode in which Good News Hyder hangs herself in order to escape the constant, mad demand upon her procreativity is a moving episode, and it corresponds to very real horrors in our society. Even the initial conception of Sufiya Zinobia as one who is struggling to let the Beast out of the Sleeping Beauty is itself in the best tradition of Grotesque Realism. These are all powerful images.

Both Bilquis and Rani are, however – when all is said and done, and quite apart from the insult and neglect they suffer at the hands of their husbands – paltry, shallow creatures themselves, capable of nothing but chirpy gossip (in 'the elite actressy manner'), inertia or, at best, a tawdry affair with the owner of the local movie-house. They are not even remotely as evil as their husbands, and while Bilquis goes increasingly to pieces, Rani at least, in embroidering her shawls, manages to maintain a sort of dignity. Even hers, however, is the dignity of resignation. In general, moreover, what we find is a gallery of women who are frigid and desexualized (Arjumand, the 'Virgin Ironpants'), demented and moronic (the twenty-odd years of Zinobia's childhood), dulled into nullity (Farah), driven to despair (Rani, Bilquis) or suicide (Good News Hyder), or embody sheer surreal incoherence and loss of individual identity (the Shakil sisters). Throughout, every woman, without exception, is represented through a system of imageries which is sexually overdetermined; the frustration of erotic need, which drives some to frenzy and others to nullity, appears in every case to be the central fact of a woman's existence. What we have, then, is a real disjuncture between particular *episodes* which can delineate quite vivid sympathies for the respective female characters on the one hand, and, on the other, a generalized *structure* of representation in which each of those same characters turns out to be at least dislikable and frequently repugnant.

## IV

The crux of the matter, however, is the characterization of Sufiya Zinobia, the girl who was supposed to have been a boy, the 'miracle which went wrong', the demented child who was born blushing, and is Shame personified. She is the one who provides the link between the stark title of the book and its many disjointed, sprawling narratives, and is at the centre of that marriage between shame and shamelessness which, the author tells us over and over again, breeds the all-enveloping violence; she blushes, we are told, not merely for herself but also, more consistently, for the world at large. In a world of utter evil, where everything that happens should evoke shame but everyone is entirely shameless, Sufiya Zinobia, this Shame personified, is no mere character; she is presented from the outset as the very embodiment of the principle of redemption – if redemption, in this altogether unheroic, unscrupulous world, is even possible.

Initially, of course, her blushes begin at birth, for the simple reason that she, like all babies, was expected to be a boy. This unending shame which begins at birth and hounds all her days on earth might well, in a different sort of trajectory, have been an appropriate metaphor for the way the generation of a sense of fundamental female inadequacy, and shame as a specifically female attribute, may be sought in the very social processes of gendering. But then two things happen. One is that she becomes ill, contracting brain fever, and thus permanently retarded, developing the brain of a six-year-old at the age of nineteen. Now, the problem with this metaphor of mental illness is that the pressures and processes of gendering – which are social and historical in character, and impose upon a great many women the possibility of deformation and incapacity, but are open to resistance and reversal by women's own actions – are given to us in the form of a *physiological* insufficiency on *her* part. The novel therefore becomes incapable of communicating to us, in whatever grotesque forms, the *process* whereby a woman's intellectual and emotional abilities may be sapped, or regained. We may be charitable and not recount here all the ways in which the fiction of women's physiological insufficiency has been mobilized in the past and present histories of gender politics. At the very least, however, this shift from the social to the physiological forecloses the possibility that the person in question can regain control of her body, let alone her brain, through her own initiative; reversals of such conditions are rare, and they require the agency not so much of the patient as of doctors and hospitals. That Bilquis, her mother, would henceforth be ashamed of the child because the child is a moron, or that Sufiya herself would become an object of medical interventions, or even that her marriage would remain sexually unconsummated, begins to make a certain sort of sense within the available social arrangements; we may now preach greater liberality of attitude towards such hapless creatures, but the essential social situation remains intractable and the novel simply fails to recover from this eliding of the social into the physiological.

In the course of the novel, moreover, Sufiya's shame comes to refer less and less to herself (her femaleness; her mental retardation) or to her family (which is ashamed of her on both counts, femaleness and retardation) and becomes increasingly focused on the world as Sufiya finds it; she becomes, almost literally, the conscience of a shameless world – a principle of honour, so to speak. This too is somewhat problematic, in the sense that when the complex moral obligations of a social conscience are reduced to the limiting emotiveness of mere shame, and when this shamed conscience is deposited in one who is physiologically incapable of intellection and sustained responsible conduct, the author precludes, by virtue of the very terms he has established, the possibility that this conscience would be capable of grappling with needs of social regeneration, or even with the sort of decency and daily heroism of which countless ordinary people are quite capable. Rushdie says over and over again, within the novel as well as in the interviews which have followed, that the encounter of shamelessness with shame can only produce violence. Precisely! But violence is not in itself capable of regeneration, and it is doubtful, Fanon notwithstanding, that violence is intrinsically even a cleansing virtue. In other words, the very dialectic – of shamelessness and shame, and their condensation in eruptions of violence – which governs the conceptual framework of the novel is fundamentally flawed; symbolic values which Rushdie assigns to Sufiya Zinobia simply exceed the terms within which he has fashioned her own existence. The double punning in her name – on the word 'Sufi' and on the name of Zainub, the granddaughter of the Prophet of Islam who is quite central to several of the popular strands derived from Sufic Islam – is, in context, excessive and merely prankish.

This becomes clear as soon as one recalls the stages in the escalation of her violences. The governing metaphor for these escalations – the Beast emerging from inside the Beauty, while the Beauty herself is anything but beautiful in any conventional sense – is again superbly within the tradition of the Grotesque, and the political idea which is inscribed within this metaphor – a woman's inherent right to be not a doll but a fighter – is equally powerful. One's sense of unease comes, however, from the irrational and spurious manner in which Sufiya's violences accumulate and from what she herself *becomes* (a destroyer of men, fields, animals; a four-legged beast herself) before she reaches her object: the murder of her husband, the 'peripheral hero', Omar Khayyam Shakil. The first such eruption comes at the age of twelve when she goes out and kills two hundred and eighteen turkeys with a certain orgiastic relish: 'Sufiya Zinobia had torn off their heads and then reached down into their bodies to draw their guts up their necks' (p. 150). The explanation for this, of course, is simple enough: 'twelve years of unloved humiliation take their toll, even on an idiot' (p. 149). The next eruption is, from the authorial standpoint, equally innocent: on the day of her sister's marriage she tries to do to her brother-in-law what she had previously done to the turkeys, but she manages only to twist his neck permanently out of shape, thus putting an end to his polo-playing career. The explanation is again quite simple: 'a pouring into her too-sensitive spirit of the great abundance of shame' at the circumstances, presumably, in which the marriage was taking place (p. 186). An instance of desolation in one case, a sense of honour in the other! But then comes something far more monumental. By then, more years have passed and she has married Shakil, who is forbidden to sleep with her and sleeps with Shahbanou, her servant, instead. She rightfully begins to wonder about sex, children, the meaning of marriage itself, and Shakil's treachery; she has, at this point, the brain of a six-year-old! One day – out of frustration and anger, it seems – she walks out of the house, picks up four men, has sexual intercourse with them, kills them, and comes home with semen and blood on her veils. The central passage in this whole episode is worth quoting:

> Shame walks the streets of night. In the slums four youths are transfixed by those appalling eyes, whose deadly yellow fire blows like a wind through the

> *latticework of the veil. They follow her to the rubbish-dump of doom*, rats to her piper, automata dancing in the all-consuming light from the black-veiled eyes. Down she lies; and what Shahbanou took upon herself is finally done to Sufiya. Four husbands come and go. *Four of them in and out*, and then her hands reach for the first boy's neck. The others stand still and wait their turn. And heads hurled high, sinking into the scattered clouds; nobody saw them fall. She rises, goes home. And sleeps; the Beast subsides. (p. 242)

In this passage, Sufiya becomes the oldest of the misogynist myths: the virgin who is really a vampire, the irresistible temptress who seduces men in order to kill them, not an object of male manipulation but a devourer of hapless men. And in thus discovering her 'true' self, she becomes the opposite not only of that other daughter in the book, Arjumand, the sexless 'Virgin Ironpants' (Rushdie's caricature of Benazir Bhutto), but also the opposite of the Muslim male who, in some interpretations of the Islamic *shari'a*, is allowed four wives: what she does to her 'four husbands' is, of course, much more extreme, perhaps because the backwardness of her mind is more than matched by the enormity of her sexual appetite as well as her malevolence.

She comes home and sleeps, but it is only a matter of time, obviously, before she escapes again, this time for good, 'because once a carnivore has tasted blood you can't fool it with vegetables any more', and because 'the violence which had been born of shame . . . now lived its own life beneath her skin' (p. 268). And she does escape, but 'what now roamed free in the unsuspecting air was not Sufiya Zinobia Shakil at all, but something more like a principle . . . a human guillotine . . . ripping off men's heads' (pp. 268–70). Soon enough, she ceases to be human even in a literal sense and becomes, of all things, 'a white panther' with a 'black head, pale hairless body, awkward gait'; 'stories about her . . . had begun to come from all over the country' (p. 280). And her achievements:

> Murders of animals and men, villages raided in the dark, dead children, slaughtered flocks, blood-curdling howls (p. 280). . . . The killings continued: farmers, pie-dogs, goats. The murders formed a death-ring round the house; they had reached the outskirts of the two cities, new capital and old town. Murders without rhyme or reason, done, it seemed, for the love of killing, or to satisfy some hideous need. (p. 287)

What the author takes to be the meaning of all this dawns, improbably enough, upon Omar Khayyam Shakil, her husband who was also her doctor, who had until then been nothing but shamelessness personified:

> For the first time in her life . . . that girl is free. He imagined her proud; proud of her strength, proud of the violence that was making her a legend, that prohibited anyone from telling her what to do, or whom to be, or what she should have been and was not; yes, she had risen above everything. (p. 281)

This is, of course, Rushdie himself speaking; there is nothing in Shakil's character to suggest that he is capable of such an act of imaginative understanding. Yet there is something profoundly unsettling about this idea of a 'freedom' which resides in rising 'above everything' (earlier in the book, we have already encountered the idea of 'floating upwards'), hence being able to commit limitless, senseless violence. And if this is indeed what Sufiya Zinobia has become, then it is very difficult, because of this moral perplexity, for a reader to sympathize with her in that last episode where she finally manages to kill Omar Khayyam Shakil himself. By then, it is no longer a confrontation between shamelessness and shame but, rather, between a man who is of course clearly a moral cripple, and a woman who has become – not in the metaphorical but in the most literal sense – a beast.

This portrayal of Sufiya Zinobia – combined with that of Bilquis and Rani, which we discussed above and that of Arjumand ('Virgin Ironpants'), which we have not had the opportunity to discuss at any length – raises a fundamental question about Rushdie's view of the world in general and women in particular. Considering that Rushdie himself has stressed the importance of women in *Shame*,[9] as well as his own conception of Sufiya as a principle of honour and redemption, he seems to have fashioned a macabre caricature of what female resistance to cruelties might be; the woman herself becomes, in this version, a rapist. For so wedded is Rushdie's imagination to imageries of wholesale degradation and unrelieved social wreckage, so little is he able to conceive of a real possibility of regenerative projects on the part of the people who actually exist within our contemporary social reality, that even when he attempts, towards the end of the novel, to open up a regenerative possibility, in the form of Sufiya's flight – and also her return, as Nemesis and all-devouring Fury – the powers which he, as author, bestows upon her in the moment of her triumph are powers only of destruction. It is indicative of the temper of the whole novel that even her innocence, up to the point where she remains innocent of the social corruptions of Rushdie's imagined world, is the innocence merely of the mad and the mentally retarded; she is doubtless the only one who finally obtains the energy to oppose and win, but this energy is itself rooted – literally, the novel tells us – in brain fever. Moreover, her power is not only purely destructive but also *blind*; even before she takes her revenge upon her tormenters, she has been on the prowl, we are told, through all the nooks and crannies of the country, eating up animals and men, destroying fields, creating terror. This kind of image, which romanticizes violence as self-redemption, has, of course, no potential for portraying regenerative processes; further, it is linked up, in a most disagreeable manner, with imperialist and misogynistic myths: the image of freedom-fighter as idiot-terrorist; the image of a free – or freedom-seeking – woman as vampire, Amazon, man-eating shrew.

What the characterization of Sufiya Zinobia illustrates once again is the limiting, even misogynistic nature of the typologies within which Rushdie encloses the whole range of women's experience. As I pointed out above, there are several episodes in *Shame* where a sense of the oppression of women is obvious enough; in one kind of response one may now pity the victims of this oppression, much in the manner of the liberal bourgeoisie which always pities the poor. It is also possible to concede within some limits, as regards the general structure of Rushdie's representation of women, that in real life many women have doubtless been driven to madness, violence, phobia, dementia. But women are not, in any fundamental sense, mere victims of history; much more centrally, women have *survived* against very heavy odds, and they have *produced* history. Madness, sexual frenzy, nullity of being, fevers of the brain, have been, by and large, very uncommon; the vast majority of women have consistently performed productive (and not only *re*productive) labour; and, like those men who also do productive work, they have retained with society and history a relation that is essentially imaginative, visionary, communal and regenerative. Erotic need has been, for women as for men, often important, but only in rare cases is it the lone desire, outside loves and solidarities of other kinds; work, in any case, has been for the great majority far more central; women are not, any more than men are, mere eroticized bodies. So there is something fundamentally awry in a system of imageries which overvalorizes, when it comes to describing women, the zones of the erotic, the irrational, the demented and the demonic. That is to say, there is something fatally wrong with a novel in which virtually every woman is to be pitied, most are to be laughed at, some are to be feared, at least some of the time, but none may be understood in relation to those fundamental projects of survival and overcoming which are none other than the production of history itself. Satirizing the masters is one thing, but it is a different matter altogether to give such chilling portraits – *only* chilling portraits – of women, in terms so very close to the dominant stereotypes.

Rushdie's inability to include integral regenerative possibilities within the Grotesque world of his imaginative creation represents, I believe, a conceptual flaw of a fundamental kind. In the book he speaks, again and again, of a 'country'; but what he gives us is a portrait, by and large, of the cruel and claustrophobic world of its ruling class. *That* world he seems to know very well, but to think of the portrait of rulers as a portrait of the 'country' itself is an error, I think, not only of politics, narrowly conceived, but also of the social imagination. Hence the remarkable fact that while Rushdie talks constantly of politics, *all* the political acts represented within the matrix of the novel are demagogic, opportunistic, self-serving, cruel, or at best petty. Politics is mostly farce, sometimes tragedy, but it is never capable of producing resistance to oppression, solidarity and integrity in human conduct, or any sort of human community; for all its marvellous humour, Rushdie's imagined world is, in its lovelessness, almost Orwellian. And that, too, fits. If the political vision of your imagined world does not include those who resist, or love, or act with any degree of integrity or courage, then you *will* conclude – as Rushdie does, in the 'worst tale in history' which comes in the final pages of the book – that it is a country in which brother has been betraying brother for generations! Now, Pakistan's history is, of course, replete with betrayals, as is India's, but it is this idea of the permanence and pervasiveness of betrayal – the Orwellian idea, in other words, that human beings *always* betray one another – which gives this book its quite extraordinary quality of lovelessness. For an equally bleak vision of human potentiality one would have to go, I think, to *Nineteen Eighty-Four* or to Naipaul's *A Bend in the River*.

There is, I believe, a connection between this view of the world and Rushdie's way of representing women. This question of the representation of women, I have argued, is important both because the issue of misogyny is always central to any kind of oppositional project and also because, in the absence of other kinds of representations of any other oppressed strata, the representation of women who *are* there in the book gives us crucial clues to the general structure of Rushdie's imaginative sympathies. Two points are, I think, worth making here. First, any representation of women, whether in fiction or in life, has to do, surely, with gender relations, but also with *more* than gender relations; it is almost always indicative of a much larger structure of feeling and a much more complex political grid. What I have attempted, in other words, is not a sufficient reading of the book but a *symptomatic* reading: the concentration on a symptom which is itself vividly central but one which may also, in the same sweep, give us some understanding of the structure as a whole. Second, politics appears to me to be a matter not so much of opposition as of solidarity; it is always much less problematic to denounce dictators and to affirm, instead, a generality of values – 'liberty, equality, fraternity', let us say, as Rushdie does indeed affirm towards the very end (p. 278) – but always much harder to affiliate oneself with specific kinds of praxis, conceived not in terms of values which serve as a *judgement* on history but as a solidarity with communities of individuals, simultaneously flawed and heroic, who act within that history, from determinate social and political positions.

## V

Quite apart from other sorts of choices Rushdie might or might not have made, that kind of politics is precluded for him by the very (post)-modernist location he chooses for himself and by the extent to which he valorizes the experience of 'migrancy' and unbelonging. This is clear enough in *Shame*, but even more visible in more direct, non-fictional kinds of writing. To illustrate this point, I want to look briefly at two pieces of his which I have selected somewhat arbitrarily: his brief essay on Günter

Grass and his succinct, delightful commentary, 'Outside the Whale', on the recent deluge of movies about the British Raj.[10] My choice is arbitrary in the sense that these are neither more nor less representative than several other of his pieces; I chose them because they came soon after *Shame* and because they are short, in some other ways delightfully inventive, and therefore disturbing for their rather flip postmodernist ambience.

The essay on Grass, for example, begins:

> In the summer of 1967, when the West was – perhaps for the last time – in the clutches of the optimism disease, when the microscopic, invisible bacillus of optimism made its young people believe that they would overcome some day, when unemployment was an irrelevance and the future still existed, and when I was twenty years old, I bought from a bookshop in Cambridge a paperback copy of Ralph Manheim's English translation of *The Tin Drum*. In those days everybody had better things to do than read. There was the music and there were the movies and there was also, don't forget, the world to change. Like many of my contemporaries I spent my student days under the spell of Buñuel, Godard, Ray, Wajda, Welles, Bergman, Kurosawa, Jancsô, Antonioni, Dylan, Lennon, Jagger, Laing, Marcuse, and, inevitably, the two-headed fellow known to Grass readers as Marxengels. . . . And my passports, the works that gave me the permits I needed, were *The Film Sense* by Serge Eisenstein, the 'Crow' poems of Ted Hughes, Borges' *Fictions*, Sterne's *Tristam Shandy*, Ionesco's play *Rhinoceros* – and, that summer of 1967, *The Tin Drum*. (p. 276)

I have quoted the last two sentences in the passage above ('Like many of my contemporaries . . . ' onwards) simply to convey a sense of the kind of influences and cultural milieux which have gone into making the type of imagination Rushdie has. Here, though, I am much more interested in the opening statements. The tone is obviously satiric, even sardonic, and the follies listed here are of course not his own but, we are told, the West's. The tone of mockery is designed, meanwhile, to destabilize the meaning of the passage itself. Despite this strategem, however, one can detect the tendency to repeat, almost unthinkingly, the commonplaces and even inaccuracies of the metropolis's High Culture. It is doubtful, for example, that something called 'the West' was, in the summer of 1967, 'in the clutches of optimism'; that was the year the Vietnamese finally began concentrating their forces for what became the Tet offensive, and at least a part of 'the West' – American imperialism, for example – was not at all 'optimistic'. It is equally doubtful that 'optimism' – the idea that 'the future still exists', the hope that we 'would overcome some day', the conviction that 'there *is* a 'world to change' – is as such a 'disease' (a 'microscopic, invisible bacillus', we are playfully told). To be amused, in retrospect, at the youthfulness of one's own youth is one thing; but to learn from maturity that a visionary relation with reality is itself folly, that literature is an antidote to such follies, is to participate, perhaps unwittingly, in precisely the kind of quietism which Rushdie himself seems formally to reject in other parts of this brief essay and in many other writings.

Despair is now, in this age of late capitalism and in the aftermath of High Modernism, so constitutive a part of contemporary bourgeois culture, and it is combined so casually with so many sorts of private pleasures, that one forgets, when one comes upon such formulations ('no future' and all that), how bleak a vision of human possibility this type of thinking signifies. And it is perhaps because of his discomfort with such bleakness that Rushdie ends the essay, formally, on the word 'hope'. But before we come to that formal ending, we see some other characteristic ways in which Rushdie participates in that cultural ambience. For example, he first speaks of Grass and of himself as 'migrants', in the literal sense of the word, as individuals who were born in one society and have migrated to another; on this score, he says some very perceptive things. But then he goes on to extend the meaning of 'migration' to a universal ontological plain: 'we are all migrants', he says, in the sense that 'we all cross frontiers'. That too is true, though in a very banal sort of way. The problem, however, comes when, having defined 'migration' as a metaphor for the human condition as such, he goes on to say that a migrant is 'a metaphorical being' and that 'the migrant intellect roots itself in itself' because it understands 'the artificial nature of reality'. Now, if a migrant is a metaphorical being, and if 'we are all migrants', then, obviously, we are all 'metaphorical beings'; and reality itself is 'artificial' not only in the sense that much of it is *made* by us but also in the much more idealistic and modernist sense that life does not exist outside its metaphors; and if reality is only 'artificial' ('artefact' is another word Rushdie uses in this context), then, obviously, the writer's intellect has no choice but to 'root itself in itself'; the tie between social despair, a literal loss of reality, and narcissism is now complete. Within these ideological predicates, what kind of 'hope' does one speak of, when one does end one's essay on that word? Here, too, Rushdie's own words, in the two sentences which precede the sentence of 'hope', are significant:

> The composition of elegies is indeed one of the proper responses for a writer to make when the night is drawing in. But outside his fiction, in his political activities and writings, Grass is making a second, and equally proper response. What this work says is: we aren't dead yet.

The presumption is that 'the night is drawing in'; again, there is no future. So far as the writing of fiction is concerned, therefore, one writes 'elegies'. Resistance, such as it is, belongs to other realms: political activities and directly political writings. In other words, art can only be an art of despair; whatever else one does, one does it elsewhere. But in that other realm, too, all one can say is 'we aren't dead yet'. The presumption again is that the apocalypse, the demonic end of the world, is at hand; we shall soon all be dead, and our laughter, if it is laughter at all, is the laughter of the day before the world ends. One acts, in other words, not because one hopes to change anything but because one is condemned, by existential necessity, to act; we are back to Beckett's formula – 'I can't go on . . . I will go on' – which Rushdie himself quotes most approvingly in his other essay, 'Outside the Whale'.

I do not have the space here to offer a detailed reading of that odd essay – odd in the sense that it is so very good in so many ways and yet, in the last instance, so profoundly marred by Rushdie's aesthetic of despair. One of the oddest things about it is that after developing a superb critique of Orwell – particularly of the essay from which Rushdie himself took his title – and after rejecting the political quietism which Orwell recommends in that essay, Rushdie goes on to display not only the same kind of sensibility we find in his Grass essay, but also his peculiar ability, which he seems to share with Orwell, to enunciate altogether antithetical ideas in one breath. Thus, one is hard put to know just where he stands intellectually when he says, for example, in consecutive sentences of a single paragraph, that 'we are all irradiated by history, we are radioactive with history and politics, which is history in action' and 'politics is by turns farce and tragedy, and sometimes . . . both at once'. Now, if 'politics is by turns farce and tragedy', and politics is also 'history in action', then what exactly is one saying about 'history' which has 'irradiated' all of us? That we are irradiated with the 'farce and tragedy' of history itself? So it is only fitting that by the end of that paragraph we find Rushdie quoting, very approvingly, Beckett's formula 'I can't go on . . . ', etc. Again, the problem is that if this kind of world-weariness is where one takes one's stand, and if history has already been dismissed as 'farce and tragedy', then why on earth does one want to quarrel with Orwell? After all, Orwell too made plenty of room in his writings for what *he* took to be 'politics', and he too thought that politics was sometimes tragic, more frequently farcical.

## VI

This parallel with Orwell is not a minor matter. Now, undoubtedly, a political discussion of Rushdie's *work* has become extraordinarily difficult in the wake of the terror unleashed against him by Iran's clerical rulers. But in those earlier days – when his own life was not so endangered, and as *Midnight's Children* and *Shame* first burst upon the international scene, receiving equal accolades from *New Left Review* and the *New York Times* – one was struck by the fact that not since Orwell had a *political* writer with a colonial background – and one who had declared himself a socialist – been so equally admired on both Right and Left. Alongside the lovelessness of the fictions, the repeated intrusions of a misogynistic streak, and a certain spontaneous belief in the universality of betrayal – which Orwell too had begun displaying since his earliest writings, from *Burmese Days* onwards – Rushdie has also deployed that same stance of unbelonging, of the lone individual occupying a moral high ground *above* the 'chimeras of politics' (Rushdie's phrase), delivering his denunciations of Left and Right alike: Indira Gandhi, the Pakistani Generals, the Communist Parties, the Naxalites, film stars, prophets, the short-lived banning of *La Prensa*. On certain *issues* – racism, religiosity, dictatorship, empire, and the like – one could take a *position*, and one could also, in a general way, speak of oneself as a man of the Left, as Orwell himself frequently did; but there was no actual Left, no existing community of praxis, within that world which had given one's imagination and fictions their energy, with which one felt in any fundamental way bonded, accepting and struggling with the risks and the restrictions and the suffering that such bonding often implies. From all such groundings one had 'floated upwards', even as one constantly thrashed about denouncing all, undifferentiatedly, that one had left behind. In an earlier time, right into the heart of modernism, such desolations of the self were still experienced quite frequently as a loss; what postmodernism has done is to validate precisely the pleasures of such unbelonging, which is rehearsed now as a *utopia*, so that belonging *nowhere* is nevertheless construed as the perennial pleasure of belonging everywhere.

In this context I can do no better than simply to quote a longish passage from that old classic, *Culture and Society*, which is ostensibly about Orwell but clearly speaks of larger things:

> Orwell was one of a significant number of men who, deprived of a settled way of living . . . find virtue in a kind of improvised living, and in an assertion of independence. The tradition, in England, is distinguished. It attracts to itself many of the liberal virtues: empiricism, a certain integrity, frankness. It has also, as the normally contingent virtue of exile, qualities of perception: in particular, the ability to distinguish inadequacies in the groups which have been rejected . . . there is an appearance of hardness (the austere criticism of hypocrisy, complacency, self-deceit), but this is usually brittle, and at times hysterical. . . . Alongside the tough rejection of compromise, which gives the tradition its virtue, is the felt social impotence, the inability to form extending relationships . . .
>
> . . . Yet we need to make a distinction between exile and vagrancy: there is usually a principle in exile, there is always only relaxation in vagrancy. . . . The vagrant, in literary terms, is the reporter, . . . it is unlikely that he will understand, in any depth, the life about which he is writing. . . . But a restless society very easily accepts this kind of achievement: at one level the report on the curious or the exotic; at another level, when the class or society is nearer the reporter's own, the perceptive critique.

Now, after Khomeini's sentencing of him, Rushdie's 'vagrancy' has turned, paradoxically and tragically, into a full-scale exile. But even that earlier condition of the production of his work need hardly be used merely to deny the breadth of his achievement, which is substantial. What

Williams's remarks on Orwell help us to understand, nevertheless, is the importance – indeed, 'the tradition' – of certain ways of living which in some cases – in Orwell's and Rushdie's, surely – have been connected with a colonial past but are in no fundamental sense limited or attributable to the colonial experience *per se*. Exile, in the true sense, is of many kinds besides the purely colonial, and in any case it rarely produces an enduring sense of great pleasure. Exile usually has, as Williams points out, a principle, and the principle prevents one from 'floating upwards' and denying the pain. Self-exile and 'vagrancy', by contrast, have become more common amongst artists in every successive phase of bourgeois culture since the early days of Romanticism, and as the experience itself has been chosen with greater frequency, the sense of celebration and of 'the migrant intellect root[ing] itself in itself' has grown proportionately. It is the palpable presence of this kind of living in Rushdie's work, with its accompanying inability to believe in any community of actual praxis, and hence the belief in the universality of betrayal, which is lost in those readings of his work which locate it primarily in the problematic of the 'Nation' and the 'Third World', even if one ends by complicating that location. Williams's summary evaluation of that 'tradition', with his highly perceptive diagnosis of its particular virtues and failings, would imply, followed in its full logic, that Rushdie's work is to be located neither in some unified and categorizable 'Third World', nor in some innocent myth of 'migrancy', as Rushdie himself would have it, nor in an empty, postmodernist 'cosmopolitanism', but in a condition which is in some basic ways older, wider, far more extreme.

# 5

# *Orientalism* and After: Ambivalence and Metropolitan Location in the Work of Edward Said

> It needs to be said that criticism modified in advance by labels like 'Marxism' or 'liberalism' is, in my view, an oxymoron. . . . The net effect of 'doing' Marxist criticism or writing at the present time is of course to declare political preference, but it is also to put oneself outside a great deal of things going on in the world, so to speak, and in other kinds of criticism.
>
> EDWARD W. SAID[1]

I have written critically of Fredric Jameson earlier in this book, and substantial portions of this chapter will be highly critical of Edward Said. One reason, simply, is that Jameson and Said are possibly the most significant cultural critics writing in the English language today for the kind of work I do in this area, and I can scarcely find my own thought without passing through theirs. Disagreeing with Jameson was easier. Writing from a Marxist position, I naturally share identifiable points of theoretical departure with him, even when – *especially* when – we disagree on the most basic issues. Said is different in this regard. I disagree with him so fundamentally on issues both of theory and of history that our respective understandings of the world – the world as it now is, and as it has been at many points over the past two thousand years or so – are simply irreconcilable, which then leads, inevitably, to differences of local interpretation and local reading so numerous that no one essay can possibly name them all.

These differences, both the general and the particular, are in any case the smaller part of my difficulty in writing about Edward Said. Much the larger difficulty resides, rather, in my sense of solidarity with his beleaguered location in the midst of imperial America. For Edward Said is not only a cultural critic, he is also a Palestinian. Much that is splendid in his work is connected with the fact that he has tried to do honour to that origin; and he has done so against all odds, to the full extent of his capacity, by stepping outside the boundaries of his academic discipline and original intellectual formation, under no compulsion of profession or fame, in no pursuit of personal gain – in fact, at frightening risk to himself. I shall come later to what all this has meant for his published work, but it is worth remarking that his eloquent and irrepressible partisanship with his national cause has earned him assassination threats, from quarters which are known to have assassinated a great many other patriotic Palestinians. Said has decided to live with such risks, and much honour – a very rare kind of honour – attaches to that decision. How, then, does one register one's many disagreements from within this solidarity? For some years I have thought that one simply could not do so, that dissenting speech would probably be a betrayal of that solidarity. More recently, though, I have come to believe that such a position of willed neutrality is politically wrong, morally indefensible. Said, after all, continues to pursue his vocation in the circumstances given to him, which is his wonderful way of answering his would-be assassins. Those of us who admire his courage and yet disagree with him on substantive issues also have to carry on our own critical pursuits. Suppression of criticism, I have come to believe, is not the best way of expressing solidarity.

## I

About the sense of that place, the question of that origin, Said has sometimes written directly: notably in his two books *The Question of Palestine*[2] and *After the Last Sky*,[3] and in numerous articles. But the awareness of it is there – at times only on the margins, in some places very much foregrounded, and increasingly so with the passage of time – in many of the writings that followed *Orientalism* (1978).[4] It is likely, in fact, that when the dust of current literary debates settles, Said's most enduring contribution will be seen as residing neither in *Orientalism*, which is a deeply flawed book, nor in the literary essays which have followed in its wake, but in his work on the Palestine issue, for example his seminal essay 'Zionism from the Standpoint of Its Victims',[5] the superbly inflected prose which he contributed alongside Jean Mohr's photographs in *After the Last Sky*, and generally the role he has played, with unrivalled energy and much salutary effect, in redefining the issue of Palestinian national liberation for Western, especially American, intelligentsias. Even though the latter parts of *The Question of Palestine* were much weaker, one could see that in Said's own intellectual biography and in the history of his sentiments, the writing of *Orientalism* had been in some ways a preparation for the writing of that essay on Zionism and its victims. One was in a sense grateful for that preparation, that will to settle the rage inside as much as possible, so that he could then speak, with scholarly precision and measured eloquence, about that most difficult place inside the self where the wound had once been, where the pain still was. And because one had already read *Orientalism*, the composure that Said had gained, the scruple he was now able to exercise, was all the more striking.

*Orientalism* marks such a radical break in Said's own intellectual career precisely because the *writing* of this book was an attempt at coming to terms with what it meant for him to be a Palestinian living and teaching in the USA, armed with not much more than a humanist intellectual training, a succesful career as literary critic, and a splendid mastery over wide areas of European literary textuality. As he puts it in the 'introduction':

> My own experience of these matters is in part what made me write this book. The life of an Arab Palestinian in the West, particularly in America, is disheartening. . . . The web of racism, cultural stereotypes, political imperialism, dehumanizing ideology holding in the Arab or the Muslim is very strong indeed, and it is this web which every Palestinian has come to feel as his uniquely punishing destiny.[6]

That is one part of his purpose: to make manifest the many strands and histories of this 'web' confronting the Palestinian. But an equally personal and more nuanced undertaking is announced, with the aid of a quotation from Gramsci, two pages earlier:

> In the *Prison Notebooks* Gramsci says: 'The starting-point in critical elaboration is the consciousness of what one really is . . . as a product of the historical process to date, which has deposited in you an infinity of traces, without leaving an inventory.' The only available English translation inexplicably leaves Gramsci's comment at that, whereas Gramsci's Italian text concludes by adding that 'therefore it is imperative at the outset to compile such an inventory.' . . . In many ways my study of Orientalism has been an attempt to inventory the traces upon me, the Oriental subject, of the culture whose domination has been so powerful a factor in the life of all Orientals. (p.25)

This passage from Gramsci seems to have meant a great deal to Said, for it reappears at the beginning of his 'Zionism' essay. Several aspects of these two passages should therefore detain us. The first is that this was the first time in Said's writings that his personal voice had intruded so sharply, was positioned so centrally, in the definition of his scholarly project. As one returns today, some twenty years later, to Said's first two books, the one on Conrad and *Beginnings*,[7] one notices the early mastery of style, but one is also struck, from today's vantage point of the *tone* of *Orientalism*, by the essentially *cerebral* character of that earlier prose: by the fact that not much more than the mind is engaged, and the mind then seemed actually to have believed that when it comes to intellectual inquiry, even in the human sciences, nothing except the mind *need be* engaged. The emphasis here, by contrast, on one's own 'uniquely punishing destiny' and the intent, then, to prepare an 'inventory' of the traces – wounds, one might say – that the destiny has inflicted upon oneself, announces the emergence of a very different kind of prose, more personal and palpable, in which erudition is poised more or less precariously against the polemical verve.

But why should this 'inventory' of traces take the form of a counter-reading of the Western canonical textualities, mainly in the cognate areas of literature and philology, from Greek tragedy onwards? The reason was again a personal one, though it was really not connected with being a Palestinian. Said had been trained primarily in the classical mould of scholarship in Comparative European Literatures, in a milieu dominated by Auerbach, Curtius and Spitzer, the German comparatists who had given to the discipline its stamp of High Humanism of a very conservative kind, more or less Tory in orientation. It was the ghost of this precise canonicity which had to be laid to rest. The particular texture of *Orientalism*, its emphasis on the canonical text, its privileging of literature and philology in the constitution of 'Orientalist' knowledge and indeed the human sciences generally, its will to portray a 'West' which has been the same from the dawn of history up to the present, and its will to traverse all the main languages of Europe – all this, and more, in *Orientalism* derives from the ambition to write a counter-history that could be posed against *Mimesis*, Auerbach's magisterial account of the seamless genesis of European realism and rationalism from Greek Antiquity to the modernist moment.

If there is an absent antihero in Said's own counter-classic, it is Erich Auerbach. If Auerbach began with Homer, Said too must begin with Greek tragedy; and a special venom must be reserved for Dante because Dante, after all, is the hero of Auerbach's account. But ghosts of that kind are not so easily laid to rest, provided that you are sufficiently possessed by them.[8] Over the past decade or so Said has recounted, most poignantly, over and over again, in several different texts, that moment in Auerbach's life when he, a refugee from fascism, sat in his lonely corner in Istanbul, cut off from the European libraries of Classical and Romance languages, and wrote *Mimesis*, his loving summation of his beloved humanist knowledge of European Literature at a time when he thought that the tradition itself was on the point of vanishing. In this narrative, to which Said returns again and again, Auerbach is the emblem of scholarly rectitude, a lone figure defending humanist value in the midst of holocaust, a scholar in the finest sense; also a surrogate, because this figure of an ultimate scholar writing his masterpiece in exile has, for Said, the stateless Palestinian and the ambitious author of *Orientalism*, a very special resonance. Outside this particular narrative of personal desolation and perseverance, however, Auerbach is also the master of European knowledge against which the counter-knowledge of *Orientalism* is assembled.

This paradoxical relationship with Auerbach, the individual master, is played out on a much more complex scale, in an equally paradoxical relationship with High Humanism as such. In the field of Cultural Studies, Said is our most vivacious narrator of the history of European humanism's complicity in the history of European colonialism. The global history of humanism doubtless includes much besides that complicity, and it is of course eminently arguable that this narrative of the convergence between colonial knowledges and colonial powers simply cannot be assembled within Cultural Studies itelf, because histories of economic exploitation, political coercion, military conquest play the far more constitutive part; those other histories are the ones which provide the enabling conditions for the so-called 'Orientalist Discourse' as such. But that argument we shall, for the moment, ignore. What is far more significant is that after Said has assembled the whole narrative of European Literature, from Aeschylus to Edward Lane, as a history of literature's complicity in inferiorization of the 'Orient', and after he has identified the Enlightenment as an unified trajectory and master sign, of both Orientalism and colonialism, he is of course faced with the problem of identifying some sort of agency that might undo this centuries-old tie between narratives of High Humanism and the colonial project. At this point we discover a peculiar blockage, for what Said now posits are the most ordinary, the most familiar values of humanist liberalism: namely tolerance, accommodation, cultural pluralism and relativism, and those insistently repeated words *sympathy*, *constituency*, *affilitiation*, *filiation*. What is remarkable about this at times very resounding affirmation of humanist value is that humanism-as-ideality is invoked precisely at the time when humanism-as-history has been rejected so unequivocally.

These ambivalences about Auerbach and about humanism in general were problematic enough, but they were then complicated further by the impossible reconciliation which Said tries to achieve between that humanism and Foucault's Discourse Theory, which no serious intellectual would want to use simply as a method of reading and classifying canonical books because the theory itself is inseparable from Nietzschean anti-humanism and anti-realist theories of representation. We encounter the invocation of Foucault as conceptual mentor early in the book, as soon as Said is done with his three definitions of the object, Orientalism, as such:

> I have found it useful here to employ Michel Foucault's notion of a discourse, as described by him in *The Archeology of Knowledge* and in *Discipline and Punish*, to identify Orientalism. My contention is that without examining Orientalism as a discourse one cannot possibly understand the enormously systematic discipline by which European culture was able to manage – and

> even produce – the Orient politically, sociologically, militarily, ideologically, scientifically, and imaginatively during the post-Enlightenment period. (p. 3)

This sense of affiliation with Foucault remains strong throughout *Orientalism*,[9] and the prose of the book is replete with Foucauldian terminology: regularity, discursive field, representation, archive, epistemic difference, and so on. Yet one is not quite sure what the relationship between Said's thought and Foucault's really is.[10] Foucault certainly knew how to be allusive, but underneath all his multiple enunciations one knows exactly what his agreements and disagreements with Marxism actually have been. His first and irreconcilable difference is that he locates Marx firmly within the boundaries of what he calls the 'Western episteme'; in its epistemic construction, he says, Marx's thought is framed entirely by the discourse of Political Economy as this discourse is assembled within that episteme.[11] From this purported philosophical difference, then, follows his equally clear disagreement with Marx over the principle that might govern historical narrativization; he radically denies that narratives of history can be assembled at the twin sites of the state and economic production, which he deems to be the exclusive originating sites of Marx's historical narrative.

I shall not examine these rather questionable propositions of Foucault here, because at the moment I am interested only in the form of Foucault's resurfacing in Said's thought. For after disagreeing with Marx on these fundamental premisses, Foucault then goes on to specify both the spatial limits and the temporal constitution of the episteme he is engaged in. He insists that it is a *Western* episteme; about the rest of humanity he makes no claims to knowledge. Second, he locates the constitution of this episteme, historically, in the processes that range from roughly the sixteenth century to the eighteenth. Foucault always sidesteps Marxist terminology, but he knows what he is talking about – namely, that emergence of bourgeois society which runs from the so-called 'primitive' accumulation up to the first Industrial Revolution. With the exception of *Histoire de la folie*, which he finished before working out his philosophical system in what became *The Order of Things* and *The Archaeology of Knowledge* – with the exception of that one book, all the narratives he had assembled before 1978 – especially the one in *Discipline and Punish*, which Said specifically mentions here –

orginate in that crucible of bourgeois beginnings. The episteme is Western *because* it is located in a transition that occurred specifically in Europe, and the narrative of incarceration and surveillance which Foucault assembles and Said invokes is designed, precisely, to demarcate the boundary between the *ancien régime* and the modern.[12]

Said uses Foucauldian terms as discrete elements of an apparatus, but refuses to accept the consequences of Foucault's own mapping of history. If Foucauldian pressures force him to trace the beginnings of 'Orientalist Discourse' from the eighteenth century or so, the equally irresistible pressures of Auerbachean High Humanism force him to trace the origins of this very 'discourse', in the conventional form of a continuous European literary textuality, all the way back to Ancient Greece. In a characteristic move, Said refuses to choose and, as we shall demonstrate below, he offers mutually incompatible definitions of 'Orientalism' so as to deploy both these stances, the Foucauldian and the Auerbachean, *simultaneously*.

Now, the idea that there could be *a* discourse – that is to say, an epistemic construction – traversing the whole breadth of 'Western' history and textualities, spanning not only the modern capitalist period but all the preceding pre-capitalist periods as well, is not only an un-Marxist but also a radically un-Foucauldian idea. The Foucault of *Discipline and Punish* simply would not have accepted that there is any kind of integral relationship between Ancient Greek and modern Western Europe, except that post-Renaissance Europe begins to trace its lineage, in a more or less fantastic manner, from that Antiquity, while reversing most of its prevailing presuppositions. And at that point Foucault never spoke of a full-fledged discourse before the sixteenth century because what he then called 'discourse' presumes, as coextensive corollary, a rationalism of the post-medieval kind, alongside the increasing elaborations of modern state forms, modern institutional grids, objectified economic productions, modern forms of rationalized planning. Said's idea that the ideology of modern imperialist Eurocentrism is already inscribed in the ritual theatre of Greek tragedy – or that Marx's passage on the role of British colonialism in India can be lifted out of the presuppositions of political economy and seamlessly integrated into a transhistorical Orientalist Discourse – is not only ahistorical in the ordinary sense but also specifically anti-Foucauldian in a methodological sense. And from the eighteenth century onwards at least, Said traces the powers and densities of this 'Orientalist Discourse' directly to what Foucault would designate as so many sites of the state – the Napoleonic invasion of Egypt, the French occupation of North Africa, the Anglo–French rivalries in the Levant, and so on – which Foucauldian positions would disqualify as constitutive sites of discourse.

I do not normally agree with most of what I find in Foucault, but I must recognize that he was on such accounts, by and large, careful in his procedures. It is not for nothing that he never constructed the history of any discourse on the basis of master-texts; Freud's psychoanalytic procedure has no privilege in Foucault's thought over the country priest who supervises the Catholic girl's confession. He always distinguishes *discourse* from canonical tradition, from mentality, from institution. His philosophical distinction between *discursive* regularity and *personal* statement, his historiographic preoccupation with specifying the *form* and *boundary* of discourse, his refusal to collapse one discourse into another – the discourse of incarceration into the discourse of sexuality, for example – are fundamental to his thought; the prolixity of his prose stands in direct contrast to the austerity of his boundaries. Said observes none of those austerities.

One of the most rigid boundaries in Foucault's thought was drawn against humanism as such; this he retained until the last few years of his life, when there were some glimmerings of recantation. On this count, most especially, Said's procedures of 1978 are radically anti-Foucauldian and are taken directly from the High Humanist traditions of Comparative Literature and Philology, which have shaped his narrative method as well as his choice of texts. For it is the proposition of this alternative, humanist tradition that (a) there *is* an unified European/Western identity which is at the *origin* of history and has *shaped* this history through its *thought* and its *texts*; (b) this seamless and unified history of European identity and thought runs from Ancient Greece up to the end of the nineteenth century and well into the twentieth, through a specific set of beliefs and values which remain essentially the same, only becoming more dense; and (c) that this history is immanent in – and therefore available for reconstruction through the canon of its *great books*. Said subscribes to the *structure* of this idealist metaphysic even though he obviously questions the greatness of some of those 'great' books. In other words, he duplicates, all those procedures even as he debunks the very tradition from which he has borrowed them. Said's narrative here presumes, as Auerbach presumes, that there *is* a line of continuity between Aeschylus and the modern European; that this sense of continuity was itself fabricated in post-Renaissance Europe is something neither Auerbach nor Said (in *Orientalism*, at any rate) would question. Like Auerbach, Said is preoccupied with the canonical author, with tradition, with sequential periodization. Auerbach *finds* humanist value in those books, Said finds only a lack; but both look for the same values, in the same books – or at least, the same *kind* of books. Said denounces with Foucauldian vitriol what he loves with Auerbachian passion, so that the reader soon begins to detect a very *personal* kind of drama being enacted in Said's procedure of alternately debunking and praising to the skies and again debunking the same book, as if he had been betrayed by the objects of his passion.

This way of alternating between inordinate praise and wholesale rejection was to endure far beyond *Orientalism*. As an example of a more recent exercise of this procedure we could cite the essay on Kipling,[13] where the criticisms of Kipling which Said offers are unsurprising since he only repeats – without acknowledgement, of course – what has been said often enough by numerous critics on the Left. But those familiar criticisms are then combined with surprisingly high and unwarranted praise for Kipling as a 'master stylist' so 'great', we are told, that

> as an artist he can justifiably be compared with Hardy, with Henry James, Meredith, Gissing, the later George Eliot, George Moore, Samuel Butler. In France, Kipling's peers are Flaubert and Zola, even Proust and the early Gide.

The list of novels with which *Kim* is then solemnly compared includes *Sentimental Education*, *The Portrait of a Lady*, and *The Way of All Flesh*. It is not entirely clear why a minor novel, which owed its wide circulation only to colonial currency, has to be thus elevated – and made worthy of the attack – before being knocked down.

The issue of trying to reconcile Auerbach with Foucault is indicative, in any case, of a whole range of problems that are at once methodological and conceptual as well as political. For Said's work is self-divided not only between Auerbachean High Humanism and Nietzschean anti-humanism (I will take up the issue of Nietzsche later) but also between a host of irreconcilable positions in cultural theory generally, from the most radical to the most reactionary, ranging all the way from Gramsci to Julien Benda, with Lukács, Croce and Matthew Arnold in between. I should like to illustrate this with some comments on Benda, whom Said has often praised as one of the examplary intellectuals of this century. That Benda, a man possessed by notions of High Aesthetics, should come in for that kind of praise is perhaps not entirely surprising, given Said's original training, his preference for High Canonicity, and the aestheticist claim of being located beyond all 'isms'. What is far more surprising is Said's habit of equating Benda with Gramsci – which is, I suppose, one way of domesticating the revolutionary content of Gramsci's thought.

One does not have to read far into *Treason of the Intellectuals*[14] to see (a) that the 'treason' of which Benda speaks is none other than the intellectuals' participation in what he calls 'the political passions'; and (b) that 'class passions' and 'racial passions' are for him among the worst, so that 'anti-semitism' and 'socialism' are said to be equally diabolical, while 'the working classes who, even in the middle of the nineteenth century, felt only a scattered hostility for the opposing class' are castigated because in Benda's own time (the 1920s) 'they form a closely-woven fabric of hatred from one end of Europe to another' (pp. 3–5). He then goes on to denounce dozens – literally dozens – of intellectuals, from all ages but especially from the modern age, who, in his opinion,

> have not been content simply to adopt passions. . . . They permit, they desire, them to be mingled with their work as artists, as men of learning, as philosophers, to color the essence of their work and to mark all its productions. And indeed never were there so many political works among those which *ought to be the mirror of the disinterested intelligence*. (p. 67; emphasis added)

There is thus boundless denunciation of all politics, especially socialist politics, in the name of the 'disinterested intelligence'; even poor Michelangelo is denounced for 'crying shame upon Leonardo da Vinci for his indifference to the misfortunes of Florence', while 'the master of the Last Supper' is commended for replying 'that indeed the study of beauty occupied his whole heart' (p. 47). One of Said's many laudatory comments on Benda runs, in turn, as follows:

> Certainly what Benda says about intellectuals (who, in ways specific to the intellectual vocation itself, are responsible for defiance) resonates harmoniously with the personality of Socrates as it emerges in Plato's *Dialogues*, or with Voltaire's opposition to the Church, or more recently with Gramsci's notion of the organic intellectual allied with the emergent class against ruling class hegemony. . . . It is also the case, both Benda and Gramsci agree, that intellectuals are eminently useful in making hegemony work. For Benda this of course is the *trahison des clercs* in its essence; their unseemly participation in the perfection of political passions is what he thinks is despairingly the very essence of their contemporary mass sell-out.[15]

The inflationary invocations of Socrates, Voltaire and Gramsci do not really help to clarify what Said really means here, even as he ends with that Orwellian phrase 'contemporary mass sell-out'. Gramsci, surely, means little if we subtract from his legacy his 'political passion' for precisely the kind of working-class politics which Benda describes as 'a closely-woven fabric of hatred from one end of Europe to another'. And so fundamental is the tie in Benda's thought between anti-communism and a general hatred of the working class on the one hand, and 'the disinterested intelligence' and the 'study of beauty' on the other, that only a very conservative mind, essentially Tory in its structure, would want to think of him as an exemplary intellectual. But then a mind of that kind would not normally want to associate itself with Gramsci. It is an index of Said's self-division that he would think of Benda, the rabid anti-communist, and Gramsci, one of the more persevering communists of the century, as occupying essentially the same theoretico-political position.[16] And it is the listing of revolutionaries like Gramsci (in the more recent work such lists would grow very lengthy indeed) which conceals how very traditionally literary-critical Said's thought actually is.

## II

What is equally striking, as one looks back on the passage I quoted above, with a quotation from Gramsci embedded in it, is Said's own formulation – 'In many ways my study of Orientalism has been an attempt to inventory the traces upon me, the Oriental subject' – which summarizes more or less accurately what the book is about, especially if we take literally the idea that the phrase 'inventory of traces upon me' refers here to Said's own quite specific grounding in – and ambivalent relationship with – the very body of knowledge which *Orientalism* interrogates. The significant move here, in any case, is Said's self-description as 'the Oriental subject'. Such self-representations are always somewhat one-sided, and therefore somewhat hazardous, for anyone whose own cultural apparatus is so overwhelmingly European and who commands such an authoritative presence in the American university. The irony of such usages in Said's case are all the greater because any careful reading of the *whole* of his work would show how strategically he deploys words like 'we' and 'us', to refer, in various contexts, to Palestinians, Third World intellectuals, academics in general, humanists, Arabs, Arab-Americans, and the American citizenry at large.[17] More to the point, in any case, are the inflations that were soon to follow, on the heels of *Orientalism*. The cursory phrase 'the Oriental subject' was then to be revamped in a number of radicalist strands in subsequent literary theory as 'the colonial subject' and, yet later, as 'the post-colonial subject'; Said's own highly tendentious uses of these latter terms will be discussed below, when I come to his schematic characterization of C.L.R James and George Antonius as the emblematic 'colonial' intellectuals, of S.H. Alatas and Ranajit Guha as the exemplary 'post-colonial' ones. The idea of the 'inventory of traces', eloquent and legitimate in itself, was to be inflated – by Fredric Jameson among others – into the idea that Third World societies are *constituted* by the experience of colonialism and imperialism. Now, the notion of a 'colonial subject' – or 'post-colonial subject', for that matter – *presumes*, of course, that we are indeed constituted by colonialism; then, in quick succession, by post-coloniality; if we are not *constituted* by colonialism, then the term 'colonial subject' is theoretically meaningless.

The original Gramscian idea of an 'inventory of traces' presumes that there is a personality, a cultural location, upon which those traces are inscribed; it presumes that there are other 'traces' into which *these* traces are woven, so that the personality that emerges out of this weave, this overlap, is conditioned not by a specific set of traces but by the whole of its history.

What this original Gramscian idea could mean, for example, is that the Italian cultural formation cannot be read back from fascism or the Risorgimento or even the failure of the Reformation – hence the unfinished character of the Italian Renaissance; that it would have to be traced all the way back, historically, to the very moment of the ascendancy of the High Church and of High Latin as the language of that Church, as well as from the histories of subordinations following thereafter; in other words, histories, and therefore subjectivities, are constituted not by what Gramsci calls 'moments' but by the always-accumulating processes of sedimentation and accretion. In relation to India, then, this original Gramscian formulation would mean, at the very least, that colonialism was doubtless a key 'moment' – even, in some specific areas, a decisive 'moment' – but the history of sedimentations which *constitutes* the Indian cultural formation includes much besides colonialism *per se*. I clarify this point here in order to emphasize that there is at least one major strand of literary theory which has developed under Said's influence – 'Colonial Discourse Analysis' – which is notable for its *separation* of the 'inventory of colonial traces' from other sorts of inventories, other sorts of traces. This, too, fits – not only in the sense that if we *are* constituted by colonialism, then the only discourse that really matters is the discourse of the colonialist, but also because of the example that Edward Said himself had set in his book.

A notable feature of *Orientalism* is that it examines the history of Western textualities about the non-West quite in isolation from how these textualities might have been received, accepted, modified, challenged, overthrown or reproduced by the intelligentsias of the colonized countries: not as an undifferentiated mass but as situated social agents impelled by our own conflicts, contradictions, distinct social and political locations, of class, gender, region, religious affiliation, and so on – hence a peculiar disjuncture in the architecture of the book. One of its major complaints is that from Aeschylus onwards the West has never permitted the Orient to represent itself; *it* has represented the Orient. I shall discuss that peculiar vision of human history below. But what is remarkable is that with the exception of Said's own voice, the only voices we encounter in the book are precisely those of the very Western canonicity which, Said complains, has always silenced the Orient. Who is silencing whom, who is refusing to permit a historicized encounter between the voice of the so-called

'Orientalist' and the many voices that 'Orientalism' is said so utterly to suppress, is a question that is very hard to determine as we read this book. It sometimes appears that one is transfixed by the power of the very voice that one debunks.

I comment below on the specific generic qualities of *Orientalism*, and then somewhat later on the conjuncture in the intellectual history of the Anglo-American academy, which, together, largely account for the book's power and reach. I must emphasize, though, that the modalities of its influence were by no means uniform. If it encouraged some to cultivate an academic kind of nationalist radicalism and very textual attitudes towards histories of colonialism and imperialism, it also enabled numerous younger academics, who had already been politicized through some other route, to arrive at new modes and areas of inquiry, mainly in the literary field. Much work was appearing at the time which had a very similar thrust,[18] but Said managed to construct a larger and more inclusive narrative, across distinct discursive fields and combining a large number of texts, to demonstrate continuities among diverse authors and the underlying mentalities. It was the book's narrative amplitude which turned out to be its most enabling quality, regardless of its principal theses. Part of the pleasure of *Orientalism* – which caused anxiety in some circles, excitement in others – was its trangression of academic boundaries. Attacks on Said on this count were numerous – augmented, two years after this prolonged orchestration, by Bernard Lewis himself, one of the doyens of Zionist historiography. His attack was unseemly on many counts, but the substantive point which Lewis raised was one of competence. What authorized Said to speak of Arab history and Orientalist disciplines? What degrees did he have? Did he know such-and-such a medieval Arabic dictionary? Did he know the meaning of such-and-such a word in the whole range of Arabic lexicography over ten centuries? Etc.[19] (In his elegant rejoinder, Said quite rightly ignored the issue of competence and authorization, while concentrating on the issue that had gone unacknowledged in Lewis's attack: namely, that Lewis's scholarly pretence was itself a camouflage for Zionist allegiance.)

*Orientalism* was clearly not a book of Middle Eastern Studies, or of any established academic discipline, but it did belong to the well-known intellectual tradition of writers debunking the great monuments of their own academic discipline or examining the complicity of intellectuals in dominant ideologies and fabrications of illegitimate power. This tradition includes such disparate writers and works as Nietzsche himself, Paul Nizan's *The Watchdogs*, Césaire's *Discourse on Colonialism*, Fanon's *Black Skins, White Masks*, Erskine Caldwell's *Notes on a Dying Culture*, a great deal of feminist writings since Kate Millett's *Sexual Politics*, and Noam Chomsky's extensive writings on the complicity of American social science in the Vietnam War. In the field of literature itself there had not, of course, been the kind of systematization that Said offers here, but there is, even within the Anglo-American tradition, actually a very *large* body of work which has previously analysed Western canonical authors and their complicity in Western colonial enterprises and ideologies. This question had been posed quite widely throughout the American and British universities, especially since the beginning of the Vietnam War, not to speak of France, where the issue had been posed even earlier, in fields as diverse as literature and anthropology, thanks also to wars of liberation both in Indochina and Algeria.

In the literary part of its undertaking, which is doubtless the largest part of the book, *Orientalism* thus belongs to a well-known lineage. If we subtract the terminological and stylistic shifts, which often regulate our impressions of novelty and originality, Said's readings of individual authors and literary texts in the impressive middle sections are politically not much more far-reaching than the kinds of readings that were common during the 1960s, such as those Jonah Raskin offers in *The Mythology of Imperialism*.[20] And if one steps out of the Euro-American traditions, one is struck by the fact that neither the architecture of *Orientalism* nor the kind of knowledge the book generally represents has any room in it for criticisms of colonial cultural domination of the kind that have been available in Latin America and even India, on an expanding scale, since the late nineteenth century. In fact, it is one of the disagreeable surprises in *Orientalism* that it refuses to acknowledge that vast tradition, virtually as old as colonialism itself, which has existed in the colonized countries as well as among the metropolitan Left traditions, and has always been occupied, precisely, with drawing up an inventory of colonial traces in the minds of people on both sides of the colonial divide.

I am not very keen on the matter of originality myself, except that when Said does return to this matter of what he might have owed to earlier critiques of colonialism and its cultural consequences for the colonies, in the well-known essay '*Orientalism* Reconsidered',[21] he deploys a characteristically contradictory rhetoric. The dominant strain in this essay is one of royal contempt, whereby all such efforts of the past are consigned to the dustbin of an undifferentiated 'historicism' which is itself declared to be twin as well as progenitor of imperialism as such. Thus, after debunking a loosely constructed geneaology which he calls 'historicism, that is, the view pronounced by Vico, Hegel, Marx, Ranke, Dilthey and others',[22] Said proceeds to posit the following:

> What, in other words, has never taken place is an epistemological critique at the most fundamental level of the connection between the development of a historicism which has expanded and developed enough to include antithetical attitudes such as ideologies of Western imperialism and critiques of imperialism on the one hand, and, on the other, the actual practice of imperialism . . .

All previous 'critiques of imperialism' are thus effortlessly conjoined with 'the actual practice of imperialism', thanks to the historicist contamination. So much for the intellectual capacities of national liberation struggles, which have often used at least the Marxist critiques of imperialism, not to speak of Gramsci's own historicism, which Said often likes to invoke!

I must confess, though, that Said's irrepressible penchant for saying entirely contrary things in the same text, appealing to different audiences simultaneously but with the effect that each main statement cancels out the other, is in evidence in this essay as much as anywhere else. The sweeping statement which I have just quoted stands in a curiously unresolved relationship with the following, which we also find in this same essay:

> At bottom, what I said in *Orientalism* had been said before me by A.L. Tibawi (1961, 1966), by Abdullah Laroui (1976, 1977), by Anwar Abdel Malek (1963, 1969), Talal Asad (1973), by S.H. Alatas (1977a, 1977b), by Fanon (1969, 1970) and Césaire (1972), by Panikkar (1959) and Romila Thapar (1975, 1978).

The most sweeping claim of originality is thus balanced against disclaimer of all originality; the most uncompromising attack on historicism is balanced against a list of authors several among whom would have little difficulty in associating themselves with historicism. The list of authors and dates is itself passing strange, I might add, since it is drawn up in the manner, more or less, of the postmodern pastiche. Tibawi, Laroui and Abdel Malek probably appear here because Robert Irwin, in his review of *Orientalism*,[23] had also raised the issue of Said's unacknowledged debts and had cited precisely these three writers. Then, as one turns to Said's actual citations of Romila Thapar, one finds that the only publications of hers that he cites are the two textbooks on ancient and medieval India which she wrote, very much on the side, for middle-school pupils. The idea that Thapar's seminal work on Indian history is to be known only through her little textbooks is somewhat breathtaking. As for his other reference to an Indian writer in this list, the whole range of Said's citations – and he *is* copious in this matter – seems to suggest that the only significant book by an Indian writer that had come his way until well after he had published *Orientalism* in 1978 was, precisely, K.M. Pannikar's good old *Asia and Western Dominance*.

Apart from the unclassifiability of genre, meanwhile, *Orientalism* had been notable also for the sweep of its contents. So majestic was this sweep, in fact, that few readers initially noticed that most of Said's references in the more substantial parts of the book were drawn from his training in comparative literature and philology. This was familiar territory for people of similar background, but those were precisely the people who were the most likely to resist the invitation to read this body of writing *not* as literature but as documents of an entirely different sort of archive, namely the *Orientalist* archive, which *they* had thought was none of their business. The Mid-East expert, on the other hand, *into* whose archive those other kinds of texts were being read, was equally displeased and bewildered, because this expert was being attacked, but with no possibility of defending himself on what he had defined as his home ground – the ground of libraries, the comparison of medieval texts, the labour of deciphering illegible manuscripts, the problems of establishing authentic texts and preparing the appropriate gloss, the learning of archaic languages, and bringing back the fruits of this labour for the enlightenment and edification of the public at large. He was, in his own eyes, a specialist, an innocent. As we well know, the effect in these fields, that of literature and of Middle Eastern studies, was electrifying, because the book did serve to open up, despite its blunders, spaces of oppositional work in both. Meanwhile, for scholars working outside the academic fields of Comparative Literature, Philology and Orientalism, the contents of the book, the sort of documents it read, were largely unfamiliar in any case. That was novelty enough. But what was even more novel was, decidedly, Said's audacity of combination. Who, after all, had ever thought that Lamartine and Olivia Manning, Chateaubriand and Byron, Carlyle, Camus, Voltaire, Gertrude Bell, the anonymous composers of *El Cid* and the *Chanson de Roland*, Arabists like Gibb, colonial rulers such as Cromer and Balfour, sundry quasi-literary figures like Edward Lane, scholars of Sufism like Massignon, Henry Kissinger – all belonged in the same archive and composed a deeply unified discursive formation! What was new, I must repeat, was the *combination*, the reach of erudition, the architecture of the book, the eloquence that went with it, even though this eloquence, too, had the tendency to be frightfully repetitive at times.

What had happened in the past was that critics who had raised these issues with reference to modern British literature rarely knew much about nineteenth-century French literature, and those who wrote about literature would rarely examine lexicography or the US State Department, even though the imperialist design would often be at issue. Said assembled these varied strands into a single narrative line, and the sense of novelty in American and British universities – and therefore also in the Anglophone ex-colonies – was greatly enhanced by the fact that the most impressive part of the book – its middle section, where Said offers readings of individual authors – was preoccupied mainly with *French* writers. The book may not have added much to our knowledge of Edward Lane or Olivia Manning, T.E. Lawrence or Henry Kissinger, but its treatment of the Bibliothèque Nationale and Chateaubriand, Nerval and Flaubert, was surely unforgettable.

Finally, the most striking novelty of *Orientalism*, which gave it its essential prestige in avant-gardist cultural theory, was methodological: not simply its wide borrowing from the constituted academic disciplines but, far more crucially, its explicit invocation of Foucault, its declaration that the object of this study, namely Orientalism, was a *discourse*, and its insistence that this was the constitutive discourse of Western civilization as such – both chronologically, in the sense that we find it there already in the oldest European textualities, and also civilizationally, since it is by defining the 'Orient' as the dangerous, inferiorized civilizational Other that Europe has defined itself. There were two distinct consequences of this novelty. One was obviously the shift from Marx to Foucault, which was clearly very congenial to the postmodernist moment. The irrefutable fact about the period before Said's intervention is that apart from the more obscurantist and indigenist kinds of anti-Westernist protests against European influence, the vast majority of the socially enlightened and politically progressive critiques of colonialism had been affiliated with either Marxism or, at least, with the general cultural anti-imperialism which Marxism, and the communist movement generally, had helped to bring about. Said's break with that political tradition was sweeping indeed. Marx himself was dismissed in the book as yet another Orientalist, Marxism was swept aside as an unsavoury child of 'historicism', and the insights which had originally emanated from that tradition were now conjoined with Foucauldian Discourse Theory.

All this fell in very nicely, as the book appeared in 1978 and began its career in a world supervised by Reagan and Thatcher, with various kinds of anti-communisms and post-Marxisms which were to grip the most advanced sectors of the metropolitan intelligentsia during the period. Alongside these large theoretical and political shifts was the matter of a certain transhistoricity which, in claiming that Europe establishes its own Identity by establishing the *Difference* of the Orient, and that Europe has possessed, since the days of Athenian drama, a unitary will to inferiorize and vanquish non-Europe, made it possible for Said to assert that *all* European knowledges of non-Europe are bad knowledges because they are already contaminated with this aggressive Identity-formation. This, indeed, was a novel idea. Numerous writers had previously demonstrated the complicity of European cultural productions in the colonial enterprise, but only the most obscurantist indigenists and cultural nationalists had previously argued – surely, no writer with any sense of intellectual responsibility had ever accepted – that Europeans were *ontologically* incapable of producing any true knowledge about non-Europe. But Said was emphatic on this point, and he mobilized all sorts of eclectic procedures to establish it.

## III

This issue of eclecticism should take us back into the text, starting with the very opening pages where Said offers not one but three – mutually incompatible – definitions of the term 'Orientalism' itself, which he then tries to deploy, simultaneously, throughout the book. In his own words, first:

> Anyone who teaches, writes about, or researches the Orient – and this applies whether the person is an anthropologist, sociologist, historian, or philologist – either in its specific or in its general aspects, is an Orientalist, and what he or she does is Orientalism. (p. 2)

In this sense, then, Orientalism is an interdisciplinary area of academic knowledge, and the terms used here – anthropology, philology, etc. – would suggest that it is a *modern* discipline. But then, in the second definition, it becomes something much more, far exceeding academic boundaries – indeed, a mentality traversing a great many centuries, if not a full-scale epistemology:

> Orientalism is a style of thought based upon an ontological and epistemological distinction made between 'the Orient' and (most of the time) 'the Occident'. . . . *This* Orientalism can accommodate Aeschylus, say, and Victor Hugo, Dante and Karl Marx. (p. 3)

We shall return to the difficulties of this particular inflation, and then to the matter of 'Dante and Karl Marx', at very considerable length later, but let me cite the third definition:

> Taking the late eighteenth century as a very roughly defined starting point Orientalism can be discussed and analyzed as the corporate institution for dealing with the Orient . . . in short, Orientalism as a Western style for dominating, restructuring, and having authority over the Orient. (p. 3)

These three definitions come on two consecutive pages, and Aeschylus and Dante are in fact mentioned as examples of the Orientalist 'style of thought' five lines before the eighteenth century is identified, in the third definition, as the 'roughly defined starting point'. Now, the demarcation of boundaries at the eighteenth century – and at the 'post-Enlightenment period' a few lines later – produces one kind of emphasis; but the naming of Aeschylus produces a very different sense of periodization, which itself goes back to the opening paragraph where we had been told, in the third sentence, that 'The Orient was almost a European invention, and had been since antiquity a place of romance . . . ' When, then, *did* this discourse of Orientalism begin? Nor is this issue of periodization a minor matter. Later on, we find this crucial statement:

> Consider first the demarcation between Orient and West. It already seems bold by the time of the *Iliad*. Two of the most profoundly influential qualities associated with the East appear in Aeschylus' *The Persians*, the earliest Athenian play extant, and in *The Bacchae* of Euripedes, the last one extant. . . . What matters here is that Asia speaks through and by virtue of the European imagination, which is depicted as victorious over Asia, that hostile 'other' world beyond the seas. To Asia are given the feeling of emptiness, loss, and disaster that seem thereafter to reward Oriental challenges to the West; and also the lament that in some glorious past Asia fared better . . .
>
> The two aspects of the Orient that set it off from the West in this pair of plays will remain essential motifs of European imaginative geography. A line is drawn between two continents. Europe is powerful and articulate; Asia is defeated and distant. Aeschylus *represents* Asia. . . . It is Europe that articulates the Orient; this articulation is the prerogative, not of a puppet master, but of a genuine creator, whose life-giving power represents, animates, constitutes the otherwise silent and dangerous space beyond familiar boundaries . . . (pp. 56–7)

The 'Orientalist discourse' has already been set in motion, then, in the earliest of the Athenian tragedies, not in general but in the specific regularities which will henceforth determine its structure: Asia's loss, Europe's victory; Asia's muteness, Europe's mastery of discourse; Asia's inability to represent itself, Europe's will to represent it in accordance with its own authority. The terms are set, and there is little that later centuries will contribute to the *essential* structure, though they will doubtless proliferate the discourse in enormous quantities. As Said puts it: 'It is as if, having once settled on the Orient as a locale suitable for incarnating the infinite in a finite shape, Europe could not stop the practice' (p.62). And: 'Only the source of these rather narcissistic Western ideas about the Orient changed in time, not their character.' This sense of an *uninterrupted* history of 'narcissistic' discourse is then made more dense with the discussion of figures like Dante, who form a kind of bridge between ancient origins and modern repetitions, as I shall clarify presently when I come to discuss Said's treatment of the *Inferno*.

Now, if there really is only this seamless and incremental history of 'Orientalist Discourse' from Aeschylus to Dante to Marx to Bernard Lewis, then in what sense could one take the eighteenth century 'as a roughly defined starting point'? In other words, one does not really know whether 'Orientalist Discourse' begins in the post-Enlightenment period or at the dawn of European civilization, whether in the period of the Battle of Plassey or in the days of the Battle of Troy. This, then, raises the question of the relationship between Orientalism and colonialism. In one sort of reading, where post-Enlightenment Europe is emphasized, Orientalism appears to be an ideological corollory of colonialism. But so insistent is Said in identifying its origins in European Antiquity and its increasing elaboration throughout the European Middle Ages that it seems to be the *constituting element*, transhistorically, of what he calls 'the European imagination'. In a revealing use of the word 'delivered', Said remarks at one point that Orientalism *delivered* the Orient to colonialism, so that colonialism begins to appear as a product of Orientalism itself – indeed, as the realization of the project already inherent in Europe's perennial project of inferiorizing the Orient first in discourse and *then* in colonization. This is, of course, doubly paradoxical, since Said is vehement in his criticism of 'Orientalism' for its highly 'textual' attitude, yet in his own account imperialist ideology itself appears to be an effect mainly of cetain kinds of *writing*.

But *why* has Europe needed to constitute – 'produce' is Said's stark word – the Orient as 'that hostile *other* world'; to 'animate', as he puts it, 'the otherwise silent and dangerous space' as 'one of its deepest and most recurring images of the Other' (p.1)? Well, because 'European culture gained in strength and identity by setting itself off against the Orient as a sort of surrogate and even underground self' (p. 3). There are many passages of this kind, and Said borrows his language from so many different kinds of conceptual frameworks and intellectual disciplines that one is simply bewildered.[24] There is, for example, enough existentialism in Said's language, derived from identifiable Sartrean concepts, which stands in a peculiar relation with Derridean ideas of Identity and Difference, all of which is mobilized to posit in some places that the West has *needed* to constitute the Orient as its Other in order to constitute itself and its own subject position. This idea of constituting Identity through Difference points, again, not to the realm of political economy – nor to those other social materialities of a non-discursive kind – wherein colonization may be seen as a process of capitalist accumulation, but to a necessity which arises within discourse and has always been there at the origin of discourse, so that not only is the modern Orientalist presumably already there in Dante and Euripides but modern imperialism itself appears to be an effect that arises, as if naturally, from the necessary practices of discourse.[25]

That is one sort of difficulty. But there is also another – namely, that the matter of Identity-through-Difference doubtless points to the primacy of representation over all other human activities. But why must representation also *inferiorize* the Other? Said again offers greatly diverse ideas, so that in quite a few places this inferiorization is shown to be a result of imperialism and colonialism in the sense in which most of us would understand these words, but in another set of formulations, which draw their vocabulary from psychoanalysis, 'the West' seems to have suffered something resembling ego-anxiety, whereby the ego is able to constitute its own coherence only through aggressive objectification of the Other, so that what Said calls 'Orientalism' appears to be a compulsive drive inherent in Europe's unitary *psyche*. When one comes upon statements like 'Psychologically, Orientalism is a form of paranoia' (p. 72), as one frequently does, there is reason enough to be disconcerted by the psychologizing impulse but, even more, one then shudders to recall that, for Said, this 'paranoia' is constitutive of all European thought. These ways of dismissing entire civilizations as diseased formations are unfortunately far too familiar to us, who live on the other side of the colonial divide, from the history of imperialism itself.

But let us return to the three definitions, especially the intermediate one which defines Orientalism as 'a style of thought based upon an ontological and epistemological distinction between "the Orient" and (most of the time) the Occident'. It is rather remarkable how constantly and comfortably Said speaks – not only in this particular sentence but throughout the book – of *a* Europe, or the West, as a self-identical, fixed being which has always had an essence and a project, an imagination and a will; and of the 'Orient' as its object – textually, militarily, and so on. He speaks of the West, or Europe, as the one which produces the knowledge, the East as the object of that knowledge. In other words, he seems to posit, stable subject–object identities, as well as ontological and epistemological distinctions between the two. In what sense, then, is Said himself *not* an Orientalist – or at least, as Sadek el-Azm puts it, an 'Orientalist-in-reverse'?[26] Said quite justifiably accuses the 'Orientalist' of essentializing the Orient, but his own essentializing of 'the West' is equally remarkable. In the process, Said of course gives us that same 'Europe' – unified, self-identical, transhistorical, textual – which is always rehearsed for us in the sort of literary criticism which traces its own pedigree from Aristotle to T.S. Eliot. That this Athens-to-Albion Europe is itself a recent fabrication, as a whole range of writers from Amin[27] to Bernal[28] have recently emphasized, and that *any* Aeschylus-to-Kissinger narrative is therefore also equally a fabrication (or a fabricated reflection of a prior fabrication), is something that does not seem to have occurred to Said.[29] The plain fact is that whatever Homer or Aeschylus might have had to say about the Persians or Asia, it simply is *not* a reflection of a 'West' or of 'Europe' as a civilizational entity, in a recognizably modern sense, and no modern discourse can be traced back to that origin, because the civilizational map and geographical imagination of Antiquity were fundamentally different from those that came to be fabricated in post-Renaissance Europe. Parenthetically, we might emphasize again that Said does *not* say that 'Orientalist' notions have beeen read *into* Greek and Latin texts; that the main regularities of the discourse are *already there* is central to his whole argument.

It is also simply the case that the kind of essentializing procedure which Said associates exclusively with 'the West' is by no means a trait of the European alone; any number of Muslims routinely draw epistemological and ontological distinctions between East and West, the Islamicate and Christendom, and when Ayatollah Khomeini did it he hardly did so from an Orientalist position. And of course, it is common practice among many circles in India to posit Hindu spirituality against Western materialism, not to speak of Muslim barbarity. Nor is it possible to read the *Mahabharata* or the *dharmshastras* without being struck by the severity with which the *dasyus* and the *shudras* and the women are constantly being made into the dangerous, inferiorized Others. This is no mere polemical matter, either. What I am suggesting is that there have historically been all sorts of processes – connected with class and gender, ethnicity and religion, xenophobia and bigotry – which have unfortunately been at work in all human societies, both European and non-European. What gave European forms of these prejudices their special force in history, with devastating consequences for the actual lives of countless millions and expressed ideologically in full-blown Eurocentric racisms, was not some transhistorical process of ontological obsession and falsity – some gathering of unique force in domains of discourse – but, quite specifically, the power of colonial capitalism, which then gave rise to other sorts of powers. Within the realm of discourse over the past two hundred years, though, the relationship between the Brahminical and the Islamic high textualities, the Orientalist knowledges of these textualities, and their modern reproductions in Western as well as non-Western countries have produced such a wilderness of mirrors that we need the most incisive of operations, the most delicate of dialectics, to disaggregate these densities.

Said's penchant for foregrounding the literariness of this so-called discourse gives rise to yet another kind of problem when he defines Orientalism, in his third definition, as 'a Western style for dominating, restructuring, and having authority over the Orient'. The surprising word, but also the key word, here is *style* – which should save us from supposing that he might be talking about the political economy or ideological constructs of colonialism and imperialism. For he says, quite directly:

> Orientalism is not a mere political subject matter or field that is reflected passively by culture, scholarship, or institution; . . . nor is it representative and expressive of some nefarious 'Western' imperialist plot to hold down the 'Oriental' world. (p.12)

So we have at least some clue as to what Orientalism is *not*: it is not what is commonly understood by colonialist – or imperialist – *ideology*. In the process, though, we come upon a strange discrepancy: it is a 'style' that has always spoken of Occident and Orient as victor and vanquished, a discourse which has always had a will to power, but expresses no imperialist design; it is full of racism, jingoism, religious bigotry, but it has no will to 'hold down' anybody. It is hard to know, therefore, what Said actually *means* – beyond, of course, the familiar Foucauldian trope of a Power which permeates everything and reproduces itself copiously in all the pores of society and textuality but has no origin, no object, even no agency. Meanwhile, Said does give us some clues as to what this book, *Orientalism*, is, and how he wishes us to read it, yet these clues tend to cancel each other out:

> My analysis of the Orientalist text therefore places emphasis on the evidence, which is by no means invisible, for such representations *as representations*. . . . The things to look at are style, figures of speech, setting, narrative devices, historical and social circumstances, *not* the correctness of the representation nor its fidelity to some great original.

The notable feature of this approach is Said's desire to combine very familiar emphases in literary-critical ways of reading ('style, figures of speech, setting, narrative devices, historical and social circumstances') with a postmodernist emphasis on 'representations *as representations*'. One of those ways of reading presses us towards the problematic of realism and mimesis, the other in the direction of non-mimetic, discursive 'truth-effects'. It would be unimaginably difficult, if not altogether pointless, I should have thought, to refer a representation to its 'setting' and 'the historical and social circumstances' of its production and dissemination without raising, in some fundamental way, the issues of its 'fidelity' and 'correctness', for, it is usually with reference to 'historical and social circumstances' that worthwhile distinctions between a representation and a *mis*representation are customarily made. I shall take up elsewhere this crucial issue of the primacy of representation, as well as Said's inability to make up his mind whether 'Orientalist Discourse' is a system of representations, in the Foucauldian sense, or of *mis*representations, in the sense of a realist problematic. For Said's deployment of this self-divided procedure leads to a great many theoretical difficulties and political confusions which are then frequently replicated and even simplified in what has come to be known as 'Colonial Discourse Analysis'. Let me say, meanwhile, that it is in the midst of all these difficulties – of definition, conception, periodization, theoretical position and political uncertainty – that Said then launches on his reading of individual authors, most of whom turn out to be the familiar canonical authors.

Many of these individual readings – of Nerval, for example, or T.E. Lawrence – are very good. One can actually say with fair certainty that with the exception of those two magnificent opening chapters in *The Question of Palestine*, where Said has handled extremely broad and complex issues altogether superbly, he still tends to be at his best when he is reading (closely) an individual canonical author, interpreting a particular canonical book, or at most preparing a focused critique of determinate issues in a particular academic discipline, such as anthropology, which has already sustained a great many trenchant critiques from which he can then borrow in distinctive ways.[30] When he exercises this skill at his best, few living literary critics can match him, for he learned this skill of close reading in the pedagogical laboratory of 'New Criticism'; has applied it in the wider and even more exacting field of comparatism; and now exercises it with wit, erudition, persuasive prose style, and liberal leanings. This skill is his achievement – but a limitation, too. For when he is at his weakest, such readings of individual authors can also be merely derivative or trite – as, for example, in his essay on *Kim*. The one on Jane Austen's *Mansfield Park* is better,[31] but Said's difficulties with the issue of gender are such that he can scarcely see the precarious ways in which women of (and around) the British propertied classes, who were doubtless complicitly benefiting from designs of empire, are nevertheless differentially located in mobilities and pedagogies of the class structure. Those, however, are difficulties of a different kind. In *Orientalism* itself, the greatest difficulties occur when Said tries to fit rather complex matters into the unilinear 'Orientalist' mode. I should like to illustrate this with some lengthier comment on his treatment of just one author: Dante.

## IV

The transition that Said makes to Dante is *strategic* on at least two counts: Dante is the central, exemplary figure forming the bridge between Antiquity and modernity and, 'Dante's powers as a poet intensify, make more rather than less representative, these perspectives on the Orient' (p. 69). The theme of transhistorical continuity is stated unequivocally:

> . . . as one surveys Orientalism in the nineteenth and twentieth centuries the overriding impression is of Orientalism's insensitive schematization of the entire Orient.
>
> How early this schematization began is clear from the examples I have given of Western representations of the Orient in classical Greece. How strongly articulated were later representations building on the earlier ones, how inordinately careful their schematization, how dramatically effective their placing in Western imaginative geography, can be illustrated if we turn now to Dante's *Inferno*. (p. 68)

There is thus an incremental history ('later representations building on the earlier ones'), 'inordinately careful' in its 'schematization', which joins the nineteenth and twentieth centuries with Dante and 'classical Greece'. Said is absolutely right, of course, in regarding the *Inferno* as a book mainly of *judgements*, and his initial comment on the poem turns, then, on Dante's treatment of Muhammad. This is predictable and unsurprising; Said is hardly the first to have noticed the inordinate horror of that passage. What is truly surprising is the way he deals with Dante's far more complex treatment of – in Said's words – 'the great Muslim philosophers and kings'.

Now, few readers of *Inferno* would find it possible to forget that Muhammad, the Prophet of Islam, is found in the eighth of the nine circles of Hell, eternally gyrating and eternally being cleft from brain to anus, in the worst punishment Dante's prolific imagination could devise. This treatment of the Prophet of Islam is, to put it mildly, indefensible, and I am entirely in sympathy with Said when he takes offence. The peculiarity, in any case, is that Ibn Sina ('Avicenna' in English, the Arab-Islamic philosopher best known for his expertise in empiricist physiology and medicine), Ibn Rushd ('Averroës' in English, the great Arab-Islamic philosopher of rationalist humanism), and Salah ad-Din (the 'Saladin' made famous by the Crusades), are found in the *first* Circle, in the company of such 'virtuous pagans' as Homer, Socrates and Plato. Now, the presence of those figures from Greek Antiquity in this mildest of all circles of Hell makes a certain sense within the Christian topography of punishments and sufferings, because they are heathens only to the extent that they came before Christ and therefore never had the benefit of Christ's teaching; this also explains the otherwise surprising decision on the part of Beatrice to appoint Virgil, himself a heathen, as Dante's guide on this eventful tour. But why Ibn Rushd? *He* came *after* Christ, and therefore had the choice of renouncing the Islamic heresy, but didn't! Dante never faces up to this question, and is benign towards Ibn Rushd ('of the Great Commentary', he specifies) despite this key difference between him and Socrates & Co. One grasps the full force of this discrepancy only if one recalls that Ibn Rushd was a splendid rationalist whose books were banned in some places by the Inquisition – not because he was a Muslim but, explicitly, because he was a rationalist. How, then, does one explain the discrepancy in the *Inferno*?

I would suggest that the discrepancy is to be understood in terms of the contradictions in Dante's own ideology, and that these contradictions stem from the fact that Dante powerfully represents that transitional moment in European thought wherein the medieval episteme is still there but on the verge of being broken up and superseded by the humanist intellectual revolution. Muhammad is eternally undergoing the most aweful punishment because predominant strands in medieval Christianity treated Islam as the most dangerous of all heresies and pronounced the Prophet of Islam the worst of all heretics. Ibn Rushd, condemned by the authority of that same medieval Christianity through the powers of the Inquisition, was nevertheless greatly respected in circles sympathetic to rationalist disputation; his book were copied and smuggled from one monastery to another. Still mired in the religious metaphysic but unable to resist entirely the strain that was eventually to blossom into a fully fledged intellectual Renaissance, and knowing that it was through their encounter with the labours of men like Ibn Rushd and Ibn Sina that a great many European thinkers were able to find their way back into Greek thought in the first place, Dante tried to devise a topography of his Hell that might do justice to these divided loyalties.

Even more notable, in fact, is the presence of Salah ad-Din ('by himself apart') who, unlike Ibn Rushd, was to be much reviled by later centuries throughout Christendom, because he was in fact a commander of the Arab-Islamic forces that were ranged against the Crusading Christians. Dante pays scant attention to that particular bigotry and delivers a 'judgement' on 'the great Muslim kings and philosophers' and on the Prophet of Islam which is, from the viewpoint of orthodox Christianity, internally incoherent. The literary-critical point I am making is that one cannot read that passage about Muhammad outside this whole range of enormous complexity. The methodological point, in Foucauldian language, is that one cannot detach a representation of Muhammad, which is produced in the discourse of Christian binaries between belief and heresy, and relocate that representation in the altogether different discourse of 'Orientalism', which – if it exists at all, and even though it may occasionally use religious forms of ideological interpellation – is a secular knowledge. Furthermore, Dante's treatment of Ibn Rushd – who is placed at least on a par with Socrates & Co., and towards whom Dante is altogether more forgiving – shows that the poet makes a severe distinction between belief and heresy, but none between Occident and Orient, as would be clear if Said were to reflect upon the fact that Judas, Brutus and Cassius do actually come even after Muhammad, in closer proximity to Satan himself. I might add that the treatment Ibn Rushd receives in Dante's imagination was no worse than the treatment he received in real life from Abu Yusuf, the Almohid King of Muslim Spain, who ordered him banished into exile and his books burned on charges of heresy. Medievality exacted its price from rationalism on both sides of the Muslim/Christian divide.

Said ignores such complexities at his own peril when he comments:

> . . . the special anachronisms and anomalies of putting pre-Christian luminaries in the same category of 'heathen' damnation with post-Christian Muslims does not trouble Dante. Even though the Koran specifies Jesus as a prophet, Dante chooses to consider the great Muslim philosophers and kings as having been fundamentally ignorant of Christianity. That they can also inhabit the same distinguished level as the heroes and sages of classical antiquity is an ahistorical vision similar to Raphael's in his fresco *The School of Athens*, in which Averroës rubs elbows on the academy floor with Socrates

> and Plato (similar to Fenelon's *Diaglogues des morts* [1700–1718], where a discussion takes places between Socrates and Confucius). (p. 69)

References to Raphael and Fenelon further illustrate Said's great erudition but contribute no insight into the substance of the argument. That Said should require this kind of literalist historicity from confessedly allegorical work is also surprising; one might as well castigate Dante for putting himself and Virgil in the same historical time and in a purely fictitious place, called Hell. Matters are made worse by the way Said construes the meaning that 'ignorance' may have in the context of religious orthodoxy, for not to *believe* in Christianity is for Dante (as not believing in Islam would have been for Sa'adi and even Hafiz) the worst kind of ignorance – worse in the case of Ibn Rushd than that of Socrates, because the former had the means to overcome that ignorance! The fact that 'the Koran specifies Jesus as a prophet' thus makes the matter of this 'ignorance' worse – though one would add, for the sake of a *modern*, irreligious discussion, that this reference to the status of Jesus himself in the literal word of the Qur'an is also irrelevant. What has been at issue in orthodox Islam is not the status of Jesus but that of Christianity, and of the way Jesus surfaces in Christian belief. For if orthodox Christianity regards Islam as a heresy, orthodox Islam has historically regarded some of the main tenets of Christianity as altogether blasphemous: the idea of the Trinity, the idea of Jesus as a *Son* of God, the further idea that Mary was a *virgin*, the even more scandalous idea of the Holy Ghost. The legacy of the Crusades lives, we might recall, on both sides of the orthodox divide.

## V

*Orientalism* appeared in 1978, a rather precise point in the history of the world, in the history of the demographic composition and reorganization of the political conjuncture in the United States, and in the history of intellectual productions in the metropolitan countries generally. Each of these aspects deserves some comment because all have some bearing on how books were being read, and how this book in particular intervened in intellectual history.

By 1978, the two great revolutionary decades, inaugurated – roughly speaking – by the onset of the Algerian War in 1954 and culminating in the liberation of Saigon in 1975, were over. The decisive turning point had come in Chile in 1973, with the defeat of *Unidad Popular*, but we did not know it then, because the liberation movements of Indochina and the Portuguese colonies in Africa were still in progress. The two revolutions of 1978–79, in Iran and Afghanistan, then made the shift unmistakable. The Khomeiniite takeover in Iran was one of those rare conjunctures in which the revolution and the counter-revolution were condensed in the same moment. In Afghanistan, the last country to have a revolution under a communist leadership, history now repeated itself, in Marx's famous phrase, both as tragedy and as farce. If the Iranian Revolution had signalled the decisive defeat of the Left in the Middle East and the rise to ideological hegemony of Islamic fundamentalism in that whole region, the history-as-tragedy-and-as-farce in Afghanistan was to contribute considerably to the collapse of what socialism there had ever been in the Comecon countries, helping to pave the way for perestroika first in the Soviet Union, then on a global scale. The savage destruction of Baghdad in 1991, the worst since the Mongols sacked that city in the thirteenth century, was the gift of this global perestroika making one recall Marx once more. As he famously put it in his correspondence on the Gotha Programme: capitalism does not lead necessarily to socialism, it may lead just as inexorably towards barbarism.

All that was to come later. What the end of the revolutionary decades did, however, was, first of all, to shift the entire balance within the metropolitan countries further to the Right. The Anglo-Saxon countries witnessed the rise to governmental power of the most reactionary ideologues, Reagan and Thatcher; movements for racial and social justice in the United States were beaten back, and the defeat of the miners' strike in Britain put an end to labour militancy there for years to come. Social Democracy itself was soon to be defeated in Germany and Scandinavia, while in Italy it submitted, under Craxi's leadership, to Christian Democracy, while the PCI retreated and was then, after 1976, decisively disorganized. Social Democracy did come to power in France, but survived by moving so far to the Right that it renounced even the autonomist positions of High Gaullism. For the backward capitalist zones, developments were far too numerous and too clearly rooted in histories of particular countries to be summarized in so short a space, but what happened in our own subcontinent is indicative. The Bhuttoite version of populist social democracy was first replaced, in 1977, by an Islamicist military dictatorship and then fleetingly reappeared in a farcical form under his daughter's regime. In Bangladesh, the progressive content of the liberation struggle was dissipated quickly, leading to a regime of right-wing military officers who had previously served in the Pakistan Army and had been trained at Fort Bragg in the United States; the widow of one of those officers is currently the Prime Minister. In India, communism has been contained in its regional locations; the social compact based on Gandhian ideas of religious tolerance has been increasingly under attack, sometimes in the name of Gandhi himself; Nehruvian models of parliamentary democracy, secularist polity, planned economy and non-aligned foreign policy have been emptied of their content, and a whole range of disorientations since the Emergency, dating back again to the mid 1970s, has moved the country and its entire political and social discourse cumulatively and decisively towards the Right.

This global offensive of the Right, global retreat of the Left, and retreat also of that which was progressive even in our canonical nationalism, is the essential backdrop for any analysis of the structure of intellectual productions and their reception in our time. Within this reorganized global conjuncture we have witnessed, in all the bourgeois countries, the ascent to dominance of an entirely new kind of intellectual within a formation which continued to call itself a Left. The characteristic posture of this new intellectual was that he or she would gain legitimacy on the Left by constantly and fervently referring to the Third World, Cuba, national liberation, and so on, but would also be openly and contemptuously anti-communist; would often enough not affiliate even with that other tradition which had also descended from classical Marxism, namely social democracy, nor be affiliated in any degree with any labour movement whatsoever, but would invoke an anti-bourgeois stance in the name of manifestly reactionary anti-humanisms enunciated in the Nietzschean tradition and propagated now under the signature of anti-empiricism, anti-historicism, structuralism and post-structuralism, specifically Lévi-Strauss, Foucault, Derrida, Glucksmann Kristeva, and so on. It is in contrast to these reactionary anti-humanisms, across the whole spectrum of cultural theories, that the rectitude in careers of people like Raymond Williams now seems so bracing.

I shall return to other kinds of determinations presently, but this matter of Nietzschean anti-humanism is of some crucial interest here, in part because of the way Said's treatment of Marx, to which I shall return in the next chapter, stands in tense balance with Nietzsche's authority, invoked indirectly through Foucault, which structures the whole book around notions of representation and discourse. This surfaces openly in a crucial passage which I shall cite below; on two consecutive pages, meanwhile, we find two rather inconsistent statements, brief and stark. First:

> as this book has tried to show, Islam *has* been fundamentally misrepresented in the past . . . (p. 272).

But then, on the very next page, we find:

> My whole point about this whole system is not that it is a *mis*representation of some Oriental essence . . .

Now, the substitution of the term 'Oriental essence' in the latter sentence for the term 'Islam' in the former does suggest that what Orientalism misrepresents is Islam itself, not an 'essence'. In a much stronger way, however, the main issue in both sentences is (*mis*)representation, not Islam or 'essence', and what Said is actually doing is drawing closer to the Nietzschean idea that no true representation is possible because all human communications always distort the facts. What happens between these two sentences is that Said raises the key question: 'The real issue is whether there can be a true representation of anything.' In other words, is it possible to make true statements? There are powerful traditions, including the Nietzschean, which have denied such a possibility. There are other powerful traditions, including the Marxist, which have said that yes, true statements are possible. Said's equivocation on this key question is delivered in what appears to be a precise formulation – namely, that the line between a representation and a misrepresentation is always very thin. That appears to me to be not a personal but a discursive statement. I would suggest, in fact, that this statement belongs directly in the Nietzschean philosophical tradition, and that Edward Said, who is here in the midst of writing a history of Orientalism, is affiliating himself with a new kind of history-writing, which was emerging more or less at this time, which goes far beyond the empirical historian's usual interrogation of and scepticism about the available evidence and the accepted modes of interpretation; and enters the Nietzschean world of questioning not merely positivist constructions but the very facticity of facts, so that it will eventually force a wide range of historians around the globe – some of the Indian Subalternists, for example – to start putting the word 'fact' in quotation marks.

With this clarification in mind, we can now turn to page 203:

> [Orientalism's] objective discoveries – the work of innumerable devoted scholars who edited texts and translated them, codified grammars, wrote dictionaries, reconstructed dead epochs, produced positivistically verifiable learning – are and always have been conditioned by the fact that its truths, like any truths delivered by language, are embodied in language, and what is the truth of language, Nietzsche once said, but
>
>> a mobile army of metaphors, metonyms, and anthropomorphisms – in short, a sum of human relations, which have been enhanced, transposed, and embellished poetically and rhetorically, and which after long use seem firm, canonical and obligatory to a people: truths are illusions about which one has forgotten that this is what they are.

This image of language as the enemy of experience, this assertion that representation is always-already a misrepresentation, this shallow pathos about the impossibility of truthful human communication, is of course a familiar Romantic trope which has undergone much aggrandizement – first in those irrationalist philosophies of the late nineteenth century and the early twentieth which preceded the rise of fascism and then again, on a much wider scale, in the reactionary anti-humanisms which have dominated many strands in contemporary avant-gardist thought. In relation to the knowledge of history, then, this image of human communication as a ruse of illusory subjectivity precludes the possibility of truthful statement on the ground that evidence, the criterion of truthful statement in history-writing, is always-already prejudiced by the very nature of language itself. It is significant that these anti-humanisms have come to dominate so much of American scholarship on the eve of the unprecedented imperialist consolidations of the present decade.

That this form of irrationalism should surface so centrally in the very book which is doubtless the most influential among radically inclined cultural theorists today should give us, I believe, some pause, but it should also help us to grasp some aspects of its enthusiastic reception and extremely widespread influence. For in one range of formulations, Said's denunciations of the *whole* of Western civilization is as extreme and uncompromising as Foucault's denunciations of the Western episteme or Derrida's denunciations of the transhistorical Logos; nothing, nothing at all, exists outside epistemic Power, logocentric Thought, Orientalist Discourse – no classes, no gender, not even history; no site of resistance, no accumulated projects of human liberation, since all is Repetition with Difference, all is corruption – specifically Western corruption – and Orientalism always remains the same, only more so with the linear accumulations of time. The Manichaean edge of these visions – Derridean, Foucauldian, Saidian – is quite worthy of Nietzsche himself.

But this vision, in the case of *Orientalism*, gains further authority from the way it panders to the most sentimental, the most extreme forms of Third-Worldist nationalism. The book says nothing, of course, about any fault of our own, but anything we ourselves could remember – the bloodbath we conducted at the time of Partition, let us say – simply pales in comparison with this other Power which has victimized us and inferiorized us for two thousand five hundred years or more. So uncompromising is this book in its Third-Worldist passion that Marxism itself, which has historically given such sustenance to so many of the anti-imperialist movements of our time, can be dismissed, breezily, as a child of Orientalism and an accomplice of British colonialism. How comforting such visions of one's own primal and permanent innocence are one can well imagine, because given what actually goes on in our countries, we do need a great deal of comforting.

But it was not within the so-called 'Third World' that the book first appeared. Its global authority is in fact inseparable from the authority of those in the dominant sectors of the metropolitan intelligentsia who first bestowed upon it the status of a modern classic; while, perhaps paradoxically, its most passionate following in the metropolitan countries is within those sectors of the university intelligentsia which either originate in the ethnic minorities or affiliate themselves ideologically with the academic sections of those minorities. In Chapter 2 above, I discussed the connection between the emergence of the category 'Third World Literature' and the key changes that occurred in the patterns of immigration from the late 1960s onwards, with substantial numbers of Asian immigrants being based now among the petty-bourgeois and techno-managerial strata. Those who came as graduate students and then joined the faculties, especially in the Humanities and the Social Sciences, tended to come from upper classes in their home countries. In the process of relocating themselves in the metropolitan countries, they needed documents of their assertion, proof that they had always been oppressed. Books that connected oppression with class were not very useful, because *they* neither came from the working class nor were intending to join that class in their new country. Those who said that majority of the populations in Africa and Asia certainly suffered from colonialism, but that there were also those who benefited from it, were useless, because many of the new professionals who were part of this immigration themselves came from those other families, those other classes, which had been the beneficiaries; Said would pose this question of the beneficiaries of colonialism in very peculiar ways in his invocation of Ranajit Guha, as we shall soon see.

Among critiques that needed to be jettisoned, or at least greatly modified, were the Marxist ones, because Marxists had this habit of speaking about classes, even in Asia and Africa. What the upwardly mobile professionals in this new immigration needed were narratives of oppression that would get them preferential treatment, reserved jobs, higher salaries in the social position they already occupied: namely, *as* middle-class professionals, mostly male. For such purposes *Orientalism* was the perfect narrative. When, only slightly later, enough women found themselves in that same position, the category of the 'Third World female subaltern' was found highly serviceable. I might add that this latter category is probably not very usable inside India, but the kind of discourse *Orientalism* assembles certainly has its uses. Communalism, for example, can now be laid entirely at the doors of Orientalism and colonial construction; caste itself can be portrayed as a fabrication primarily of the Population Surveys and Census Reports – Ronald Inden literally does this,[32] and Professor Partha Chatterjee seems poised to do so.[33] Colonialism is now held responsible not only for its own cruelties but, conveniently enough, for ours too. Meanwhile, within the metropolitan countries, the emphasis on immigration was continually to strengthen. I have written on one aspect of it in relation to Salman Rushdie, but it is worth mentioning that the same theme surfaces with very major emphases in Said's latest essays, with far-reaching consequences for his own earlier positions, as we shall see.

The perspectives inaugurated in *Orientalism* served, in the social self-consciousness and professional assertion of the middle-class immigrant and the 'ethnic' intellectual, roughly the same function as the theoretical category of 'Third World Literature', arising at roughly the same time, was also to serve. One in fact presumed the other, and between the two the circle was neatly closed. If *Orientalism* was devoted to demonstrating the bad faith and imperial oppression of all European knowledges, beyond time and history, 'Third World Literature' was to be the narrative of authenticity, the counter-canon of truth, good faith, liberation itself. Like the bad faith of European knowledge, the counter-canon of 'Third World Literature' had no boundaries – neither of space nor of time, of culture nor of class; a Senegalese novel, a Chinese short story, a song from medieval India, could all be read into the same archive: it was all 'Third World'. Marx was an 'Orientalist' because he was European, but a Tagore novel, patently canonical and hegemonizing inside the Indian cultural context, could be taught in the syllabi of 'Third World Literature' as a marginal, non-canonical text, counterposed against 'Europe'. The homogenizing sweep was evident in both cases, and if cultural nationalism was the overtly flaunted insignia, invocation of 'race' was barely below the surface – not just with respect to the United States, which would be logical, but with reference to human history as such. Thus, if 'Orientalism' was initially posited as something of an original ontological flaw in the European psyche, Said was eventually to declare: 'in the relationship between the ruler and the ruled in the imperial or colonial or racial sense, race takes precedence over both class and gender . . . I have always felt that the problem of emphasis and relative importance took precedence over the need to establish one's feminist credentials.'[34] That contemptuous phrase, 'establish one's feminist credentials', takes care of gender quite definitively, as imperialism itself is collapsed into a 'racial sense'. In a Nietzschean world, virtually anything is possible.

## VI

Said's interventions since the initial publication of *Orientalism* have doubtless been prolific and diverse. *The Question of Palestine* and *Covering Islam*, as they came in quick succession thereafter, were explicitly conceived as volumes in a series inaugurated with *Orientalism*. *After the Last Sky* and *Blaming the Victims*, which came some years later, may also be considered as parts of that same integrated *œuvre*. Surrounding this impressive array of books are essays, articles and reviews on cognate themes in a great many periodicals, political journals and newspapers, not to speak of unpublished interventions in scholarly conferences and public forums of various kinds, including very effective television appearances, so numerous that they could easily fill two or three volumes. About *Orientalism* I need not say more, and *Covering Islam* is undoubtedly Said's most forgettable book, so defensive is it about Islamicist kinds of politics and Khomeiniite kinds of criminalities (only after the sentencing of Salman Rushdie did Said begin to take public note of the terror which had by then enveloped tens of thousands within Iran). By contrast, the writings which deal directly with Palestine constitute not only the most enduring part of Said's work but also, by any standards, the most persuasive insertion of a national-liberation struggle into the American imagination, which is otherwise substantially formed by Zionist-colonial presumptions.

Almost equally extensive – though far more problematic and at times even disconcerting – are Said's publications in the field of literary and cultural studies. Central to this other work, of course, is his 1983 volume *The World, the Text, and the Critic*, which brings together essays written between 1969 and 1981. But there are also numerous other essays which have appeared in journals but have not yet been collected in a single volume; a few of these, too, have been included in volumes edited by others. The book includes at least two major pieces, 'Raymond Schwab and the Romance of Ideas' and 'Islam, Philology and French Culture: Renan and Massignon', which are thematically connected with *Orientalism*, even though some of the formulations in those essays are considerably different; the essay on Schwab, written much earlier but collected in a book more recently, makes very odd reading indeed, considering that the charitable view of Schwab's work which we find there has no analogue within

*Orientalism* itself.[35] Two other essays in the book, which are in fact the best-known and the most influential – 'Criticism between Culture and System' and 'Travelling Theory' – were evidently written some time after *Orientalism* and are notable not so much for explicating Said's preference for Foucault over Derrida as for his partial distancing of himself from Foucault. This distancing is facilitated by his reliance on criticisms of Foucault which had been framed already by Poulantzas[36] and Chomsky, whom Said cites directly, and part of what Said now says about Foucault is uncannily similar to some points I have raised above about *Orientalism* itself. The following extract from 'Travelling Theory', intended to express reservations about Foucault and his notion of Power, applies almost exactly to Said himself and his conception of Orientalism:

> Foucault's eagerness not to fall into Marxist economism causes him to obliterate the role of classes, the role of economics, the role of insurgency and rebellion in the societies he discusses. . . . The problem is that Foucault's use of the term *pouvoir* moves around too much, swallowing up every obstacle in its path, . . . obliterating change and mystifying its microphysical sovereignty. . . . Foucault's history is ultimately textual or rather textualized; its mode is one for which Borges would have an affinity . . . they [his archaeologies] make not even a nominal allowance for emergent movements, and none for revolutions, counterhegemony, or historical blocs.[37]

Since those two essays are only tangentially connected with the aspects of Said's work with which I am most concerned here, I shall not offer any reading of the remarkable ambivalances one finds in them; in any event, it is simply not possible within the space of one chapter – even an inordinately lengthy chapter such as this one – to give detailed accounts of each significant item in an ouput so substantial, distinctive and diverse.

This partial distancing from Foucault is in fact part of a number of shifts that have occurred in Said's more recent writings, which includes a retreat from the Nietzschean position of all representations being misrepresentations and admits, concomitantly, the possibilities of resistance from outside the colonial discourse. Meanwhile, his rereading of both Foucault and Derrida, and his many convergences with diverse postmodernist positions, then culminate in the insistence that the double task of responsible knowledge is to resist the pressures both of the dominant culture and of what would now increasingly be dubbed 'system', 'theory', 'grand theory', 'disciplinary knowledge' and several even more colourful epithets – referring frequently to Marxism in particular, but also to any other way of being-in-the-world which seeks to establish theoretical as well as narrative intelligibility of history as such, and then identifies collective agents (such as class, gender, nation) as bearers of resistance and political action. All such *systems* are rejected, in the characteristic postmodernist way, so that resistance can always only be personal, micro, and shared only by a small, determinate number of individuals who happen, perchance, to come together, outside the so-called 'grand narratives' of class, gender, nation.[38]

Ambivalences on this question are already notable in 'Travelling Theory', but even more representative in all this is the essay 'Opponents, Audiences, Constituencies and Community',[39] where Said first speaks derisively of 'the self-policing, self-purifying communities erected even by Marxist, as well as other disciplinary, discourses', and then goes on to specify what he considers to be a key project that needs to be posed against the 'disciplinary' character of Marxism, etc.: 'to restore the nonsequential energy of lived historical memory and subjectivity . . . to tell other stories than the official sequential or ideological ones produced by institutional power'. I am not quite sure what this last formulation actually means, but it would not, I think, be unfair to say that the sense in which Marxism is said to be 'self-policing, self-purifying', as well as 'disciplinary', 'institutional' and 'ideological', applies inescapably to particular tendencies – notably the socialist tendencies – within feminism too. Meanwhile, theoretical eclecticism runs increasingly out of control: sweeping, patently poststructuralist denunciations of Marxism can be delivered in the name of Gramsci, using the terminology explicitly drawn from Althusser, and listing the names of communist poets like Aimé Césaire, Pablo Neruda and Mahmoud Darwish to illustrate the sites of resistance.

The largest shift, however, has been on the issue of nationalism. In the years immediately following the publication of *Orientalism*, Said's position was indistinguishable from straightforward Third-Worldist cultural nationalisms, and what we used to get was an unselfcritical narrative of European guilt, non-European innocence. This has shifted dramatically, beginning in about 1984 and growing increasingly more strident in rejecting nationalism, national boundaries, nations as such, so that one now has reason to be equally alarmed by the extremity of this opposite stance. Characteristically, though, the most sweeping statements about 'nation' and 'state' as 'coercive identities' are frequently delivered alongside resounding affirmations of national liberation, of the Palestinian *intifada* in particular, and the right of the Palestinian people either to obtain a nation-state of their own or, alternatively, to live as coequals in a binational state. It is this growing ambivalence about nation and nationalism – combined with an even more surprising shift from a wholesale rejection of 'the West' to an equally wholesale assertion that the *only* authentic work that can be done in our time presumes (a) Third World origin, but combined with (b) metropolitan location – which should bear some scrutiny. The intellectual cited as an exemplary figure of our time in this latest construction, is, of course, Ranajit Guha, who is commended both for this initial origin in the Indian upper class and for his later location in the metropolitan university, but the autobiographical self-referentiality is quite unmistakable.[40]

Among the numerous essays by Said which have appeared in journals over roughly the past decade but have not yet been collected into a single volume are a dozen or so that are thematically organized around the relationship between imperialism and (mainly) literature. Some of these happen to be on highly canonical figures (Jane Austen, Kipling, Yeats, Camus, Verdi); others are of more general import. Among the essays on individual figures, the one on Verdi[41] is my favourite – not because I wholly understand operatic language, or have ever actually seen *Aïda*, but because I quite follow Said's highly convincing argument. With all the knowledge he accumulated in the course of writing *Orientalism*, with his great competence as a pianist and his passion for opera, he is peculiarly well situated to write about this masterpiece of European classical music composed specially for the opening of the Suez Canal, and he accomplished the task with verve and rare wit. However, I must perforce again skip readings of particular authors, and it is from among essays that fall in the latter category, those with a certain generalizing sweep, that I should like to examine only two: 'Figures, Configurations, Transfigurations', cited above, and 'Third World Intellectuals and Metropolitan Culture'.[42] Of the two, the 'Figures' essay appears to be chronologically earlier and was originally delivered as a lecture at the Conference of the Association for Commonwealth Literature and Language Studies, held at the University of Kent in August 1989. Such Associations are usually very conservative and mindless affairs, so the radicalism of a great many things Said says in his essay is salutary. My interest in these essays, however, is of a slightly different kind.

Both essays, like several others in recent years, register some real advances over *Orientalism*. There had been, for example, no evidence until after the publication of that book that Said had read any considerable number of non-Western writers. By contrast, references to principal figures of the counter-canon of 'Third World Literature' surface very regularly in his more recent writings, even though not even one of them has yet been treated with the hermeneutic engagement and informed reading that Said offers so often for scores of Western canonical figures; in the rare event that he actually refers to particular texts – as in the case of George Antonius or Ranajit Guha in the essay we shall soon discuss – none receives the kind of detailed scrutiny which Said routinely accords to a wide range of European writers, from Swift to Renan to Schwab to Kipling. His engagement, both as activist and as scholar, with the Palestinian Liberation movement has been extended, meanwhile, to regular expressions of solidarity with anti-colonial movements in general, and a basic respect for figures associated with such movements. These partial gains in the range of engagements and sympathies stand, however, in peculiar and paradoxical relation with the freshly acquired but altogether irrepressible rage *against* the peoples, societies, national boundaries, reading communities and literatures of Asia, Africa, and 'the Islamic world'; the enormous privileging of a handful of writers, strictly those who now live in the West, over those societies and literatures; and the conception of the 'Western centre' as the only site where 'contests over decolonization' can now take place. The enormity of this shift is puzzling. The continued American hostility towards the Arab world on the one hand, the sentencing of Rushdie by Ayatollah Khomeini on the other, combined with the failure of most people in Asia, Africa and the Arab world to do combat on Rushdie's behalf, seem to have given rise to an extraordinary fury against West and non-West alike, with the figure of the lonely writer in the Western city –

and the uncommitted reader of novels in that same city – eventually emerging as the only figures of redemption.

## VII

These ambivalences are fully played out only in the address on Commonwealth Literature, but some of the key formulations are found in the essay on 'Third World Intellectuals and Metropolitan Culture', which we shall take up first. The latter half of this essay consists of the entirely salutary recommendation that non-Western writers be taken seriously by Western readers. The main burden of the argument, however, rests on a rather strange distinction between what are called 'colonial' and 'post-colonial' intellectuals; cryptic references to four books to furbish this sweeping typology; and a resounding affirmation of the acquisition of Western 'technique' and personal location in 'the Western centre' as the prerequisites of 'insurgency' and 'contest over de-colonization'. Before we come to all that, however, it may be useful to indicate the breezy way in which generalizations are handled, as in the following rather interesting passage which opens the third paragraph:

> Resistance to imperialism does not, of course, only involve armed force or bands of guerrillas. It is *mainly* allied with nationalism and with an aroused sense of aggrieved religious, cultural, or existential identity. In its pantheon are great warriors like Abdel Qader of Algeria, prophets and priests like the Mahdi and Gandhi, a phalanx of nationalist writers – Tagore, Yeats, Neruda, Aimé Césaire, Leopold Senghor – and dozens of intellectual figures like Marti, Mariategi, Fanon, Cabral and others, whose major role in the creation of an emergent and alternative discourse cannot be minimized. (pp. 27–8; emphasis added)

Gandhi's appearance here in the category of 'prophets and priests' is odd. Meanwhile, the affirmation of 'nationalism', here as in several other places, stands in curious relation to the debunking of national identity which we shall see in the other essay. My immediate interest, however, is in the list – compiled in the genre of the postmodern pastiche – of nine names, joined in the infinite category of 'others', bringing together communists and anti-communists, pacifists and Marxists, five of whom actually either led or participated in guerrilla warfare, all mobilized to posit the idea that imperialism is *mainly* a cultural phenomenon to be opposed by an *alternative discourse*. What is important about Cabral, evidently, is his *discursive* position, not that he launched and led the armed struggle which brought about the liberation of his country and contributed decisively to the liberation of all the Portuguese colonies in Africa, not to speak of the collapse of fascism in Portugal itself.

With this insight in hand, Said then goes on to specify a certain typology of two kinds of intellectual: the colonial and post-colonial. In all, he discusses four authors. Into the category of the colonial intellectuals fall C.L.R. James, the Trinidadian communist and famous author of *Black Jacobins*, and the Arab nationalist historian George Antonius, the author of the equally famous *The Arab Awakening*. In the category of post-colonial intellectuals come the Malaysian writer Alatas and the Indian writer Guha. Among the four, the globe is nicely covered, as are political ideologies, notably Marxism and nationalism. Before going on to the theoretical import and the arbitrariness of Said's usage in this context, it is necessary to clarify what these terms 'colonial' and 'post-colonial' actually mean in political theory. For these are key analytic categories which are used for periodization of history as regards the rule over peoples of particular countries by ruling classes of other countries; for the fundamental shifts that take place with decolonization in forms of state and relations between different national formations, units of capital, classes, and economies; for the internal reorganization of state personnel, modes of governance and appropriation as well as circulation of surpluses nationally and internationally, when sovereign regimes are constituted in former colonies. This analytic distinction rests upon the fundamental fact that the ruling class of a colony is located outside that colony, and the colonial state is the instrument of that externally based ruling class; with decolonization, this structural feature of the dominated formation no longer applies and the formation therefore ceases to be colonial, regardless of any other kind of dependence.

In political thought, these categories have a precise meaning because they refer not to the date of decolonization but to identifiable structural shifts in state and society, and in the hierarchy of systemic determinations which structure the relations between the imperialist bourgeoisie and the direct producers of the imperialized but sovereign nation-state of what was previously a colony. To describe, on the other hand, a critic as 'post-colonial' simply because he/she came of age after decolonization is a tautology; to ascribe a shared cultural attitude towards Western dominance to *all* intellectuals who begin writing after decolonization, and a structurally different attitude to all those whose intellectual formation was completed under colonial rule, regardless of their individual social and political locations, is the most arrant idealism and facilitates a very peculiar kind of ahistorical levelling. I might add that this way of deploying the terms 'colonial' and 'post-colonial' for self-projection, and for defining locations within the profession of cultural criticism, is now quite widespread among literary theorists.

These categories have no analytic value, or theoretical status, when they are mobilized to homogenize very complex structures of intellectual productions or the trajectories and subjectivities of individual writers and critics or broad intellectual strata, of the kind Said suggests in his essay. For particular intellectuals or clusters of them, colonial cultural ambience can last far beyond the moment of decolonization; for others, rejection of cultural dominance of the colonizing country can take place – and often does take place – well before the actual dissolution of the colonial state. Careers of historians and teachers like Susobhan Sarkar, sociologists like A.R. Desai, militants and intellectuals like E.M.S. Namboodripad, not to speak of D.D. Kosambi – mathematician, Sanskritist, anthropologist, historian of ancient India – span many years of both the colonial and the post-colonial periods, and none of them, let alone scores of others, displays the kind of cut-and-dried characteristics that Said attaches so neatly to his category of 'colonial' and 'post-colonial' intellectuals. Kosambi started writing roughly at the same times as C.L.R. James, Irfan Habib roughly at the same time as Ranajit Guha; the kind of distinction Said makes tells us nothing about these other trajectories. He simply inflates differences of individual formation and attitude into meaningless global typologies.

What Said tells us is that colonial intellectuals – by which he simply means non-Europeans who wrote during the colonial period, be they nationalists or Marxists – always write within the cultural perspectives of

European dominance, identifying themselves with European culture and thinking of the colonizing country as 'Mother Country'. As he puts it:

> For James and Antonius the world of discourse inhabited by natives in the Caribbean and the Arab Orient was honorably dependent upon the West. . . . There is no sense in their work of men standing *outside* the Western cultural tradition, however much they think of themselves as articulating the adversarial experience of colonial and/or non-Western peoples. (pp. 33–6)

This may well be true of the individual authors Said cites, but the generalization which is intended here simply boggles the mind, for it is so obviously contrary to what one knows about numerous intellectuals of the colonial period who never thought of themselves as ever standing *inside* the 'Western cultural tradition'. Nor is one quite sure how Said can later describe Guha squarely as a 'poststructuralist' and at the same time designate him the examplary 'post-colonial' intellectual standing *outside* the Western cultural tradition; where, one wonders, is that line of demarcation between poststructuralism and the Western cultural tradition? Post-colonial intellectuals are in any case said both to be *outside* Western cultural tradition *and* to have an even better command of the weapons of European critical thought; their real distinction is that they turn these weapons against their own tutors. No one in the past, during the colonial period, apparently did that! Criticism of the most fundamental aspects of Europe through criticial methods learned initially in the European institutions was, one would have thought, a favourite pastime of a great many communists and nationalists in the colonial period.

More significant is Said's very special way of according absolute centrality to those intellectuals of non-European origin who command a high degree of technical competence and have chosen, both in the colonial and post-colonial periods, to locate themselves in the West:

> These figures address the metropolis using the techniques, the discourses, the very weapons of scholarship and criticism once reserved exclusively for the European, now adapted either for insurgency or revisionism at the very heart of the Western centre. (p. 29)

Both James (the 'colonial') and Guha (the 'post-colonial') have written significant books, but to designate the writing of such books as acts of 'insurgency' appears excessive, not least because words of that kind should be applied to the act of writing sparingly, lest not only acts but even words become devalued. Castro's writing of 'History Shall Absolve Me' or Mao's writing of 'The Hunan Report' were certainly acts of insurgency, as is the act of writing whenever it can constitute a challenge to the existing structure of rule and a risk to one's security, but scholarly works on events of the late eighteenth and early nineteenth century do not fall in that category. Guha did, after all, publish his study of the late-eighteenth-century Permanent Settlement, to which Said refers, some sixteen years after decolonization, when enormous quantities of writing in India as well as in Britain, during the colonial as well as the post-colonial periods, had demonstrated how much Indian agriculture had suffered from that Settlement. What brings about such inflationary tendency in Said's language here is probably the great importance he attaches to the very act of 'addressing the metropolis . . . at the very heart of the Western centre', and it is probably this need to be 'at the very heart of the Western centre' which accounts for the emphasis on 'the techniques, the discourses, the very weapons of scholarship'; if 'addressing the metropolis' is what one does, then one had better have those 'techniques', those 'discourses'. (In all fairness to Guha, though, it should be pointed out that he moved permanently to 'the Western centre' some years *after* writing the said book.) This migration of the superior scholar from non-Western countries to Western ones is what Said calls *the voyage in*; he describes it as follows:

> . . . the voyage in constitutes a specially interesting variety of hybrid cultural work. And that it exists at all is a sign of adversarial internationalization in an age of continued imperial structures. (p. 31)

That is a nice phrase: 'adversarial internationalization'. Unfortunately, its novelty serves to conceal the fact that there is usually no relationship between 'the voyage in' and any 'adversarial' activity. Said speaks, inexplicably, of 'intellectual and scholarly work from the peripheries, done either by immigrants or by visitors, both of whom are generally anti-imperialist' (p. 30). That is not even remotely accurate. The vast majority of immigrants and visitors' who go from 'the peripheries' to the 'Western centre' in the United States either take no part in politics and scholarly endeavour or turn out to be right-wing people, well represented in the field of literature by Bharati Mukherjee; that a few do produce oppositional work should not serve to conceal the fact that the 'scholarly work . . . by immigrants or by visitors' is overwhelmingly in the mould of mainstream Anglo-American scholarship. Far from being 'generally anti-imperialist', most of them want to be part of the 'centre'; the last thing they want is 'adversarial internationalization'. Said seems not to know the immigrant communities on whose behalf he speaks, and one does indeed need a great distance from the reality of those 'voyages', made overwhelmingly in pursuit of material and professional success, if one is actually able to formulate the following declarative: 'The contest over decolonization has moved from the peripheries to the centre' (p. 30). The force of that word 'moved' takes one's breath away. The struggle against imperialism now simply does not take place in the countries that are actually imperialized; it is a movable feast, and it goes where the experts go! In this sort of formulation the 'contest over decolonization' becomes mainly a literary and literary-critical affair, and the elite academic intelligentsia claims for itself, in an amazing gap between fact and self-image, the role of the world's revolutionary vanguard. The statement is definitive enough but we may still ask: why is Ranajit Guha deemed so uniquely endowed to represent the 'post-colonial' intelligentsia?

The first formulation we get is the following: 'Guha's book is, in ways that later poststructuralist writers (including Guha himself) would recognize, an archeological and deconstructive study . . . ' (p. 32). Archaeology (Foucault), deconstruction (Derrida and friends) and poststructuralism generally seem thus to guarantee the personal affinity, and Said also approves of Guha's writing in his capacity as literary critic: 'narrative is replaced by irony,' says Said admiringly of Guha's style, and makes much of his postulate that 'post-colonial' history-writing of the kind Guha practises has ceased to be built around narratives and is far more interested in language itself. Literary criticism, in other words, is the desired model for the writing of history.

But what fascinates Said about Guha, above all, is the issue of class origin, social and geographical location, and the accompanying mastery of research techniques and Western knowledges. Said does not talk about the substance of Guha's book, and it remains unclear whether he has actually read it. What he talks about, rather, is the fact that Guha comes from a family that was notably a beneficiary of the same Permanent Settlement of which Guha offers his fulsome critique; that he then moved to Western countries to carry on his work; and that Guha's mastery of technique and archive is equal to that of any Western scholar. In a rhetorical inflation characteristic of the contemporary Third-Worldist intellectuals located in 'the Western centre', Said then goes on to erase the fundamental political distinction between immigration and exile, when he simply declares Guha to be an 'exile figure'. With the personal choice one has absolutely no wish to quarrel, and I certainly neither know nor wish to judge the circumstances which lead any individual to emigrate from one country to another; those are strictly private matters. By the same token, however, it is best not to misrepresent personal preference as fate ordained by repression. Yet the 'exile figure' is central to the persona Said ascribes to Guha. For it is in this combination of comprador class origin, Western location, exiled self, and mastery of techniques that Said locates the productive and oppositional energies of the Subalternist project and its putative ability to overturn the entire trajectory of all the schools and tendencies previously obtaining in Indian historiography.

The social context of thus privileging Guha is of considerable interest. There are several references to *Subaltern Studies* in these essays, but with the exception of a passing reference to Guha's own brief introductory note in Volume I, Said does not even cite any of the individual texts which constitute this project, let alone give evidence of any detailed engagement with its premisses or products or, especially, with what may signify its difference from – purported superiority over – other kinds of historiography in India. One is not sure what it is in the work itself that is being singled out for praise in this foregrounding. Even in the singular case of Guha, where a particular book – *A Rule of Property for Bengal* – is mentioned, two facts stand out. One is that this is an early work by Guha, published some two decades before the launching of the Subaltern project, based upon his research of the 1950s within what one may loosely call the main traditions of Indian historiography, not entirely indifferent to premisses shared with teachers like Susobhan Sarkar or approximate contemporaries like Irfan Habib. It is significant that Said is so notably silent about Guha's more recent work in the actual Subalternist mould.[43] Then, even with reference to *A Rule of Property*, Said quotes only from the introduction and only the biographical detail; he is curiously indifferent to the immense body of writing on the Permanent Settlement which has accumulated in India over the decades, before Guha's book and since.

Given this pattern of invocation and affiliation, the actual content of what Guha or the general Subaltern tendency actually does cannot be an issue here, and all that matters is Said's own construction of it. One comes away with the impression that the paramount fact for him is the structure of conversation, conference and personal encounter currently available in the American university, and the increasing presence of the Subaltern Group in that particular milieu; this, then, is cemented by the matter of 'poststructuralism'. The main source of attraction, in any case, is the biographical one: class origin, privileged access to 'technique' and 'discourse', the imaginative construction of 'exile', and the subsequent relocation. The irony of this personally felt and highly valorized biographical detail is that Said has given us, probably without Guha's consent, the portrait of a typical upper-layer bourgeois; for it is that kind of individual who has typically mobilized the accumulations achieved during the colonial period to acquire the most modern Western technology, to launch upon collaborative competition with the metropolitan bourgeoisie, from the margins of global capitalism.

There is, of course, a trenchant irony in the obviously paradoxical relationship between the way the Subalternist project would define itself and the way Said defines it – as an upper-class, émigré phenomenon at odds with its own class origin and metropolitan location. Suffice it to say that there is a very considerable resonance in this narrative of class origin, the migration as a *voyage in*, and preferred metropolitan location – the pleasures of self-exile much more often than those of forced exile – and the subsequent professionalization and hybridization ('cultural amphibians' is Said's laudatory description) which far exceeds the terms of any personal choice that Ranajit Guha might or might not have made, even though he is the one who is singled out. One of the few features that these more recent essays share with *Orientalism* is that they continue to speak to the existential situation – the class privilege, the presumed oppositional and beleaguered situation, the technical ability to collaborate as well as compete, the professional location – of the more privileged sections of the incoming immigrant in the United States. What is significant in terms of authorial intentions, meanwhile, is the fact that the turn from a wholesale denunciation of the West, so uncompromising in *Orientalism*, to an equally sweeping desire for a location *in* the West, which these latest essays assert, is now complete.

## VIII

Predilections of this kind are what Said brings to the even more complex and internally far more riven essay 'Figures, Configurations, Transfigurations', which is notable for its high estimation of Western canonicity, its debunking of the non-West, its handsome praise for the civilizing mission of English, its advocacy not only of literature's aesthetic pleasures but also of the central importance of fiction as a vehicle for consuming the world. Reversals of a great many earlier positions are simply astonishing.

Said starts by commending the 'salutary and invigorating quality in the very notion of Commonwealth literature today', which is surprising for anyone on the Left, since all that is wrong with the category 'Commonwealth Literature' begins with the *notion* that it should exist at all. Said, however, sees in this construct an 'invigorating' civilizational mission:

> If configurations like Commonwealth or world literature are to have any meaning at all, it is . . . because they interact ferociously not only with the whole nationalist basis for the composition and study of literature, but also with the lofty independence and indifference with which it has become customary Eurocentrically to regard metropolitan western literatures.

Now, 'Commonwealth Literature' is a construct pretty much of the British Council and is limited largely to its clients, who themselves construe it as a meeting-ground for discrete 'national' traditions; the 'ferocity' Said imputes to it is at best imaginary, and it is at the very least astonishing that Said posits this cultural hangover of the British Empire as a credible alternative to 'the nationalist basis'.

This civilizing mission is said to reside, further, in the very global pre-eminence of the English language itself: 'What gives the actuality of Commonwealth literature its special force is that, of all languages today, English is, properly speaking, *the* world language.' The Kenyan writer Ngugi Wa Thongo is then invoked to make the point that this global circulation of English enables us to 'decolonize' our minds through study in the same language that was used to colonize us. This too is somewhat surprising, both because Ngugi has over the last several years made the point that in order fully to decolonize his mind he must, rather, write in Kikuyu, and because this beneficent role of English as vehicle of enlightenment and world culture is at the very least overstated. In present-day India, surely, English occupies a much more contradictory space: as simultaneously a language for the production of knowledge , a means of connecting the country with currents around the world, both good and bad, and as a line of demarcation, a cultural boundary between privilege and dispossession; for many among the literati, it is also the language of Raj nostalgia. Said, however, is insistent on this point of the civilizing ethos. He recounts a visit to a national university in one of the Gulf States and, having registered the fact that the English Department attracted the largest number of students, goes on to bemoan two things: that so many students took English not for its literature but as a technical language needed for professional advancement; and that 'English, such as it was, existed in what seemed to be a seething cauldron of Islamic revivalism'. Both these laments deserve some comment.

Said's main statement about the use of English in the Gulf State runs as follows:

> This all but terminally consigned English to the level of a technical language almost totally stripped not only of expressive and aesthetic characteristics but also denuded of any critical or self-conscious dimension. You learned English to use computers, respond to orders, transmit telexes, decipher manifests and so forth. That was all.

Said's lament is quite unmodulated by any awareness that English has become a 'world language', a fact which he celebrates not because of its 'aesthetic characteristics' or 'critical dimension' – that is, not owing to its literature and literary critics – but because of its centrality in the administrative and capitalist enterprises in the most powerful empires of past and present, hence as a language of rule ('taking orders') and of command in global grids of telecommunications, airlines, administration, transnational corporations. The poor student whom Said so derides in fact makes a rational choice, in his own circumstances, in learning the technical aspect and ignoring the aesthetic one.

The main comment on the beleaguered situation of this 'world language' in the midst of a 'seething cauldron' runs, meanwhile, as follows:

> Either it is a technical language with wholly instrumental characteristics and features; or it is a foreign language with various implicit connections to the larger English-speaking world, but where its prsence abuts on the much more impressive, much more formidable emergent reality of organized religious fervor. And since the language of Islam is Arabic, a language with considerable literary community and hieratic force, English seems to me to have sunk quite low . . .

Against this debasement and overwhelming of the 'world language' by 'organized religious fervor' are ranged 'smaller literate groups that are bound together not by insensate polemic but by affinities, sympathies and compassion'. A particularly important member of these 'smaller literate groups' is Salman Rushdie, whom Said has defended most fervently, in this article as well as in every other available public forum, partly because 'That the novel [*The Satanic Verses*] dealt with Islam in English and for what was believed to be a largely western audience was its main offence.'

Said's way of posing English against Arabic is odd. In Arabic-speaking countries, certainly, the characterization of Arabic as the language of Islam (as of everything else) may be substantially true, but in so far as he speaks constantly of larger things (Asia and Africa, Commonwealth Literature, Rushdie and 'the Khomeini threat') it may be worth recalling that the vast majority of Muslims in the world neither speak nor understand Arabic. More to the point, any number of studies exist to show that the urban petty bourgeoisie which normally constitutes the cutting edge of 'organized religious fervor' in a number of countries is educated in English as much as in any other language; in the 'Islamic world', certainly, English-knowing professionals occupy key positions in such movements, and the representatives of orthodox Islam who led the campaign against *The Satanic Verses* in

England knew English very well, while a great many knew no Arabic. And it is entirely to be doubted that such representatives of orthodox Islam, including the Iranian clerics, would have been any the more forgiving if *The Satanic Verses* had been written in Arabic, Farsi, Urdu or any other language, for Asian and Arab readerships; what caused the outrage was the book's heresy and its direct representation of the Prophet of Islam and his family in the most vulgar fashion possible, not its language of communication. That it was written in English, by a writer of Muslim origin with immense prestige in the Western countries, and was made available by powerful Western publishing industries to the international media and the British state, to be used against the immigrant communities inside Britain as well as for certain kinds of representations of Muslim people in the imperialist countries generally – all that, of course, greatly complicated the issue of the heresy. The odd thing, of course, is that Edward Said, who had given us such a powerful narrative of literary representations as integral to the imperialist systems of power, and who in writing *Covering Islam* had been so very sensitive about the coverage of Islam in the Western media as to have ignored the domestic criminalities of Islamic regimes in the course of his denunciations of those media, now championed, because the superior sanctity of *literature* was involved, the novelist's absolute right to write as he pleases, regardless of the novelist's own location in relation to the corporate world of global representations and the British imperial state.

Denunciations of the Irani state for passing the death sentence and whipping up assassination squads were, of course, entirely in order, but Said went far beyond that. The issue of rising, or failing to rise, in Rushdie's defence became for him the touchstone for moral rectitude on the part of writers in a host of countries. The fact that most writers located in Asia and Africa failed to rise to this grand duty is said to indicate, then, that this intelligentsia is possessed, on the one hand, by networks of multinational information (CNN, NBC, etc.), and, on the other, complicities with their own states and regimes, with the result that

> in the relatively open environment postulated by communities of readers interested in emergent postcolonial Commonwealth and Francophone literature, *the underlying configurations on the ground* are directed and controlled not by processes of hermeneutic investigation, nor by sympathetic and literate

> intuition, nor by informed reading, but by much coarser and instrumental processes whose goal is the mobilization of consent, the eradication of dissent, the promotion of an almost literally blind patriotism. (emphasis added)

Those readers who are interested in 'Commonwealth Literature', we are being told, 'postulate' 'open environments' but these readerly islands of liberality are besieged by 'configurations on the ground' based on 'blind patriotism'; bureaucrats of the British Council who invented the category 'Commonwealth Literature' feel, I am sure, the same way. There is even a hint of nostalgia: 'environment' was once 'open', but 'intuition' has now ceased to be 'literate', and communities have become incapable of 'hermeneutic investigation' and 'informed reading'; what once had the potential to become refined has become 'much coarser'. The issue of the 'state' will come up soon, but what is lamented here is 'the underlying configuration on the ground' – that is to say, the state of mass culture itself, exemplified by those students who read English for technical purposes ('instrumental process') and not for its aesthetic beauty (through 'hermeneutic investigation'). The Arnoldian problematic of culture and anarchy is here in full bloom. Once these 'communities' can be accused of lacking all that the literary critic most values – literate intuition, hermeneutics, informed reading – they obviously become 'literally blind'. The evidence of this literal blindness, of course, is 'the quite stunning acquiescence of the Islamic world to the overall prohibitions and proscriptions as well as threats pronounced against Salman Rushdie', a lone genius whom an entire world ('Islamic world') fails to appreciate because of its blindness, its coarseness, its lack of hermeneutic finesse. Apart from the damning fact that they have come to regard English only as a 'technical language' while disregarding its 'aesthetic characteristics', the main problem of these communities is that they identify too closely with their state, not realizing that 'the chief, most official, forceful and coercive identity is the state with its borders, customs, ruling parties and authorities'. We shall not comment here on the double-edged meaning of the word 'customs', but that a stateless Palestinian, longing always to have a state of his own, should describe the state – *all* states; the state *as such* – as a 'coercive identity' signifies a paradox too painful to bear comment. It is as well to remember, however, that multinational capital registers exactly the same objection against sovereign states of Asia and Africa: they have their governments, customs duties, borders, and so forth, so that free movement of capital and commodities is impeded.

The price of not possessing hermeneutics but being enclosed within the borders and customs of Asian and African countries is not only that they fail to recognize a genius when they see one – Salman Rushdie in this case – but that the literature they themselves produce within those frontiers is fated to remain for ever inferior:

> I think it is a mistake to try to show that the 'other' literatures of Africa and Asia, with their more obviously worldly affiliation to power and politics, can be studied respectably, that is, as if they were in actuality as high, as autonomous, as aesthetically independent and satisfying as French, German or English literatures. The notion of black skin in a white mask is no more serviceable and dignified in literary study than it is in politics. Emulation and mimicry never get one very far.

Naipaul, surely, never made a judgement more damning. The key word here, of course, is 'respectably'; people of Asia and Africa who produce literature within their own borders and according to their own 'customs' simply are not worthy of respect, because they are mimic men, all. In direct contrast, we get – from the author of *Orientalism*, no less – the characterization of 'French, German and English literatures' as not only 'high' but also 'autonomous', 'aesthetically independent' and 'satisfying'. Now, satisfaction is doubtless a personal matter, but may one ask: 'autonomous' and 'independent' of what? The whole point of *Orientalism*, one would have thought, was that these literatures were *not* autonomous; that they were too complicit in colonialism to be spoken of primarily in terms of 'high' aesthetics.

All such mimicries (African and Asian literatures) and such coercive identities (the state, certainly, but also nation, gender, class) must be left behind. Once these are shed, the real business of literature can begin:

> The reader and writer of literature . . . no longer needs to tie him or herself to an image of the poet or scholar in isolation, secure, stable, national in identity, class, gender, or profession, but can think and experience with

> Genet in Palestine or Algeria, with Tayeb Salih as a black man in London, with Jamaica Kincaid in the white world, with Rushdie in India and Britain, and so on. . . . To paraphrase from a remark made by Auerbach in one of his last essays, our philological home is the world, and not the nation or even the individual writer.

Rarely in the latter half of the present century has one come across so unabashed a recommendation that the world, especially the 'Orient' – Palestine, Algeria, India – and indeed all the races, white and black, should be *consumed* in the form of those fictions of this world which are available in the bookshops of the metropolitan countries; the condition of becoming this perfect consumer, of course, is that one frees oneself from stable identities of class, nation, gender. Thus it is that sovereignty comes to be invested in the reader of literature, fully in command of an imperial geography. All that seems to have changed since Auerbach made that recommendation, in the name of philology, is that London itself – Britain, the white world – has become an object among other objects of consumption, quite on a par with India. This is the imperial geography not of the colonial period but of late capitalism: commodity acquires universality, and a universal market arises across national frontiers and local customs, while white trade rejoins black trade. When cultural criticism reaches this point of convergence with the universal market, one might add, it becomes indistinguishable from commodity fetishism.

## IX

So one returns, inevitably, to the question of Marxism. In the essay 'Secular Criticism', which serves both as dossier of his basic theoretical position and as introduction to *The World, the Text and the Critic*, Said had said:

> . . . it may seem that I am an undeclared Marxist, afraid of losing respectability . . .
>
> . . . on the important matter of a critical position, its relationship to Marxism, liberalism, even anarchism, it needs to be said that criticism modified in advance by labels like 'Marxism', or 'liberalism', is, in my view, an oxymoron.

> The net effect of 'doing' Marxist criticism or writing at the present time is of course to declare political preference, but it is also to put oneself outside a great deal of things going on in the world, so to speak, and in other kinds of criticism. (pp. 28–9)

But supposing that what Marxists write was not to be prejudiced and already disparaged as 'doing', in quotation marks; and supposing also that Marxism itself, when used alongside criticism, would be neither marked in similar fashion nor described as a 'label', would it not then be possible to face the problem squarely? I shall not raise the problem of 'losing respectability', because that is always a personal and therefore very touchy matter, though I must confess that I cannot help being reminded of the passage I quoted a little earlier, where Said declares that those '"other" literatures', Asian and African, cannot be read '*respectably*' as being on a par with the European.

I must mention some other problems. The problem one creates for the coherence of one's own thought when one refuses to acknowledge the full import of the fact that Gramsci was a communist militant, so that the word 'Marxist' would quite accurately describe the nature of his undertaking, and when one tries to claim, instead, that Gramsci was just another Julien Benda, another Matthew Arnold. The problem of accepting far too much from the dominant American ideology when one gives oneself the right to use the term 'Secular Criticism' as the title of a chapter; when 'oppositional criticism' can be recommended; when Guha can be lauded for being a 'poststructuralist writer' – when one regularly has recourse, in other words, to the common practice of putting two words together in order to specify lineages of theoretical or political position in all kinds of other situations – but the use of the word 'Marxist' before the word 'criticism' is declared 'oxymoronic'. Why should one *not* attach the word 'Marxist' – not the label, but the word – and attach it consistently, without quotation marks, to everything Lukács wrote after he had in fact become a Marxist, and then try to think through *his* Marxism, *one's own* Marxism if one has any, the Marxism *in general*? What sanctity attaches to this word 'criticism', which is elevated by the term 'oppositional' or 'secular', but defiled by the term 'Marxist'?

The larger issue, admittedly, is that of one's willingness – or lack of it –

'to put oneself outside a great deal of things going on in the world'. The pain of any ethical life is that all fundamental bondings, affiliations, stable political positions, require that one ceases to desire, voraciously, everything that is available in this world; that one learns to deny oneself some of the pleasures, rewards, consumptions, even affiliations of certain sorts. This much Said must have learned himself through his consistent anti-Zionism. Why is Marxism singled out for this pain – and joy – of choosing? Rather, why is Marxism alone associated only with the pain, but not the joy and the ethical need, of choosing? Is it that the secular and the religious, even the Zionist and the anti-Zionist, can equally respectably partake of the imperial geography and the consumption of a 'great deal of things', and it is only a fundamental acceptance of a Marxist position, with all its consequences, which entails an unbearable self-denial?

Like all political positions which are ethically viable, the Marxist one also closes off certain possibilities and opens up certain others. In choosing such a position, one chooses the closures, certainly, but one also chooses the potentialities. Said's warning – which is also a self-warning – that a choice for Marxism entails putting 'oneself outside a great deal of things' points towards a possible inventory of renunciations; it is a pity, though, that Said never takes stock of what Marxism might have made possible, nor of what one actually *loses* when one puts oneself *inside* too many things. Having access to a 'great deal of things' always gives one a sense of opulence, mastery, reach, choice, freedom, erudition, play. But resolution of the kind of ambivalences and self-cancelling procedures which beset Said's thought requires that some positions be vacated, some choices be made, some of these 'great deal of things' be renounced.

# 6

# Marx on India: A Clarification

There is a large and by now fairly old tradition of cultural criticism which addresses the issues of empire as well as the uses of literature and the knowledge industry that generates imperialist ideologies both for domestic consumption within the metropolitan countries and for export to the imperialized formations, not to speak of the complicity of particular writers, scholars and scholarly disciplines. In other words, the body of work on cultural imperialism is very copious. Until about the mid 1970s, most of that scholarship had been produced by people who were either Marxists themselves or were quite prepared to accept their affinities with Marxist positions on issues of colony and empire; much useful work of that kind continues to be done even today. Within mainstream scholarship, the usual way of marginalizing that work was either to ignore it altogether or to declare it simple-minded and propagandistic. Dismissal by the post-structuralist critic is as a rule equally strident, though the vocabulary has of course changed. Instead of using words like 'simple-minded' or 'propagandist', one now declares that work of that kind was too positivistic, too deeply contaminated with empiricism, historicism, the problematics of realism and representability, the metaphysical belief in origin, agency, truth.

It has been Edward Said's achievement to have brought this question of cultural imperialism to the very centre of the ongoing literary debates in the metropolitan university by posing it in terms that were acceptable to that university. Sections of the Right could still attack him, as they loudly did, but the liberal mainstream had to concede both that he knew his

Spitzer and his Auerbach as well as they did, and that he certainly was not 'propagandistic' in the way the 1960s' radicals usually were. One of Said's notable contributions to the American Left, in fact, is that he, perhaps more than anyone else, has taught this Left how to build bridges between the liberal mainstream and avant-garde theory. The range of erudition has been a considerable asset, though not everyone who wrote from the Marxist position was necessarily less erudite. And there certainly is an eloquence, a style. But the notable feature, underlying all the ambivalences, is the anti-Marxism and the construction of a whole critical apparatus for defining a postmodern kind of anti-colonialism. In this Said was certainly among the first, and a setter of trends. The Marxist tradition had been notably anti-imperialist; the Nietzschean tradition had had no such credentials. Now it transpires that that is precisely what had been wrong – not with the Nietzschean intellectuals but with anti-imperialism itself. It *should* have been Nietzschean and now needed to do some theoretical growing up.

For buttressing the proposition that Marxism is not much more than a 'modes-of-production narrative' and that its opposition to colonialism is submerged in its positivistic 'myth of progress', it is always very convenient to quote one or two journalistic flourishes from those two dispatches on India, the first and the third, which Marx wrote for the *New York Tribune* in 1853 and which are the most anthologized on this topic: 'The British Rule in India' and 'The Future Results of the British Rule in India'. That Said would quote the most-quoted passage, the famous one on 'the unconscious tool',[1] is predictable, and there is no evidence in *Orientalism* that he has come to regard this as a *representative* passage after some considerable engagement with Marx's many and highly complex writings on colonialism as such and on the encounter between non-capitalist and capitalist societies. This is certainly in keeping with Said's characteristically cavalier way with authors and quotations, but here it gains added authority from the fact that it is by now a fairly familiar procedure in dealing with Marx's writings on colonialism. The dismissive *hauteur* is then combined in very curious ways with indifference to – possibly ignorance of – how the complex issues raised by Marx's cryptic writings on India have actually been seen in the research of key Indian historians themselves, before the advent, let us say, of Ranajit Guha. What this *hauteur* seems to suggest is that neither Marx's writing on India nor what Indian scholarship has had to say about that writing is really worth knowing in any detail; the issue of Indian scholarship is in fact never raised – not even by remote suggestion. This, too, is curious. One would have thought that if some 'Orientalist' view of Indian history were in question, one obvious place to start looking for a discussion of that 'Orientalism' might well be the writings of precisely those anti-imperialist Indian historians who have been most concerned about the structure of pre-colonial Indian society and its contrasts with Europe at that stage – superb historians, I might add, by any reckoning.

It is not my purpose in this chapter to address the whole issue of Marx's writings on India, or to review the many Indian debates which have a bearing on the subject; that would be quite beyond the scope of the present argument. Rather, I should like to examine Said's summary way of dealing with this complex and highly contentious matter, to summarize some minimal background for putting Marx's journalism in perspective, and then to cite some representative opinions from the main currents of anti-colonial historiography in India, in order to illustrate the curious fact that Said's understanding is quite the opposite of what Indian historians have usually had to say about this question. This clarification is necessary because Said's position on this matter is both authoritative and influential, while the procedure in his treatment of Marx is a familiar one, as we saw in the case of Aeschylus and Dante in the previous chapter: he detaches a certain passage from its context, inserts it into the Orientalist archive and moves in different, even contradictory, directions.

The larger section of the book in which Said's comments on Marx are enclosed actually deals with English and French literary travellers in the Near East – Edward Lane, Nerval, Flaubert, Lamartine, Burton, and others. The appearance of Marx in this company is surprising, since he was not 'literary' in that sense, nor did he ever travel anywhere south of France. The distinction is important because the theme of the section is *testimony* and *witness* brought back in the form of travelogue, fiction, lyric, linguistic knowledge, to say 'I was there, therefore I know'. Marx clearly made no such claims. Said none the less goes on to quote the overly famous passage:

> Now, sickening as it must be to human feeling to witness those myriads of industrious patriarchal and inoffensive social organizations disorganized and

> dissolved into their units, thrown into a sea of woes, and their individual members losing at the same time their ancient form of civilization and their hereditary means of subsistence, we must not forget that these idyllic village communities, inoffensive though they may appear, had always been the solid foundation of Oriental despotism, that they restrained the human mind within the smallest possible compass, making it an unresisting tool of superstition, enslaving it beneath the traditional rules, depriving it of all grandeur and historical energies . . .
>
> England, it is true, in causing a social revolution in Hindustan was actuated only by the vilest interests, and was stupid in her manner of enforcing them. But that is not the question. The question is, can mankind fulfil its destiny without a fundamental revolution in the social state of Asia? If not, whatever may have been the crimes of England she was the unconscious tool of history in bringing about that revolution.

Now, it is obviously true that colonialism did not bring us a revolution.[2] What it brought us was, precisely, a non-revolutionary and retrograde resolution to a crisis of our own society which had come to express itself, by the eighteenth century, in a real stagnation of technologies and productivities, as well as regional and dynastic wars so constant and ruinous as to make impossible a viable coalition against the encroaching colonial power. Likewise, it is doubtless true that the image of Asia as an unchanging, 'vegetative' place was part of the inherited world-view in nineteenth-century Europe, and had been hallowed by such figures of the Enlightenment as Hobbes and Montesquieu; it is also true – though Said does not say so – that the image of the so-called self-sufficient Indian village community that we find in Marx was lifted, almost verbatim, out of Hegel. All this had been reiterated for the Left, yet again, by Perry Anderson in his *Lineages of the Absolutist State* (1975), which had circulated widely while *Orientalism* was being drafted. Said's contribution was not that he pointed towards these facts (he emphasized instead, in literary-critical fashion, Goethe and the Romantics) but that he fashioned a rhetoric of dismissal, as we shall see presently.

In that rhetoric, moreover, there really was no room for other complexities of Marx's thought. For it is equally true that Marx's denunciation of pre-colonial society in India is no more strident than his denunciations of Europe's own feudal past, or of the Absolutist monarchies, or of the German burghers; his essays on Germany are every bit as nasty.[3] His direct comments about the power of the caste system in the Indian village – 'restrain[ing] the human mind within the smallest possible compass, making it the unresisting tool of superstition, enslaving it beneath the traditional rules, depriving it of all grandeur and historical energies' – are, on the one hand, a virtual paraphrase of his comments on the European peasantry as being mired in 'the idiocy of rural life' and remind one, on the other hand, of the whole range of reformist politics and writings in India, spanning a great many centuries but made all the sharper in the twentieth century, which have always regarded the caste system as an altogether inhuman one – a 'diabolical contrivance to suppress and enslave humanity', as Ambedkar put it in the preface to *The Untouchables* – that degrades and saps the energies of the Indian peasantry, not to speak of the 'untouchable' menial castes. Conversely, the question Marx raises towards the end of that passage – 'can mankind fulfil its destiny without a fundamental revolution in the social state of Asia?' – may be objectionable to the postmodern mind because of its explicit belief, inherited from the more decent traditions of the Enlightenment, in the unity, universality and actual possibility of human liberation, but it is surely not generated by the kind of racism Said ascribes to Marx, as we shall soon see. It is also worth recalling that those particular questions – Is human liberation possible without the liberation of Asia? What transformation will have to take place *within* Asian societies in order to make that liberation possible? – have been posed again and again in our own century: most doggedly in China, Korea, the Indochinese countries, but also in those revolutionary enterprises which were defeated so many years ago that barely a memory now remains – in Malaya, Indonesia, the Philippines, India.

I shall return to the issue of accuracy, or lack of it, in Marx's judgement presently. (Now, after the experience of the history that Britain in fact made, *who* could possibly *want* an 'unconscious tool' of that sort?) The first issue, again in the Foucauldian terms that *Orientalism* popularized, is the methodological one: what mode of thought, what discursive practice authorizes Marx's statement? Said, of course, locates it in 'Orientalism'. In my view, the intemperate shrillness of those denunciations belongs to an altogether different theoretical problematic – or 'discourse', as Said uses the term. The idea of a certain progressive role of colonialism was linked, in Marx's mind, with the idea of a progressive role of capitalism as such, in comparison with what had gone before, within Europe as much as outside it. In context, any attempt to portray Marx as an enthusiast of colonialism would logically have to portray him as an admirer of capitalism as well, which is what he wanted Germany to achieve, as quickly as possible. This idea of a colonial society giving rise to brisk capitalist development was also connected, in Marx's mind, with the North American experience. At the time when he was writing those much-too-well-known journalistic pieces on India, in the 1850s, the full colonization of Africa was still some years away, and although the process in Asia generally – and especially in India – was much further advanced, there was no *past* experience of fully fledged colonization in these two continents that was available for summation; the long-term consequences of full colonization in our part of the world were still a matter for speculation. Rammohun himself, indulging in the worst kind of speculation, had *recommended* the settling of British farmers and the insertion of British capital into the Indian economy, in order to buttress the 'constructive mission' of British colonialism, some thirty years before Marx offered his generalities. In other words, from the historical point of view, the status of Marx's writings on the possible consequences of British colonialism in India is not theoretical but conjectural and speculative.

What gave these speculations their particular, progressivist slant, apart from a positivist faith in the always-progressive role of science and technology, was the prior experience of the United States, where a powerful capitalist society was then emerging out of a brutal colonizing dynamic – more brutal, in fact, than that in India – and was even then, during the 1850s, in the process of completing its bourgeois revolution, in the shape of the impending Civil War. Marx was wondering, even as the conflict in India waxed and waned, whether India might not, in the long run, go the way of the United States. The idea of 'the transplantation of European society' grew out of that analogy, which now appears to us altogether fantastic, but it is worth recalling that the gap in material prosperity between India and England was narrower in 1835 than it was to become by 1947, on the eve of decolonization. Marx was particularly concerned with the anachronisms of our pre-capitalist societies, the dead weight of our caste rigidities, the acute fragmentation of our polities, the primacy of military encampment over manufacture in our mode of urbanization, the exhaustion of the urban artisanate – due as much to levels of direct appropriations as to the inability to find markets in the countryside – and other such distortions of development in nineteenth-century India, because these distortions were seen as impediments in the path towards a true bourgeois revolution. We need to keep the whole range of these complexities in mind while reading those journalistic pieces, even though Marx's understanding of Indian society was on some crucial points factually quite incorrect; indeed, the hope of brisk industrialization under colonialism turned out to be so misplaced that Marx himself seems to have abandoned it in later years. Here, in any event, is Said's main comment on Marx's passage:

> That Marx was still able to sense some fellow feeling, to identify even a little with poor little Asia, suggests that something happened before the labels took over . . . only to give it up when he confronted a more formidable censor in the very vocabulary he found himself forced to employ. What that censor did was to stop and then chase away the sympathy, and this was accompanied by a lapidary definition: Those people, it said, don't suffer – they are Orientals and hence have to be treated in other ways. . . . The vocabulary of emotion dissipated and it submitted to the lexicographical police action of Orientalist science and even Orientalist art.

Several things in Marx's passage are – to me, at least – disagreeable, including its positivist belief in the march of history, and I shall return to some of my own reservations about Marx's writings on India. But having read it countless times over some twenty years I still cannot find in that passage even a hint of the racist 'lapidary definition' which Said claims to find there: 'Those people don't suffer – they are Orientals and hence have to be treated in other ways.' There is a different kind of blindness in that passage, but racism – and racism of that order – there is not. What is also striking about Said's comment is its reckless psychologizing impulse – not that Marx held certain views about historical development which led inevitably to this passage, but that something happened to him *emotionally*, *psychologically*. I should rather think that Marx's passage needs to be placed, if one wishes to grasp its correlates, alongside any number of passages from a wide variety of his writings, especially *Capital*, where the destruction of the European peasantry in the course of the primitive accumulation of capital is described in analogous tones, which I read as an enraged language of *tragedy*, – a sense of colossal disruption and irretrievable loss, a moral dilemma wherein neither the old nor the new can be wholly affirmed, the recognition that the sufferer was at once decent and flawed, the recognition also that the history of victories and losses is really a history of material productions, and the glimmer of a hope, in the end, that something good might yet come of this merciless history. One has to be fairly secure in one's own nationalism to be able to think through the dialectic of this tragic formulation. Amilcar Cabral emphasized as much in his famous essay 'The Weapon of Theory', which he first delivered as a talk in Havana at a time when he was leading Southern Africa's most highly developed struggle against Portuguese colonialism.

Said's treatment of Marx is too impressionistic ever to come down to any real chronology, but if I understand him correctly he seems to be asserting that Marx *started* with 'some fellow feeling' for 'poor Asia' but then gave in to a 'censor' (Orientalism) which served to 'chase away the sympathy' and replaced it with that 'lapidary definition'. Marx, it seems, started in one place and arrived at another: what is rehearsed here for us appears to be a *chronology* of submission, or at least blockage. May one, then, quote from a letter he wrote to Danielson in 1881:

> In India serious complications, if not a general outbreak, are in store for the British government. What the British take from them annually in the form of rent, dividends for railways useless for the Hindoos, pensions for the military and civil servicemen, for Afghanistan and other wars, etc., etc., – what they take from them *without any equivalent* and *quite apart* from what they appropriate to themselves annually *within* India, – speaking only of *the value of the commodities* that Indians have to gratuitously and annually *send over* to England – it amounts to *more than the total sum of the income of the 60 million of agricultural and industrial laborers of India*. This is a bleeding process with a vengeance.[4] (original emphasis)

This letter was written towards the very end of Marx's life, and the 'lapidary definition' which Said puts into the mouth of Orientalism ('Those people don't suffer – they are Orientals') does not seem to have prevented Marx from describing colonialism as a 'bleeding process with a vengeance', the 'lexicographical police action' notwithstanding. Between the dispatch of 1853 from which Said quotes and the letter of 1881 cited above, there had also been – in terms of chronology – the great Rebellion of 1857. This is not the place to review the complexities of Marx's analyses of that event, but it is worth recalling that he declared it a 'national revolt' and welcomed it as part of what he took to be a great Asian upheaval, indicated to him first by the Taiping Rebellion, against Europe – which was certainly more than what was said by the whole of the emergent modern intelligentsia of Bengal, which remained doggedly pro-British.[5]

Nor was Marx alone in this, either in the earlier or the latter part of his life. Engels, who had virtually forced Marx to take up that journalism in the first place, had this to say about what we today call 'national liberation':

> There is evidently a different spirit among the Chinese now. . . . The mass of people take an active, nay, a fanatical part in the struggle against the foreigners. They poison the bread of the European community at Hongkong by wholesale, and with the coolest meditation. . . . The very coolies emigrating to foreign countries rise in mutiny, and as if by concert, on board every emigrant ship, fight for its possession. . . . Civilization mongers who throw hot shell on a defenseless city and add rape to murder, may call the system cowardly, barbarous, atrocious; but what matter it to the Chinese if it be but successful? . . . We had better recognize that this is a war *pro aris et focis*, a popular war for the maintenance of Chinese nationality.[6]

That is a wonderfully contemptuous word for the colonizers: 'civilization-mongers'! What one wishes to emphasize here is that the writings of Marx and Engels are indeed contaminated in several places with the usual banalities of nineteenth-century Eurocentrism, and the general prognosis they offered about the social stagnation of our societies was often based on unexamined staples of conventional European histories. Despite such inaccuracies, however, neither of them portrayed *resistance* to colonialism as misdirected; the resistance of the 'Chinese coolie' was celebrated in the same lyrical cadences as they would deploy in celebrating the Parisian communard. On the whole, then, we find the same emphases there as Cabral was to spell out a century later: colonialism did have, in some limited sense and in some situations, a 'progressive' side, but 'maintenance' of 'nationality' is the inalienable right of the colonized. For Indian historiography, meanwhile, this issue of the partially progressive role of colonialism has been summarized by Bipan Chandra, our foremost historian of anti-colonial thought of the Indian bourgeois intelligentsia, who is himself sometimes accused of being too nationalistic:

> . . . most of the anti-imperialist writers would agree with Marx. They all, without exception, accept that the English introduced some structural changes and nearly all of them welcome these changes. . . . Their criticism was never merely or even mainly that the traditional social order was disintegrated by British rule but that the structuring and construction of the new was delayed, frustrated, and obstructed. From R.C. Dutt, Dadabhai Naoroji and Ranade down to Jawaharlal Nehru and R.P. Dutt, the anti-imperialist writers have not . . . really condemned the destruction of the pre-British economic structure, except nostalgically and out of the sort of sympathy that any decent man would have, that, for example, Marx showed for the 'poor Hindu's' loss of the old world.[7]

I shall have more to say about some other Indian historians and political leaders in a moment, but let me return to the passage from Marx which Said quotes, and to the methodological problem of how we read particular statements in relation to discursive practices, in terms to which Said would appear to subscribe. It seems fairly clear to me that what authorizes that particular statement – to the effect that the replacement of village society by industrial society is historically necessary and therefore objectively progressive – is by no means the discourse of 'Orientalism' (Britain, Marx says, is pursuing the 'vilest interests') but what Foucault would designate as the discourse of political economy. In other words, Marx's statement follows not *anecdotally* from Goethe or German Romanticism, nor discursively from an overarching 'Orientalism', but *logically and necessarily* from positions Marx held on issues of class and mode of production, on the comparative structuration of the different pre-capitalist modes, and on the kind and degree of violence which would inevitably issue from a project that sets out to dissolve such a mode on so wide a scale. One may or may not agree with Marx, either in the generality of his theoretical construction or with his interpretation of particular events, but the question about Said's method remains in any case, as much here as in the case of Dante: if particular representations and discursive statements – if in fact they *are* discursive statements – can float so easily in and out of various discourses, then in what sense *can* we designate any one of them a discourse in which the whole history of Western enunciations is so irretrievably trapped?

The Foucauldian objection, in any case, is not the only possible one – to my mind, not even the more important one – against Said's procedure here. At the one point in *Orientalism* where he registers a considerable difference with Foucault, Said emphasizes his own belief in 'the determining imprint of individual writers' (p. 23). Yet when he sets out to debunk Dante or Marx or a host of others, what he offers us are decontextualized quotations, with little sense of what status the quoted passage has in the work of the 'individual writer' or what sort of 'imprint' he might have left – what responses the writing might have evoked – among scholars and thinkers outside 'the West'. These are complicated histories and this is not the place to examine all of them, but to the extent that Said's summary dismissal is fairly characteristic of some current radical understandings in the Anglo-American milieu – in its dismissal and its summary brevity – a few facts may be usefully cited.

Marx sent, in all, thirty-three dispatches on Indian affairs to the *New York Tribune* ('this wretched paper', as he unjustly called it in a letter to Engels in 1858) and thought of the whole enterprise as 'a great interruption' to the economic studies he was then undertaking, having put the defeats of 1848–49 behind him after writing *The Eighteenth Brumaire*. The likelihood is that the journalism might not have come if he had not needed the money so very desperately. Twelve of those dispatches were written in 1853, fifteen in 1857, six in 1858. The first thing to be said for this overly famous series, which got going with the dispatch of June 1853, is that there is no evidence that Marx was taking any regular interest in India before the beginning of that year; it was the presentation of the Company Charter to Parliament for renewal that gave him the idea of attending to this matter in the first place. That he read much of the Parliamentary Papers and the *Travels* of Bernier, the seventeenth-century French writer and medicine-man, very carefully before writing the first dispatch is clear enough, and his acuteness of mind is equally obvious from the great insights which are scattered throughout the series. But the overall status of that journalism cannot be separated from its immediate purpose, the general state of knowledge about India prevailing in England at the time (which was far more considerable than Said would grant, but still patchy and frequently misleading), the web of prejudice which enveloped that knowledge (but the prejudice was not the only and not even an isolable fact), the relative novelty of the subject matter for Marx himself, and the stage in his own development at which these pieces begin; the drafting even of the *Grundrisse*, let alone *Capital*, was still some years away.

No careful reader of *Orientalism* need be surprised by the fact that Said hangs the whole matter on a quotation from the first, most widely anthologized of those dispatches, without any effort to contextualize the writing.[8] How little Marx knew about India when he started writing those pieces is indicated by the fact that he thought the title for all agricultural land was held by the sovereign;[9] he had picked up this idea from Bernier and others, and the British authorities had done much to propagate it, since *they* were now the new rulers. Only four years later, when he came to write the second series of his dispatches on India, he had realized that this had been at best a legal fiction, but he still did not even begin quite to grasp the complex land tenure system in pre-British India and began having some sense of the intricacies only much later, after he had read Kovalevsky's *Communal Landholdings* (1879), when his main interest had shifted to the Russian *mir* and India figured in his studies only as a comparative case.[10]

The point is neither to suggest that those dispatches should be simply ignored as mere juvenilia, nor to argue in favour of an onward march in Marx's thoughts on India, from precocious insight to final clarities. The point, rather, is to emphasize far greater complexity than Said's summary procedures admit, and even to register a certain affinity with Harbans Mukhia when he remarks, in the course of what is clearly one of the definitive summations of how one is now to view Marx's writings on India in the light of more modern researches:

> The notion of significant changes in pre-colonial India's economy and society is a recent entrant in Indian historiography; and no hard effort is called for to explain Marx's ignorance of it. . . . Yet the significant difference implied by Marx in the pace and nature of changes in pre-colonial Indian society *vis-à-vis* premodern Europe remains an important pointer to the different paths of development that those societies have followed for entering into the modern world.
>
> Europe's stages of historical development – slavery, feudalism and

> capitalism – are clearly enough marked. . . . Changes in India are long-drawn and gradual; they have the effect of modifying the existing production techniques and social organization of production; but they rarely overthrow an existing social and economic structure and replace it by a new one, by a new mode of production. *This is especially true since the seventh century* A.D. (emphasis added)

Then, after summarizing some of the social conflicts which beset India over the next millennium, from the seventh to the seventeenth century, Mukhia goes on to say:

> As a consequence of these conflicts, the means of production were never redistributed until after the onset of colonialism; what was distributed and redistributed was the peasants' surplus produce. It was thus that even when crises created by such momentous events, as the collapse of the Mughal empire, occurred during the early eighteenth century, the empire was succeeded by the resurgence of the class of zamindars everywhere; the crisis, in other words, led to the resurgence of an old property form rather than the emergence of a new one.[11]

We might add that Mukhia's is a very cautious and authoritative evaluation, by no means simply adulatory; he carefully documents how Marx was at least partially wrong on every count. He disagrees with Irfan Habib in matters both of detail and of emphasis in the latter's interpretation both of medieval India and of Marx's writings on the subject, but he, like Habib, rejects the idea of the so-called Asiatic mode of production as well as the alternative notion that pre-colonial India was somehow 'feudal'; these agreements and disagreements aside, he and Habib are entirely in accord on what Mukhia has to say in the above passage.[12] These two are, of course, among contemporary India's distinguished historians for the pre-colonial period and both doubtless write, even as they periodically disagree with each other on some key issues, from recognizably strict Marxist positions. Ravinder Kumar, an equally distinguished historian of both the colonial and the post-colonial periods who writes from within that other tradition also descended from strands in classical Marxism, the tradition of Left-liberal social democracy, basically confirms the same substantive prognosis:

> . . . substantially self-regulating village communities, scattered over the face of the subcontinent, and characterized by relatively weak economic and cultural interaction with one another, constituted the distinctive feature of rural society over the centuries. Hence the vision of a timeless and static world which surfaces again and again in the historical literature on Indian civilization. The classic formulation of this vision is to be found in the memoranda penned by British civilians of the nineteenth century, who, while they overstated the case for changelessness, nevertheless grasped an essential truth about the structure and configuration of rural society in India.[13]

Marx's famous view of colonialism's 'double mission in India: one destructive, the other regenerating', which Said takes to be the epitome of 'the Romantic Orientalist vision' in which Marx's 'human sympathy' is 'dissolved', is thus one that has been debated very, very extensively, in explicit as well as implicit ways, by India's own most notable political thinkers (from Gandhi to Namboodripad) as well as Indian historians. It is unfortunate that Said is unaware of these complex intellectual and political traditions. There are innumerable things to be learned from them, but as regards the positions that have been given such credence by Edward Said and the subsequent Colonial Discourse Analysis groups, at least two general principles which govern the principal historiographic traditions in India – essentially humanist, rationalist and universalist principles – may be emphasized. One is that the right to criticize is a universal right, which must be conceded to everyone, European and Asian alike; what is objectionable is not the European's right to criticize Asians, past or present, but those particular exercises of this right which are manifest and arbitrary exercises of colonial or racial or any other kind of prejudice. In other words, criticism itself must be evaluated from some objective criterion of validity and evidence. The accompanying principle, necessarily conjoined to the first, is that the archive which we have inherited from our colonial past is, like any substantial historical archive, a vast mixture of fantastic constructs, time-bound errors and invaluable empirical information. This, too, must be subjected to the same kind of discrimination that we require for any other kind of historical investigation, whether the writer in question is European or non-European.

Before we go on to offer some comments on the politically contrasting traditions, from Gandhi to Namboodripad, it may be useful here, without attempting a full résumé, to specify that Marx's position was in fact the exact opposite of what can accurately be called the *Orientalist* position in India, and that Marx self-consciously *dissociates* himself from that position when he declares earlier, in that very first dispatch: 'I share not the opinion of those who believe in a golden age of Hindustan.'[14] The idea of a golden age in the remote past which India now needed to reconstitute – one that sections of Orientalist scholarship had inherited from strands of High Brahminism – was to bequeath itself to a great many tendencies in Indian nationalism, as we shall soon see. But then Marx moves quickly to dissociate himself also from the opposite position – most famously enunciated by the anti-Orientalist Macaulay – which saw British colonialism as a benign civilizing mission. Against that Marx is equally unequivocal, in the very next paragraph: 'the misery inflicted by the British on Hindustan is of an essentially different and infinitely more intensive kind than all Hindustan had to suffer before.' In short, the idea of 'the double mission' was designed to carve out a position independent both of the Orientalist–Romantic and the colonial–modernist.

The dispatch from which Said quotes was drafted on 10 June 1853, and Said has the liberty to believe that Marx's 'human sympathy' had, by the end of that piece, been 'dissolved'. The other piece by Marx, 'The Future Results of the British Rule in India', which has become equally famous, was drafted a few weeks later, on 22 July. Here, too, Marx says some very rude things, and he certainly has no 'sympathy', either for India –

> . . . the whole of her past history, if it be anything, is the history of the successive conquests she has undergone. Indian society has no history at all, at least no known history. What we call its history, is but the history . . . of the successive intruders who founded their empires on the passive basis of that unresisting and unchanging society. (p. 29)[15]

– or for Britain:

> The profound hypocrisy and inherent barbarism of bourgeois civilization lies unveiled before our eyes, turning from its home, where it assumes respectable forms, to the colonies, where it goes naked. (p. 34)

In between, he also speaks frankly of 'the hereditary division of labour, upon which rest the Indian castes, those decisive impediments to Indian progress and Indian power',[16] but then comes the final judgement on the 'double mission':

> All the English bourgeoisie may be forced to do will neither emancipate nor materially mend the social conditions of the masses of the people . . .
>
> The Indian will not reap the fruits of the new elements of society scattered among them by the British bourgeoisie, till in Great Britain itself the new ruling classes shall have been supplanted by the industrial proletariat, or till the Hindus themselves shall have grown strong enough to throw off the English yoke altogether. (p. 33)

Three things need to be said about this judgement. First, no influential nineteenth-century Indian reformer, from Rammohun to Syed Ahmed Khan to the founders of the Indian National Congress, was to take so clear-cut a position on the issue of Indian Independence; indeed, Gandhi himself was to spend the years during World War I recruiting soldiers for the British Army. Second, every shade of Indian nationalist opinion as it developed after 1919 – from the Gandhian to the communist, and excluding only the most obscurantist – would accept the truth of that statement, *including* the idea that colonial capitalism *did* contribute 'new elements of society' in India, some of which have a very great need to be preserved. Finally, it should be of some interest to us here that Marx speaks of the 'proletariat' in the English context but of the 'Hindus' (by which he simply means the inhabitants of the country) in the context of India. In other words, only five years after his hopes for a European revolution had been dashed, Marx is hoping for three things in the short run: a socialist revolution in Britain, a nationalist revolution in India, and the break-up of the caste system. Those, he thought, would be the preconditions for 'the masses of people' even to start reaping any sort of 'benefit from the new elements of society'. Now, much later, India has of course become independent, but those two other issues – of class in Britain and caste in India ('the hereditary division of labour', as Marx puts it) – are yet to be resolved; and the resolution of the class question in India doubtless passes, even today, through the caste question.

This is hardly a 'Romantic, Orientalist vision'. But if we do want to have some sense of what a particularly Tolstoyan version of a Romantic, Orientalist statement in the Indian situation may have been like, we need go no further than the following from *Hind Swaraj*, by Gandhi, the admirer of Emerson and Tolstoy and Ruskin:

> The more we indulge in our emotions the more unbridled they become. . . . Millions will always remain poor. Observing all this, our ancestors dissuaded us from luxuries and pleasures. We have managed with the same kind of plough as existed thousands of years ago. We have retained the same kind of cottages that we had in former times, and our indigenous education remains the same. . . . It was not that we did not know how to invent machinery, but our forefathers knew that, if we set our hearts after such things, we would become slaves and lose our moral fibre. They, therefore, after due deliberation, decided that we should do what we could with our hands and feet. . . . They further reasoned that large cities were a snare and a useless incumbrance and people would not be happy in them, that there would be gangs of thieves and robbers, prostitution and vice flourishing in them, and that poor men would be robbed by rich men. They were therefore satisfied with small villages.[17]

Said has recently included Gandhi in the category of 'prophets and priests'. I am not sure whether the above is to be read as prophecy or priestcraft, but Gandhi did write it, originally in Gujarati, in 1909. What is remarkable about this passage is that whether or not Gandhi knew it, he seems to be refuting Marx on every count. If Marx raved against the slow ('vegetative') pace of change in India, Gandhi admires precisely that kind of stasis, while his sense of India's eternal changelessness is much more radical than Marx could ever muster: that the Indian peasant has used the same kind of plough for 'thousands of years', while the education system has also remained the same, is said to be a *good* thing. The reason India did not have an industrial revolution (and was therefore particularly vulnerable to colonial capital, Marx might have added) is not that the antiquated systems of production and governance did not allow it, but that 'our forefathers', in their superior wisdom, had decided that it should be so; and we should of course follow in the footsteps of 'our forefathers'. If Marx had debunked the mode of medieval India's urbanization for being based upon royal courts and military encampments and conspicuous waste of the agrarian surplus,

Gandhi simply denies the existence of cities in our history altogether: no cities, no thieves, robbers, prostitutes, or divisions between rich and poor; only the idyllic village community, based on 'moral fibre'.

Gandhi, like Marx, was an extremely complex thinker, and I have no wish to reduce him to this quotation. I should clarify, therefore, that what I am illustrating here is not Gandhism as such but a certain way of idealizing a past by eliminating all its material co-ordinates – that is to say, a certain strand of obscurantist indigenism which unfortunately surfaced in Gandhi's thought much too frequently; which was radically opposed to the way Marx thought of these matters; and which still lives today, in many forms, under the insignia, always, of cultural nationalism and opposed, always, to strands of thought derived from Marxism.

As a counterpoint to that kind of indigenism, it might be useful briefly to recapitulate the views of an eminent intellectual of the political Left – E.M.S. Namboodripad, who recently retired from his post as the General Secretary of the Communist Party of India-Marxist (CPI–M) – and who has written precisely on these same themes. In the course of a brief intervention in a seminar on Indology, Namboodripad speaks first of 'the kernel of truth concerning Indian society revealed by Marx', and then goes on to say, unwittingly shedding some light on that same paragraph which Said, unknown to Namboodripad, interprets in his own way:

> Indian society had, for several centuries, remained in a stage of stagnation and decay; its destruction had come as the order of the day. Since, however, there was no internal force which could destroy the stagnant and decaying old society, the external force that appeared on the scene, the European trading bourgeoisie who came to India in the 15th and 16th centuries, particularly the most modern and powerful of them, the British trading-cum-industrial bourgeoisie, were the 'unconscious tools of history'. Marx the revolutionary therefore did not shed a single tear at this destruction, though with his deep humanism and love for the people, he had nothing but sympathy for the Indian people who were undergoing – and hatred for the British who were inflicting – immense suffering on them.[18]

Later in the same essay, having pointed out the progressive role Bhakti had played in the rise of the post-Sanskritic modern languages, Namboodripad goes on to reflect upon the overall impact of colonialism on language and literature in India:

> The efforts of the early European trading companies to popularize the Christian faith and the subsequent measures adopted by the British rulers to establish educational institutions in order to create a stratum of educated employees of the company, led to the development of a language and literature which was as popular in style as the earlier Bhakti works, but free from the limitations of the latter which was, by and large, confined to Hindu society and culture . . .
>
> The development of the world market and the slow but sure integration of the Indian village into that world market broke the self-sufficient character of India's village society which has now become part of the growing world capitalist society . . .
>
> This naturally reflected itself in the field of literature. Eminent writers in all the languages of the rapidly-growing world capitalist system were translated into, and exercised their influence over, the new generation of Indian writers. In other words, the world of Indian literature could free itself from the shackles of the caste-ridden Hindu society and its culture only when its economic basis – the self-sufficient village with its natural economy – was shattered by the assault of foreign capitalism. (pp. 42–3)

This 'assault', then, contributed to the widening of cultural horizons: a 'progressive' role, clearly, even though one has considerable reservations about some simplification here. But Namboodripad then specifies yet another dialectic specific to colonialism: the growth, on the one hand, of a dependent, comprador intelligentsia – 'the foreign and foreign-trained intellectual elite' who emerged as 'the dominant force moving the new bourgeois literature and culture of India' and were 'interested in decrying all that was Indian . . . as "barbarian" and "uncivilized"' – and, on the other, a 'false nationalism' which defended everything Indian, old and new, and relied for its arguments, ironically, upon that other body of imperialist scholarship which had taken to idealizing 'ancient Hindu society'. The praxis of the socialist revolution is then seen, in the closing paragraphs of Namboodripad's brief text, as the negation of the *whole* of that colonial dynamic, and as the precondition for 'that final defeat of the stagnating and decadent society and culture, inherited by the Indian people from their several-centuries-old development since the pre-historic tribal societies were disintegrated and class society was formed under the garb of caste society'. This formulation, too, is notable for three different emphases. Some fundamental aspects of decadence and stagnation are acknowledged to be much older than colonialism itself; these aspects are not dissolved into the comforting category of the 'colonial legacy'. Meanwhile, colonialism itself is recognized as having come and gone without destroying 'the stagnating and decadent society'; colonialism's potential for constructive destruction was, after all, very limited. Finally, Namboodripad emphasizes that same tie between class and caste in India which we have noted above in the case of Marx and Ambedkar.

What Namboodripad specifies at the end is a particular contradiction in the cultural logic of colonial capitalism: a certain democratization of language, some secularization of ideological parameters, some denting of insularity; but also, decisively, the creation of a dominant intelligentsia which merely oscillates between ideological dependence on the fabrications and sophistries of advanced capitalism on the one hand, and indigenist, frequently obscurantist nostalgia on the other. The issue he finally raises is that of agency. To what extent can even the patriotic section of the bourgeois intelligentsia, divided as it is between metropolitan theorizations and idealized indigenisms, fulfil the tasks of the very anti-imperialism it so stridently preaches? Through what location, affiliation, praxis?

The basic thrust of Namboodripad's argument is unassailable, even though he makes at least two sizeable errors: in exaggerating the 'self-sufficiency' and 'natural economy' of the pre-colonial Indian village, and in assigning too one-sided a role in the democratization of language and literature to the missionaries and the colonial educational apparatus. We shall touch upon the latter issue at slightly greater length in the next chapter, but it is worth emphasizing that neither error is a matter of 'Orientalist' or any other a priori discursive position. They can be seen as errors thanks to the historical research which has become available especially over the past thirty years, and the same criteria of validation and evidence apply in Namboodripad's case as in any other.

That Marx picked up some phrases from the Romantic lexicon is in fact a minor matter, and whatever injury is done to one's national pride can easily be overcome by recalling the colourful epithets he uses for the European bourgeoisie. Two other kinds of problem are in fact much more central to what went wrong in Marx's writings on India. The first is the issue of evidence. Modern research shows that each of the props of Marx's general view of India – the self-sufficient village community; the hydraulic state; the unchanging nature of the agrarian economy; absence of property in land – was at least partially fanciful. Research in all these areas is still far from adequate, but the available evidence suggests that the village economy was often much more integrated in larger networks of exchange and appropriation than was hitherto realized; that the small dam, the shallow seasonal well and the local pond built with individual, family or co-operative labour were at least as important in irrigation as the centrally planned waterworks; that property in land and stratification among the peasantry was far more common than was previously assumed; and that agrarian technology was, over the centuries, not nearly as stagnant. The fact that Marx did not have this more modern research at his disposal explains the origin of his errors, but the fact that he accepted the available evidence as conclusive enough to base certain categorical assertions on it was undoubtedly an error of judgement as well.

But this error of judgement was also a theoretical error and a violation of the very materialist method which he did more than anyone else to establish in the sciences of the social as such. The danger in the practice of any materialism is that whereas it begins by opposing all those speculative systems of thought which make universal and categorical claims without the necessary physical evidence for the grounding of such claims, its own sustained oppositional practice tends to push it in a direction where it is impelled to assert universal laws of its own, different from those it opposes, but without sufficient evidence of its own; a materialism which does not sufficiently resist such pressure, and does not recognize the gap between the validity of a universalist aspiration and the paucity of both evidence and method that might in fact give us a universal history of all humankind, becomes speculative in its own way. The period of Marx's work in which those journalistic pieces were drafted is riven with contrary pulls towards the most concrete engagements, as in the *The Eighteenth Brumaire*, and brilliant but flawed speculations about a systematic, universal history of all modes of production, as in *Pre-Capitalist Economic Formations*. The drafting of *Grundrisse* – which Marx started after writing his 1853 articles on India, and which ranges from broad summations of transcontinental systems to the most minute movements of commodities – was in a way the transitional text. By the time he came to write *Capital*, the aspiration to formulate the premisses of a universal history remained, as it should have remained, but the realization grew that the only mode of production he could adequately theorize was that of capitalism, for which there was very considerable evidence as well as a largely adequate method, which he himself had taken such pains to formulate. It is from the theoretical standpoint of *Capital*, as much as from the empirical ground of more modern research in past history, that one can now see the brilliance, but also the error, in many a formulation about India.

# 7

# 'Indian Literature': Notes towards the Definition of a Category

One of my difficulties with the *theoretical* category of 'Third World Literature', it should be clear enough, is its rather cavalier way with history; its homogenization of a prolix and variegated archive which is little understood and then hurriedly categorized; its equally homogenizing impulse to slot very diverse kinds of public aspirations under the unitary insignia of 'nationalism' and then to designate this nationalism as the determinate and epochal ideology for cultural production in non-Western societies; its more recent propensity to inflate the choice of immigration into a rhetoric of exile, and then to contrive this inflation as the mediating term between the Third World and the First. Kosambi once said: 'The outstanding characteristic of a backward bourgeoisie, the desire to profit without labour or grasp of technique, is reflected in the superficial "research" so common in India.'[1] Ironically enough, so much of what is published in the metropolitan countries displays this very characteristic of the 'backward bourgeoisie' when it comes to the 'Third World'.

I find it all the more difficult to speak of a 'Third World Literature' when I know that I cannot confidently speak, as a theoretically coherent category, of an '*Indian*' Literature. The purpose of this chapter, therefore, is not to pose, category by category, an 'Indian Literature' (the national specificity) against 'Third World Literature' (the tricontinental generality) but, rather, to explore some of the difficulties we currently have in constructing such a category. One of my arguments here is that we cannot posit a *theoretical* unity or coherence of an 'Indian' literature by assembling its history in terms of adjacent but discrete histories of India's major language–literatures. A 'national' literature, in other words, has to be more than the sum of its regional constituent parts, if we are to speak of its unity theoretically. Given this position, I could not possibly be arguing at the same time that if we can assemble the historiographic knowledge of discrete national literatures in these tricontinental zones, we shall somehow arrive at a 'Third World Literature'. In other words, I emphasize not just the obvious lacunae in our empirical knowledge but also that (a) developments during the colonial period are everywhere embedded as much in the pre-colonial legacies as in the colonial processes as such; and (b) cultural productions everywhere greatly exceed the boundaries set by the colonial state and its policies, so that the highly diverse historical trajectories may simply not be available for generalizing theoretical practices and unified narratives on the tricontinental scale.

A literature exists as a theoretical object to the extent that its productions can be examined in relation to their objective determinations by the development of the culture as a whole, so that periodization comes to rest on shifts more fundamental than mere breaks in chronology and is able to account for the dominance of the major generic forms, their uneven developments in terms of period and region, as well as the material conditions for the subordination of other generic forms in the course of historical development. The possibility of that kind of objective determination in the process of the material development of a culture can certainly exist across languages and state boundaries. Culture and literature, in other words, are not necessarily coterminous with linguistic formation and state boundary, especially in historical epochs preceding the emergence of the bourgeois nation-state and, in countries like India, even after the emergence of such a state; the rise of print capitalism is a variable but by no means an invariable determinant. The difficulty in thinking of an 'Indian' literature, therefore, is not that it is spread over many languages, with histories of very uneven development, nor that the state boundaries which have historically contained these literary productions have been shifting through all the centuries we know of. The difficulty lies, rather, in the very premisses that have often governed the narrativization of that history, which has (1) privileged High Textuality of a Brahminical kind to posit the unification of this literary history; or (2) assembled the history of the main texts of particular languages (in a very uneven way) to obtain this unity through the aggregative principle; or (3) attempted to reconstruct the cross-fertilization of genres and themes in several languages, but with highly idealistic emphases and with the canonizing procedures of the 'great books' variety, with scant attempt to locate literary history within other sorts of histories in any consistent fashion.

I shall discuss these ways of narrativizing Indian literary history at some length below. Theoretically advanced work in histories of political and economic structures has shown that it *is* possible to speak of an Indian history which is not the history of mere rulers and empires and religions, and is not composed of discrete developments in sectors and geographical regions. This work, most notably of the Marxist historians,[2] has laid the basis for future work of the empirical kind and created the possibility of theoretical abstraction and generalization, hence for the plotting of periodization as regards the main forms of production and property, as well as their regional and temporal variants, gaps in knowledge and disagreements among the historians themselves notwithstanding. It is in comparison with these other kinds of histories that the relative underdevelopment of the research genre of literary history in India stands in sharpest relief, especially as regards its theoretical premisses. One of the consequences of these very uneven developments is undoubtedly that it is in these other kinds of histories, rather than the straightforward literary histories, that one comes across some of the most profound insights about what we could generally designate as 'literary', especially for the earliest centuries. My own attempt here, in any case, is not to chalk out a full theoretical position, which for me would be at the very least premature, nor to examine in detail the existing approaches, but simply to demarcate some areas which I find especially troublesome.

## I

At some level, of course, every book written by an Indian, inside the country or abroad, is part of a thing called 'Indian Literature'. But the institutions that could produce a coherent and unified knowledge of the various language–literature clusters in India, either in a strictly comparatist framework or as a unified, albeit multilingual object of knowledge, have had a rather sporadic development, so that despite superb work by individual scholars there are very few *institutional* sites where such knowledges may be systematized and disseminated among large numbers of students and teachers. As a result, the intelligentsia that could reproduce these knowledges on an extended scale remains quite dispersed and in some key areas largely undeveloped, leading to several kinds of difficulty.

There are major languages and literatures for which no comprehensive history is really available. The tradition of circulating texts through the various linguistic communities of India by means of mutual translations, without the mediation of English, is so weakly developed that even where such historical research does exist, it is rarely accessible to readers outside the particular linguistic community. The tradition of any sustained effort to study the literatures of the various languages in mutual relation, as overlapping realities constituting a unified configuration, is even weaker, so that we have, as a rule, a peculiar disjunction between an assertion that there *is* an '*Indian*' literature, and the actual production of a knowledge which refers essentially to discrete archives of individual languages, with principles of aggregation either absent or very weakly developed. This replicates in some ways those other conceptual frameworks which produce the category of a 'European Literature' both as a civilizational unity and as a comparatism of discrete national literatures. Like most analogies this one has its uses, but one of the distortions which result from confusing an analogy with a *model* is that the modern languages of India are then seen as discrete and markedly differentiated entities, as if the relationship between, say, Hindi and Urdu, or between modern Hindi and the half a dozen languages which have historically composed it and continue to have extremely diverse relations with Hindi itself, as well as with each other, were of the same order as, say, that between English and French, or Italian and Spanish.

These confusions and inadequacies of reliable information as to texts, authors, genres, modes of transmission, audiences, and so on, are most marked with respect to those early periods when what we now know as our modern languages emerge out of complex and prolonged processes of mutual influences and differentiations. And of course, these processes have been regionally very uneven. Tamil in the South undoubtedly had a much more autonomous development and became a court language very early, alongside Sanskrit in the North, so that the earliest extant texts can be dated more or less precisely, in the first century BC or thereabouts, even though much has been destroyed by the passage of time and unreliable modes of transmission, leaving large lacunae. For Kannada, the earliest inscription is from the fifth century AD, though large bodies of writing came only much later. We have only scant studies, available in other Indian languages, of the process whereby languages of the South got their differentiated identities; of the role of Sanskrit in the succeeding centuries in affecting the *linguistic–literary*, as distinct from the religious, ambience of these languages (8 per cent of the vocabulary in Malyalam is said to be of Sanskrit origin, but what is the literary significance of this linguistic property?); or of bodies of literature, notably Sangam literature[3] in Tamil, which remains much less studied in both literary and historiographic aspects than the contemporaneous Sanskrit literature. The transition from Sangam to Bhakti, which was also a Tamil phenomenon, is known only in very broad outline, but not really as a *transition*, more as a discrete epochal shift, after a gap of centuries and the intercession of an 'epic' tradition. Nor is it clear how this phenomenon of Tamil origin spread through the Deccan plateau and then across the Vindhyas, eventually to all corners of the land – if, indeed, the Northern forms of Bhakti *were* in some fundamental way a continuation of the Southern, which is again not entirely established, except through discrete pieces of evidence in the work of individual poets.

In the North itself, the gradual differentiation between the various forms of *upbhranshas* which led eventually to the consolidation, more or less, of the modern languages is also known only in outline, with very uneven bodies of information for the various linguistic regions. We do know that it happened; that the initial phase of key differentiations spans roughly the tenth to the twelfth centuries; that it was a prolonged and uneven process, with the consolidation of some modern languages (e.g. Bengali) taking place much sooner than the differentiation between some others (e.g. between Hindi and Urdu, which is an ongoing affair, starting in the late nineteenth century), while many such questions have remained unsettled into the present (the shift of millions of people in Uttar Pradesh from Hindustani to Hindi and Urdu in the 1961 Census, and in Bihar from Hindi to Maithili, are cases in point).[4] The gaps in knowledge, as well as the great fluidity and unquantifiability of what is known, should be chastening for anyone who sets out to theorize about 'Indian Literature'. Even plain historiography is at a very preliminary stage, given the large gaps in existing bodies of documentation, so that even a descriptive kind of knowledge about 'Indian Literature' as to its unities, its essential periodizations, the relationships between various sets of writings which are available from the same period, the circulation of principal genres through the overlapping linguistic clusters, and about scores of other such issues, is still of a very uncertain nature. Yet histories of individual languages as discrete entities also tend to be misleading, since multilinguality and polyglot fluidity seem to have been chief characteristics – possibly *the* characteristics – which give 'Indian Literature' its high degree of unification in the premodern phase. Unilinguality seems to have been the aspiration only of certain kinds of canonical scholasticism, whereas mass literary cultures, and even many of the elite formations, remained polyglot well into the nineteenth century, when the insertion of print capitalism, modern forms of unilingual vernacular education, the rise to literary predominance of professional petty-bourgeois strata, and the rise of many regional and religious particularisms speeded up the process of linguistic differentiation and the attendant claims – objectively fabricated and subjectively felt claims – of unilinguality. For the earlier period, Mohan Singh Diwana states the matter eloquently:

> . . . there were hardly any poets from Gorakh of the 10th century to Ghulam Farid in the early half of the nineteenth century belonging to Maharashtra, Gujarat, Bengal, Agra, Oudh, Bihar, Delhi, Punjab or Sindh, who had not written in three languages – the mother tongue, the provincial language and the common Hindustani language, Hindui, besides Persian or Sanskrit, such as he could command. Even Zafar and Sauda wrote in Punjabi; even Guru Gobind Singh wrote in Persian, in Braj, in Rekhta and in Khyal; even Guru Nanak Dev wrote in Persian, in Sanskrit, in Kafi, in Lahndi; even Namdev, Kabir, Raidas and Dadu wrote in Punjabi and Hindui. In Bengal the writers of Brajbuli thrived. Miran wrote in Rajasthani, in Gujarati and in Hindui.[5]

Among Mughal kings one might have mentioned Akbar, who is said to have composed in Braj some verses in the Bhakti mould which are now irretrievably lost, and for Bengal one could name Vidyapati himself, who is claimed by Hindi and Maithili as well as Bengali; the list, in other words, could be virtually infinite. Even the linguistic categories are so fluid that the three languages for Miran are named by Umashankar Joshi, alternatively, as 'Rajasthani, Vraj and Gujarati'[6] – the line between 'Hindui' and 'Vraj' undoubtedly being very thin. And, as I have pointed out elsewhere,[7] even Diwana's own insistence on broad and opulent heterogeneity, which is itself entirely well placed, is unfortunately too contaminated with the restrictive triadic category – 'the mother tongue, the provincial language and the common Hindustani language' – which was invented, in a more or less fantastic manner, in the course of the nineteenth century through a shifting but always unholy alliance between indigenous linguistic fundamentalists and colonial demographers, to be recovered in post-colonial policy in the liberal three-language formula. On none of the cases where Diwana himself notes the languages in which individual poets wrote does this fixed tripartite division have any bearing; linguistic fluidities have been historically of a very different kind. It is in negotiating those fluidities, so naturally embedded in the versions of the poems we now have, so bewildering for the untrained modern reader, that the initial *linguistic* aspect of comparative work begins.

This question of overlapping multilingualities remains as well for the more modern archives as they have been assembled since the introduction of print and the classificatory practices of the nineteenth century, but it also takes some new forms. Because the major languages are now much more clearly demarcated in terms of individual competences, print archives, authorial *œuvres* and reading publics, the question of translations, back and forth, among the different Indian languages becomes at once more complex and far more pressing. This machinery of translations for the circulation of literary works within the various literary communities is poorly developed, being left in a significant degree to individual industry and preference, with little institutionalized and systematic effort. I know from experience, for example, that the whole range of publishing in Urdu gives us no sense of literary developments in Kashmiri or Punjabi or Modern Hindi or Telugu, even though the Urdu *language* has always existed in regions and states where these other languages are also spoken and written, often by a majority of the people. All the Urdu academies, all the Departments of Urdu in colleges and universities, have failed to sponsor any real project of comparative scholarship, research and translation, aimed at a fuller understanding of the composite linguistic and cultural milieux in which they operate. I believe this emphasis on exclusivity is by no means unique to Urdu institutions, even though the situation is different in different linguistic communities. Translations from other Indian languages are more common in Telugu and Bengali (mainly through initiatives from the literary intelligentsias themselves) as well as Hindi (owing both to state sponsorship and to individual initiatives), but this is not work that receives much emphasis in most languages.

Lacking such public institutions for overlapping translations, direct knowledge of an '*Indian*' literature presumes the knowledge of so many languages that only rare specialists could command them all, and considering that public rewards for such labours are minimal, competences of that kind presume rare kinds of linguistic abilities combined with very exceptional kinds of individual industry and devotion – indeed, most of the work in this *integrated* field has been done by individuals who managed this rare combination. Meanwhile, it is in English more than any other language that the largest archive of translations has been assembled so far; if present trends continue, English will become, in effect, the language in which the knowledge of 'Indian' literature is produced. The difficulty is that it is the language least suitable for this role – not because it was inserted into India in tandem with colonialism, but entirely because it is, among all the Indian languages, the most removed, in its structure and ambience, from all the other Indian languages, hence least able to bridge the cultural gap between the original and the translated text. This disability is proportionately greater the closer the original text is to the oral, the performative, the domestic, the customary, the assumed, the unsaid; Miran in any other Indian language would make sense; in English nothing much better than doggerel is really possible without fundamentally altering the original to the point of unrecognizability. Certain kinds of modern, realist narratives work perfectly well in English; the rest works very infrequently. This is quite additional to the fact that the vast bulk of the literary intelligentsia in India is not and has not been very proficient in English, even as a reading public, regardless of what the upper layers of half a dozen cosmopolitan cities may believe.

My third example of the kind of comparatism we need in order to establish both the heterogeneity and the fundamental unity of 'Indian Literature' refers to genres and forms of composition. We know that the *pada*, for example, became a translinguistic, often very flexible genre for the Bhakti poets, as did the *doha*; we also know that the *doha* – like the *barahmassa*, which was also a favourite translinguistic form for these polyglot poets – survived well into the contemporary period, in less and less religious forms, becoming more and more secular: *doha* more in oral traditions, *barahmassa* in lengthier and therefore in slightly more formal ways, both oral and written. What are the histories of the genesis of these respective forms, their properties, their usages, their alterations over time and across language–literature clusters? Which social grids and belief systems produce them, which ones account for their mutation, decline, replacement? What happens to the *barahmassa*, for example, as it evolves in Hindui, develops in one direction into what was increasingly differentiated into Hindi and Urdu, lived in Urdu in close proximity with the other generic form, *mathnavi*, as it was initially imbibed from Farsi but as it drew closer, first metrically and then in systems of belief and imagery, to genres like *barahmassa*? How does one locate, then, Daya Shankar Nasim's famous (and in Urdu the first major) *mathnavi*, entitled *Gulzar-e-Ishq* (Garden of Love) in these systems of generic – and more than generic – overlaps?

One could ask similar questions about the more modern period, in terms of both thematics and generic shifts. What happens, for example, to Indian narrative traditions in the nineteenth century when the idea of companionate marriage is introduced, as a necessary form of the household in bourgeois society, across regions and languages, into the imaginative universe and the narrative structures of the newly emergent, modern Third Estate? We need to assemble these genealogies of genres, as well as their sociology, not for any formalistic reasons but because the genre often serves as the very horizon which defines the general semantic field, the presumptions of belief systems, the politics of transgression and containment, and the very possibilities of what are called the aesthetic effects of individual utterances, as well as of authors and *œuvres*. For instance, if the name 'Kabir' can simply become a collective signature for certain kinds of utterances, partly erasing the distinction between the poet and the *panthi*, that is because in certain kinds of belief communities the sharing of specific generic features of some existing utterances generates the possibility of more such utterances so profuse that only the act of compilation and transmission sets the limits of their reproduction. By the same token, the possibility of generating more and more such utterances disappears or becomes transmuted only when the belief community which gave the genre its stability disappears or shifts to markedly different systems of belief and utterance. That is why merely enumerating the compositional forms, classifying their aesthetic effects and properties, and slotting various available works under the various generic designations – which is what our literary history generally does when it addresses the question of genre at all – while it may often be of much empirical value, remains, from the standpoint of history itself, merely tautological.

## II

Let me illustrate this problem of historicizing the linguistic layerings and of generic unclassifiability, as it confronts someone with a mainly literary training in an age of print capitalism, by citing only two of the well-known properties of even those pre-modern literary texts which have already gained canonical status; these properties would obviously be there to negotiate, in equally difficult ways, for any student of literature who approaches the literary culture of the contemporary popular classes as well. I will ignore for the moment the obvious fact that a great many of these texts are implicated – and are generally recognized to be implicated – in histories of philosophy and religion, and that the disciplines both of Ancient History and of Anthropology routinely rely on these texts. Let me raise only the 'literary' question. It is well enough known, first, that a great many of the constitutive texts of our literary traditions, the *Ramayana* and the *Mahabharata* included, consist of centuries of sedimentation, in all aspects of their composition from the linguistic to the ideological, with the ideological frequently embedded in the linguistic itself; it is also well enough known that regardless of the enormous machinery of textual standardizations and commentators' glosses that all such texts have undergone, their essential status in the culture at large, century after century, has been fundamentally performative; hence the durability of their imaginative re-enactment, the always local and immediate construction of their meaning, the flexibility of their assimilation into the felt life, as well as their irretrievable mutability as written texts – until the much more recent phenomena of cinema and television began attempting a centrally produced, technically infinitely reproducible celluloid performance that could now aspire to displace both the mutability and the agential immediacy of all local performances and figurations.

Meanwhile, numerous Bhakti poets present us with the added difficulty, apart from the frequent impossibility of fixing individual authorship even when the signature line is there, that not only their overall *œuvres* but even individual compositions have embedded in them, compositely, earlier versions of not one but several of what we now know as our modern languages, and that the poetry itself has always belonged fundamentally to the oral–performative domain, to the extent that not only the producer, the performer or the audience but even the subsequent scribe(s) would continually amend it both textually and performatively. Considering just these two facts, one may well ask what there *is* in the disciplinary knowledge of a literary critic, other than the presumed sensitivity to ranges of verbal meaning in the printed form, which prepares one to approach such artefacts. Literary criticism, a product of print capitalism, presumes the existence of printed texts; it presumes stable textual objects, even when comparison of texts is to be undertaken and the objective is, precisely, to establish a stable text; it distinguishes itself from other ways of knowing by choosing for itself objects which are said to disclose their meanings primarily through their verbal construction; at its widest, it admits biographical background, social origins of the author, the sociology of aesthetic effects; but it presses us to return, always, to poems as printed units in relation to other poems, also as printed units. The pedagogy of 'New Criticism', which is the dominant and frightfully universal pedagogy of English Departments, especially in India, narrows these engagements as much as possible, through what is called 'close reading'. What happens to this pedagogy, into which we are all recruited, when we approach texts which are forever distributed between word and performance, where layers of language may be several even in the strict philological sense, where authorship is itself frequently layered and sedimented, where undeterminable contradictions of authorial location introduce equally difficult problems of both sociological origin and ideological locations – even of periodization – of individual texts, authors, *œuvres*, given that we often know little about the immediate circumstance of composition even for the text as it comes to *us*?

Linguistic and philological problems are myriad, and they exist at one level of difficulty; but one would need to know, in the same sweep, the aesthetic densities of certain kinds of music, dance, gesture, ritual, on the local as well as the trans-Indic plane; the anthropology of certain kinds of recitation and locution; the social history of certain kinds of belief; the genealogies of temples, *maths*, communities, pilgrimages; the hard economy of materialities out of which arise certain kinds of images and addresses, certain generic expressions of grief or joy, which now come to us primarily as aesthetic form – and because we, as progeny of the wider culture, do *feel* the power of many of them, we often make the mistake of thinking, carelessly, that we know their origins, the whole range of their powers and meanings, and the modalities of what they have been in the past or may now be in other locations of class and community even today. It is the purest error of the literary-critical mind to think that the structure of such cultural artefacts, the central documents of our literary tradition, is essentially verbal, linguistic and therefore apprehensible as *poetry* – though, of course, it *is* poetry in the most fundamental sense of that word. My suggestion, however, is not that each one of us has to develop all these other kinds of abilities before we qualify to speak of this history; that would be nonsense. My sense, rather, is that mere literary-critical abilities simply will not do, that the requisite kind of work can be done, individually and collectively, only across disciplinary boundaries and through undertakings which submit 'literary criticism' to a whole range of the expressive arts and the human sciences.

But we need also to take the measure of what the development of print capitalism, which has become increasingly the determining material condition for India's literary development over the past two centuries, has done to our sense of what literature and the site of its production *is*. As we look back at some of the most powerful developments up to the eighteenth century, we find that the locus of literary production – certainly for those immense movements which changed the face of India in their own time – was most frequently not the urban elite but the life-process of the artisanate, the peasantry, the women, the *shudras*, the precariously located clusters of dissent. With the arrival of the printing presses, however, 'literary' has come to mean that which we see in printed form, and because of this privileging of print in a predominantly non-literate society, the social weight in the very process of literary production has shifted towards the leisured class and the professional petty bourgeoisie, away from the alternative modes of preservation and transmission which do not involve print and are then involved also in modes of evaluation rather different from those of the print culture. The gap, within the vernaculars, between the popular and the petty-bourgeois forms and vocabularies has widened to such an extent that all progressive cultural work is beset, to a lesser or greater degree, with the problem of *finding* a vocabulary of forms and enunciations that may bridge it. The question of the relationship between oral–performative and print – which in the urban setting of High Culture is seen as a relation between 'literature' and the other arts (theatre, most often) but is more fundamentally a relation between rural and urban, popular and elite, that which is *authorized* as 'literature' and that which is not – must be posed in some different ways as regards, precisely, the modern.

The other emphasis of my argument here, on bi- and multilingualities, surely has to do with our personal lives – for rare would be an Indian with any degree of urban or periurban experience who functions with only one language – but also with the very shapes of our collectivity, past and present. For unlike that of the West European countries, where the historical movement which consolidated them as nation-states was also, in each case, the one that constituted their national literatures, the principle of our unity was civilizational and historical for many centuries before it came to be contained in the national form, so that the 'national' literature of India finds its principle of unity not in linguistic uniformity but in civilizational moorings and cultural ethos, hence in histories of 'literary' movements and even compositional forms which have crisscrossed geographical boundaries and linguistic differences. In this respect, the marked difference of Indian political culture from the European one is that the period in which print capitalism established its power in India is precisely the one in which a multilingual anti-colonial nationalism spread from one end of the country to the other; even the divisions which came within that nationalism – on religious, communal, class lines – were themselves multilingual. This civilization has been a composite one precisely to the extent that it has possessed, in the cultural domain, a remarkable history of an essential unity in structures of feeling, yet great diversity in forms of belief and utterance, which have then *travelled* through and across linguistic ensembles; the stresses which have in the past and may again in the future blow apart those unities have taken many forms, but hardly ever exclusively, or even predominantly, the linguistic. Multiplicity of languages is the fundamental characteristic of this civilization, this nation, this literature, and the structure of its unity is positivistically far less quantifiable than in Europe or in Europe's offshoots in North America. I might add that this characteristic of loose and diverse unities is by no means unique to India, since it obviously exists in several other Asian and African countries as well; the *scale* on which this fact needs to be addressed here, however, is historically unprecedented.

## III

There is doubtless the generally undisputed idea that an 'Indian Literature' exists, whether definable and quantifiable or not in generic or any other terms, one whose unity resides in the common national origins of its authors and the common civilizational ethos of the Indian people. This is neither better nor worse than the way national literatures are usually defined, even though the civilizational depth in this case is far greater than most, and even though our actual knowledge or understanding of this unity, as regards 'Literature', remains more or less opaque. Many of these gaps in our knowledge are inevitable results of very incomplete kinds of evidence which have survived, or of the inevitable inadequacy of a still developing tradition of literary historiography; these material conditions one accepts. What is disconcerting, however, is that much of the existing and ongoing research seems to be governed by the ideology of the literary text as a discrete, aesthetic object – partly canonical in the New-Critical way, partly spiritual in the iconographic mould – and of literature as a treasure-chest, virtually a temple, of such objects. The histories of various language–literatures, from Assamese to Telugu, which Sahitya Akademi is in the habit of issuing from time to time, are marvels of this discreteness of texts, genres, periods, linguistic formations – even of 'Literature', most of the time, from the non-literary. Within these broad predicates, meanwhile, we have at least two different ways of demarcating this literature.

The more traditional one, which has endured for a remarkably long time, privileges the classical texts and then follows them up with some eclectic selection of a few medieval and modern texts, bestowing upon them a vast canonicity, with little regard to the possible relationship between the canonized text and the larger, obscured networks of literary productions and their social groundings; what often seems to hold this canon together is a preference for religion and metaphysics, so that it is said to exude, transhistorically, some essential Indianness in the form of an abiding spiritual ethos. This privileging of antiquity and preponderant citation of Sanskrit classics as the unique repertoire of 'Indian Literature' is there not only in those (frequently German) Orientalists, from Wilhelm von Schlegel to Maurice Winternitz, who played a key role in constructing the category in the first place,[8] but in full splendour also in such legendary nationalists as Aurobindo Ghosh.[9] Winternitz did devote one of the three volumes of his history to the early Buddhist and Jain classics, so that the emphasis on Sanskrit becomes less exclusive, but it is significant that 'Indian Literature' to him still meant, in the first decades of the present century, predominantly a universe of Vedic, Sanskritic, religious and metaphysical texts of North Indian antiquity.[10] Tamil literature seems not to have interested this tradition of Orientalist High Textuality, despite its own antiquity, perhaps because of the inherent Northerly/Sanskritic bias of the Indo-Aryan philological construct, perhaps because of late availability of the Sangam anthologies even in printed Tamil, and, conceivably, because the secularity and this-worldliness of Sangam poetic traditions really do not appeal to the kind of mind for which the outstanding attribute of the Indian tradition is its purported spirituality. It was not, of course, possible for Winternitz, in the first quarter of the present century as bourgeois nationalism got going inside India, to ignore entirely the plain fact that India did continue to have a history after the seventh century as well, so that subsequent developments, spread over some fifteen hundred years and in scores of languages, do appear in his book – in a brief appendix.

Quite apart from being astonishingly ahistorical, these Orientalist ways of privileging the early tradition so entirely at the expense of later ones are doubtless highly obscurantist and even repressive in their own special ways, as my later comments will indicate. It is worth remarking, though, that these emphases were nevertheless infinitely superior and infinitely more productive than the colonial–modernist positions of Macaulay, who famously declared that he had 'never found one among them [i.e. the Orientalists] who could deny that a single shelf of a good European library was worth the whole native literature of India and Arabia', and then went on to conclude that he 'would at once stop the printing of Arabic and Sanskrit books'.[11] The irony of such a statement is not only that it is so outrageously wrong in its devaluation of those traditions and texts, but also that it grossly misrepresents the Orientalist viewpoint, which emphatically insisted on printing, reprinting, translating, studying and putting those very texts on those very shelves of any 'good European library'. The original Orientalist position, diametrically opposed to Macaulay's, was stated with no less rhetorical flourish by William Jones in his address to the Bengal Asiatic Society in 1776: 'the Sanskrit language, whatever be its antiquity, is of wonderful structure, more perfect than the Greek, more copious than the Latin, and more exquisitely refined than either.'

It is true, of course, that there is much in Jones's own work which graphically illustrates a great many of the ways in which colonialism substantially derailed, inside Europe and elsewhere in the world, that universalist outlook and humanist aspiration of the better tendencies in the Enlightenment which often surface in writers like Vico, as for example in his contention that 'there must in the nature of human institutions be a mental language common to all nations, which uniformly grasps the substance of things feasible in human social life and expresses it in as many diverse modifications as these same things may have diverse aspects.'[12] In the Indian context, Macaulay's was the canonical statement of the colonialist negation of that universalist aspect of the Enlightenment project. Orientalist scholarship itself was often tainted by that very negation – came to have, through much of its career, the colonialist institution as the site of its own reproduction – but it would be simply mindless to deny that there were also aspects of this Orientalist work on Sanskrit that bore the impress of the more universalist aspirations of the Enlightenment. Much of that scholarship is in fact riven, within its own textual body, by the contending pressures of colonialist Eurocentrism and universalist humanism and rationalism – and riven also, in far more complicated ways, between colonialist modernity and the obscurantist tendencies in which European Romanticism often overlapped with Indian Brahminism. Nor is it deniable that in collecting those textual materials from Sanskrit the Orientalists brought together and made available to a public domain texts that had been widely scattered, often in sacrosanct possession of sundry sectarian groupings, and thus performed a task of collation and dissemination for which many of those sectarian groupings were scarcely willing. The Brahminical stamp and generally metaphysical bias (medievalist, since much of Romanticism was itself often attracted by medievalism) remained strong in that body of scholarship, but it is also true that in transferring those texts to some of the modern languages – albeit the European ones – the Orientalist scholar played a useful role in freeing them, however partially, from that sectarian, ecclesiastical stranglehold and made them accessible, in whatever layered wrappings, for the scrutiny of the modern, secular, critical intelligentsia.

The damage Orientalism often did can now be undone by superior scholarship, if and when we ourselves produce such scholarship, but the Orientalist scholarship as such cannot simply be dismissed as an exercise of bad faith, any more than the first Farsi translations of some of those same texts can be dismissed because they were done under Muslim kings in a 'foreign' language.[13] The translation of many of those same Sanskrit texts into many of the *modern* Indian languages, in fact, played a considerable role in the process of the consolidation of these languages as well, even though the translations of Christian texts done under European missionaries received far greater emphasis in our literary historiography. A study of these various traditions of translation – under the Mughals in Farsi, in English and German during the British period, and into modern languages of India from numerous sites during the nineteenth and twentieth centuries – would in fact constitute an important area of comparatism in the study of Indian Literature, and might demonstrate the weaknesses as well as the strengths of Orientalist scholarship in ways that have been suppressed in contemporary debates.

The inadequacy of the model developed by nineteenth-century Orientalism for narrating the history of Indian literature is emphasized often enough by many contemporary writers,[14] but the criticism of that model remains restricted, as a rule, to the predictable objection that it neglects later developments in Indian Literature. The actual etiquettes of the Orientalist readings, selections, emphases, meanwhile, are hardly ever interrogated, nor is it common to challenge the ideological grid which accounts for assembling that particular kind of narrative, which itself greatly contributes to creating a *single* canonicity of the literary and the religious texts. For the historical moment in which this particular idea of an 'Indian Literature' came into being was also that same moment in which a canonical kind of 'Hinduism' ('syndicated Hinduism', in Romila Thapar's telling phrase) was also assembled, more or less on the model of the Semitic religions, with notions of uniform beliefs, canonical texts, prophetic traditions, clerical institutions, adjudicable bodies of prescriptions, and all the rest. Overlaps in the fabrication of literary canonicity and religious canonicity were intense, as is evident in the standard anthologies of 'Indian Literature', 'Indian Tradition' and 'Hindu Religion' in which a great many items, especially those that receive the most emphasis, tend to be the same, with the difference that the former two types of anthology would make room for some 'Muslim' items for the 'Muslim' period and thereafter. In constructing this overlapping literary–religious canonicity, the work of the Orientalist itself overlapped with the ambitions of a great many of the Hindu reformers and revivalists alike, with the distinction between reformism and revivalism becoming in most instances less and less clear.

Aurobindo's emphatic notion – stated at considerable length in his *The Foundations of Indian Culture* – that the *Mahabharata*, Valmiki's *Ramayana* and (much less so) the plays of Kalidasa sufficiently constitute the essence, the difference and the achievement of Indian Literature presumes this narrowing of canonicity and the substantial overlap of the literary and the religious; apart from some general comments on narrative realism, what Aurobindo emphasizes most strongly, in the manner of a great many elite traditions, is precisely their metaphysical grandeur and spiritual timelessness. This then privileges certain kinds of readings and disallows others. Characteristically, then, the religiously canonized text can be read as 'literature' primarily for its sublimity but not in the modern sense of secular or profane writing: not only is the *Bhagavad-Gita* privileged over other Gitas found in the same *Mahabharata* tradition, but its sublimity as 'literature' is so thoroughly framed by its supremacy as metaphysic that it cannot be read in relation to the secular conditions of its own production, nor as an ideological text whose main task is to offer an imaginary resolution for real conflicts in the secular, familial, material domains. Even to read properly the fissures of its own metaphysic would be, in this overlap of the literary and the sacred, not only an irreligious but also-already an inferior form of reading. In an expanding circle of interpellations, then, the whole of the *Mahabharata* gets bathed in sacrality and becomes, simultaneously, over a period of time, the constituting epic of the nation and its literature, a self-proclaimed *pancham Veda* (fifth Veda, after the four strictly Vedic texts), a flamboyant television spectacle of unspeakable violence and kitsch, as well as a structure of belief and the authorizing text of Bharatya Janata Party's *Hindutva* – whose *rath yatra* then condenses, incongruously, the symbology of Lord Krishna's charioteering for Arjun, the all-purpose *trishul* of Lord Shiva, the various travels of Rama (the Lord and the Prince), the Dwarka-to-Ayodhya medieval pilgrimages, in precisely that *syndication* of Hinduism which, in the more otherworldly ideologies of the scholastic type, is said to be the essence of Indian Literature.

The upshot of this simultaneity in constructing the literary and the sacred canonicities is that a certain kind of sanctity comes to be attached even to those cognate texts which are not so central in the specifically religious canon, while the sacred comes to be uniquely privileged in texts which are riven between the sacred and the profane, and are of enduring importance for the reconstruction of our secular histories. Implicit in all Hindu nationalisms is the notion, confirmed in much Orientalist writing, that the entire tradition of high textuality in India up to the Turko–Persian (called simply 'Islamic') invasions expresses *a* Hinduism. In this enlarged version, which elevates certain kinds of Brahminical ideas to canonicity while assimilating all other cultural tendencies under its own dominance, Buddhism, Jainism and all other large and small dissents, religious and not so religious, are obscured into secondariness but also assimilated into processes of syndication. This religious hegemony is then brought forward to normalize later centuries as well, so that the diverse tendencies of Bhakti are recouped, too, as so many moments of a Hindu spirituality which is distributed between the High tradition and the Low, between the philosophical (e.g. Vedantic) and the narrative (e.g. the Puranic genealogies) and the populist-lyrical (e.g. Bhakti), but remains essentially the same.

Literary and cultural writings which then address those documents of High Canonicity replicate the methods of both literary aestheticism and speculative thought in detaching the documents from their historical locations and the determinate conditions of their production, in order to contemplate them as detached moments in which the Indian spirit sets out to delight the senses, instruct the mind and satisfy the soul's inexhaustible yearning for lassitudinous metaphysic. Only in the more materialist school of modern Indian historiography, and in writings which have emerged under the influence of that school of historians of Ancient India, do we find sustained efforts to lift such fog.

## IV

The other, relatively more sober version of an 'Indian Literature' is the one that is in fact composed of discrete language–literature traditions, so that the word 'Indian' is superimposed upon diverse texts drawn, say, from the various periods of the development of Dogri and Bengali and Marathi, much as anything written in any corner of Africa is immediately slotted into something called 'African Literature'. In the routine manifestations of this latter version, the unity of the object called 'Indian Literature' appears to be an effect of geography and the nation-state. At its best, though, this second version does make a great deal of sense, in so far as only by assembling the documents and literary histories of the different languages and literatures of India would it be possible actually to examine and historicize their overlaps, if we are to see at all whether or not they do add up to a unified history, however diverse in its constituent units. In other words, it is only by passing through the comparatist method that a knowledge of the unity can be obtained. The empirical value of such work, therefore, is enormous. What is often lacking, however, is the sense that a shift from Marathi or Bengali or Urdu to 'Indian' is both aggregative and *qualitative*, and that the shift from quantity to quality, from mass to composition, requires altogether different kinds of conceptual apparatuses and theoretical principles of narrativization.

It *is* possible, as a matter of contrast, to speak of a European Literature, for example, because European universities constantly produce and reproduce large numbers of intellectuals, each of whom knows several European languages, who can together, through a complex grid of textual exchanges, produce a unified body of knowledge about literary production in the various linguistic formations of Europe; this is supplemented, then, by a brisk industry of translations, back and forth. It is because of these institutional structures that a thing called 'European Literature' does exist, albeit with its own system of exclusions and stratifications, both as a comparatist discipline and as a unified object of critical knowledge. That we cannot hope to match the *scale* of such institutions in the advanced capitalist countries is doubtless a matter of scarce resources. Nor do we need to replicate either the canonizing procedures of Europe's famous comparatists, such as Curtius or Spitzer, or the ethnocentric racisms which are so central in the construction of European uniqueness as that comparatism construes it in the High Imperial fashion. The past and present cultural boundaries of India are in fact very indeterminate. The traffic between India and its neighbours in both western and eastern Asian zones is infinitely more complex than the problematics of Aryanization, or Islam, or marauding tribes and armies, would signify; the history of Buddhism alone would show that the migration of ideas and peoples took many directions and forms. Even in the much narrower frame of twentieth-century narrative literature, Russian and French influences have been quite as fundamental as British–colonial. And of course, the major thrusts of our cultural productions which we loosely call 'literary' have been essentially anti-canonical. The point, in other words, is not the replication of European ideologies and procedures.

Given our own multilingualities, however, the fact that the existing and proliferating institutions would not even be *structured*, on whatever scale, to produce comparatist knowledges of the various literatures of India is, I believe, a systemic distortion. The lamentable underdevelopment of Indian Literature as a scholarly discipline – reflected in the relative obscurity of those Comparative Literature Departments which focus on Indian Literature at all, as compared with the size, number and prestige of English Departments – reflects this distortion. I know, of course, that there are *individuals* – gifted and resolute individuals – who have sought to do this kind of work, either on their own or with some minimal institutional support, or through oppositional networks. I also know that there are *some* university departments and institutes where a few dents are being made. What I am deploring here is that the Literature Departments in our universities have not been reorganized more fundamentally; that there are not more, more highly developed and better-funded institutes for this purpose – so that this kind of work could be done not only by some devoted individuals but by a whole category of a new type of schooled, institutionally supported intelligentsia that could then give us adequate knowledge of this prolix thing called 'Indian Literature'. Lacking any nationwide network of such institutions, we can assert the category 'Indian Literature' as a necessary corollary of the very real civilizational unity of our peoples, or as a consequence of the equally real centralizing imperatives of the modern nation-state, but of the thing itself, 'Indian Literature' – its historic constitution and generic composition, its linguistic overlaps, its supposedly unified and unifying practices – we still know relatively little.

Not that a more complex sense of this unity/diversity problem, or of the need for a comparatist method for reading a period and a genre on as wide an Indian scale as possible, is altogether lacking.[15] The erudition and confidence, but also the sobriety and modesty, of Sisir Kumar Das in his recent detailed survey of modern Indian Literature[16] is, however, exemplary in this regard, hence very chastening. He makes two preliminary observations. One is that the last volume, pertaining to the Modern Period (1800–1910), has been completed first because work on the others is so much more difficult. But he also points out that all the present state of our collective knowledge permits, even for a scholar as encyclopaedic as himself – who, for once, did have institutional support and the co-operation of a whole team – and for so recent a period, is the preparation of a comprehensive Chronology and the charting out of the main trends; *analytic* history on any comprehensive scale, he says, can come only in the future. The work is proportionately more difficult for earlier periods, when print played no role in circulation of texts and even precise dating is hard, let alone the task of collation. Can we, then, in the present state of our knowledge, really speak of 'Indian Literature' as an object already there, available for theorization? Sisir Kumar's very thoughtful observations would seem to suggest that descriptions of various kinds are certainly possible, and theoretical speculations about specific and delimited areas may be offered most fruitfully, but the present state of our empirical knowledge does not really warrant confident theorization on too broad a scale.[17] One might, therefore, venture the generalization that the much more difficult task of assembling a history of 'Indian Literature' which does not derive its sense of unity from some transhistoric metaphysic nor from the territoriality of the existing nation-state, nor by simply assembling discrete histories of the different linguistic traditions, but traces the dialectic of unity and difference – through systematic periodization of multiple linguistic overlaps, and by grounding that dialectic in the history of material productions, ideological struggles, competing conceptions of class and community and gender, elite offensives and popular resistances, overlaps of cultural vocabularies and performative genres, and histories of orality and writing and print – has barely begun. Nor can it be otherwise.

## V

Part of the problem arises, of course, from the residual effects of imperialist scholarship, colonially determined educational apparatuses, and the colonial etiquettes of mapping our history, in cultural as much as the political domains. The consequences of the colonial periodization of Indian History into the so-called Hindu, Muslim and British periods are well enough known for the discipline of historiography, not to speak of the consequent disorientations of consciousness at large, at both elite and popular levels. The best of our historians also emphasize that a mere shift in nomenclature which substitutes the terms Classical, Medieval and Modern for that same Millsian sense of periodization does not really help, even though it takes some of the communalist sting out of these procedures. In the cultural domain, this pattern of periodization was further buttressed by the colonial preoccupations with High Textuality, mechanisms of monarchical and imperial centralization, and languages of command, in both religious and material spheres. These preoccupations led – naturally, as it were – to the privileging of the Vedic and Sanskritic texts for the Hindu/Classical period, the Persian and Mughal texts for the Muslim/Medieval period, and the pre-eminence of English texts for the British/Modern. This was the conceptual universe in which the colonial apparatuses of research and education were first assembled, as the career of William Jones or the whole complex history from, let us say, the founding of Fort William College in 1800 up to the establishment of the first three modern universities in 1857–58, with Macaulay's Minute of 1835 in between, would amply demonstrate. But the actual elaboration of colonial society was contradictory, and both the Christian missionary and the colonial officer were soon to discover that neither Sanskrit nor Persian nor even English could serve at the time as a language of command, in the administration of souls and bodies, so far as the masses of Indians, or even the colonial clerks, were concerned; they *had* to be spoken to in the languages they themselves spoke – in what we now call 'the regional languages'.

The early history of the printing presses and grids of colonial education demonstrates this fact clearly enough. An English-language press, of course, kept evolving, and much was imported from England for the British themselves as well as the emergent Indian Third Estate, but the first two printing presses, at Serampore and Fort William, came into being for publication of material primarily in the Indian languages, for both Indians and Europeans, and the history of all subsequent developments of printing presses in various parts of the country is inextricably linked with the need for textbooks and other educational materials – in the fullness of time, for the pedagogies of reformist 'literature' very centrally – in the indigenous languages. This was obviously connected also with the evolving educational structures, sponsored by the colonial state, the Christian missionaries and the Indian reform movements, in which most of the education and instruction were carried out in the indigenous languages, Macaulay or anyone else notwithstanding. Specialized training in the classical languages of India – Sanskrit, Farsi, even Arabic – was imparted in the Oriental Colleges and the academies which were established for this purpose, but most such scholarship survived mainly through more traditional institutions and privately organized circuits, even though some instruction in these languages was available in some of the regular schools and colleges as well. English became the language of higher education, especially at university level; while normal schooling was carried out everywhere in what was taken to be – and was therefore greatly standardized as – the local vernacular. Only in the handful of highly exclusive public schools was English taught in an exclusive way. There, a key sector of the dominant intelligentsia evolved which was actually removed from any productive relation with any other of the Indian languages.

Considering that barely 15 per cent of the population was in any sense literate by the time of decolonization, the failures of the system are obvious enough, and in some senses all of this literate segment of the population could be construed as some kind of 'elite', since even bare literacy did help in the long-term dynamics of social mobilities. In terms of decisive class privilege, however, which combined *higher* education with considerable property and/or income, the real 'educated elite' was a mere fraction of that 15 per cent. Basic education did reach sizeable proportions of the underprivileged strata, especially through the schools established by the reform movements and philanthropies and local entrepreneurs, secondarily through mission schools, but also through government schools, which were few in number but heavily subsidized. The bulk of the literate population came out of these schools, knowing a little English (sometimes enough, often not even enough for colonial service); but they were schooled in the indigenous languages, and this vernacular schooling was then greatly supplemented by the evolving vernacular print networks. Even the most elite colleges – e.g., Presidency (Hindu) in Calcutta, Elphinstone in Bombay, Government College in Lahore – produced bilingual intelligentsias and scores of writers of Bengali, Gujarati, Marathi, Urdu, Hindi, Punjabi, and so on. For those who came out of other kinds of colleges, which were by far the majority and were established most often by indigenous reform movements and philanthropies, moorings in English were even less secure. This education system corresponded fairly accurately to the system of colonial administration itself, which was conducted in English only at the upper levels where British personnel were directly involved. The rest was conducted either bilingually, through intermediaries at the median levels, or in the indigenous languages, by Indian personnel at the lower levels; this constituted the vast bulk of the administrative machinery. Conversely, publishing too – newspapers, journals, the book trade – was preponderantly in the indigenous languages, even though the English-language press commanded, and still commands, a disproportionate degree of influence. The issue of 'literature' must be viewed in this broad context.

The constitutive logic of Colonial Discourse Analysis is such that significant practitioners of it have come to construe the English language in India as a pure colonial imposition, and English literature itself as some kind of central enterprise of the colonial state in its bid for the construction of consent in India. Both these propositions are substantially inaccurate. It is of course true, in some partial way, that English was an imposition, but the more remarkable fact is that in the entire history of Indian reformism, from Rammohun to Vivekanand to Sir Syed to Tilak and Gandhi, there is always an attachment to and a competence in one or two Indian languages, but never any rejection of English as such; virtually all of them *wanted* it, not as a literary language but as a window on the most advanced knowledges of the world, mainly in the physical and social sciences, in historiography, in the technical fields. Even Gandhi's most extreme statements of obscurantist nationalism in *Hind Swaraj* (1909) – where he fumes against the railways as carriers of communicable diseases and for violating caste purities, while he also dismisses the whole range of modern professions such as law and medicine – are remarkable for the absence of the English teacher as an object of ridicule; the purported claim that English is superior because of its European origin or that any social superiority attaches to an Indian who learns it is rightfully debunked, but there is no sense that English as such has no rightful place in India. That kind of opposition to English came only from those even more rigidly obscurantist circles – located for the most part in the overlap of extreme religiosity, pre-capitalist landed property and small-scale commercial capital – which were opposed to a great many reforms of Indian society as such, whether advocated by the British or by the more advanced sectors of Indian society.

To the extent that English *was* imposed by the British, it was imposed primarily as the language of administration, management, modern professions such as law and medicine, technical fields, central surveys, and so on. The introduction of literary texts into various sorts of syllabi was primarily a means towards such ends, the zeal of particular ideologues notwithstanding. Inculcating a belief in Christianity or in the grandeur of British civilization was obviously an important goal for a colonizing power that saw itself as carrying out a civilizing mission among the heathen, and zealots doubtless made much of it. But a traditional British pedagogy also held that the best way to improve one's knowledge of a language, especially a foreign language, once you have mastered the basic vocabulary and simple grammar, is through stylistically accessible poems such as Wordsworth's 'Lucy' sequence, or through fables or historical romances. The role of literary compositions in the school curricula for Indian children was one expression of that pedagogy, but language teaching for British personnel at Fort William College was also organized according to that same principle. Thus a number of books, such as *Aaraish-e-Mehfil* or *Bagh-o-Bahar*, which eventually came to be included among the key classics of Urdu prose, were initially composed as textbooks for British personnel who needed to learn the language and know its cultural ambience. It was similarly believed that a mastery of Milton's poetry might or might not make a Christian out of anyone, but it would certainly improve one's understanding of the English grammar and one's ability to write the compound sentence. It was in the teaching of the compound sentence that the ways of God were seen to be highly justifiable.

Only in selected social strata did any appreciable number of Indian intellectuals come to believe in the intrinsic literary superiority of the English language to the extent of desiring to write in it, even though it was generally recognized that the physical and social sciences, the technical fields, historiography, lexicography, urban planning and numerous other areas of modern knowledge were much more highly developed in Britain than in India. The sense of the superiority of Western knowledges was thus established not in the literary but, generally, in the cognitive and technical fields. This can easily be witnessed in the fact that compared to the vast numbers who wrote in the older indigenous languages and actively participated in the emergence of modern literatures in those languages, relatively few Indian writers during the colonial period took to writing poems and fiction in English, even though many came to love this foreign literature which had in some ways become their own; whereas, in direct contrast, English became the predominant language both for the higher levels of administration and for writing in a whole range of fields other than the literary. In the field of literature, English had its greatest impact not directly as a language of composition but through some specific genres which the Indian writers now encountered for the first time: the Homeric epic, the sonnet, tragedy in both its Greek and its Shakespearian variants, blank verse, the prose essay, Bunyan-like allegory, the historical romance, the many kinds of prose fiction. Virtually all these compositional forms were tried, at one time or another, by one writer or another. But the encounter that proved decisive was with realism, especially in its Russian and French variants, albeit in English translation. Most other forms came and went, but realism remained, mainly because its ways of apprehending the world corresponded to that historic moment within Indian society when it was undergoing its first bourgeois upheavals, obtaining its own class structure and household arrangements of the capitalist type, forming its own self-consciousness as a society beset with revolutionary crises, albeit in a colonial setting.

## VI

From contradictions of this kind came broad, essentially class-based divisions of intellectual function among the new intelligentsias which arose out of the apparatuses of colonial education.[18] The development of these intelligentsias was highly uneven both regionally and sectorally, and we still need far more accurate monographic studies of the social history of their development in terms of regional roots, class origins, religious or caste affiliations, social mores, schooling patterns, and linguistic competences. So one can never be sure, but certain patterns can be summarized. The dominant, more privileged strata among these *new* intelligentsias – often reflecting a nexus of class, caste, college degrees, and the upper layers of colonial service – acknowledged the three-part division, came to adopt English as the main language of public function, but sometimes learned Sanskrit or/and Persian also, as the languages of scholastic and courtly eminence in India's own past, while retaining the indigenous language for common discourse in household and community. These clusters tended to produce not 'writers', in the literary sense, but 'scholars' in the Humanities and the Social Sciences – or (a favourite pastime) translators of either a *modern* European text into an Indian language or a *classical* Indian text into English, more or less in the Orientalist genre.

Concurrently, however, clusters of a new type of professional petty bourgeoisie were also assembled in the various regions of the country, which then found themselves functioning with a new kind of bi- and even trilinguality, whereby *professional work* was done in a mixture of English and the indigenous languages, which gave them a Bhadralokish window on English *literature* as well. *Cultural life* was lived, by and large, in the language(s) of locality and region, while for the majority of those who were thus incorporated into these new, regional clusters – often drawn from the impoverished sections of the upper castes, or from the middle castes and petty property – any real, working knowledge of Sanskrit or Persian was either fragmentary or nonexistent. As often happens in the case of professional strata which are drawn from diverse classes and social groups, there was considerable traffic and overlap between the dominant and the middling layers, but they were also, in their respective generalities, *structured* into distinct layers. Meanwhile, the establishment of printing presses in different linguistic regions was revolutionizing the means of literary and journalistic production, turning the new professional strata and the propertied classes generally into 'reading publics', for English often enough but, on a far greater numerical scale, for the 'regional' languages – albeit very unevenly in the different regions: earlier and far more extensively for Bengali, more than a century later in Kashmir.

Meanwhile, the education system was such that the thin upper crust of the highly Anglicized urban elite which went to the more exclusive convents and the select public schools were hardly ever encouraged to specialize in *any* Indian language, classical or modern, and either made do with English alone or fell back on family networks and private instruction for indigenous language(s), while the traditional sectors of those same dominant classes developed institutions for the dissemination of literary productions in the indigenous languages, outside the apparatuses of the colonial state. The fact that these upper *classes* frequently coincided with upper *castes* meant that, regardless of the exact nature of their relationship with the upper layers of the colonial apparatuses which had the English language at their epicentre, many of them came out of family traditions which included a knowledge of Sanskrit and/or Persian. This was particularly true in the case of those *scholastic* fractions which had been located in either the religious or the judicial institutions of pre-colonial society, or were closest to the courts either at imperial or regional and local levels. 'Court' in pre-capitalist society, we must remind ourselves, went down to the level of individual fief-holders, and the scholastic caste fractions were quite widely spread.[19]

Contradictions of the education system, however, were felt most acutely among the petty bourgeoisies, of both the traditional (propertied) and the new (professional) kinds, because the dynamic of their schooling and professional ambition drove them towards English, while the cultural pressures of their own lives kept them rooted in their own linguistic communities. The pattern of their schooling served only to deepen these contradictions, since the link with the spoken and lived language was strongest at the lower levels, while English kept taking over more and more as they went further up into colleges and universities. It was mainly, though by no means exclusively, in the hands of these culturally beleaguered individuals, belonging neither to the colonial elite nor to the truly oppressed classes, who were themselves riven by the contradiction between the language of administrative command and the language of felt life, that the print literatures of India, in languages of our own speech, were first assembled on any appreciable scale. Thus it was not primarily in the institutions of colonial *education*, nor even in the expanding philological researches of Western Orientalists who doubtless did much useful work, but in the productions and investigations of those who actually *produced* literature in the modern languages of the land that the question of the relationship between their own spoken tongues and their immediate linguistic precursors in the pre-modern, medieval languages of India – not just Farsi, the language of command in many regions but a language of felt life only for a few, but all those *lived* linguistic histories that came between the classical past and the modern speech – was first productively and systematically posed, in the terms of a modern scholarship.

The literary clusters which arose in the so-called 'regional' languages during the colonial period were drawn preponderantly from the emergent Third Estate, typically combining medium-scale property with professional or commercial location and a mixture of knowledges drawn from English as well as the vernacular; the relatively impoverished sectors of those upper castes which had traditionally occupied intellectual functions in pre-colonial society dominates this new formation.[20] To the extent that the majority of them did not come from the upper layers of the traditional landowning classes, many thought of themselves as part of a democratizing dynamic that arose from inside the crisis of pre-capitalist society. Many felt oppressed by the proximity and power of that moribund structure, so that various rhetorics of reform, in both enlightened and mystificatory ways, came more or less naturally to them. In turn, they were often deeply responsive to those particular parts of our medievality which were most closely connected with the idioms and beliefs of the popular classes. Since these literatures arose in *regional* languages at a time when India was experiencing both a colonial subjection of subcontinental scale and a historically unprecedented kind of *bourgeois* unification, affected partly by colonial administration and the development of a basically capitalist structure of economy and partly by the anti-colonial movement itself, the producers of these literatures often had a deep investment in negotiating the relationship between our regional particularities and our civilizational unity. Furthermore, it was also in the latter decades of the colonial period, especially with the rise of the communist movement and its concomitant cultural clusters, that India began to witness the gradual emergence of full-scale literary cultures that were, in many of their articulations, not only struggling against religious particularity and obscurantism, which many kinds of both personal and collective dissidence had attempted in innumerable ways in the past as well, but were also groping, for the first time in our history, towards secular historicization and non-religious narrativization of the material world.

It is small wonder, then, given this whole range of their own engagements, that many of these new intellectuals came to have a very special interest in those many strands of our medievality which we cumulatively call 'Bhakti'. For Bhakti had been associated, on the whole, with an enormous democratization of literary language; had pressed the cultural forms of caste hegemony in favour of the artisanate and the peasantry; had been regionally dispersed on both sides of the Vindhyas; was ideologically anti-Brahminical; had deeply problematized the gender construction of all dialogic relations, whether of love or worship or speech itself; and was highly ecumenical in its philosophical inspirations. In other words, it was these democratizing and somewhat liberating aspects of Bhakti – not its final metaphysical determination but its overall anti-Brahminical character; its peculiarly irreconcilable tension between consent and transgression; its status as a *bridge* between our modernity and our classics, planked with the perspective and speech of the popular classes; its cumulative formation as a cluster of regional and even individual specificities which nevertheless was dispersed throughout the land, more or less – that gave it a special significance for a whole range of modern writers, both in the broadly cultural and the strictly political arenas, in the twentieth century even more than the nineteenth. In a different emphasis, of course, Bhakti was also attractive for all kinds of indigenisms and nationalist aporias of consent and organicity, including Gandhi's own, which we shall for the moment ignore. Regardless of the contradictory modern uses to which the ideologies of Bhakti were to be subjected, it was in tandem with the emergence of the modern literatures of India in the nineteenth century that attempts were first made to assemble a systematic as well as modern, even secular, knowledge of the medieval antecedents of these languages and literatures.

## VII

Into this complex and contradictory cultural landscape, however, came three further and quite different kinds of pressures. First there was the pressure of the nineteenth-century *reform* movements, which were almost always movements of *religious* reform, some of them deeply tinged with revivalism of one kind or another, even when their actual analyses and projects spilled far over into social and political domains of a secular type. Some of these, notably Brahmo, functioned as much through English as through the old and modern languages of India, but the great majority of these movements – Arya Samaj and Sanatan Dharm, for example, or the Dar-ul-Ulum of Deoband and (somewhat later) the Nadwat-ul-Ulema of Lucknow for Muslims – had the effect, first, of pressing the modern Indian languages into service for proselytizing, and, second, of greatly enhancing, at the same time, the prestige of scholarship in the classical language (Vedic and Sanskritic knowledges for Hindus, Arabic and Persian for Muslims) as the language of religious textuality; reform, after all, could not be carried out without linguistic mastery – and a certain absorption in the reliving, albeit somewhat differently – of that which was to be reformed.

This whole dynamic was greatly strengthened by the further tie between religious reform and educational reform. Many of the educational institutions which came into being outside the directly colonial apparatuses – and indeed, these private institutions came to be far more numerous than the government schools and colleges – were established by religious reform societies, with the project of ensuring that even as the sons and daughters of the traditional petty bourgeoisie went in for acquiring modern professional skills, their social being and ideational universe would remain traditional and religious. If this tie between religious and educational reform stood, on the one hand, in tense relation with the rise of modern communalism, it was also, on the other hand, a rearguard defence against Western missionaries who had also concentrated their extraordinary powers, frequently reaching deep into the countryside, in the twin fields of religion and education.[21] Given the cultural ambivalences of the colonial bourgeoisie, the interlocutors of reform movements were often much too ready to be co-opted back into conservative structures, while numerous educational enterprises were established or came to be controlled by the most reactionary religious elements who were themselves organized, just as frequently, along lines of caste, sect and faction. To the extent that even the modern languages were thus pressed so widely into the service of *religious* scholarship, sectarian education and proselytizing, such movements had the effect of reinvesting these modern idioms with lexicons and sensibilities derived from the universe of religious discourse, and privileging the religious text, along with all the paraphernalia of priestly gloss and commentary, within the literary canon. This effectively checked, with devastating effect, the impulse towards democratization and secularization of literature which we have noted above.

That *dominant* sector of the modern intelligentsia which was the best-schooled in the modern scientific and critical disciplines and was often employed in the privileged professions (the Indian Civil Service [ICS] officers, for example, or the more sophisticated in the professoriate) tended also to be drawn from those upper castes which already had family traditions of classical scholarship. Individuals among them produced a new kind of scholarship of classical texts which was informed by the modern disciplines of Philology, Textual and Literary Criticism, Anthropology, and so on. Considerable new work appeared, much of it very good in terms of solidity of research, but it usually bore a conservative, British stamp, and it almost always favoured the traditions of High Textuality and an uncritical acceptance of the revivalist forms of celebrating our 'tradition'.

There were also the many strands of social and political movements which now, after decolonization, we have come to think of as, simply, 'the national movement'. The mass character of these movements required the use of modern, spoken languages, both in print and in social action, and it is arguable that nothing contributed – in areas as diverse as journalism, literature, social and historical sciences, public oration, the labour movement, the nitty-gritty of political mobilization – so much to the development of the modern/'regional' languages of India as did the political mobilization of the masses of Indian people during the half-century or so leading up to the moment of decolonization. We tend to ignore, however, the fact that many of the tendencies which went into constituting what can now be described as our canonical nationalism were deeply implicated in various kinds of revivalisms – and if they were not revivalist in the narrow religious sense, they nevertheless thought of the 'greatness' of India's past almost always in terms of its dynastic splendours, its high-caste textualities, its priestly pieties, its elite Sanskritic past. Rare would be a text of our canonical nationalism (witness, for example, the agnostic, socialist Mr Nehru's *Discovery of India*) which did not in some way assume that 'spirituality' was the special vocation of the Indian in world history. Positivist kinds of secularism and modernism which grew during the same period often found it difficult to withstand these pressures for identifying Indian cultural nationalism with metaphysics and revivalist tendencies.[22] At the very least, a sort of bargain was struck whereby a secular, even non-religious sphere was gained by conceding that the hallowed religious texts were never to be challenged directly and were always presumed to be 'great' because, after all, they were the great monuments of our 'tradition'. Relatively – though not always – more consistent were the 'progressive' literatures which arose during the 1930s and after, directly inspired by the communist movement; these were able to carry on the democratizing processes in linguistic and literary arenas, while remaining largely free of the revivalist taint.

Certain *broad* features of this highly complex and contradictory situation as it prevailed at the moment of decolonization can thus be identified here, though only schematically. First, so far as university levels were concerned,

'English' was the only literary institution which was developed throughout the country, in all its regions, through an enormously powerful grid of educational apparatuses and professional expertise. Second, a strong tradition of modern, textual and critical scholarship about our Vedic and Sanskritic traditions, and of Mughal heritage as well as the medieval analogues of popular culture as such, already existed during the colonial period and has been greatly improved since, in the modern Indian languages but also especially in English – though the bulk of this scholarship is itself replete with preferences of the speculative, religious-minded, idealist and/or Orientalist kind. Third, the last two hundred years have also witnessed developments of historic proportions in the modern/'regional' languages, but with several historically determined peculiarities, only some of which can be cited here. These developments were regionally uneven, with some – Bengali, Tamil, both the Hindi and Urdu variants of Hindustani – experiencing far greater elaboration of schooling, printing and literary production than many others, such as Oriya or Punjabi or Kashmiri. Fourth, these respective modern traditions are composed much more of literary *production*, while branches of literary *scholarship* – philology, criticism, theory, history, translation, comparative study – were in most regions relatively far less developed. Fifth, a systematic knowledge of any one of these literary traditions remained confined largely to its own region, some polyglot scholars and some sporadic translations notwithstanding. Sixth, the trajectory in the writing of literary history has been in some ways the opposite of the prevailing trend in areas of economic and political history. In the early phase, emphasis in the writing of our political and economic history was on the grand narrative, with the belief that vast epochs of Indian history and diverse regions of this subcontinent were directly accessible for that kind of narrativization, in the manner of Mill or Moreland. It was only much later that emphasis shifted towards regional and local histories, and to the specialized monograph. In matters of literature, by contrast, many more studies are by now available for particular regions and for developments in some specific languages, usually *within* each language, with far fewer attempts to connect these discrete histories into the sweep of overall perspectives.

The lack of a common, 'national' language has doubtless played its part in this lack of analytic and theoretical aggregation, for – and this is our seventh point – it appears plausible, on an even broader level of historical generalization, that the emergence of an 'Indian Literature' as a coherent object of theoretical knowledge has been greatly obstructed because the entire development of the (bourgeois, colonial and then post-colonial) nation-state in modern India has been such that it has failed to give rise to a linguistic formation *shared* by all – or even close to a majority – of Indians, even at the level of basic literacy or comprehension of daily speech. In most of these areas – for example the training of a sizeable number of *scholars* in the regional languages; the compilation of the histories of regional literatures; the establishment of institutions for comparative study, research and publication in the various Indian regional literatures – any systematic efforts have been made, on whatever limited scales, only since decolonization, and informal networks assembled by the writers themselves seem to have played a far greater role in opening up these possibilities than have the formal networks which have arisen out of the cultural policies, such as they are, of the post-colonial state.

## VIII

These gaps in our knowledge, compounded by traditions of High Textuality which have assimilated so many of the earlier literary texts to contemporary religious and even fundamentalist purpose, pose one whole set of problems in thinking of an 'Indian' literature as a historically structured and theoretically coherent category. Another set of problems is related, meanwhile,to the shape of literary education, and the role of English literature, in modern India. The only *national* literary intelligentsia that exists in India today – an intelligentsia constituted as a distinct social stratum and dispersed in all parts of the country, which brings to bear upon its vocation and its work a *shared* body of knowledge, *shared* presumptions and a *shared* language of mutual exchange – is the one that is fairly well grounded in English; and the only literature that is *taught* through the length and breadth of the country is English Literature – and that too not in the shape mainly of what gets written in India but of what comes from elsewhere.

As I pointed out above, the underdevelopment of departments for comparative study of Indian languages and literatures becomes altogether clear if we compare their growth or size with that of the English Departments. From what institution or network of institutions, then, may one expect a sustained production of systematic knowledges about 'Indian' literature, not as an eclecticism of individual texts – Valmiki or Kabir here, Tagore or Anita Desai there – but as a structured body of knowledge and a coherent object of theoretical study? The present structure of English Departments in our universities becomes an issue here in a peculiarly contradictory way. In a sense, these are the only departments of literature which exist in the shape of a unified literary institution through the entire organization of higher education in India, designed to impart analogous kinds of literary training in the various universities and at least the elite colleges. Not even remotely can the Departments of Hindi, for example, supposedly the 'national' language, let alone our Departments of Comparative Literature, begin to compete with this power of English in the reproduction of the literary intelligentsia across the land. These same Departments require, nevertheless, that the professional attention of their personnel be focused *away* from India, on to Dickens or Fielding or, better yet, Sidney's *Arcadia*. It is only by resisting the very thrust of one's education and profession that a teacher of English literature manages to refocus attention on matters closer to home. Even this refocusing comes in large measure, given the institutional constraints, not inside the classroom but outside it.

In context, the situation of the English teacher who aspires to be a critic of literature oscillates, in relation to the profession, between the poignant and the absurd. In an earlier time, not so long ago, pressures on the profession were not, so to speak, so professionalized. The relation between the college teacher and the university faculty, even where such distinctions existed, were not so acutely hierarchical; there was no such emphasis on acquisition of PhDs, mainly from abroad, for teaching in the more highly regarded universities; nor such pressures for publication, certainly no clear distinction between 'professional' and 'non-professional' publications; seminars, conferences, and so on, were rare, not terribly professional, and quite outside the main business of teaching in any case.

A typical college teacher of English in an earlier generation was an activist of the nationalist or communist parties (sometimes both), or a crusader for civic reform. He was likely to be teaching English mainly to earn a living and to satisfy his love of this foreign literature which he had in some ways made his own, but he was likely either not to write at all or to write about the literature of his own indigenous culture, probably in the language of his family; equally likely, he would teach English in accordance with the English literary canon but *write* not criticism, not English, but poetry or fiction in his own tongue. This kind of bilinguality – the felt cultural distance between the language of the taught text and the language of one's own sense and inwardness, hence one's own writing – was all the more probable if he did not come from the upper class, and virtually inevitable if he were of the progressive political persuasion. So readily and completely would his own social milieu then reaffirm that cultural distance that he would not feel it, subjectively, as a split within himself.

The profession of English teaching in our own day has not yet been quite fully professionalized, especially outside the elite institutions, and some of the power of those earlier trajectories has remained, especially among those younger teachers who have found their personal locations within traditions of the Marxist Left. But the pressure of professionalization is increasing rapidly, very much on the metropolitan model of higher degrees, professional publications and conference-hunting, especially for those who wish to teach in the more prominent universities. Consequently, that earlier kind of teacher, and that sort of assured self, is less common now, and institutional pressure to keep such people at lower or at best middling levels of the hierarchy is much sharper. Today, if he were to teach English and write, let us say, only in Hindi or Telugu, the bureaucrats of English might well pronounce him unfit to teach at the university. With increased professionalization, and with increasing Americanization of the profession, he is pressed to write exclusively, or at least predominantly, in the language of the profession and mainly within his 'field'; if he is truly inclined to make a mark in this 'field' and obtain the higher appointments, he feels pressed to publish in professional journals abroad. Responding to more complex pressures of that same market – the pressure of 'Third World Literature', for example – he may occasionally write on some topics pertaining to India as well, but only on one or two of the handful of topics which the market would bear or encourage. The directions of research and writing for the best and the brightest, the most ambitious, are thus increasingly controlled by the local academic bureaucracy and the foreign publishing industry; an active kind of bilinguality is by and large suppressed, and 'Indian' literature remains at best a side issue because India is not his 'field'. This pressure not to drift too far out of Eng. Lit. comes not only from Departments of English but also from all those who, pressed by the same processes of professionalization, are diligently ploughing their own 'fields', in History or Social Science or whatever.

Within the terms of this context, it seems to me, nothing of much worth can be done; the bond market would probably be more profitable. Literary study in our time and place, more than ever and more than elsewhere, needs to be transgressive, and the very first transgressions need to be, in the most obvious and literal senses, against 'English' and against 'Literature'. No solid scholarship of an 'Indian Literature' is possible unless we recoup, in active and viscerally felt ways, as much for reading and writing as for speech, our bi- and multilingualities. Nor is a full reappropriation of our older literatures, classical or medieval, possible unless we are willing to wander across all sorts of boundaries that are said to separate History from Philosophy, Anthropology from Linguistics, Religion from Economics, and 'Literature' from all these and much else besides. Vast resources of what one could reasonably call 'Indian Literature' are scattered through half a dozen disciplines – Anthropology, Religion, History, Comparative Philology – and we need not only to recover those 'literary' texts from a broad range of fields but, even more urgently, to reconstitute literary study itself in a fundamentally non-literary way, at the boundaries and cross-sections of the whole range of the human sciences, so that the methods and purposes of our reading may begin to correspond to the ranges and condensations of meaning – social and historical, physical and metaphysical, symbolic and lexical – which are embedded in this thing, 'Indian Literature', which is currently dispersed into so many disciplines precisely because this literature itself is so much more than simply 'literary'.

## IX

What I have in mind is a very different kind of Literary Study which would be, on the one hand, simply a subdiscipline within a much broader, far more integrated Historical and Cultural Studies, and would, on the other hand, subsume and reorganize what we currently know as Departments of English. Briefly put, my sense of the matter – of the teaching of *English*, that is to say – is that both the language *and* the literature need to be taught, but for radically different reasons, and therefore in radically different ways. The reason why the English *language* should be taught is that it has simply become, for better or worse, one of the *Indian* languages, even the key professional language and certainly the main language of communication between the schooled sections of the different linguistic regions. The recognition of *this* purpose would mean, for example, that in teaching the history of the English language, focus would shift to the history of the language here, in India, not in the British Isles or North America; and in so far as English has expanded here not as the main language of literary production but as the dominant expressive medium of discursive thought, modes of governance and organizations of profession, focus in teaching would also shift from the literary to the social, the political and the discursive. Meanwhile, if the objective is the dissemination and expanded reproduction of knowledges about *Indian* literatures, English would be taught not as the primary, privileged focus but in a comparatist manner, in relation to other Indian languages and literatures, depending upon linguistic region and historical period.

Meanwhile, English *Literature* also needs to be studied in India, but the reasons for doing so would again be radically different from those we subscribe to at present. The first major reason for such an undertaking should be the same that was operative when Marx, in writing *Capital*, chose to study English political economy: Britain was the first country of capitalist industry, hence the leading colonial power on the one hand and the first country, on the other, of organized labour movements as well as the modern democratic demand. The literary texts of this 'tradition' are among the most vivid inscriptions of that very complex history of capital and labour, coercion and democracy, colony and empire. Raymond Williams once called that complexity (a little too charitably, I believe) a 'Long Revolution', and Williams himself is no doubt the best single guide in deciphering that complexity. *We* need to know this history, however, because it has had as many consequences for us as for Britain itself. But that deciphering is impossible if it is undertaken simply as a *literary* enterprise, as a homage to our colonial connection, and impossible, surely, through those etiquettes of colonial education in which the teaching of English in India is still so mired. In a parallel undertaking, English Literature needs to be studied in close relation with the history of modern literatures in India itself, and indeed all forms of Indian writing, because of the substantial place that not just the English Language but English Literature has had in the schooling of some key sections of the modern Indian intelligentsia, hence in defining the very terms of its thought, since at least the second quarter of the nineteenth century. The history of English Literature is now woven into the very modalities of many strands of Indian thought, and no disaggregation of these elements is possible without detailed and subtle understanding of the verities of this influence. It is only by submitting the teaching of English Literature to the more crucial and comparatist discipline of Historical and Cultural Studies, and by connecting the knowledge of that literature with literatures of our own, that we can begin to break that colonial grid and to liberate the teacher of English from a colonially determined, subordinated and parasitic existence. In the process, we might learn a thing or two about 'Indian Literature' as well.

In all this, the source of inspiration and the very model of scholarly rectitude for me remains the figure of the late Professor Kosambi. As a polyglot scholar and a distinguished scientist who held the Chair of Mathematics at the Tata Institute of Fundamental Research for sixteen years, one whose very last book was on Prime Numbers, Kosambi's exacting and irreverent mind wandered over large areas of knowledge – Genetics, Statistics, Numismatics, Archaeology, Prehistory – but his main gift to those of us who do not know much about the physical and mathematical sciences came in the shape of his textual criticism, editions and interpretation of some key classical texts, which is fully reflected in his English writing as well; his lucid, firm, delightfully polemical readings of crucial and hallowed texts, including the *Bhagavad-Gita* itself; and, above all, his revamping of the whole history of Ancient India, the study of which relies considerably – alongside other kinds of written documents, of course – upon what we loosely call 'literature', even though he himself held emphatically that no evidence about the ancient period drawn from *writing* could be taken entirely for granted unless it was corroborated with material evidence drawn from archaeology, numismatics, and so on.[23]

What one finds so liberating in Kosambi is definitely the *combination*: the solidity of scholarship on the one hand; the absolute determination, on the other, to ground all sorts of texts – whether books or coins or customs or stones – in the material history of our people and in the conflicts that history engendered, beyond all spirituality and all humbug. Equally liberating is the sense of the man as it saturates the very tone and texture of his writing: at once a physical scientist and a Sanskritist, crisscrossing between the scholarly detail and the political co-ordinates of that scholarship, thoughtful, intemperate, and so uncompromising both in his Marxism and in his other kinds of scholarship as to have rebuked S.A. Dange publicly, *in those days*, for the latter's much-too-widely-read inaccuracies about Ancient India.[24] And his advice, reflected fully in his scholarship: no usable knowledge of India is possible without actually looking at the people who inhabit this land and then working across the boundaries of the constituted academic disciplines. One does not always agree with Kosambi, either in his conclusions or in his points of departure; there are occasions, in fact, when one feels as quarrelsome towards him as he frequently does towards others. But he is to my mind, generically, what all literary critics, theorists, and so on, in India today should aspire to be.

I invoke the name of Kosambi here not merely to make explicit my own debt, which is incalculable, nor simply to emphasize the obvious fact that the discipline of History in India is much more advanced than Literary Studies and can therefore teach us much, but also to point to a methodological achievement which belongs to him even more than to any other in the distinguished tradition of Marxist historiography in India. For Kosambi was able to produce *in a single sweep* both a narrative of the empirical facts of Ancient India and the theoretical position, the very organic principle of narrativization, from which that narrative was to be assembled. He knew just as thoroughly the coins and the crops and the stones which he studied as he knew his Marxism, and he gave us, without compromising the one or the other, a Marxism that was appropriate to *those* coins, *those* crops, *those* stones. So appropriate was the method to the evidence, so intimate the link between study and political purpose, that the products of his study were always seamless. He never ranted against Orientalism, for example, even acknowledged the debts that deserved acknowledgement, but the knowledge he himself produced was so radically different, so sufficient for part of the same terrain, that he simply displaced those Orientalist ways of knowing our own ancient past. As we engage in the study of 'Indian Literature', the insufficiencies we grapple with are of both the empirical and the theoretical kinds. Even more than the search for more texts and more coherent narratives of their production, we need far greater clarity about the theoretical methods and political purposes of our reading. We need not only to write but also to rewrite; not only to discover but also to displace, as Kosambi did, in a single sweep.

# 8

# Three Worlds Theory: End of a Debate

Those categories and debates that were once centred on a tripartite division of the world may well appear antiquated after the global restructuring of the past few years. The temptation, surely, is to declare that history itself has settled the debates. The difficulty with theoretical debate, however, is that it can neither ignore the facts nor be simply settled by them; thought, one knows from the prehistory of one's own thought, tends always to exceed the facts, in more ways than one. Only in the more doggedly empiricist epistemologies do facts provide sufficient conditions for corrections of theory. My own sense, rather, is that theory can correct itself only through self-correction, with reference, *simultaneously*, to the history of facts as well as to its own prehistory and present composition. In the absence of such an operation, the correction of a past theory straightforwardly by the current facts becomes a mere repression, which then keeps returning to haunt and disrupt the present both of theory and of history itself. A knowledge of the world as it now is presumes corrections in the knowledge of the world as it – the world, and the knowledge of it – previously was.

## I

The range of positions from which Third-Worldist ideology has surfaced in literary-critical theories of culture can be summarized, schematically speaking, by recapitulating the contrasting ways in which Fredric Jameson and Edward Said have, respectively, deployed it.

Jameson is clearly much more capable of rigorous theoretical work, as the magisterial breadth of his *œuvre* amply demonstrates, and it was precisely the lack of such rigour in his formulations about Third World Literature which prompted me to take issue with him on that score. For one of the chief characteristics of Jameson's essay which I analysed in Chapter 3 is the contradiction between his embarrassed awareness, in the opening section, of the basically untheoretical character of the category of the 'Third World' (hence his assertion that he is using the term for purely 'descriptive' purposes) and his tendency, on the other hand, both to attribute quite exact theoretical meaning to the term and then to apply it, in the rest of the essay, to show a fundamental generic difference between literatures of the First and the Third Worlds. Most of the ensuing difficulties have been identified already. What interests me here, rather, are the very terms of his mapping, the fundamental ways in which these terms are different from those of Edward Said; the way Jameson, once he has adopted this category, is forced, however, by the very ideological interpellation inherent in it, to declare, exactly as Said does in *Orientalism*, that nationalism is the determinate political position and cultural energy of the epoch. He has two key differences with Said: he associates the Second World explicitly with socialism, and he dissociates himself equally explicitly from the Maoist idea of 'convergence' between the United States and the Soviet Union. This is a fundamental difference: as late as 1986, Jameson neither adopts the rhetoric of 'Soviet imperialism', first made fashionable by Maoists and then adopted fairly generally in metropolitan radicalisms, nor attempts to designate either the Soviet Union or China as more 'socialist' than the other, while continuing to speak of a 'socialist Second World' despite the first rumblings of perestroika, the endemic Sino-Soviet conflicts, and the triangular contests between Khmer Cambodia, Vietnam and China. Yet, thanks to the theoretical primacy of the 'Third World', the key cultural category that is produced by that primacy and posited against late-capitalist postmodernism is that of national *allegory*.

I have referred to the category of nationalism throughout this book, but this generic specification is itself significant. Jameson himself remarks that allegory is 'a form discredited in the west and the specific target of the Romantic revolution of Wordsworth and Coleridge' as he goes on to caution against 'Our traditional concept of allegory' based on 'an elaborate set of figures and personifications to be read against some one-to-one table of equivalences'.[1] This warning against a 'one-to-one table of equivalences' is shrewd, for it opens up a path for more diverse ways of allegorization to be recognized as such. But the essential underpinning of a representational relation between the individual tale and the essence of a whole remains, as is evident in a later formulation: 'what I call narrative allegory (namely the coincidence of the personal story and the "tale of the tribe", as still in Spenser)'.[2] This drawing of the decisive line at Spenser is also accurate, as was the identification of the Romantics as especially averse to allegory.

But why does this form decline in the First World after Spenser and re-emerge in the Third in the era of colonialism and imperialism, specifically in the national(ist) form? If nationalism constitutes it in the latter case, what constituted it in the former? And if nationalism has this capacity in the Third World, then what explains the fact that it is precisely in the nineteenth century, the age of European nationalisms *par excellence*, that allegory is attacked most vehemently? Why this tie between nationalism and allegory in the one case and utter antipathy between the two in the other? Jameson does not face up to any of these questions. The plain fact is that the cultural products of European medievality are permeated with allegory, in the proper sense, because those products presume a universe of meaning integrated by a constituting metaphysic, specifically of a religious kind, which could be rehearsed narratively as 'character' based on tables of virtues and/or vices and as 'events' which signify the stages and signposts of particular kinds of quests; allegorical arrangements of symbologies and fictional narratives decline after Spenser precisely to the extent that secular historicization begins to displace that integrated metaphysic. Then, it is the full emergence of the masses as historical subjects in the process of the late-eighteenth-century revolutions which breaks up that metaphysic – hence its typical representational form – *decisively*. Allegory would thereafter exist only as an element within some other narrative form, as a trope of allegori*zation*, or not at all. In other words, it is in the emergence of secular histories, and in society's self-consciousness of being irretrievably divided into several kinds of secular antagonism (feminism and the modern novel were born, significantly, in the same revolutionary moment which gave classes and nations their social organization and self-consciousness as distinct historiographic entities), therefore in the convergence of the mimetic form with historicism proper, that allegory as the cultural dominant is dissolved; the more powerful narratives would henceforth foreground not a metaphysical unity but historicized contradiction. To say that allegory is the main form of writing in the Third World, and to declare that nationalism is the organizing narrative principle of this allegory, is to bestow upon Third World nationalism the quasi-religious function of a metaphysic, of the same kind that Christianity held for medieval Europe. This particular way of mapping the disappearance of allegory in Europe after the Renaissance and its reappearance in the contemporary Third World also tends to extend, with a peculiar twist, those tendencies in European Romanticism which often sought in non-Europe that 'organicity' which was said to have existed once but then to have been lost within Europe – not to speak of the familiar liberal idea, recouped with great flair and given much currency on the Left by Benedict Anderson, that the 'imagined community' of the nation comes up, chronologically later but to satisfy some of those same needs of belonging, when (and where) the 'sacred communities' of religion break up.[3]

The pressures of the Three Worlds Theory account for the paradox that Jameson, a perfectly secular intellectual who himself identifies the 'utopian moment' in modern politics not with nationalism but with socialism, is compelled by the logic of that theory to bestow upon nationalism the quasi-religious status of a unifying metaphysic, across countries and classes, the many nuances of his argument notwithstanding. The formal consequence for reading the fictions of this world, of course, is that novels written in Asia or Africa simply cannot be read within the problematics of bourgeois realism and mimetic representation of secular divisions, far exceeding any unifying metaphysic. In mapping the world itself, meanwhile, and in so far as he identifies the Second World strongly with the bloc of socialist countries, he gives us – more or less unwittingly, I think – a version of the theory which came out of a certain convergence between the Soviet and what one may call the mid-fifties-Nehruvian position, as my later comments on these positions will clarify.

Edward Said is, by contrast, theoretically much more eclectic, and had been – when he wrote *Orientalism* – ideologically far more responsive to many forms of straightforward Third-Worldist nationalism, unmediated by any socialist desire. He therefore makes a characteristically less nuanced statement in celebrating the spirit of Bandung:

> By the time of the Bandung Conference in 1955 the entire Orient had gained its political independence from the Western empires and confronted a new configuration of imperial powers, the United States and the Soviet Union. Unable to recognize 'its' Orient in the new Third World, Orientalism now faced a challenging and politically armed Orient.[4]

I shall return to the Bandung Conference at some length presently. But it simply is not true that 'the entire Orient', whichever way one draws the map, 'had gained its political independence' by 1955: the Algerian War, for example, had just started; and Palestine, of course, so central for so many Orientalist mappings, has yet to gain such 'independence'. Significant for our present argument, in any case, is the yoking together of the United States and the Soviet Union as 'a new configuration of imperial powers'. Said has none of Jameson's difficulties about such unequivocal declarations, since for him socialism is not even an issue. The rhetoric of *two* imperialisms here is simply taken over from some well-known Maoist positions, even though Said himself is far from subscribing to Maoism as such and therefore takes the purely nationalist aspect of the Three Worlds Theory without bothering about China being the 'true' socialist country. In short, he advocates precisely that theory of American–Soviet convergence from which Jameson carefully dissociates himself.[5]

One may also quite legitimately ask: what is it, according to Said, that had rendered the Third World so 'armed' and 'challenging'? Most of *Orientalism* was written during 1975–76, Said tells us in his acknowledgements. There were then, and had been for many years before that, many kinds of *arms* in many regions of Asia, Africa and the Middle East: in Vietnam, Laos, Cambodia, which were liberated during those years, as well as in all the Portuguese colonies in Southern Africa, which were also liberated; in the Arab world, when the Egyptian armies crossed the Suez in 1973, and generally in the hands of the Palestinians; and in the hands of the ANC for the liberation of South Africa. Those had been, overwhelmingly,

Soviet arms. That may be easy to forget now, in this new epoch of global perestroika; but that lapse of memory as early as 1975–76 is surprising. Within the Arab world, that view of the Soviet Union as an imperialist power had surely by then become quite widespread, endorsed not by the PLO but by the partnership between Anwar Sadat and the Saudi monarch.

Said, in any case, uses that word 'armed' simply as a literary metaphor, and the weapon to which he alludes is nationalism, which in Jameson's more sedate prose had been mainly a metaphysic. Whether a weapon or a metaphysic, the question remains: *whose* nationalism is it?

## II

The striking feature of the Three Worlds Theory as it passed through its many versions was that this theory, unlike all the great modern theories of social emancipation – for democratic rights, for socialist revolution, for the liberation of women; indeed, anti-colonial nationalism itself – arose not as a peoples' movement, in an oppositional space differentiated from and opposed to the constituted state structures, but, in all its major successive variants, as an ideology of already-constituted states, promulgated either collectively by several of them, or individually by one distinguishing itself from another. Even its ways of mapping the world kept shifting, and it had neither a central doctrine nor a fundamental core which constituted it theoretically; the Soviet and Chinese versions of the theory were so constitutively hostile towards each other that they simply did not share a common starting point. To the extent that it invoked the ideology of anti-colonial nationalism, its most striking feature was that the invocation came at a historical juncture and from particular countries when, and where, the revolutionary content of that anti-colonial ideology – namely, decolonization – had already been achieved. This lack of an articulated central doctrine and the generality of an anti-colonial stance in the post-colonial period gave to the so-called Theory the character of an open-ended ideological interpellation which individual intellectuals were always free to interpret in any way they wished, which in turn made the Theory particularly attractive to those intellectuals who did not wish to identify themselves with determinate projects of social transformation and determinate communities of political praxis, retaining their individual autonomies yet maintaining a certain attachment to a global radicalism.

In most versions of the Theory which gained popular currency, meanwhile, the agency for fundamental transformations was said to reside in the nation-state itself – namely, in the nation-state of the technologically backward societies in collaborative competition with the states of technologically advanced formations. It is significant that the Theory was advanced precisely at the point when states of the national bourgeoisie had already emerged and were consolidating themselves, frequently through a mix of strong state sectors with generalized private enterprise, in a number of the newly independent countries. An ideological formation which redefined anti-imperialism not as a socialist project to be realized by the mass movements of the popular classes but as a developmentalist project to be realized by the weaker states of the national bourgeoisies in the course of their collaborative competition with the more powerful states of advanced capital served the interest both of making the mass movements subservient to the national bourgeois state and of strengthening the negotiating positions of that type of state in relation to the states and corporate entities of advanced capital. It was this sectoral competition between backward and advanced capitals, realized differentially in the world, owing partly to colonial history itself, which was now advocated as the kernel of anti-imperialist struggles, while the national-bourgeois state was itself recognized as representing the masses. None of the variants of the Theory said anything of the kind, of course, which indicates its mystificatory character, but this was in some crucial ways an extension, into the post-colonial phase, of the dominance the national bourgeoisie had been able to establish over most of the anti-colonial movements in the colonial period itself.

Like most mystificatory ideologies, Three Worlds Theory has often mythified its origins.[6] The implication in Said's statement cited above is that the Bandung Conference was in some way the moment of its immaculate birth, and that, indeed, is the common wisdom. Some clarification about that moment of origin is therefore in order. Held in April 1955 in the Indonesian city of Bandung, it was a Conference strictly of the independent countries of Asia and Africa. South Africa and Israel were excluded for obvious reasons, the two Koreas were also excluded for reasons of controversy, but the Indochinese countries and three African colonies which had not yet become entirely sovereign were included because they were soon expected to gain their independence. No country was invited from Latin America. China was invited, and Zhou En Lai in fact played a very considerable role, despite the fact that China was the world's largest communist country; Pakistan (one of the hosts) and several such countries were also there, despite their military alliance with the United States. Marshal Tito, who was soon to emerge as a major architect of the Non-Aligned Movement, was not there, because Yugoslavia is neither Asian nor African. The actual activities of the imperialist countries could not be discussed in the sessions of the Conference because it was a Conference of governments, Nehru said emphatically, to general approval. It was not proper, he said, for representatives of governments to discuss the policies of governments of those other states which were also members of the United Nations; no one, of course, controlled the informal discussions. None of the senses in which the term 'Third World' is now used – non-alignment, a global space other than capitalism and socialism, the tricontinent – would apply to this event.

Alfred Sauvy claimed that he had coined the term 'Third World' in 1952, modelled on the conception of the French Third Estate. In French journalism at least, the term had been used well before Bandung. The phrase was thus of European coinage, and owed its currency to European mediology; but this we shall ignore. The overlap of certain other kinds of background is far more significant. The Korean War had ended, and China needed to normalize its presence in the community of African and Asian states, not as a communist giant but as a neighbour. Both China and India had been prominent in the recently concluded Geneva Conference on Indochina, and both needed a forum where they could assert their leadership – part collaborative, part competing – in the region. The Manila Treaty had been concluded, paving the way for the emergence of the Southeast Asian Treaty Organization (SEATO) in that vicinity, while in West Asia the groundwork was being laid for what was to soon become the Baghdad Pact; Pakistan's membership of both these interlocking Anglo-American military alliances had worried Nehru a great deal, and he wanted to build a structure of Afro-Asian pressure on Pakistan.

SEATO was also exerting considerable pressure on Sukarno, who was heading a neutralist government in the vicinity of that organization, and quite apart from whatever personal predilections he might have had, he simply was in no position to reconsider that neutrality, given that Asia's second-largest Communist Party – second only to the Chinese – was operating in his country. The leaders of countries in his immediate neighbourhood (for example Thailand, the Philippines), also invited to the Conference, had meanwhile scrambled into American protection against what appeared to be a communist wave, emanating from China and the Indochinese countries which had just defeated the French, as well as the very substantial communist movements in their own territories. The Burmese government, too, was nervous about being perhaps gobbled up by their huge Chinese and/or Indian neighbours, perhaps swept away by the impact of the revolutions in Indochina. Between China and India, there was an ongoing border dispute (to erupt into full-blooded war in 1962); between India and Pakistan, there was the issue of Kashmir (site of battle in 1948, and again in 1965 and 1971). The 'Five Principles of Peaceful Coexistence' sponsored jointly by China and India, to be adopted by the Conference as a whole, certainly had a visionary edge, but in view of the regional realities of mutual suspicion, competition and threats of war, the declaration had the air of an informal undertaking that armies should not soon march against neighbours for acquisition of territory.

This undertaking, minimal and informal, hardly corresponded to the fanciful idea of a unified Third World (the reborn 'Orient', politically armed with a shared nationalism, ready to do combat against Orientalism, Western imperialism, imperialist Bolshevism), even though the Conference had taken place in the midst of what came to be known as the Cold War, in the perspective of a *felt* threat of a Third World War and uses of far deadlier atomic weapons than had been dropped on Japan towards the end of World War II. The elder statesmen at the Conference, Nehru and Zhou En Lai in particular, were certainly aware of this added dimension when they pleaded against foreign bases in Afro-Asian regions. A key element in this emphasis on the military aspect was that the Korean War which had just ended had cost a million Chinese deaths, the Soviet Union had developed its atomic and hydrogen bombs, and there was a powerful argument in the United States, gripped at the time by Dulles-style hysterical anti-communism, to annihilate the Soviet Union before it became a full-scale nuclear power; similar scenarios for the annihilation of

China had been put forward all through the Korean War. Those urgent matters were part of that political moment in which Nehru, certainly, visualized a bloc of Afro-Asian countries interposing themselves between the United States and the Soviet Union.

Since the Western media were less interested in regional realities and saw those realities through the prism of Soviet–American contentions, it was particularly keen to pick up this singular aspect and conjured up a tripartite division of the world, with the 'Third World' being the world of military non-alignment. In this characterization, the American world was First not because capitalism was superior but because its interlocking military alliances, from NATO to SEATO, were more powerful, with fully global reach; the USSR was Second because it had only the Warsaw Pact, with a comparatively very inferior technological base; the Third World was composed of those countries which were militarily not aligned with either the United States or the USSR and could therefore be a force for peace. The fact that this key element of non-alignment did not fit half the governments represented at Bandung did not much bother the media, and it has not bothered the scholars who have inherited that tradition of representing Bandung. In the context of the severity of the Cold War, this Third World was presented as the one that was going to prevent what was said to be the inexorable logic of military madness of the First and Second Worlds, otherwise leading them inevitably towards World War III.

Even in this initial mediatic presentation, this tripartite division of the world had nothing to do with modes of production, or with social systems, or even with structures of feeling, as this division would later be conceived by theorists of literature. 'Third World' was simply another name for military non-alignment. (Later, when a fully fledged Non-Aligned Movement emerged and the term 'Third World' became attached to it more or less permanently, the presence of Tito as one of the moving forces belied its identification with non-Europe; exclusion of numerous countries like Pakistan, which were members of formal alliances, also belied its identification with *all* of non-Europe; while the inclusion of a whole range of countries from Cuba to Saudi Arabia indicated how merely *formal* and flexible the notion of alignment had by then become.)

Such were the intra- and international pressures and configurations at Bandung, and their reflections in the Western media. Since, however, these very complex configurations were being represented, within the problematics of the Conference, primarily at governmental levels, language itself came to have a peculiarly overdetermined, archaic character, perfectly transparent to the initiated, always in need of decoding by all others, with words constantly exceeding their meanings, at once slippery and hermeticized. How complex the pressures were in the actual situation prevailing in any given country, and what ranges of meaning were embedded in what appeared to be transparent statements of belief, we can illustrate with reference to Nehru and a rather simple sentence he uttered at Bandung.

## III

'We do not agree with the communist teachings, we do not agree with the anti-communist teachings, because they are both based on wrong principles,' Nehru is reported to have said. If we were to read a sentence of this kind in the New-Critical fashion, overvalorizing the verbal surface and detaching the sentence from the system of enunciations and the series of political contexts in which it belongs, it would be perfectly possible to read into it the precise meaning that Said conveys in *his* sentence about the 'Orient', reborn as a Third World, asserting itself against the new configuration of two imperial powers. But who is this 'we' in Nehru's sentence? This needs some decoding, because Nehru was undoubtedly the main luminary at the Conference, but before we make the mistake of having this 'we' represent the Conference as such, hence the generality of a 'Third World', it is best to recall that Zhou En Lai occupied almost an equal eminence and a statement of that kind ('communist teachings . . . based on wrong principles') simply could not have been made on his behalf. And, of course, Nehru had been the first to underline the fact that it was a conference of *governments*. Nehru's sentence, in other words, is a governmental sentence. The 'we' is, in the first instance, the government of India. In this first instance, it presumes that it speaks on behalf of *all* of India; government, in other words, claims to *be* the nation.

I shall come soon to the several meanings of this sentence as it is enunciated by the *we* which claims a perfect identity of government and nation. But what the governmental assertion conceals is a second instance of this *we*, which is Nehru as the head of the Congress Party, one political party among others in India, representing one political position among others, and soon to face elections in the newly created states of, first, Andhra (later that same year) and then Kerala (two years later, in 1957), where the Communist Party of India was expected to win, Congress to lose. In this latter instance of that same pronoun, Nehru speaks to the electorates of those states inside India, from the august podium of an international conference – the media there to construct it as the glorious birth of the 'Third World' – asserting the convergence of the Congress Party, the government, the nation on a single ideology: *we* don't believe in 'communist teachings/wrong principles'; that is to say, voting for the Communist Party of India is *ipso facto* an anti-national activity. In a very subsidiary register, though, he is also speaking to the Communist Party itself, opposing it but also reassuring it that he will not go so far as actually to join the American camp (the 'anti-communist teaching' is *also* wrong, Nehru says; A.K. Gopalan, a leading member of the party, had after all visited him just before the Conference to assure him that despite bitter contentions within the country, the party did support him in his policy of non-alignment). But he is speaking, above all, to that mass of the electorate which is *between* Congress and Communists, and whom he educates in the *falsity* of communism – in this sense the statement is pedagogical, delivered with the full authority of an international conference, Zhou En Lai sitting close by – but whose anti-imperialism he must respect, lest he lose them altogether (hence the deliberate distancing from 'anti-communist teachings' as well, a phrase which simply meant, in this register, the American camp, the Dulles brothers, McCarthyism, SEATO, the Baghdad Pact). At the same time Nehru is speaking to that right wing of his own party, which had been greatly disturbed by the beginning of large-scale Soviet aid to India only two months earlier, in February 1955. Simply put, that half of the sentence which debunks 'communist teachings' is meant to convey that closer state-to-state relations with the Soviet Union and inviting China to the Conference, despite explicit objections from both Britain and the United States, did *not* mean any concessions to the Communist Party of India – quite the contrary, as we shall see.

But that turn towards the Soviet Union had been very, very recent;

Nehru had spent the first few years after Independence seeking an alliance with the Anglo-American bloc, and there was some anxiety in the country that he might revert to this position at any time, as indeed he did during the Galbraith ambassadorship, in the Kennedy years; his disavowal of 'anti-communist teachings' was meant to address that anxiety. This design of the sentence which addresses the nation from an international forum shows quite clearly that the nation is itself riven with contentions; that the only statement which claims to be a truthful statement and aspires to speak *for* and *to* this nation has to balance, at the very least, the clauses. (In the event, Congress won in Andhra a couple of months later by a much wider margin than even Nehru could have anticipated, but then the Communists won in Kerala in 1957, establishing the first non-Congress government in independent India and the first elected Communist government anywhere in the world. The calculus of electoral factors underlying those losses and gains are complex indeed, but Namboodripad, who took over as Communist Chief Minister in Kerala, does suggest that the lustre Nehru had gained at Bandung was a distinct element in the Andhra elections which followed immediately, but not in Kerala two years later.[7])

But I also pointed out above a certain doubling of the voice in that sentence, addressed by the head of the largest party to the political divisions inside the country but also addressing the world as the unified voice of a self-identical nation-state. The international situation in which that sentence was enunciated was certainly not external to its meaning. On this score we may take the matter of China first, since Zhou was the other main presence at the Conference and since China is present in the sentence itself in the characteristically pedagogical formulation, 'communist teachings'. The very Nehruvian author of Nehru's standard biography[8] tells us that when Communists took power in Beijing barely two years after Indian Independence, Nehru's main thoughts were about the Sino-Indian border, so he instructed his diplomats to offer '*cautious* friendship'. During the Korean crisis the next year, the Indian government accepted both the key Security Council Resolutions, of 25 and 27 June 1950, which paved the way for the thin veiling of the US invasion as a United Nations force. When the United States started scrambling for military contingents from other countries to bestow an international semblance upon the American invasion, Nehru had instructed his ambassador to emphasize to the

Americans that India's 'moral support' was worth many a contingent from lesser countries. It was only India's mediating role towards the end of the Korean War, supplemented then with Sino-Indian co-operation during the Geneva Conference on Indochina, which had created a sense of neutrality and even a certain partnership with China. When Nehru met Zhou in October 1954, the latter had remarked that the existing maps were not very accurate because much of the Sino-Indian border simply was not demarcated, to which Nehru had replied, just as politely, that there was no reason to worry because everyone knew where the borders were. The subject had been dropped, but the great divergence between these two positions was obvious enough and tensions had remained – right into Bandung, where a certain meaning of that sentence is that the apparent amity between China and India should not be taken at face value, as some sort of enduring alliance between these two great Asian countries (no united, reborn 'Orient' here).

The matter of the Soviet Union had been even more complex during those same months. The Conference was held in April and, as I mentioned above, substantial Soviet aid had begun in February of that year (a projected steel mill with a production capacity of one million tons annually); Nehru then visited the Soviet Union in June, and both Khrushchev and Bulganin came to India that winter; their tour climaxed in Calcutta, where two million people came out to greet them. The pace and scale of *rapprochement* was decidedly unexpected, and the streets of Calcutta were not under Nehru's control, but events nationally and internationally were such that Nehru had certainly desired the normalization of relations between the two countries.[9] Towards the end of that visit, in December, he was to extract from the Khrushchev–Bulganin team the explicit affirmation that the Soviet Union had given no financial aid to the CPI and would maintain no significant links with it; how Nehru was to deal with the party, for good or ill, would have no effect on Indo-Soviet relations. The sentence quoted above is perched, so to speak, between the steel mill and the millions who welcomed the Soviet leaders; it anticipates the visit, fixes its meaning in advance. And, to the extent that the areas of co-operation and distance were demarcated in relation to China and the Soviet Union, those same demarcations were there for scrutiny by the SEATO countries, and by Burma, Britain, the United States.

But where did Bandung fit into Nehru's tenure as first Prime Minister of independent India? His later power has obscured the fact that Nehru had come to occupy that office from a position of great weakness, and only because Gandhi had chosen him. The Congress Party was much more firmly in Patel's control, a fact which Patel later demonstrated by getting Parshotam Das Tandon elected as party president despite Nehru's public opposition; Nehru was to describe that election as a 'slap in my face'. Under the circumstances, Gandhi's assassination in January 1948 was a very personal blow to him, and it was only Patel's own death in December 1950 which secured his unchallenged supremacy within Congress. Meanwhile, it is not entirely clear why Nehru had insisted on keeping Mountbatten as Governor-General and retaining the British Service Chiefs. Among all the Congress leaders, Nehru was the one Mountbatten had found the most congenial, and we know that Nehru relied on the latter's friendship and advice both before and after Independence. It may well be that a weak Prime Minister was using a British Governor-General to shield himself from the majority of his own party. What must be emphasized is that this was entirely consistent with Nehru's personal culture and initial vision of India's international ties after Independence.

After his famous radicalization of 1933–36,[10] Nehru had shifted back into a very Fabian kind of socialism, more and more normalized as the years went by, so that the mix between the state and private sectors which the Planning Committees of Congress drafted under his guidance had the full and explicit support of the Indian bourgeoisie. For independent India, he had visualized close co-operation with the Anglo-American bloc, and he kept hoping for American support until at least 1950, when consistent American preference for Pakistan and the American effort to build up Liaqat, Pakistan's Prime Minister, as an alternative Asian leader finally disillusioned him. When Radhakrishnan, India's ambassador to the Soviet Union (later to emerge as President of the Republic), suggested a Treaty of Friendship between the two countries, Nehru refused, for fear of offending the Americans; he got India to join the restructured British Commonwealth instead, in April 1949, and even accepted the King as 'Head' of the Commonwealth, mainly with a view to cultivating the Anglo-American bloc and over strenuous objections not only from the Communists but even from such Socialists as Jayprakash Narayan. The record suggests that it was

American intransigence, in the grip of McCarthyism and then generally of the Dulles–Nixon variety of the extreme Right, which forced Nehru's hand. Had there been even a faintly liberal American administration in place, Nehru would probably have settled down into a close co-operative relationship, as happened with John Kennedy's victory in 1960, when Galbraith arrived in India as ambassador and was immediately given pride of place both in personal counsels and in consultations over economic policy. The dilemma, in other words, was that the Anglo-American bloc was simply not willing to accept the facts of India's sovereignty, the aspirations which flowed directly both from the size of the country and its relatively well-developed bourgeoisie which demanded room for some autonomous growth, or the limits on Nehru's choices placed by the size of the Left.

The combination of such elements proved decisive for Nehru's calculated leftward turn after the 1952 elections. By then, the ban on the Communist Party had been lifted and it emerged as the second largest party in Parliament, followed closely by the Socialist Party in third place; Congress itself got less than half the votes polled in that year, when the deaths of Gandhi and Patel had left Nehru wholly in charge of the party and in a position to claim unchallenged leadership of the nationalist legacy. The Socialists' departure from Congress in 1948 had infuriated Nehru a great deal, and their relatively good showing at the polls sealed the possibilities of their return; Nehru's fear was that both the Communists and the Socialists might expand their electoral bases substantially over the next five years, while many of the right-wing elements in his own party might gravitate towards the newly founded Jan Sangh, so that Congress might possibly not get enough parliamentary seats even to form a government.

Rebuffed by the Americans, taken aback by the Left's impressive electoral showing in India's first elections based on universal suffrage, and fighting to retain a majority in Parliament, Nehru made the bold decision to move leftward simply by taking over the entire platform of the Socialist Party, with the power of the state at his command to implement at least a part of that platform; the scope of this leftward shift is clear if one compares the preparatory documents for the Second Five-Year Plan, drawn up after the 1952 elections, with the First Plan which had been drawn up before those elections. It was a spectacularly well-calculated strategy. Socialists were now free either to join up or to be marginalized. Even the Communists were placed in a quandary. Their mass base had been decimated during the suppression of the 1948–51 uprisings, and the defeat of the peasant movement in Telengana had left them with few choices outside the parliamentary mould. Having recovered part of that mass base in electoral contests, legal trade-union work and peaceful peasant mobilization, they could not now afford to be seen as opposing a Prime Minister who was himself moving so much towards the Left, lest they be branded permanent ultras; but without such an opposition they could hardly expect to enlarge their own base substantially. Internationally, meanwhile, American intransigence was such that Nehru lost nothing much by drawing closer to the Soviet Union and staging mass spectacles of Sino-Indian fraternity. Bandung, which came exactly between the two elections of 1952 and 1957, was part of this domestic and international realignment, and it helped to propel Nehru from a beleaguered Prime Ministership to the status of a world leader, rivalled in the Afro-Asian continents only by Zhou En Lai. In the domestic sphere, it was the Second Five-Year Plan which won over most of the urban intelligentsia and secured for him a much larger populist base than ever before. As he had calculated, he won his largest electoral mandate in 1957, even though he lost Kerala. Congress was to remain hegemonic for the next twenty years and more. When he made his peace with America some three years later, with the onset of the Kennedy years, and when he sent thousands of Communists to prison after the Sino-Indian War, none of it made any difference to that hegemony.

Bandung was thus no logical step that flowed directly from some generalized Third-Worldist nationalism; it was embedded, for Nehru, in specific compulsions, both internal and external. And, of course, other leaders brought to Bandung their own compulsions, which were equally complex but will be indicated here only in broad outline. Sukarno, for example, was heading a *nationalist* government against what was, outside China and the Soviet Union, the largest Communist Party in the world, and a party which was deeply Maoist. Zhou En Lai's announcement of a partnership with Sukarno-style Indonesian nationalism and the consequent eulogy for an undifferentiated 'peace' had the effect of signalling a *peaceful* road for Indonesian communism and a united front with Sukarno – which eventually contributed, of course, to the largest single bloodbath of communists in any military coup in history. It was the factor of Chinese guidance and the consequent complete reliance on Sukarno which led KPI to ignore the possibility of the coup even as it stared them in the face; in the event, the coup swept off Sukarno himself, along with some half a million of them. Nasser's own coup and subsequent anti-British moves had been designed largely to pre-empt the possibility of a communist revolution from the Left, as well as to neutralize the Muslim Brotherhood [*Ikhwan-ul-Muslimun*] on the Right. When he came to Bandung, barely a year after consolidating power in Egypt, he desperately needed an international profile and a bloc of support for a showdown with the British over Suez the next year, which was to lead to nationalization of the Canal, the tripartite invasion of Egypt, the building of the Aswan Dam and the Halwan steel complex with Soviet aid, and Nasser's rise to unassailable hegemony in Arab nationalist politics for the next fifteen years; those golden years of Nasserite nationalism during the late 1950s were also those when he broke the Communist Party of Egypt with unspeakable brutality. Bandung was inseparable from such exigencies of the main leaders. Nehru managed not to be swept away like Sukarno, and he was more subtle, far less brutal, than Nasser; but all three came to Bandung with distinct agendas which happened, in the short term, to overlap.

## IV

Such were the beginnings in Egypt, in Indonesia, in India. The term 'Third World' had come into mediatic parlance even before the Non-Aligned Movement fully got going. Soon enough, however, this nomenclature was given a very different theoretical content by the Soviet Union, as the Soviet self-conception came to be redefined in the wake of the Twentieth Party Congress. The *main* contradiction was now said to be not between capital and labour, nor between the capitalist and the socialist systems of *production*, but between the socialist and capitalist system of *states*, condensed in the competition between the United States and the USSR. This thesis basically preserved the idea – developed during the Stalin era – that the defence of the USSR, as the first socialist country, was the primary form of class struggle on the global scale; for that idea, too, Indian communism had paid a heavy price, during the 'Quit India Movement' and for a decade or more thereafter. But after 1956 this Stalinist idea suffered several complications.

First, after World War II a *system* of socialist states had come into existence; this was now said to be in a position to compete with the capitalist system and eventually to overthrow it. Second, the invention of atomic (and then thermonuclear) weapons had made a war between the two systems impossible, so the competition had to be peaceful. Third, a large number of independent states had come into existence during the same postwar years, in Asia and increasingly in Africa as well, and if these underdeveloped but sovereign states could be made to ally themselves not with the USA but with USSR – if not militarily, then at least economically – the global balance of economic power could be shifted in favour of the socialist states and capitalism could gradually be eliminated as a rival, through peaceful competition. The task of the working classes of these newly independent countries was therefore to pressurize the states of their national bourgeoisies to remain militarily neutral between blocs and integrate themselves economically into the system of socialist rather than capitalist states. Internally, the working classes were to take up arms, where feasible, only against the remaining colonial authorities and, in extremity, where imperialism intervened militarily. For the rest, the struggle for socialism had to be peaceful, through parliaments where such were available.

The main point in all this was that the struggle between capitalism and socialism was to be waged (peacefully) between the (capitalist) First World and the (socialist) Second World, and the progressive character of any regime in the (nondescript) Third World was to be determined by the character of its foreign policy and external relations. If it remained militarily non-aligned and expanded its economic relations with the socialist countries, then it could be called a *National* Democracy (a 'progressive' state based upon the nationalism of the national bourgeoisie, as distinct from a *People's* Democracy, where a Communist Party was already in power), while an expanding state sector could even launch it on the road to socialism, through 'non-capitalist' development; Nehruvian India was often said to be verging on this 'non-capitalist' development, which overlapped nicely with Nehru's description of his own planned economy as 'socialist*ic*', with state monopoly and private enterprise (itself often monopolistic) finely balanced. In other words, the Third World was not uniformly progressive, but any state within it could choose to become so, regardless of its domestic structure, by choosing a *nationalist* – that is to say, pro-Soviet – foreign policy.

The true prestige of the Three Worlds Theory came, in any case, only with the Chinese Cultural Revolution, when the definition of the world was most thoroughly revamped. The First World now included only the United States and the USSR, the two equally dangerous imperial powers; the Second World was composed of other industrialized countries, which were said to be potential allies in a struggle against the imperialisms of what were now called the two superpowers; the Third World was composed of the predominantly agricultural and poor countries, which now together constituted the 'countryside' and were destined to surround and smash the 'cities': namely, the United States and the Soviet Union. Significantly, China again ended up in the Third World. At a later stage, of course, the USSR was declared 'fascist', which seemed to leave it alone, in a class unto itself, with the United States becoming an ally in the anti-fascist struggle. It is worth mentioning here that it was not the Soviet version of the Theory, with its partial truths and opportunistic twists, which seized most radical imaginations in subsequent years. Rather – with all kinds of anti-communism assuming merely an anti-Soviet form, and with even the most fantastic forms of the Maoist ideology taking hold of impressive sections of campus radicals from the latter 1960s onwards – it was the Chinese version of the Three Worlds Theory which had the widest global currency.

Now, some of us may well feel wounded by so stark a recapitulation of recent history. Maoism, after all, is not something entirely external to the practices and debates that have shaped large parts of our own political culture over the past two decades. The reason why those of us who came of age in the late 1960s or the early 1970s need to come to terms with this prehistory of our own intellectual and ideological formation is that this prehistory has endowed us with vocabularies and styles of thought which are so global in their dispersion, so much a part of what one might call the modern Leftist common sense, that we absorb them on a daily basis, without giving them so much as a thought. Not all of us are equally gripped by it, but at least some elements of it – some variant of the Three Worlds Theory, mostly in the Maoist reformulations – are inscribed now, sometimes despite ourselves, in the political unconscious of all we write, think, say about the global dispersion of powers and cultures.

In other words, this term, the 'Third World', does not come to us as a mere descriptive category, to designate a geographical location or a specific relation with imperialism alone. It carries within it contradictory layers of meaning and political purpose. In the conception of its chief *nationalist* exponents – Nehru, Nasser, Sukarno – the term was indissolubly linked to the containment of communism and a 'mixed' economy of the private and state capitalist sectors. In the Soviet variant, it came to have the practical significance of approving precisely such regimes – such as the Nasserite one – regardless of their domestic policies towards the working classes or Left parties and organizations, so long as they were aligned with the Soviet Union internationally and had large state sectors. In the Maoist version, the originary presuppositions of this term *include* a large degree of distancing – that is, a *world* of difference – from those other countries which might also have been groping towards a socialist future, and have been constructed, in the prehistory of this term, as (a) a military bloc which endangered the very existence of the human species; (b) an imperial system, with the Soviet Union commanding a host of colonies, from Eastern Europe to Cuba to Vietnam; and (c) a fascism.

In two of these variants, the Maoist and the straightforwardly nationalist, the term also presupposes that the 'Third World', with its existing state and class formations, and regardless of the deformities of these formations, is a real alternative; indeed, a locus of resistance – that is, *a world unto itself*, something to be preserved and strengthened – against encroachments by the other two worlds. Not socialism but *nationalism* has always been designated by the propagators of this term – even in the post-Twentieth-Congress, Soviet variants of it – as the determinate, epochal, imperative ideology of the Third World. (There is, of course, yet another usage of this term which makes no theoretical pretence and applies the nomenclature 'Third World' simply to the so-called developing countries, from Cuba to Saudi Arabia and from China to Chad. That is a polemical use, a matter simply of common parlance, and I use it myself in that sense often enough.) The difficulty with deploying this term, 'Third World', as a *theoretical category*, however, is that its career has been so contradictory, so riven with detailed contention, that one would first have to specify, with *some* degree of theoretical rigour, the very grid – Nehruvian, or Maoist, or Soviet, or some other – which underlies one's own deployment of it. Meanwhile, the fact that *all* the theoretical variants emphasize the nationalist character of the term's politics should necessarily mean that it is really not possible to adopt the category itself, as the basis of one's theoretical work, and simultaneously to break away from that originary underlying presupposition. In order to think of the world differently, one would have to forgo the theoretical category itself. Marxists who subscribe to the idea of socialism, deploy the Three Worlds Theory, identify socialism with the Second World, uphold Third-Worldist nationalism as the determinate ideological imperative of our epoch, and posit this nationalism as the *real* alternative to the postmodernist American culture, render the discussion not less but *more* eclectic and incoherent.

## V

The power of this terminology would have declined, one would have thought, with the general decline of explicitly political Maoism which began in the mid 1970s, but that power remained. A great many intellectuals who renounced their formal ties with organized Maoism nevertheless continued to function through those same categories of thought – now as 'independents'; by the early 1980s, quite a few of them were joining what now came to be known as 'social movements'. The upshot was that while the politics of Maoism declined, its social and cultural impact among the middle-class intelligentsia remained, in many versions. The fact that the term 'Third World' was used as much by regimes of the national bourgeoisie as by the Soviet-style regimes and parties bestowed upon it overlapping layers of self-evident legitimacy, which could be used equally by the communist and the anti-communist, even though the individual theorist who used the term theoretically could not always tell what it meant. A Third-Worldist nationalism was a convenient position for intellectuals who represented themselves as anti-imperialist radicals, while also participating in the anti-communist ambience of the culture at large; but a certain valorization of nationalism was also the homage that left-wing academics paid to the burgeoning power of the national bourgeoisies from the late 1970s onwards. Now, the collapse of the 'Second World' has, of course, made a shambles of the 'Three Worlds Theory', but how does one understand the world as it actually exists, especially now? One may fruitfully begin this discussion by looking at the range of responses to the sea-change that has taken place in the erstwhile Comecon countries.

There is, first, the triumphalism of the bourgeoisie; all sections of it, in all parts of the world, seem quite agreed that Marxism, socialism, communism have passed away. Second, the diverse postmodernist/post-Marxist currents in contemporary (literary) theory, which were all already agreed that Marxism is not much more than a 'progressivist master-narrative of modes of production', and therefore no sort of answering critique of capitalism or an alternative to it as such, are now likely to speak even less often of socialism as a determinate negation of bourgeois society and much more frequently of 'democracy', 'social movements' and 'dispersed sites of struggle'. These responses to the dissolution of the 'Second World' were predictable enough, and we surely have, on the other side, analyses from Marxist positions as well. There have been three other responses, however, which I think are even more interesting in the present context.

There is, first, the pre-existing Maoist theory of 'convergence' between the capitalist United States and the social–imperialist Russia which can now claim – not from Beijing, where that kind of Maoism receded some years ago, but from other global sites – that what has happened now had been foreseen by protagonists of the Chinese Cultural Revolution. Second, however, there is also the 'Islamic' interpretation, which holds that a great revolution is sweeping the world from the Atlantic shores of the Maghreb through the whole of the Middle East and West Asia, dipping down into West Africa on one side of the Sahara, into the Sudan and Somalia on the other, then rising into the Asian Republics of the erstwhile Soviet Union and the vast Sinkiang region of China, curving into the twin regions of Kashmir and Bangladesh on the two flanks of India, then marching on to Malaysia, Indonesia, and so on – against which the two Satans (the superpowers; the First and Second Worlds) are converging. This is not the

'Three Worlds Theory' as the Left normally knows it, but surely an uncanny version of sorts (with the two worlds of Christian capitalism and godless communism converging against the third, the Islamic Ummah).

But then, alongside these Maoist and Islamicist interpretations one also encounters a third explanatory model of 'convergence' based upon the idea of an emerging global confrontation between two monoliths, one white and industrialized, the other non-white and non-industrialized, uniting the First and Second Worlds against the post-colonial Third World. There is actually some truth in this latter explanatory model, but that truth-portion is submerged in three quite sizeable misconceptions. First, there is a *racist* characterization of the new global conjuncture which is partially false in the sense that there is doubtless a heightened racial arrogance in American triumphalism as well as a distinct racist edge in Gorbachevian rhetoric of a 'common European home' and of 'common civilization' shared by all of Europe and North America, but this racist convergence is not at the origin but a consequence of imperialist triumph and the readmission of Southeastern Europe into its hegemony – in a distinctly inferior and subordinate position, of course. Furthermore, this model borrows from the 'Three Worlds Theory' the propensity to think of global divisions in monolithic terms, with the difference only that instead of three worlds there are said now to be only two: white/non-white, industrialized/non-industrialized. And, like the Maoist and the Islamicist, this model too thinks of the dissolution of the Soviet Union simply as a 'convergence' with the United States, without taking into account the key fact of a victorious imperialism subordinating and assimilating into its own structure the adversary of yesteryear. What is remarkable about these three explanatory hypotheses of convergence is that they all, from the Muslim to the Maoist, share three things: (a) the idea of a tripartite division of the world, in which a 'Third' World is pitched against the combined (and increasingly converging) resources of the First and the Second; (b) the tendency, in each variant, to see this 'Third World', whether defined as Islamic or as non-white or as non-industrialized, as a homogeneous entity; and (c) a conception of a certain kind of transnational nationalism – achieved on the basis of religion, or racial difference, or presumably shared national poverties – as the determinate answer to the momentous changes currently taking place. It is doubtful that any of these hypotheses will achieve any sort of theoretical rigour, but each seems to draw upon pre-existing notions of a tripartite global division and of 'nationalism' as the appropriate answer.

Surely, the historic transformations in Eastern Europe and the break-up of the Soviet Union do not by any means constitute a 'convergence', in the sense of a partnership, with the United States. The evolving relationship is, rather, in the nature of capitulation, fragmentation, incorporation, subordination, and what in an entirely different context Andre Gunder Frank once called 'the development of underdevelopment', so that those countries can either be simply taken over (e.g. East Germany) or restructured into a backward zone on the immediate periphery of the more advanced Western Europe. Gorbachev, of course, imagined that if his regime unilaterally dissolved the existing social organization of production and power in the Soviet Union, the country would painlessly become part of what he calls, in somewhat racist terms, 'our common European home', with its global position intact, quite unmindful of the obvious fact that the global position rested directly on that internal social organization; without it, neither the position nor the country itself, even in the most basic territorial arrangements, could remain what it was. Subordination has been inherent in the way the project of perestroika has unfolded, even for the technologically more developed among the states that are now arising out of the ruins of the Soviet Union. Meanwhile, the punishing logic of the capitalist market that is being imposed upon Eastern Europe today is neither structurally different from nor less brutal than the logic that was imposed, say, in Egypt after Nasser or in Chile after the defeat of *Unidad Popular*. In other words, racism is certainly a considerable component in the ideologies and cultures of the imperialist countries but the logic which determines the exercise of their power is a capitalist logic, so that the reincorporated countries of Eastern Europe are being treated structurally, according to their economic problems and capitalist potentials, much in the same way that Latin American countries or any other country of the zones of backward capitalism may be treated.

## VI

The capitalist world today is not divided into monolithic oppositions:

white/non-white, industrialized/non-industrialized. Rather, its chief characteristics in the present phase are (1) that it is a hierarchically structured global system in which locations of particular countries are determined, in the final analysis, by the strengths and/or weaknesses of their economies; and (2) the system itself is undergoing a new phase of vast global restructuring. The United States occupies a unique position in this hierarchical structure – first, because of the hegemonic dominance it enjoyed for roughly the first thirty years after World War II and the residual strengths which that long wave of prosperity has left behind; and second, because of the *unique combination* of the size of its domestic economy, the breadth of its global economic power, and the vast superiority of its military machine as compared even to those of its closest economic competitors, Japan and Germany. The *relative* economic decline of the United States – relative both to the preceding long wave of its own prosperity and to the growth rates of its main competitors – means, however, that it no longer commands the hegemonic position it commanded previously, and that key decisions affecting global economy cannot now be made unilaterally in Washington and New York, but must be made, rather, by several regimes of advanced capital in several countries, collectively and simultaneously.

We thus have a situation in which the three countries at the apex of economic power – the United States, Japan and Germany – hold the key positions but must co-ordinate their policies among themselves, as well as with other centres of advanced capitalism, in order to manage the global economy as a whole and to design imperialist interventions in the economies of the subordinated backward capitalist countries. These subordinated countries, I might add, are ranged across a very wide spectrum. From the petroleum economies of the Gulf to the substantially industrialized societies of the East Asian Pacific Rim, such as South Korea or Taiwan or Singapore; and from India to countries of Sub-Saharan Africa, there are vast differences in demography, sociohistorical formation, economic scale, levels of accumulation, and modes of articulation into the world economy. The rentier bourgeoisie of Saudi Arabia is simply not comparable to the industrial bourgeoisie of India, nor is the scale of demography, economy and technical labour in India comparable to similar factors in Sub-Saharan Africa. The position that any given country occupies in the hierarchical structure of global capitalism is determined by a host of such factors. In other words, the tendential law of global accumulation functions not towards greater homogenization or similarity of location in zones of backward capitalism, but towards greater differentiation among its various national units.

The hierarchical nature of this structure is itself intertwined with the rapid rate of its global restructuring. Some of the key elements in this restructuring are as follows. For the first time in over a century, this system no longer faces a major, fundamental challenge from organized labour movements, and for the first time in roughly half a century it no longer faces a systemic challenge from a global space largely outside its control. Conversely, *advanced* capital has now reached a level of global self-organization where conflicts between its national units cannot be settled through warfare because supranational interpenetrations of its national capitals are now such that the nation-state has ceased to be the discrete site for the reproduction of *advanced* capital, which must now survive as a global system or not at all. This factor has given the imperialist countries a kind of unity that was inconceivable even fifty years ago, let alone in Lenin's time, thus producing what one may legitimately call, in the Kautskyian language of the Second International, a 'Super Imperialism'. The unification of Germany; the impending unification of Europe, essentially on German terms; the utilization of the Security Council and the unification of West European and Japanese positions under US military command against Iraq – all are stages in the construction of this superimperialism – with internal contradictions, granted, but largely unified in its will to weed out all opposition in all parts of the globe and to dominate collectively the backward capitalist countries, with no small degree of racist arrogance as well. Third, this emergent superimperialism has been vastly strengthened by the collapse and reincorporation of the erstwhile Comecon countries, which not only consign *them* to a Latin American-style dependence, but also greatly undermine what little negotiating positions other countries of backward capitalism ever had; this applies, objectively, as much to India, which had friendly ties with those countries, as to the Philippines, which has lost its key strategic value in the containment of communism; as much to Syria, whose own strategic calculations had previously assumed the continued stability of the Warsaw Pact, as to any country or political movement for which the Soviet Union had been a source of weaponry and/ or alternative technology.

Interwoven into all the above factors is the increasing unification of Europe, both political and economic. If the sheer *size* of the North American economy has exerted its own pressure upon Western Europe to obtain corresponding economies of scale, the spectacular growth of West European capital and its increasing unification exerted, in turn, unbearable pressures upon the Comecon countries, becoming the immediately proximate external factor contributing to the dissolution of their existing economic organizations. In Asia and Africa, decolonization within a global capitalist framework had, of course, greatly contributed to the unification of a single global market as well as to the intensification of capitalist relations in individual countries, for it had meant the dissolution of protected markets for individual colonizing countries – India for Britain, Niger for France, and so on – into a single market open to circulation of all commodities on a global scale. The national bourgeoisies which took hold of the newly independent countries have favoured the generalization of capitalist relations to whatever extent it is possible; various kinds of new protectionisms or the residual ties inherited from the past have sought to impede these processes but have failed to arrest the basic trajectory. In the process, manufacture has become a fairly worldwide phenomenon, *some* of the backward capitalist countries have experienced quite spectacular levels of industrialization, all the larger agrarian economies have witnessed increasing capitalization of agriculture through new technologies, and the juridical as well as social relations of capitalism have tended to dominate and subsume even pre-capitalist productions throughout Asia and Africa, even though low levels of accumulation frequently foreclose the possibility of a proper industrial transition. The cumulative effect of these changes has been to *increase* differentiations between classes and among regions within countries, as well as among the many countries of these backward capitalist zones.

## VII

This system of globally differentiated restructuring faces two fundamental problems today. One pertains to the structural distortions in the advanced economies themselves, leading to a situation where all these economies – now even the Japanese – are slowing down, while each recessionary cycle tends to be both more intense and more prolonged. These economies are facing the possibility, not of intra-imperialist war but of a collective slowdown, with unpredictable kinds (and degrees) of instability in their own economic structuration. Whether or not the factors more favourable to further expansion and consolidation in the contemporary dynamics of advanced capitalism which we have enumerated above will help the system to overcome its structural distortions is yet to be seen.

The second problem is far less open to long-term remedy. While the logic of capital is now irreversible in Asia and Africa, the great majority of these countries simply cannot make a fully fledged capitalist transition of the European type, now or at any point in the foreseeable future. European transition occurred when there were no external, imperialist, far more powerful capitalist countries to dominate and subjugate the European ones; when the world's resources – from minerals to agricultural raw materials to the unpaid labour of countless millions – could form the basis for Europe's accumulation; when vast reservoirs of European populations could simply be exported to other continents; when the European working classes could be pressed into service for commodity exports to the markets of the world, establishing a global hegemony of European capital. Where can India send the approximately five hundred million people for whom Indian capitalism simply cannot provide, and whose minerals is the Indian bourgeoisie to extract to fuel our economy and guarantee our balance of payments for the next two hundred years? It has only its own forests to ravage, its own mountains to denude, its own rivers to dam up and pollute, its own countryside to consign to generalized filth, its own cities to choke with carbonized air – in a subordinated partnership with imperialist capital. Lacking the historically specific global conditions which proved to be the nursery for European capital, most of the Asian zones simply cannot ever hope to develop stable capitalist societies, and the devastating combination of the most modern technology and backward capitalist development is likely to inflict upon these societies, on lands and peoples alike, kinds and degrees of destruction unimaginable even during the colonial period. Given the existing differentials of accumulation, gaps between the various layers of world capitalism – as regards not only nation-states but also populations and classes and regions within nation-states, from the most advanced to the poorest – are likely to increase.

This structural inability of capitalism to provide for the vast majority of the populations which it has sucked into its own dominion constitutes the basic, incurable flaw in the system as a whole. Such a contradiction can be overcome neither by the will of the national bourgeoisies nor by the edicts of the IMF and the World Bank, nor indeed by all the governmental and non-governmental agencies of advanced capitalism, so long as the system itself remains. Negation of this contradiction can come only from outside the terms of this system as such, because the backwardness of the backward capitalist countries, hence the poverty of the majority of the world's population, cannot be undone except through a complete redistribution of wealth and an altogether different structuring of productions and consumptions on a global scale, among classes, regions, countries and continents of the world. Socialism is the determinate name for this negation of capitalism's fundamental, systemic contradictions and cruelties, and the necessity of this negation will remain, regardless of the fate of the Soviet Union as such.

If this analysis, however schematic, is broadly correct, then, in sharp contradistinction to the Three Worlds Theory, several propositions and their virtually axiomatic corollaries naturally follow. First, the world is not divided into monolithic binaries; it is a hierarchically structured whole. The corollary of this first proposition, then, is that the answering dialectic in its broader and transnational sweep must also be global and universalist in character – not human*ist* in the bourgeois sense, surely; but, equally surely, encompassing humanity in general. Second, if the universalist character of the answering dialectic – namely, socialism – implies an international character of the revolutionary project, the fundamental and irresolvable contradiction of global capitalism – the fact that it cannot provide for the vast majority of the direct producers in the backward formations – equally implies that it is the struggles of those direct producers in the backward formations which constitute the primary site for struggles towards the realization of the socialist project. The corollary of this second proposition is that the bearers of the socialist project could come as much from the advanced as from the backward zones of capitalism, but it is the issue of imperialism – the historically structured system of inequalities, between classes and between countries, between men and women, and between the working classes themselves of the different zones of the global system – which is the primary object of socialist resistance. To the extent that the metropolitan Left has come to concentrate so entirely on improvement in the quality of life in the respective metropolitan countries, speaking of social movements within the national boundaries of imperialist countries and the perfection of democracy for the historic beneficiaries of imperialism as the immediate goal, it has abandoned the fundamental project of socialism, which is none other than the destruction of the imperialist character of modern capital. Third, the nation-state is neither the site for the reproduction of capital in the zones of advanced capitalism nor the primary site of resistance to imperialism in zones of backward capitalism; decolonization is now too firmly behind us, the logic of capital is now too deeply entrenched in all our societies, for nationalisms of the kind which are centred on the existing state apparatuses to *be* the answering dialectic, if they ever were.

The corollary of this third proposition itself has two quite different aspects. On the one hand, one cannot think of the systems of oppression and exploitation in terms of opposing systems of nation-states or even clusters of transnational entities – the First and Third World, or whatever the nomenclature for such conceptions may be – because it is not at the level of the post-colonial national-bourgeois state but at the level of the popular political forces, which are by the very nature of things in conflict with that state, that a nationalism can actually *become* an anti-imperialism. Yet, to the extent that contemporary imperialism's political system takes the form of a hierarchically structured system of nation-states, it is only by organizing their struggles within the political space of their own nation-state, with the revolutionary transformation of that particular nation-state as the immediate practical objective, that the revolutionary forces of any given country can effectively struggle against the imperialism they face concretely in their own lives. In other words, the socialist project is essentially universalist in character, and socialism, even as a transitional mode, cannot exist except on a transnational basis; yet the *struggle* for even the prospect of that transition presumes a national basis, in so far as the already existing structures of the nation-state are a fundamental reality of the very terrain on which actual class conflicts take place.

# Notes

## Introduction: Literature among the Signs of Our Time

1. Gerald Graff, 'Why Theory', in Lennard J. Davis and M. Bella Maribella, eds, *Left Politics and the Literary Profession* (New York: Columbia University Press, 1990).

2. The initial impact of Althusserian positions in British cultural criticism and literary theory came from such journals as *Screen* (founded in 1971) and through such writers as Stephen Heath and Colin MacCabe. The combination in which this impact was embedded was accurately summarized by Heath somewhat later as 'the encounter of Marxism with psychoanalysis on the terrain of semiotics' (*Questions of Cinema*, London: Macmillan, 1981, p. 201). MacCabe's work, ranging from essays in *Screen* to the influential book *James Joyce and the Revolution of the Word* (London: Macmillan, 1978), provided the crucial bridges first between film theory and literary theory, and then at a later stage between the remnants of Althusserian Marxism and a fully fledged poststructuralist location. Terry Eagleton's *Criticism and Ideology* (London: New Left Books, 1976) was, of course, the first fully Althusserian intervention in British literary studies, even though his formal political association had been with Trotskyism, a Marxist tradition towards which Althusser had been at least indifferent; by the time *Literary Theory: An Introduction* appeared (Oxford: Basil Blackwell, 1983), Eagleton had drawn, by his own account, closer to Foucault than to Althusser. The positive contribution of the Althusserian position in British Marxism, in a nutshell, was that it helped retrieve many debates from the anti-theoretical ambience and a very lax kind of Left populism which had become the hallmark of the British Communist Party and tendencies influenced by it; at its worst, British Althusserianism tended towards a very hermetic, theoreticist and anti-historical alibi of pure structures – as in the work of sociologists like Hirst and Hindess. The latter kind of work took from Althusser virtually none of the conjunctural political charge, which had defined a *political* intervention in the French CP, and was fascinated purely by Althusser's structuralist abstraction. Perry Anderson's *Arguments within British Marxism* (London: New Left Books and Verso, 1980), largely written in response to E.P. Thompson's inordinately piqued and lengthy denunciation of Althusser in *The Poverty of Theory and Other Essays* (New York: Montly Review Press, 1978), offers judicious and sympathetic readings of Althusser, registering agreements as well as closely argued reservations, but is so preoccupied with Thompson alone that it fails in the end to offer a real reading either of Althusser or of British Althusserianism. Needless

to add, none of these writers – MacCabe or Eagleton, Hindess and Hirst, unfortunately even Anderson himself – has displayed any notable interest in issues of colony and empire, except occasionally in the instance of Ireland. See also Michael Sprinker's book of a decade later, *Imaginary Relations* (London: Verso, 1987) for an even more sustained and spirited engagement than Eagleton's with the Althusserian position, in the American context of literary theory.

3. Perry Anderson, *Considerations on Western Marxism* (London: New Left Books, 1976; first Verso reprint 1979). See, in particular, Chapter 4, entitled 'Thematic Innovations'. Originally, of course, it was in the latter 1920s that the term 'Western Marxism' was used by a number of Soviet critics to deride the work of Korsch, Lukács and others. Hence the ironic invocation of the term by Merleau-Ponty, in the second chapter of his *Adventures of the Dialectic* (Evanston, IL: Northwestern University Press, 1973; original French publication 1955) as he registers his agreement with some propositions of Lukács and prepares his own attack on Sartre's 'ultrabolshevism'.

4. Some of these matters, and especially the *differences* between the American and the British developments, are addressed at some length in Chapter 1. The lack of any lived connection between the cultural radicalism of the American academy and any home-grown labour movement is well indicated in the fact, for example, that Harry Braverman's seminal work on the restructuring of the American working class throughout this century, but then more markedly in the postwar phase of American capital, simply does not serve even as a reference or a problem for American literary theory.

5. I do not mean to imply that work which seeks to periodize shifts in ideological ensembles and cultural productions in terms of their eventual determination by shifts in the larger structure of global productions and politics in general is altogether absent from contmporary cultural theory. Jameson's exploration of postmodernism as the cultural logic of late capitalism and David Harvey's superb book *The Condition of Postmodernity* (Oxford: Basil Blackwell, 1989) are among distinguished examples of work of this kind. None of that work, however, examines the issue at hand – i.e. the determination of literary theory itself, as it negotiates the issues of colony and empire, by the conditions of its production and by the location of its agents in specific grids of class and institution. A notable feature of Harvey's work, of course, is that while he charts the passages from modernism to postmodernism and as he periodizes the shifts in regimes of accumulation, late capitalism is treated by and large as a discrete structure comprising of the advanced capitalist economies and cultures alone, not as a hierarchically structured system of *global* productions and cultural articulations which is, in fact, unintelligible except as a contradictory unity on a global scale.

6. It is, of course, to Perry Anderson that I owe the brilliantly adequate phrase, 'exorbitation of language'.

7. According to Ranajit Guha, described on the blurb of *Subaltern Studies VI* (Delhi: Oxford University Press, 1989) as 'guru', the colonial nation was characterized by the 'coexistence' of two 'domains', 'elite' and 'subaltern', structurally connected by the category of 'domination'. The former includes all the colonizing personnel as well as both the 'traditional' and the 'modern' 'elites', communist cadres and Marxist historians; the latter, whose 'domain' is said to be 'autonomous' and traceable to pre-colonial society, includes all the rest. See, for an initial statement, 'On Some Aspects of the Historiography of Colonial

India', in *Subaltern Studies I* (Delhi: Oxford University Press, 1982). Page 8, where Guha tries to define these terms, is remarkable for its contortions as he undertakes to reconcile a language taken partly from Gramsci and partly from American sociology with the Maoism of New Democracy and 'contradictions among the people', at the founding moment of a project which has subsequently come to be assimilated into a very hybrid and largely dependent kind of poststructuralism. For a lengthier statement – hence for compounded problems – see 'Dominance without Hegemony and its Historiography' by the same author in vol. VI, cited above.

8. Many ramifications of the confusion about 'culture', 'nationalism' and 'tradition' as they surface in Anglo-American literary theories will be detailed elsewhere in this book. Within Indian debates, this inversion of the tradition/modernity binary may be found in very diverse kinds of writing: not only in many of the articulations of the Hindu communalist Right, nor only in the neo-Gandhians such as Ashish Nandy, but also in many 'subalternist' writings. Partha Chatterjee's outright hatred of Nehru as a 'modernizer' and his privileging, by contrast, not only of a certain version of Gandhi but even of Bankim Chattopadhyay over Nehru, in his *Nationalist Thought and the Colonial World: A Derivative Discourse* (London: Zed Books, 1986; Delhi: Oxford University Press, 1986), is replete with that kind of inverted logic.

9. The emphases in this sentence can easily be documented from numerous sources, ranging from Ho Chi Minh and Le Duan to Amilcar Cabral, and from Mao to any number of documents of the various cultural organizations and fronts of the Communist Party of India during the colonial period, not to speak of virtually all the major Marxian tendencies which have developed in predominantly agrarian societies. Detailed examination of these very large and diverse theoretical formations would, of course, show great unevenness of conception, clarity and practice.

10. Of course, Marxism itself theorizes states and nations as structures of force, but with two fundamental differences. What Marxism poses against these structures is not 'the individual', the categorical universal of bourgeois epistemological abstraction, but the dialectic of *class* revolution and *universal* liberation. And since the class relations of imperialism are themselves structured through a hierarchy of nation-states, the anti-imperialist revolutionary project passes through the historic phase of *national* liberation and the construction/defence of the revolutionary *state*. Universal liberation, which is the only guarantee of freedom for 'the individual' (conceived not abstractly in the self-image of the bourgeoisie, but with reference to the species-being of Marxist epistemology) doubtless presupposes the destruction of the imperialist system of nation-states as much as it presupposes the conquest of scarcity.

11. Edward W. Said, *Orientalism* (New York: Vintage, 1979), pp. 153–6.

12. See, for a recent treatment of the rise of the most conservative neo-liberalism in the wake of poststructuralism in France of the 1980s, George Ross, ' "Intellectuals Against the Left": The Case of France', in *The Socialist Register 1990* (New York: Monthly Review Press, 1991), pp. 201–27. For a convenient summary of slightly earlier trends, see Peter Dews, 'The "New Philosophers" and the End of Leftism', in Roy Edgley and Richard Osborne, *Radical Philosophy Reader* (London: Verso, 1985).

13. Michel Foucault, *The Order of Things: An Archeology of the Human Sciences* (New York: Pantheon, 1971; (translation of *Les Mots et les choses*, Paris 1966). See, in particular, pp.

260–62, where Marx is summarily dismissed with the following rather fantastic formulation:

> . . . the alternatives offered by Ricardo's 'pessimism' and Marx's revolutionary promise are probably of little importance. . . . At the deepest level of Western knowledge, Marxism introduces no real discontinuity; it finds its place without difficulty, as a full, quiet, comfortable and, goodness knows, satisfying form for a time (its own) within an epistemological arrangement which welcomed it gladly.

How *satisfying* the European bourgeoisie found Marxism, and how *gladly* they accepted it, is now a matter of historical record! Foucault's statements tended to become far more extreme in the aftermath of 1968, converging with those of Bernard-Henri Lévy and the other 'New Philosophers'. See, for example, his interview entitled 'Powers and Strategies' with the *Révoltes Logiques* collective, in Meaghan Morris and Paul Patton, eds, *Michel Foucault: Power, Truth, Strategy* (Sydney: Feral Publications, 1979).

14. Among recent Indological writings, Nicholas Dirks's *The Hollow Crown: Ethnohistory of an Indian Kingdom* (Cambridge: Cambridge University press, 1987) is characteristic. It begins with a quotation from Foucault before even the table of contents, which serves as a methodological statment (not 'a theory of power' but 'an analytic of relations of power'). The passage from Marx which Said quotes in *Orientalism* reappears on the first page of Dirks's introduction, and Said himself is then cited on the next page as authorizing the view that all prevailing conceptions of the Indian state and society are derived from the 'Orientalism' which is shared between Marx, Weber and Dumont, among others. Ronald Inden, who was certainly Dirks's senior colleague and perhaps also a dissertation adviser in Chicago, comes in for extensive citation throughout the book. In his more recent *Imagining India* (Oxford: Basil Blackwell, 1990) Inden does not cite Dirk but announces his own affinity with Said not only very directly, on pp. 37–8, but even in the second sentence of the introduction: 'The specific object of my critique is the Indological branch of "orientalist discourse" . . . ' Foucault is then invoked on p. 2. The entire range of Marxist historiography of ancient and medieval India which has been produced in India is dismissed later in just over two pages (pp. 154–6). See my 'Between Orientalism and Historicism: Anthropological Knowledge of India', *Studies in History*, vol. 7, no. 1 (New Delhi 1991) for extended commentary on Inden's book.

15. Among the voluminous writings on the growth and crisis of peripheral industrialization, see in particular Alain Lipietz, *Mirages and Miracles: The Crises of Global Fordism* (London: Verso, 1987) and Section III of Arthur MacEwan and William Tabb, eds, *Instability and Change in the World Economy* (New York: Monthly Review Press, 1989). So rapid is the deterioration in the economies of these countries that India, which had been singled out by Lipietz (p. 153) as the country most successful in maintaining rising investment rates and an extremely low ratio of debts and debt-servicing to both GDP and exports, now faces, less than five years later, a far worse crisis than Mexico or Brazil.

16. Michael Hudson's little-known book *Super Imperialism: The Economic Strategy of American Empire* (New York: Holt, Rinehart Winston, 1972), with its thesis that the inter-imperialist rivalries of the kind Lenin theorized at the height of the colonial period had effectively ended with World War II and that a syndicate of imperialist powers was now

ready to exploit the rest of the world jointly and co-operatively, makes eerie reading now, even though the book itself was written in the closing years of American hegemony and before even the christening of the Trilateral Commission.

17. It is, of course, eminently arguable that imperialist success against socialism's global project began in the aftermath of World War I itself, when the Hungarian, Italian and German uprisings were beaten back quite easily, while the crisis of Bolshevism precipitated by the Civil War and Allied intervention paved the way for the rise of Stalinism within the Soviet Union and for the incorporation of West European social democracy within the structures of advanced capital. We are concerned here, however, with the post-1945 period.

18. It is now strictly impossible to calculate, for instance, the degree and variety of distortions that crept into every aspect of Soviet society and economy owing to the single, glaring fact that the country undertook for forty years an altogether unsustainable competition for parity with NATO's war machine, which served the contradictory function of extending the scope for autonomy for progressive states and movements around the globe (the survival of the revolutionary regime in Cuba and the ability of Vietnam to sustain itself through the revolutionary war are really unthinkable without the fact of that military balance) while also becoming a structural imperative for the reproduction of the techno-bureaucratic state within the Soviet Union.

19. In the well-known Bettleheim–Sweezy exchange on the nature of the Soviet-type 'post-revolutionary' society, I am generally in agreement with Sweezy. But it does no violence to Sweezy's own argument to underscore what Bettleheim points out and documents: much of the small Bolshevik vanguard, especially at levels lower than the top leadership, had already been decimated by the end of the first imperialist intervention while Lenin was still alive, so that virtually 90 per cent of the officialdom which came to run the Soviet state on a day-to-day basis was Tsarist in origin. Those kinds of costs are hardly ever calculated in the famous 'failure of communism'. See Charles Bettleheim, *Class Struggles in the USSR, First Period: 1917–1923* (New York: Monthly Review Press, 1978.)

20. E.P. Thompson, 'The Ends of Cold War', *New Left Review*, no. 182, July–August 1990.

21. In the years immediately preceding the advent of perestroika, Western analyses of Soviet economy used to run on two simultaneous tracks: one speaking of utter stagnation and imminent collapse, the other documenting enormous industrial power with dire pressures upon the West. Gorbachev's advisers settled early for the first of these tracks, in a stunningly self-fulfilling prophecy. Among the more sober analysts, the Soviet dissident Zhores Medvedev and the Western economist Alec Nove, deeply critical of the Soviet regime themselves, may be cited. In his assessment of Brezhnev's rule in 1979, Medvedev was to emphasize that agricultural output had risen by 70 per cent and industrial output had doubled in fifteen years, while population had remained basically constant; in cybernetics and computer technology, the Soviet Union was said to be two to three years behind the United States – a substantial gap, but narrowing. Some months later, Nove was to summarize his own conclusion thus:

> there is no catastrophe imminent, the system is not in chaos, the quality of its planning and of its production are not in decline. Indeed, quality is actually improving . . . even if growth stays at the modest levels of 3% per annum over the

> next few years (which seems to be a reasonable forecast to make), this may contrast favourably with Western economies.

See Zhores Medvedev, 'Russia under Brezhnev', *New Left Review* no. 117, September–October 1979; and Alec Nove, 'Soviet Economic Prospects', *New Left Review*, no. 119, January–February 1980. Within the next three years, Gorbachev and his advisers were to declare that whole era to be a 'period of stagnation', and chaos was said to reign supreme.

22. A careful study of Solzhenitsyn would reveal how a career starting in a leftist kind of anti-Stalinism came eventually to espouse, on it way to spectacular fame and influence, the most reactionary ideas celebrating the Tsarist past, the Orthodox Church and the Great-Russian variety of racism. At the other (postmodernist) end of the spectrum, Milan Kundera's vision of a 'Europe rooted in Roman Christianity' leaves little room for either the countless millions of non-Europeans who now reside permanently in Europe or for those even more numerous Europeans who have sought to rid themselves precisely of that sort of Europe.

23. A very vicarious kind of jubilant triumphalism has been the characteristic response of numerous groupus such as the Democratic Socialists of America (DSA), even as the unification of Germany has had the effect of strengthening not social democracy but Kohl's Christian Democrats. For a more sober but not fundamentally different response from leading activists of the European Nuclear Disarmament (END), see contributions by Mary Kaldor and E.P. Thompson to *Europe from Below: An East–West Dialogue*, ed. Mary Kaldor (London: Verso, 1991); these writers take great pride (somewhat exaggerated, I believe) in their own contribution to the East European events. Thompson chooses to doubt that East European regimes intend to build market economies, while Kaldor goes on to suggest that we stop speaking about 'socialism' and take to struggle for 'justice'. More surprising are writers like Alex Callinicos, whose very sectarian kind of anti-Stalinism blinds them to the reactionary character of the regimes and movements which have now engulfed so much of Eastern Europe. See Chapters 1 and 3 in Alex Callinicos, *The Revenge of History: Marxism and the East European Revolutions* (University Park, PA: Pennsylvania State University Press, 1991).

24. With his characteristically inflated sense of the centrality of 'literature' in human affairs, Salman Rushdie, in his Herbert Reade Lecture of February 1990, stated this desire to be liberal-capitalism's clarifying helper with rare eloquence:

> It seems probable . . . that we may be heading towards a world in which there will be no real alternative to the liberal capitalist social model. . . . In this situation, liberal capitalism or democracy or the free world will require novelists' most rigorous attention. . . . 'Our adversary is our helper', said Edmund Burke, and if democracy no longer has communism to help it clarify, by opposition, its own ideas, then perhaps it will have to have literature as an adversary instead. (Cited in Alex Callinicos, *The Revenge of History*, p. 11)

25. See, for example, Sumit Sarkar, 'Popular Movements and National Leadership 1945–47' in his *A Critique of Colonial India* (Calcutta: Papyrus, 1985), for a little-known

speeding-up of that kind in India where the Indian National Congress was otherwise very much in control of the anti-colonial movement.

26. That this moment of decolonization came much earlier in Latin America – not much later than in the United States, well before much of Africa and Asia was fuly colonized, and at a much earlier conjuncture in the history of capital as such, hence giving the national bourgeoisie of that continent a markedly different character and role during the whole of the imperialist epoch – is well enough known, but almost always ignored in Third-Worldist perspectives.

27. Algeria was a very special case within this very complex trajectory. Socialist elements were doubtless strong in the movement itself, and the predominant role of state property (so often and so misleadingly associated, there and elsewhere, with 'socialism') in post-colonial Algeria was surely a legitimate way to resolve the problem of the *colon* properties left behind. The key fact, however, is that the moment of decolonization brought to power that core of externally based military officers and leaders of the FLN which became the social basis for the emergence of a bureaucratic bourgeoisie as the new ruling class. The gigantic ambiguities of Fanon's work, papered over by many of the proponents of cultural nationalism and Colonial Discourse Analysis, reflect the formative phase of that conjuncture, while some sections of *Wretched of the Earth* appear to foretell precisely that outcome.

28. See Edward W. Said, *Covering Islam: How the Media and the Experts Determine How We See the Rest of the World* (New York: Pantheon, 1981).

29. Part of the difficulty in engaging with the poststructuralist philosophical positions, especially as they resurface in Anglo-American literary theory, is that their exaggerated claims of novelty and their propensity to reduce all prior philosophical positions to a mere caricature pre-empt such an engagement. As regards the caricature of Marxism as a 'progressivist modes-of-production narrative', for example, Marx's own critique of the positivist notions of progress begins in his earliest writings and can be traced all the way through his notes on the Russian peasants' commune towards the end of his life. This critique is extended within the Marxist tradition in a great many places, including *History and Class Consciousness* (Cambridge, MA: MIT Press, 1971; original German edition 1923) by Lukács, about whom then, Merleau-Ponty makes the following approving remark in his own *Adventures of the Dialectic*:

> He says that the idea of progress is an expedient which consists in placing a contradiction which has already been reduced to a minimum against the backdrop of an unlimited time and in supposing that it will there resolve itself. Progress dissolves the beginning and the end, in the historical sense, into a limitless natural process . . . (p. 35)

30. For Edward Said's celebration of what he approvingly calls the 'gradual disappearance of narrative history' and his emphasis on irony as the desirable historiographic mode ('Narrative is replaced by irony'), see his essay 'Third World Intellectuals and Metropolitan Culture', which I discuss at some length in Chapter 5.

31. For this practice of 'theory' as 'travel', see in particular James Clifford and Vivek Dhareshwar, eds, *Traveling Theories, Traveling Theorists, Inscription* 5, an occasional volume

brought out by the Group for the Critical Study of Colonial Discourse and the Center for Cultural Studies, Oakes College, University of California at Santa Cruz, 1989.

32. Fredric Jameson is exceptional in this regard in the sense that he does make a limited attempt of this kind, most obviously in 'Periodizing the 60s' (his prospectus-essay of 1984, reprinted in *The Ideologies of Theory, Volume Two: Syntax of History* (Minneapolis: University of Minnesota Press, 1988) and in lesser detail wherever he addresses this question. This awareness on his part that periodization is fundamental for anyone who sets out to historicize relations between politics and culture is particularly salutary in a context where literary theorists who address questions of colony and empire are generally given to the broadest assertions, with little regard to the interplay between specificity of periods and multiplicity of determinations. But so preoccupied is Jameson with establishing the discreteness of 'the 60's' (which, he quite rightly argues, began with the Algerian War and the Cuban Revolution, and ended in the early 1970s) that one gets neither a sense of before and after (the essay *was* written, the book says, in 1984, and 'the 60s' did inherit a world that had undergone fundamental changes after World War II) nor a sense of how the elements he enumerates led, by 1984, to imperialism's decisive triumph. The overarching Third-Worldism, as well as some curiously archaic and incoherent postmodernist reformulations of Marxism (e.g. 'Late Capitalism may be described as the moment when the last vestiges of Nature which survived on into classical capitalism are at length eliminated: namely the Third World and the unconscious': p. 207), then went into the essay published two years later, which I discuss in Chapter 3.

33. Althusser's is in some ways a peculiar and even poignant case. He remained a lifelong member of the French Communist Party because he believed in the centrality of the working class in the making of history, yet he advocated the idea of 'history as a human-natural process' which had neither subject nor goal. His highly nuanced essay 'Contradiction and Overdetermination' (*For Marx*, London: New Left Books, 1977) is notable for affirming, against the contemporary radical currents, a final determination by the economic, but his even more influential essay 'Ideology and Ideological State Apparatuses' (*Lenin and Philosophy and Other Essays*, London: New Left Books, 1971) assigns so vast a space to the state that any methodological distinction between state and not-state as differential sites for ideological production and reproduction becomes difficult to maintain. Inside France, his philosophical positions were forms of intervention in the politics of the Communist Party, with at least a few of them obviously designed to challenge the Stalinist legacies within the party. His chief critic in Britain, E.P. Thompson, denounced him, on the other hand, as a Stalinist, while some of his key admirers, Hirst and Hindess among them for some years, sifted out the political charge of Althusser's interventions and invoked him, instead, for the worst kind of structuralist constructs, static and anti-historical. If the injection of Althusser's work into Anglo-American debates initially had the salutary effect of forcing greater theoretical rigour, 'theoretical practice' became, in most of the British (and then American) appropriations, an excuse for the worst kind of academic professionalization of Marxism.

34. See Section IV of the essay 'Marxism and Humanism' in Althusser, *For Marx*, which includes a very peculiar passage on the role of ideology 'in a society in which classes have disappeared':

> If, as Marx said, history is a perpetual transformation of men's conditions of existence, and if this is equally true of socialist society, then men must be ceaselessly transformed so as to adapt them to these conditions: if this 'adaptation' cannot be left to spontaneity but must be constantly assumed, dominated and controlled, it is in ideology that this demand is expressed . . . (p. 235)

In other words, there is no end to domination and control, even in a classless society; human beings simply cannot be 'left to spontaneity', nor can they *live* the relations of knowledge (which come only through theoretical practice and are not, in any case, *lived*). This entrapment of humankind in ideology, now and for ever, is eerily close to Foucault's notion of the power of discourse.

35. Althusser, 'Ideology and Ideological State Apparatuses'.

36. This is not the place to delve into the vexed question of 'humanism', but it is necessary to stress the distinction between the epistemological and the practical (i.e. political and ethical) issues involved. Marx breaks entirely from that humanist epistemology which takes the 'individual' to be the locus of experience and knowledge, and no variant of Marx's writings on ideology and consciousness – on the opacity of experience to itself, and on the social determination (hence the provisional character) of all knowledge – is reconcilable with that bourgeois category of the 'individual'. It is in relation to the constructedness of history (unauthored but humanly made) and the ethical life of the species-being (the struggle from necessity to freedom) that Marxism recoups its humanist energy.

37. Gender specification for non-specific persons in the third person singular is an unfortunate but mandatory aspect of the English language. I tried writing this book with the 'other' gender specification: *she*, *her*, etc. That exercise turned out to be equally disagreeable – and unnecessarily provocative in an entirely different way.

## 1 Literary Theory and 'Third World Literature'

1. This chapter substantially reproduces the notes I first made for a Seminar at the School of Languages, Jawaharlal Nehru University, and kept revising for subsequent uses elsewhere in Delhi. In revising that material for present publication, I am now quite unable to find a voice that presumes no audience.

2. See Raymond Williams's, fine essay 'Cambridge English, Past and Present', in his *Writing in Society*, for a judicious summation of the decisive contributions – but also the ultimate failures – of Richards, and of much besides, in Cambridge and beyond.

3. 'New Criticism', with its considerable borrowings from Richards, Eliot and Leavis, turned out to be far more sweepingly hegemonic in the United States than 'Practical Criticism' ever was in Britain, though the American Left (with the single exception of Kenneth Burke) never defined its own terms of contestation against it as the British Left – Williams, Terry Eagleton, Mulhern and others – were to define in relation to Leavis in particular and 'Practical Criticism' and the technicist variants of 'close reading' generally. The most substantial challenge to 'New Criticism' came, rather, from individuals like

Krieger (*The New Apologists for Poetry*, 1956), Frye (*Anatomy of Criticism*, 1957), Kermode (*The Romantic Image*, also 1957) and Graff (*Poetic Statement and Critical Dogma*, 1970) or, as a sustained position, from deconstruction, which partly explains the American Left's own symbiosis with these positions, especially the deconstructionist one.

4. By far the most sustained critique of the Leavis tendency has been assembled by Francis Mulhern, though it must be said that his own magnificent essay 'English Reading' in Homi K. Bhabha, ed., *Nation and Narration* (London: Routledge, 1990) is qualitatively superior to his own previous book, *The Moment of 'Scrutiny'* (London: Verso, 1979), which had seemed definitive.

5. Mulhern is especially good in deconstructing the masculinist aspects of this populism, enacted in the personal life and public personae of F.R. and Q.D. Leavis in valorization of the ideologies of the athletic male and the good housewife. This particular variant of masculinism underlies, one need hardly add, Leavis's inordinate admiration of Lawrence and his reading, especially, of *Women in Love*.

6. See, for example, Williams's introductory remarks in *Marxism and Literature* about the isolation he faced at the time, in literary studies specifically.

7. *Monthly Review* also started publication – in New York, in 1949 – in the period of the HUAC hearings and the onset of the Cold War. That journal, preoccupied more with political economy than with history, and engaged in defining a Marxism much sharper and broader than that of the official Communist Party, shared with its publishing house an influence that was by no means insignificant in its own terms. Compared with the British developments of the same time, however, that influence remained confined to a much narrower intellectual stratum in the United States, making hardly a mark on the culture at large – and it was the *literary* Left that remained the least affected.

8. See, for example, Dobbs's *Political Economy and Capitalism* (1937) and Hill's *The English Revolution 1640* (1940).

9. There is, of course, his superb *Milton and the English Revolution* (1977) as well as the lesser-known *Some Intellectual Consequences of the English Revolution* (1980), not to speak of the equally superb *The Experience of Defeat: Milton and Some Contemporaries* (1984). The point, nevertheless, is that Hill's entire *œuvre* is really an engagement, using the tools of a magnificently careful historian, with that particular point of confluence at which culture *becomes* history.

10. See *William Morris: Romantic to Revolutionary* (originally published 1955, revised 1977). A comparative reading of the two texts provides fascinating and essential clues to Thompson's own intellectual trajectory over roughtly a quarter-century, from communism to a certain kind of Left Labourism.

11. Richard Hoggart later emerged as a founder of the Centre for Contemporary Cultural Studies. Among his publications, *The Uses of Literacy* (1957) is, of course, something of a classic.

12. Eliot's monarchist and colonialist persuasions are well enough known, and these surface in *The Waste Land*, in the most disagreeable ways, alongside his contempt for the sexuality of poor and working women, which is constrasted in the structure of the poem with the calm splendours of – of all the people – 'Queen Elizabeth and Leicester/Beating oars'. See, in particular, the third section of the poem, subtitled 'The Fire Sermon'. In Pound's case, shrill support for Mussolini is a mere tip of the iceberg; the entire structure of

*The Cantos* is inseparable from his affiliations with fascism, anti-Semitism, racism of various sorts, and his general preference for authoritarian, aristocratic rule in all epochs and civilizations.

13. It is symptomatic of the whole drift of American Left Criticism that Frank Lentricchia's *After the New Criticism* (Chicago: University of Chicago Press, 1980), surely the central and in some ways a genuinely brilliant summation of the vast changes that have occurred in US literary criticism and theory in the two key decades between 1957 and 1977, makes scant effort to locate the disciplinary developments in any history other than the literary-theoretical. It is only by holding on to one's own memory and by fixing this memory on stray remarks here and there that one recalls, while reading the book, that these same twenty years were known in other kinds of narratives for quite other sorts of developments, such as the revolutions in Algeria, Cuba, Indochina and Southern Africa.

14. *After the New Criticism*, p. xii.

15. The sense in which I use the convenient term 'Western Marxism' here was given the widest currency and almost self-evident meaning by a number of writers associated with *New Left Review*, most notably Perry Anderson. For an anthology of some articles which contributed to the construction of the category, see *Western Marxism – A Critical Reader* (London: New Left Books; Verso 1983). For categorical definition and a certain kind of summation, see Anderson's own *Considerations on Western Marxism* (London: New Left Books, 1976; Verso 1979). There is, of course, an earlier history of this term, dating back to the 1920s, but we are not concerned with that here.

16. See *The Savage Mind*, (French publication 1962; English translation 1966), especially the concluding chapter, in which Lévi-Strauss mounts a savage attack on historicism in general and on Sartre's construction of it in particular. Sartre had exchanged famous polemics in previous years as well, notably with Camus and Merleau-Ponty, but the attack by Lévi-Strauss proved decisive, in the sense that it inaugurated a shift in intellectual hegemony among the most influential stratum of Parisian intelligentsia as such, in favour of structuralism, with consequences for the English and American avant-gardes as well.

17. See, for this last point about 1968, Régis Debray's 'A Modest Contribution . . . ', *New Left Review*, no. 115, May–June 1979. Elsewhere, in his delightful polemic on the vicissitudes of the French intelligentisa, *Teachers, Writers, Celebrities: Intellectuals in Modern France* (French publication 1979; English translation 1981), Debray establishes three periods in the history of this intelligentsia, from 1880 onwards: the first (1880–1930) dominated by schools and universities; the second (from 1930 to the 1960s) dominated by publishing; and the third (inaugurated by the Events of 1968 and still ascendant) dominated by the media. This last one might designate a dark age perpetrated by the silver screen.

18. I know that my polemic here lumps together diverse positions, but lack of space makes it impossible to develop the argument. Among the voluminous writings on the subject, I could confirm my own very considerable agreement with at least two. Perry Anderson's Wellek Library Lectures of 1982, *In the Tracks of Historical Materialism* (Chicago: University of Chicago Press, 1984) would be to my mind, but for those pages on Habermas, an exemplary introduction. Peter Dews's *Logics of Disintegration* (London: Verso, 1988), deliberately narrower in focus, is written with less verve but is essentially sound and illuminating, especially on Lyotard.

19. 'New Left' means a great many different things in different contexts, but as a distinct political tendency within the plethora of diverse radicalisms which arose in this period, the term has to have, I believe, some claim to an affiliation with Marxism, however the affiliation or the Marxism may be conceived. In Britain, surely, the roots go back to at least the consequences of 1956 (Suez, Hungary, the Khrushchev Report). In the USA, the Cuban Revolution was perhaps more decisive, even though *Monthly Review* had started even earlier to define an alternative kind of Marxism, different from the Stalinist one. It is possible to argue, in any case, that while the *origins* of the 'New Left' may be traced back even to the 'Old Left' of the 1930s, it was in 1967–68 that it first made major interventions in most Western societies, especially the universities.

20. The category of 'Commonwealth Literature' came to play the same function of affirming beleaguered identities – and, in the fullness of time, opening up careers – for immigrant intelligentsias in Britain. It was on the prior basis of 'African Literature' and 'Commonwealth Literature' that the category of 'Third World Literature' first arose, often duplicating those very pedagogical procedures and ideological moorings.

21. See Edward Said's essay 'Metropolitan Intellectuals and Third World Culture', which is discussed at some length in Chapter 5.

22. These familiar themes of recent French theory were then applied to matters of colony and empire, in both the literary and the sociological theories, in characteristically subordinate and dependent modes, by a number of the Indian members of this 'post-structuralist' avant-garde, from Homi Bhabha to Partha Chatterjee. For the latter's highly derivative debunkings of 'the Enlightenment', 'myths of progress', etc., see *Nationalist Thought and the Colonial World: A Derivative Discourse* (London: Zed Press; Delhi: Oxford University Press, 1986).

## 2 Languages of Class, Ideologies of Immigration

1. Some of these issues and conceptual categories will be clarified in Chapter 7 – see Section VI in particular.

2. Franklin Frazier's classic little book *Black Bourgeoisie: The Rise of a New Middle Class* (New York: The Free Press, 1957) is among the many studies which make it quite clear how narrowly based, precariously balanced, and essentially lower-petty-bourgeois this stratum in the United States was until after the war. It is only since the Civil Rights Movement of the 1960s that any appreciable expansion of the African-American middle class in the USA has taken place in ways even remotely comparable to that of the white middle class.

3. Alaine Locke, ed., *The New Negro* (New York: Boni, 1925; Atheneum, 1968) is, of course, the classic anthology inaugurating the Harlem Renaissance as a self-conscious movement. The reference here is to Locke's own essay of the same title, highly perceptive in its own way but arguing for inclusion in the American canon on the existing terms: 'we're good enough', 'just like you', so to speak. The contrast with the 'New Black Renaissance' of the 1960s becomes altogether clear if we look at some of the typical anthologies of this latter period: LeRoi Jones and Larry Neal, eds, *Black Fire* (New York: William Morrow, 1968); Clarence Major, ed., *The New Black Poetry* (New York: International Publishers, 1969); Ed Bullins, ed., *New Plays from the Black Theater* (New York: Bantam, 1969); June Jordan, ed.,

*SoulScript: Afro-American Poetry* (New York: Doubleday, 1970); Orde Coombs, ed., *We Speak as Liberators* (New York: Donald Meade, 1970) – and many others. Locke, of course, does not represent the *whole* of the Harlem Renaissance (McKay, to take one example, was very different); nor do I intend a generalization about the pre-1960s developments in Black Literature.

4. Anthologies are always interesting barometers of changes in perception, social location and market demand. I have cited some above. The increased embourgeoisement of a whole stratum of Black writers from the 1970s onwards is reflected well in the one edited by Terry McMillan, *Breaking Ice: An Anthology of Contemporary African-American Fiction* (New York: Penguin, 1990). In the introduction she cites Trey Ellis, who 'has coined a phrase which he calls "The New Black Aesthetic" ' (NBA) and quotes him approvingly:

> 'For the first time in our history we are producing a critical mass of college graduates who are children of college graduates themselves. Like most artistic movements, the NBA is a post-bourgeois movement; driven by a second generation of [the] middle class. Having scraped their way to relative wealth and, too often, crass materialism, our parents have freed (or compelled) us to bite those hands that fed us and sent us to college. We now feel secure enough to attend art school instead of medical school.' (p. xx)

After some more commentary on this new comfort and opportunity, McMillan goes on to say, in her own words:

> If a writer is trying hard to convince you of something, then he or she should stick to non-fiction. These days, our work is often as entertaining as it is informative, thought-provoking as it is uplifting. Some of us would like to think that the experiences of our characters are 'universal' . . . (p. xxi)

5. For more discussion on this point, see my comments on Edward Said's essay 'Third World Intellectuals and Metropolitan Culture', in Chapter 5.

6. See in particular the two statements, editorial and authorial, which bracket the beginning and ending of Henry Louis Gates, Jr, ed., *'Race', Writing and Difference* (Chicago: University of Chicago Press, 1986). Gates, of course, uses the term 'Third World' quite freely, but for him it is not so much a political category as yet another semantic construct in the infinite play of poststructuralist 'Difference' in the articulations of 'minority literature'.

## 3 Jameson's Rhetoric of Otherness

1. *Social Text*, Fall 1986, pp. 65–88.
2. Edward W. Said, *After the Last Sky: Palestinian Lives* (New York: Pantheon, 1986).
3. Timothy Brennan's *Salman Rushdie and the Third World: Myths of the Nation* (New

York: St Martin's Press, 1989), based upon that dissertation, appeared after the publication of this chapter in *Social Text*.

## 4 Salman Rushdie's *Shame*

1. It is to Brennan's credit that he does not locate Rushdie's kind of authorial project primarily in the undifferentiated counter-canon of 'Third World Literature'. Instead, he coins a new subcategory of 'Third World cosmopolitans', which encompasses, in his own words, 'those writers Western reviewers seemed to be choosing as the interpreters and authentic public voices of the Third World'. See Timothy Brennan, *Salman Rushdie and the Third World: Myths of the Nation* (New York: St Martin's Press, 1989, p. viii). His thematic preoccupations and the very terms of his thought, probably dictated by the very milieu in which he did the research, are well illustrated, however, in the very title of the book and in such chapter headings as 'National Fictions, Fictional Nations' or 'The National Longing for Form'.

2. 'A Dangerous Art Form', an interview with Salman Rushdie, *Third World Book Review*, vol. 1, no. 1 (London 1984).

3. In view of the discussions that followed the initial publication of this chapter as an essay, it seems necessary to reiterate the obvious fact that it is not about Rushdie's work in general but only about certain aspects of *Shame* and the authorial practices which saturate that book. The couple of interviews and essays which I discuss here belong to the same phase of his writing, which ends very dramatically with the appearance of *The Satanic Verses*.

4. Asked directly 'How closely can this narrator be identified with the author, with yourself?' Rushdie responded as follows: 'Pretty closely. Much, much more closely than you could identify Saleem Sinai. But beware of total identification. This is a novel, which means it is invented, and that includes the bits that appear not to be invented.' (See the interview cited in Note 2 above.) Some of the details have certainly been reshuffled, and I would not want to suggest an identification between author and narrator throughout the book. In the passages I cite here, however, this identification is quite compelling.

5. All references to *Shame* in this essay are to the Vintage/Ventura edn (New York: Random House, 1984).

6. See 'Such Angst, Loneliness, Rootlessness', an interview with Salman Rushdie, *Gentleman*, February 1984.

7. For Moretti's use of the term 'spell of indecision', see Chapter 9 of his *Signs Taken for Wonders* (London: Verso, 1983).

8. Rushdie says in his interview with *Gentleman*: 'I am one of those writers who believes that a writer has a public function. . . . It becomes almost an obligation of writers who know what is going on.' But then he resolves the relationship (or lack of it) between his 'socialism' and his 'writing' in a curious way. In his interview with *Third World Book Review*, for example, he comments: 'I would describe myself as a socialist, but I do not write *as* a socialist any more than I write *as* a member of the group which is 5'9" tall, or any other group. I write as a writer.' The difficulty with that kind of formulation is that physical height does not normally indicate the nature of one's social commitments, whereas terms like 'socialist' are meant to indicate those very sorts of things. Nor is membership of a

'group', *any* group, the issue; the ways of being a socialist in our time are actually far too diverse. The questions are rather different. What relationship might there be between these two practices, being a socialist and the assembling of political narratives? Does one contradict, or exclude, the other? Does a writer leave behind the one when she or he undertakes the other? And what history of discourse generates simple statements like 'I write as a writer'?

9. Thus, towards the end of the book, Rushdie declares:

> I had thought, before I began, that what I had on my hands was an almost excessively masculine tale. . . . But the women seem to have taken over; they marched in from the peripheries of the story to demand inclusion of their own tragedies, histories and comedies, obliging me to couch my narrative in all manner of sinuous complexities, to see my 'male' plot refracted, so to speak, through the prisms of its reverse and 'female' side. It occurs to me that the women knew pecisely what they were up to – that their stories explain, and even subsume, the men's. (p. 189)

10. 'On Günter Grass' was originally published in *Granta*, vol. 15 (1987). 'Outside the Whale' was first published in *Granta*, vol. 11 (1983) and appeared again in *American Film* (January–February 1985). Both essays have been reprinted more recently in *Imaginary Homelands* (London: Viking, 1990), a collection of Salman Rushdie's non-fiction pieces, from which quotations have been taken.

## 5 *Orientalism* and After

1. Edward W. Said, *The World, the Text and the Critic* (Cambridge, MA: Harvard University Press, 1983), pp. 28–9.

2. Edward W. Said, *The Question of Palestine* (New York: Doubleday, 1980).

3. Edward W. Said, *After the Last Sky: Palestinian Lives* (New York: Pantheon, 1986).

4. Apart from scores of articles and interventions in the journalistic media, see in particular *Blaming the Victims: Spurious Scholarship and the Palestinian Question* (London: Verso, 1987; co-authored with Christopher Hitchens).

5. Edward W. Said, 'Zionism from the Standpoint of Its Victims', in the inaugural issue of *Social Text*, Winter 1979, later integrated into *The Question of Palestine*.

6. Edward W. Said, *Orientalism* (New York: 1979), p. 27.

7. Edward W. Said, *Joseph Conrad and the Fiction of Autobiography* (Cambridge, MA: Harvard University Press, 1966); *Beginnings: Intention and Method* (New York: Basic Books, 1975).

8. Twelve years after the publication of *Orientalism*, in his essay entitled 'Figures, Configurations, Transfigurations' (*Race and Class*, vol. 32, no. 1, 1990), where the title itself plays on the philological trope of 'figuration', Said uses the verb 'revere', with its inescapably religious connotations, for describing his own sense of awe when he thinks of Auerbach and Spitzer.

9. Said's pairing of those books of Foucault is curious for its lack of interest in how much

the latter book contradicts the procedures and formulations of the former. If *The Archaeology of Knowledge* proclaims the entrapment of all human volition in structures of discourse, *Discipline and Punish* inaugurates for Foucault, even in its stunning opening section, a kind of history-writing which negotiates the *relation* between the discursive and the non-discursive.

10. For a scrupulous examination of Said's highly questionable uses of Foucault, albeit with very different emphases from mine, see 'On Orientalism' in James Clifford's *The Predicament of Culture* (Cambridge, MA: Harvard University Press, 1988).

11. Said, of course, locates Marx not in what Foucault calls the 'discourse' of Political Economy but in the *literary* ambience of what Said himself designates as an 'Orientalist discourse', without even addressing the question, as any Foucauldian obviously would, whether or not statements, and their authors, can actually circulate so very freely between discursive fields which are otherwise mutually so distinct and discontinuous. For more on the treatment of Marx in *Orientalism*, see the next chapter.

12. By the time he came to write his *History of Sexuality* Foucault had, of course, abandoned this strict sense of periodization, just as he had also begun to relent on the question of 'humanism'. But all that came later. My concern here is with the Foucauldian positions before the composition of *Orientalism*.

13. Edward W. Said, '*Kim*, The Pleasures of Imperialism', *Raritan Quarterly* 9:3, Winter 1990, pp. 27–50.

14. Reference here and in subsequent quotation and pagination is to the Norton paperback edition of 1969, which is a reprint of the original 1928 translation by Richard Aldington.

15. *The World, the Text, and the Critic*, pp. 14–15.

16. We might recall here a trenchant remark that Williams once made in a very different context, to the effect that those literary critics who claim to be beyond all 'isms' rarely examine the 'ism' of their own 'criticism'. See Raymond Williams, 'The Crisis of English Studies', *New Left Review*, no. 129, September–October 1981.

17. The later pages of Said's famous essay 'Representing the Colonized: Anthropology's Interlocutors' (*Critical Inquiry*, no. 15, Winter 1989), which was originally, delivered as an Address at the 86th Annual Meeting of the American Anthropological Association in Chicago, 21 November 1987, may fruitfully be consulted for this use of the collective pronoun.

18. *The Myth of the Lazy Native* (London: Allen & Unwin, 1977) by S.H. Alatas and *Marx and the End of Orientalism* (London 1978) by Brian S. Turner appeared while Said's book was in press, indicating the range of analogous ideas which were very much in the air.

19. Bernard Lewis, 'The Question of Orientalism', *New York Review of Books*, 24 June 1982.

20. Jonah Raskin, *The Mythology of Imperialism* (New York: Random House, 1971).

21. First presented at the Essex University Conference on 'Europe and Its Others' in 1984, six years after the original publication of *Orientalism*, this essay has been reproduced widely: for example, in the American journal *Critical Inquiry* and the British journal *Race and Class*, as well as in books such as Barker, Hume, Iversen and Loxley, eds, *Literature, Politics and Theory* (London: Methuen, 1986).

22. Elsewhere, of course, it is precisely Vico's 'historicist' statements which Said would

invoke for high praise. See, for example, *The World, the Text, and the Critic*, pp. 290–91, where he explicates one of his favourite quotations from Vico, as well as the superb passage on p. 114, where he makes a crucial point about Vico's idea of history through a wonderfully inflected reference to Bach's *Goldberg Variations*.

23. See 'Writing about Islam and the Arabs: A Review of E.W. Said, *Orientalism*', in *I & C*, no. 9, Winter 1981/2. It might be helpful to know that *I & C* was previously published as *Ideology and Consciousness*, but was then reduced to mere initials after the editors lost their nerve about the categories of both 'ideology' and 'consciousness'.

24. Said keeps shifting, throughout the book, between one set of statements in which 'the Orient' is said 'always' to have served for Europe as the image of an absolute Other, inferior and exotic and alien and insufferable because of this inferiority; and another set of statements which suggest that 'the West' has 'always' sought to represent 'the Orient' as a partial self-image, not necessarily inferior (e.g. 'To the Westerner, however, the Oriental was always *like* some aspect of the West; Indian religion was essentially an Oriental version of German-Christian pantheism' [p. 67]). One might note in passing, though Said does not say so, that at least some of those Romantics regarded the 'Indian religion' as the purer, higher form.

25. Variants of the following statement, for example, can be found throughout the book: 'To say simply that Orientalism was a rationalization of colonial rule is to ignore the extent to which colonial rule was justified in advance by Orientalism, rather than after the fact' (p. 39).

26. See Sadek el-Azm's review essay 'Orientalism and Orientalism-in-Reverse', *Khamsin*, no. 8 (London: Ithaca Press, 1981), there is much in el-Azm's essay that I would disagree with, but his discussion of Said's treatment of Marx is fruitful and he is right, on the whole, about the convergence between Said's procedures and those of his adversaries.

27. Samir Amin, *Eurocentrism* (New York: Monthly Review Press, 1989).

28. Bernal demonstrates convincingly that the fabrication of Ancient Greece as an originary and autonomous cultural formation, its sundering from the composite Mediterranean culture in which it had been placed overlappingly with Egyptian and Levantine Antiquities, and its relocation as the fount of a West European history rather than at the Afro–Asiatic–European confluence – i.e. the mapping of an Athens-to-Albion cultural grid which demarcates Europe from Asia – is really a product of the late eighteenth century onwards, after the main European interests (in both senses of the word) shift from Egypt to India, and when the Indo-Aryan linguistic model gets going as the basic explanatory model for cultural unities and mobilities. See Martin Bernal, *Black Athena: The Afroasiatic Roots of Classical Civilization*, *Volume 1: The Fabrication of Ancient Greece 1785–1985* (New Brunswick: Rutgers University Press, 1987).

29. Fabrications, of course, have their own uses and consequences, quite as dense as those of facts. The Aristotle-to-Eliot tradition of literary criticism, for example, is an utter fabrication but one with consequences which every student of English literature knows, painfully, by heart. My point here is that Said takes a fantastic, and rather late, fabrication for a real genealogical history, hence disabling himself as regards the history of fabrication *qua* fabrication and settling down, instead, to reading modern history back into Antiquity, as is the wont of humanist scholars. I wonder what Foucault might have made of these after-the-fact surfaces and genealogies.

30. For a survey of a field in which originality resides mainly in the way Said draws upon prior critiques, see his 'Representing the Colonized: Anthropology's Interlocutors', *Critical Inquiry*, Winter 1989.

31. Edward Said, 'Jane Austen and Empire', in Terry Eagleton, ed., *Raymond Williams: Critical Perspectives* (London: Polity Press, 1989).

32. See my 'Between Orientalism and Historicism: Anthropological Knowledge of India' *Studies in History* vol. 7, no. 1, (New Delhi 1991) for detailed comments on Ronald Inden's *Imagining India* (Oxford: Basil Blackwell, 1991).

33. See Partha Chatterjee, 'Caste and Subaltern Consciousness', in Ranjit Guha, ed., *Subaltern Studies*, vol. VI (Delhi: Oxford University Press, 1989).

34. 'Media, Margins and Modernity: Raymond Williams and Edward Said', Appendix to Raymond Williams, *The Politics of Modernism: Against the New Conformists*, (London: Verso, 1989), pp. 196–7. The transcript of that public discussion – and, indeed, the whole book – ends on that sentence about 'feminist credentials'.

35. This essay has also appeared as an introduction to Schwab's own *The Oriental Renaissance: Europe's Rediscovery of India and the East, 1680–1880*, translation of *La Renaissance orientale* (1954) by Gene Patterson-Black and Victoria Reinking (New York: Columbia University Press, 1984).

36. In his last book, *State, Power, Socialism* (London: New Left Books, 1978; translation by Patrick Camiller of *L'Etat, le Pouvoir, le Socialisme*, published in Paris that same year), Poulantzas offers a critique of Foucault from a Marxist position but tries also to find common ground between the two. See, in particular, the section on 'Law' in Part One and the one entitled 'Towards a Relational Theory of Power?' in Part Two. This critique, in the book that is theoretically the most eclectic in Poulantzas's overall *œuvre*, was probably not available to Said when he was writing *Orientalism*.

37. *The World, the Text and the Critic*, pp. 244–6. This distancing from Foucault was then to be repeated in the more recent essay 'Foucault and the Imagination of Power', in David Couzens Hoy, ed., *Foucault: A Critical Reader* (Oxford: Basil Blackwell, 1989), which also says less than what is already there in Poulantzas.

38. This emphasis on 'resistance' outside the 'grand narratives' is not notably different from the one Foucault (partially aided by Deleuze) delineates in a great many places, including the two interviews published as the concluding chapters of Michel Foucault, *Language, Countermemory, Practice*, ed. Donald Bouchard (Ithaca, NY: Cornell University Press, 1977).

39. See Edward W. Said, 'Opponents, Audiences, Constituencies and Community', *Critical Inquiry*, no. 9, 1982; reprinted in Hal Foster, ed., *The Anti-Aesthetic: Essays in Postmodern Culture* (Port Townsend, WA: Bay Press, 1983), pp. 135–59.

40. Ranajit Guha, editor of the series *Subaltern Studies* and author, most notably of *A Rule of Property for Bengal* (1963) and *Elementary Aspects of Peasant Insurgency in Colonial India* (1983), taught history for many years at Sussex University in Great Britain before moving in 1980 to the Australian National University, Canberra.

41. See Edward W. Said, 'The Imperial Spectacle', *Grand Street*, vol. 6, no. 2, Winter 1987.

42. *Raritan*, Winter 1990.

43. The more recent *Elementary Aspects* would be a closer approximation of the

Subalternist approach ('poststructuralism', as Said designates it), but the mongraph *An Indian Historiography of India: A Nineteenth Century Agenda and its Implications* (Calcutta: K.P. Bagchi, 1988); the superb essay, possibly Guha's best work in the past quarter-century, entitled 'Chandra's Death' (*Subaltern Studies* V, Delhi 1987), and the recent, much lengthier and much more problematic essay 'Dominance without Hegemony and its Historiography' (*Subaltern Studies* VI, Delhi 1989) would have been even more representative.

## 6 Marx on India

1. See *Orientalism*, pp. 153–7, for the quotation and Said's treatment of it.

2. Some awareness of this fact in sections of even the British-educated intelligentsia in India is virtually as old as colonialism itself, and thus predates Marx. Criticisms of the British land settlement and revenue system are already there in Rammohun Roy and his colleagues. See, for example, Rammohun's 'Questions and Answers on the Revenue System of India', composed in 1832, in *English Works of Rammohun Roy*, vol. 3 (Calcutta 1947). Bipan Chandra's *The Rise and Growth of Economic Nationalism in India* (New Delhi 1966) is a convenient summary of the criticisms of the British obstruction of Indian industry and finance among the intellectuals and entrepreneurs who grew up under the shadow of 1857. Enormous evidence, too vast for convenient citation, of what I have called colonialism's non-revolutionary resolution of the Indian crisis has accumulated since that early phase. Among the ongoing researches, see in particular A.K. Bagchi's distinguished work on the nature of private investments, deindustrialization and structural distortions in the colonial economy in, among other writings, *Private Investments in India 1900–1935* (Cambridge: Cambridge University Press, 1972) and such of his essays as 'De-industrialization in India in the Nineteenth Century: Some Theoretical Implications', *Journal of Peasant Studies*, January 1976 and 'Colonialism and the Nature of 'Capitalist' Enterprise in India', in Ghanshyam Shah, ed., *Capitalist Development: Critical Essays* (Bombay: Popular Parkashan, 1990).

3. This particular point – that Marx had equal contempt for European and non-European pre-capitalist structures – was initially made in response to Said by the Syrian intellectual Sadek el-Azm in his essay 'Orientalism and Orientalism-in-Reverse', *Khamsin*, no. 8 (London: Ithaca Press, 1982).

4. Marx and Engels, *On Colonialism: Articles from the 'New York Tribune' and other Writings* (New York: International Publishers, 1972), p. 339.

5. This loyalism at the time of battle was to give rise to a fully fledged sense of guilt among that first generation of Bengali nationalists which grew up in the shadow of 1857. For a preliminary statement of the facts, see Benoy Ghosh, 'The Bengal Intelligentsia and the Revolt', in P.C. Joshi, ed., *Rebellion 1857* (New Delhi: People's Publishing House 1957).

6. Frederick Engels, *Persia and China* (1857) pp. 123–4.

7. Bipan Chandra, 'Reinterpretation of Ninteenth Century Indian Economic History', *Indian Economic and Social History Review*, March 1968; reprinted in his *Nationalism and Colonialism in Modern India* (New Delhi: Orient Longman 1979). Quotation from the 1981 paperback edition, p. 43.

8. It should be said, in all fairness, that the practice of speaking of 'Marx' on the basis of these two well-anthologized journalistic pieces is by no means peculiar to Said; it is in fact quite the norm. Bill Warren, whose argument is the exact opposite of Said's, does the same thing in *Imperialism: Pioneer of Capitalism* (London: New Left Books, 1980). For a discussion of Warren, see my 'Imperialism and Progress' in Ronald Chilcote and Dale Johnson, eds, *Theories of Development: Mode of Production or Dependency?* (Beverly Hills, CA: Sage, 1983).

9. So cursory was Marx's knowledge of the facts and so offhand his attitude towards the journalism, that he simply lifted entire formulations from Engels's letter of 6 June 1853, and inserted them into his own dispatch of 10 June. As luck would have it, some of those epistolary/journalistic amalgams became overly famous.

10. By the time Marx came to write the letter of 1881 from which we have quoted above (about 'railways useless for the Hindoos', etc.), he had developed a great interest in the communal form of landholdings in the less industrialized countries as a possible basis for socialist transition, perhaps because it had become obvious by then that West European capital was not going to 'transplant' industrial society in the dependent countries like Russia and India. See, for an illuminating exploration, Teodor Shanin, *Late Marx and the Russian Road: Marx and 'The Peripheries of Capitalism'* (New York: Monthly Review Press, 1983).

11. Harbans Mukhia, 'Marx on Pre-Colonial India: An Evaluation', in Diptendra Banerjee, ed., *Marxian Theory and the Third World* (New Delhi: Sage, 1985), pp. 181, 182.

12. See Irfan Habib's two fundamental essays, 'Problems of Marxist Historical Analysis in India', *Enquiry*, Monsoon 1969, pp. 52–67; and 'Potentialities of Capitalist Development in the Economy of Mughal India', *Enquiry*, Winter 1971, pp. 1–56. The classic triangular debate on pre-colonial Indian formation between Mukhia, Habib and R.S. Sharma – with some contributions by others – which was triggered initially by Mukhia's famous essay 'Was There Feudalism in Indian History?', is available in T.J. Byres and Harbans Mukhia, eds, *Feudalism and Non-European Societies* (London: Frank Cass, 1985). Marx figures only peripherally in that debate, but the clarifications which the debate provides are germane to evaluating Marx's ideas about India.

13. See Ravinder Kumar, 'The Secular Culture of India', in Rasheeduddin Khan, ed., *Composite Culture of India and National Integration* (Delhi: Allied Publishers, 1987), pp. 353–4. The passage quoted above is immediately followed by an approving quotation from the Minute by Sir Charles Metcalfe dated 17 November 1830. Now, there is no reference to Metcalfe in Marx's articles or letters on the subject, but it was a famous Minute and Marx very probably knew it; what Metcalfe says is, in any case, almost identical. Ravinder Kumar is too erudite a historian not to be fully aware of this overlap, and the choice of Metcalfe appears deliberate, so that he can avoid an unnecessary controversy about Marx but make the same point.

14. Karl Marx and Frederick Engels, *The First Indian War of Independence: 1857–1859* (Moscow: Progress Publishers, 1959), p. 14. Marx and Engels, in fact, composed no such book. Editors in Moscow simply put together some – not all, only some – of Marx's journalistic pieces, personal notes and private letters, and gave the collection an inordinately imposing title.

15. We should emphasize that these dispatches belong to the same period of Marx's thought which had been inaugurated with the magisterial pronouncement in *The Communist*

*Manifesto*: 'The history of all hitherto existing society is the history of class struggles.' When the *Manifesto* was to be reprinted in 1886, after Marx's death, the only revision Engels proposed (but then dropped) was to add the word 'written' before 'history', so that the phrase would then be 'the written history of all hitherto existing society'. Marx's outrageous statement that 'India has no history at all, at least no known history' gets a very peculiar twist from the fact that the history of class struggles in pre-colonial India was in fact not 'known' in his time.

16. It is as well to recall that Ambedkar, whose portrait now hangs prominently in the hall of the Indian Parliament, was to make a much harsher judgement a century later. The Indian caste system was worse than slavery, he said, because it was 'a system of exploitation without obligation'.

17. From *Hind Swaraj* in *The Collected Works of Mahatma Gandhi*, vol. 10, p. 37.

18. E.M.S. Namboodripad, 'Evolution of Society, Language and Literature', in Debiprasad Chattopadhyaya, *Marxism and Indology* (Calcutta: K.P. Bagchi, 1981); pp. 35–44.

## 7 'Indian Literature'

1. See Kosambi's brief review of Dange's *India from Primitive Communism to Slavery*, in A.J. Syed, ed., *D.D. Kosambi on History and Society: Problems of Interpretation* (Bombay: University of Bombay, 1985), pp. 73–8. The sentence from which this observation is taken closes the second paragraph.

2. D.D. Kosambi, Romila Thapar, R.S. Sharma, Irfan Habib, K.M. Ashraf, Nurul Hasan, Satish Chandra, Harbans Mukhia, Bipan Chandra and Sumit Sarkar are, of course, among the most eminent, but the work that has gone into establishing the main contours of the material history of the Indian is in fact much more vast than any list of names could indicate and, as the short list above reveals, Marxist contributions hae been central to these researches.

3. This term is used for the earliest body of extant Tamil writing. I have come across different transliterations for the word, but I simply write 'Sangam' to indicate the prevailing pronunciation. See A.K. Ramanujan, *Poems of Love and War* (New Delhi: Oxford University Press; reprint, n.d.; New York: Columbia University Press, 1985) for matchless translations of a selection from those classical anthologies, and for commentary at once moving and erudite.

4. See Ashish Bose, 'Some Aspects of the Linguistic Demography of India', in *Language and Society in India*, Proceedings of a Seminar (Simla: Indian Institute of Advanced Study, 1969).

5. Mohan Singh Diwana, 'Indian Socio-Linguistic Background', in ibid. Bahadur Shah Zafar was the last Mogul king and a substantial poet in Urdu. Sauda was also an early-nineteenth-century Urdu poet and notable member of a Sufic guild in Delhi. The confluence of ecstatic Sufism and Bhakti, as we find it in the much earlier work of Amir Khusrow, is quite evidently combined in some of Sauda's work with the direct influence of Nirguni Bhakti, which matured in Urdu *ghazal*, oddly but for specific historical reasons, mainly in the Deccan.

6. Umashankar Joshi, *The Idea of Indian Literature*, Samvatsar Lectures (New Delhi: Sahitya Akademi, 1990), p. 30.

7. 'In the Mirror of Urdu: Reorganization of Nation and Community', forthcoming as

an Occasional Paper in the 'History and Politics' Series from The Centre for Contemporary Studies, Nehru Memorial Museum and Library, New Delhi.

8. Schlegel was probably the first scholar to use the term 'Indian Literature', in 1823, and he meant Sanskrit. Albrecht Weber's *The History of Indian Literature* (original German, 1852; 1875 English translation reprinted by Kegan Paul, Trench, and Trübner & Co., London 1978) is the classic full-length study based on this identification between 'Indian' and Sanskrit.

9. *In Defence of Indian Culture* (New York: Sri Aurobindo Library, 1953).

10. See Maurice Winternitz, *History of Indian Literature*. The work appeared originally in German in three volumes published in 1907, 1920 and 1922, respectively. Publication of English translations began in Calcutta in 1926 and was completed forty years later, in Delhi in 1966, by Motilal Banarsidas, foremost publishers of Indological work.

11. The quoted words here are taken, obviously, from Macaulay's much-reproduced Minute of 1835. See Chapter 6 for some additional comments on the key distinction between the Orientalist and the modernist projects within the colonial dynamic.

12. *The New Science of Giambattista Vico*, unabridged translation of the third edition (1744), by Thomas Goddard Bergin and Max Harold Fisch, revised and expanded paperback edition, Ithaca, NY: Cornell University Press, 1984.

13. It is as well to note here a fact which few scholars even in India know or fully grasp: that so widespread was the work of writing and translating in Farsi in India, over so many centuries, and so often accomplished by the scholastic castes of Brahmins and Kayasthas, that a distinct form of Farsi, often highly differentiated from the Iranian evolution, came into being and was generally referred to as 'subuk Hindi', i.e. 'refined Hindi', with connotations of that same class-based superiority and that same 'refinement' which is inherent in the word 'Sanskrit' itself, which distinguished it from less 'subuk' Prakrits and *upbhranshas*.

14. See, for example, Sisir Kumar Das, Sujit Mukherjee and Umashankar Joshi, as cited in Notes 16 and 17 below.

15. See Meenakshi Mukherjee, *Realism and Reality: The Novel and Society in India* (New Delhi: Oxford University Press, 1985) for an attempt to define the moment of the emergence of the modern novel in India in terms of a basic set of thematics across language clusters. As an extreme example of thematic formalism, see Satendra Singh, 'Towards a Concept of the Indian Novel: A Thematic Construct', in Amiya Dev and Sisir Kumar Das, eds. *Comparative Literature: Theory and Practice* (New Delhi: Allied Publishers, 1989).

16. Sisir Kumar Das, *A History of Indian Literature*, vol. VIII (New Delhi: Sahitya Akademi, 1990).

17. Among the more thoughtful writings on the conceptual approach towards an integrated sense of an *Indian* literature, as distinguished from the sense of a comparatism of discrete linguistic–literary formations in the subcontinent, see in particular Umashankar Joshi's two distinguished lectures, entitled *The Idea of Indian Literature* (New Delhi: Sahitya Akademi, 1990); Suniti Kumar Chatterjee's *Language and Literature of Modern India* (Calcutta: Bengal Publishers, 1963); and Sujit Mukherjee, *Toward a Literary History of India* (Occasional Papers, Indian Institute of Advanced Study, Simla 1975).

18. The emphasis here is on *functions*, and on the determination of these by the social division of labour. By the term 'intelligentsia' here I do not simply mean 'writers', less still

'littérateurs'. The term includes, rather, all those whose function in the social division of labour is (a) to produce ideas and (b) to *lead* the institutions of state and society on the basis of claims of knowledge. In a colonial society, state-associated strata occupy key positions in this social category, and the upper layers of such strata function under a professional compulsion to use mainly the language of the colonizing country in the public sphere; in private life, and in activities associated with leisure time, they may continue to use their own language(s). For these upper layers, then, the linguistic differentiation between public and private spheres, with the concomitant tendency of the public sphere determining in the long run the social mores of the private sphere, is a structural feature of this colonial matrix, individual exceptions notwithstanding. In the middling layers, meanwhile the salaried strata are also often impelled to perform multiple and even contradictory functions. The fact that a particular individual writes for publication in two languages, or publishes in one language but writes in another in the course of the bureaucratic function, is significant in the aggregation of biographies but does not alter the objective determination of social functions and the corresponding distribution of social agents.

19. It is significant that what one might call the first Indian *novel* – Syed Hasan Shah's *Nashtar* – was written in Farsi. See Qurratulain Hyder's acceptance address at the Jnanpath Award ceremony, exerpted in *Times of India*, 3 February 1991.

20. I use the term 'Third Estate' here to designate a broad social category in the urban life of early colonial transition, wherein a nucleus of the professional petty bourgeoisie has been assembled in urban society but is yet to assume a full-fledged class character because most members of this emergent social category continue to overlap quite decisively with commerce and ground rent. Since industrial development was obstructed by the same colonial transition which had laid the basis for the genesis of the capitalist ground rent in India, the professional classes were increasingly detached from pre-capitalist agricultural bases yet remained rooted in the ground rent, predominantly rural but also urban, which in turn overlapped frequently with petty commercial enterprise and/or was consumed in the process of securing a genteel life despite low professional incomes.

21. This traditionalist turn in defence against European missionary pressure is there already in Rammohun, whose Vedantic studies were directly in response to that kind of pressure. On the other hand, however, these nativist revivalisms also gained greater authority among sections of the colonially minded Indian intelligentsia because Orientalist scholarship could always be invoked to attach the aura of modern scholarship to texts of indigenous orthodoxy.

22. Bankimchandra Chattopadhyay (1834–94) is himself, of course, the supreme example of this very uneasy coexistence between positivist modernity and revivalist phantasmagoria, culminating in a fully fledged articulation of Hindu communalist idealogy.

23. A working bibliography of Kosambi's writings can be found in R.S. Sharma, ed., *Indian Society: Historical Probings – In Memory of D.D. Kosambi*, (New Delhi: People's Publishing House, 1974).

24. See Note 1 above. The opening sentence is fairly indicative of the temperature of the whole piece. It begins: 'This painfully disappointing book by one of the founders of the Communist Party of India would not have been worth reviewing, but for the fact that to let such a performance go unchallenged would bring Marxism into disrepute.'

## 8 Three Worlds Theory

1. Fredric Jameson, 'Third World Literature in the Era of Multinational Capital', *Social Text*, Fall 1986, p. 73.

2. Fredric Jameson, 'A Brief Response', *Social Text*, Fall 1987, p. 26.

3. Benedict Anderson, *Imagined Communities: Reflections on the Origin and Spread of Nationalism* (London: Verso, 1983). This displacing of the religious and the dynastic–imperial by the national, via print capitalism, is the central proposition of the book, explicated in its treatment of sacred and secular languages, pilgrimages, etc., and summarized at one point thus: 'the very possibility of imagining the nation only arose historically when, and where, three fundamental cultural conceptions, all of great antiquity, lost their axiomatic grip on men's minds. The first of these was the idea that a particular script-language offered privileged access to ontological truth. . . . It was this idea that called into being the transcontinental sodalities of Christendom, the Ummah Islam, and the rest' (p. 40). That breeziness of 'the rest' leaves one somewhat short of breath, but the idea that the nation arose where religion had once been is unmistakable.

4. Edward W. Said, *Orientalism*, (New York: Vintage, 1979), p. 104.

5. The paradox in discussing the issue of 'convergence' now, after the restructurings of recent years, is of course that a convergence of sorts – a capitulation, really – has indeed taken place, but only after the systematic dismantling of that specific Soviet state which had been portrayed at that time as the imperialist superpower and an alter ego of the United States in the logic of global exterminism.

6. In designating Three Worlds Theory as an ideology, I mean not to erase the difference between theory and ideology but to emphasize the purely ideological character of the theoretical claim. This Theory offers false knowledge of imperialism but nevertheless derives its emotive power from the directly phenomenal experience of the difference between the advanced and the backward capitalist societies, and from the fact that advanced capital is imperialist capital. The mystificatory function of this false knowledge resides in concealing the fact that in sovereign post-colonial societies, imperialism functions through the national-bourgeois state itself, and in its claim, instead, that the role of the national-bourgeois state is to resolve the contradiction between imperialism and the masses of the imperialized formations in favour of the latter.

7. E.M.S. Namboodripad, *Nehru: Ideology and Practice*, (New Delhi: National Book Centre, 1988), pp. 246–52.

8. Facts about Nehru in this and subsequent paragraphs can easily be confirmed from the standard and very Nehruvian four-volume work by Servepalli Gopal, *Jawaharlal Nehru: A Biography*. See, in particular, volume 2 (New Delhi: Oxford University Press, 1979) for the crucial 1947–56 period.

9. We shall return to the American dimension presently. Inside India, the Ranadive line of frontal assault and insurrection had been withdrawn, and with the most militant phase of the Telengana uprising already in the past, the Communist Party of India was poised to transform itself into a predominantly parliamentary opposition – and Nehru had a great many reasons to encourage that process. Internationally, there had been a sea-change in the policies of the Soviet Union and China, which were now willing to extend long-range co-operation to non-aligned states regardless of their domestic policies. The Nehru

government, which had been dismissed at one time as a stooge of imperialism, was seen now as a potential ally in a progressive international alliance. Nehru's leftward turn at this juncture was in part a response to these domestic and international shifts.

10. See, for a summary treatment of that radical interlude, Bipan Chandra, 'Jawaharlal Nehru and the Capitalist Class, 1936', in his *Nationalism and Colonialism in Modern India*, (New Delhi: Orient Longman, 1979). The essay itself was first published in August 1975 (*Economic and Political Weekly*, vol. X, nos 33–5). Professor Chandra has, of course, retracted his own earlier interpretation of that phase and replaced it with a far more laudatory summation of Nehru's career in his recent *Jawaharlal Nehru in Historical Perspective*, D.D. Kosambi Memorial Lectures (University of Bombay: Department of History, 1989).

# Index